From Rainforest

to Cane Field

in Cuba

Envisioning Cuba

Louis A. Pérez Jr., editor

FROM RAINFOREST TO CANE FIELD IN CUBA

REINALDO FUNES MONZOTE

Translated by Alex Martin

The University of North Carolina Press
Chapel Hill

An Environmental History since 1492

© 2008 The University of North Carolina Press
All rights reserved
Manufactured in the United States of America
Originally published in Spanish with the title *De bosque a sabana: azúcar, deforestación y medio ambiente en Cuba, 1492–1926*, © 2004 Siglo XXI Editores, S.A. de C.V.
Designed and typeset in Minion Pro and Scala Sans by Eric M. Brooks

This book was published with the assistance of the Anniversary Endowment Fund of the University of North Carolina Press and a grant from the Social Science Research Council.

The paper in this book meets the guidelines for permanence and durability of the Committee on Production Guidelines for Book Longevity of the Council on Library Resources.

Library of Congress Cataloging-in-Publication Data
Funes Monzote, Reinaldo, 1969–
[De bosque a sabana. English]
From rainforest to cane field in Cuba: an environmental history since 1492 / Reinaldo Funes Monzote; translated by Alex Martin.
p. cm. — (Envisioning Cuba)
Includes bibliographical references and index.
ISBN 978-0-8078-3128-1 (cloth: alk. paper)
ISBN 978-0-8078-5858-5 (pbk.: alk. paper)
1. Sugarcane — Cuba — History. 2. Sugarcane industry — Cuba — History. 3. Forest management — Cuba — History. I. Title.
SB229.C9F8613   2008
333.75′137097291 — dc22   2007026916

cloth   12 11 10 09 08   5 4 3 2 1
paper   12 11 10 09 08   5 4 3 2 1

THIS BOOK WAS DIGITALLY PRINTED

A MI MADRE

siempre en mi memoria

CONTENTS

Figures, Tables, and Maps

Figures

Tables

Maps

Preface

This book was first published by Mexico's prestigious Siglo XXI Editores, thanks to a 2003 UNESCO/State of Quintana Roo/Siglo XXI Book Prize for Caribbean Thought, Environmental Category. The opportunity presented by this new English-language edition has given me time for a critical rereading. I have made some changes to the earlier text that, although they do not alter the general structure, do introduce new aspects, revise others, and make the book more concise. For this magnificent opportunity, I thank the University of North Carolina Press, particularly the staff and board members responsible for the series Envisioning Cuba, as well as the Cuba Program of the Social Science Research Council for funding the translation.

Years of help from numerous colleagues in Cuba and abroad made this book possible. I would first like to thank José A. Piqueras Arenas, both for what he has taught me about the historical profession and for the support that enabled me to obtain a scholarship from the Spanish Agency for International Cooperation, which made possible a long stay at the Universidad Jaume I and allowed me to consult Spanish archives and libraries. I was aided by Miguel Angel Puig-Samper, of the Department of the History of Science at the Consejo Superior de Investigaciones Científicas (Superior Council for Scientific Research) in Madrid, to whom I also express my gratitude. I also thank Josefina Gómez Mendoza, Joan Martínez Alier, Manuel González de Molina, Luis Urtega, and Vincent Sanz, who made valuable suggestions.

I began this research while in the Department of the History of Science at the Carlos J. Finlay Historical Museum of Science in Havana. During this period of my study I had important conversations on the topic with Pedro M. Pruna, Leida Fernández, Mercedes Valero, Rolando Misas, Orieta Alvarez, Rosa María González, and Alfredo Alvarez. At different times while working toward my doctorate in Cuba I received moral support from Carmen Almodóvar, Onaney Muñiz, María del Carmen Barcia, Eduardo Torres Cuevas, Camilo Pérez Casal, and particularly the Antonio Núñez Jiménez Foundation for Nature and Mankind through its president, Lupe Velis, and its vice president, Liliana Núñez.

At the Universidad Jaume I, I was well cared for by the director's offices and secretariats of the Department of History, Geography, and Art, the Faculty of the Humanities, and the Vice-rectorate for Research. It would be impossible to mention everyone, so I will limit myself to those colleagues and friends who had the most impact on the results of my work: Imilcy Balboa, Vicent Sanz, Salvador Broseta, Enrique Montón, Isabel Andúgar, Begoña García, and Jovino Pizzi. In other Spanish cities I was helped by Consuelo Naranjo, Joan Casanovas, Antonio Santamaría, María Dolores González-Ripoll, Luis Miguel García, Martín Rodrigo, and Nadia Fernández de Pinedo. A scholarship from the School for Hispano-American Studies in Seville allowed me to consult its library and the Archive of the Indies.

In Cuba I have benefited from the painstaking attention that I have always received from library staff members. I extend my gratitude especially to Julio Vargas and Jorge Macle of the Cuban National Archives. I would also like to mention in particular Arturo Sorhegui. Among others who contributed in one form or another, I would like to thank Carlos Venegas, Mercedes Córdova, Marial Iglesias, Mercedes García, Fe Iglesias, Hernán Venegas, and Enrique del Risco Rodríguez.

Various colleagues at universities in the United States and Canada contributed to the fruit of my work. Among these scholars of the history of Cuba and the Caribbean, I am indebted to Arcadio Díaz Quiñones, Laird W. Bergad, José F. Buscaglia, Rebecca Scott, Franklin Knight, Louis A. Pérez, Javier Figueroa, Ada Ferrer, David Sartorius, Lillian Guerra, and Dale Tomich. A number of environmental historians working on Latin America gave me useful suggestions and valuable bibliographic help, even though some did not know me personally. They include Kate Christen, John Soluri, Stuart McCook, John McNeill, Christian Brannstrom, Bert Kreitlow, and Richard Tucker. I have a similar debt of gratitude to Latin American colleagues such as Guillermo Castro, José Augusto Padua, Stefanía Gallini, Mauricio Folchi, Claudia Leal, Regina Horta, and Bernardo García Martínez.

Finally, this book would not have been possible without the support of my family, from the motivation to choose this vocation given by my grandfather to the professional example of my parents. My brother Fernando and my sister-in-law Claudia helped me in some of my bibliographic searches. I would especially like to dedicate this book to Déborah, for her constant professional and personal support and for all her efforts to help me complete this project, which entailed three years of separation from her and from our young children, Laura and Daniel.

From Rainforest
to Cane Field
in Cuba

INTRODUCTION

In April 1926 the president of the Republic of Cuba prohibited the indiscriminate cutting and burning of forests to clear fields for sugarcane. His decree reversed a policy more than one hundred years old. In August 1815, after a long struggle with his royal navy, the Spanish king had granted property owners complete freedom to fell trees on their land. From that point on, sugar plantations grew unhindered, at the expense of the abundant forests that covered most of the Cuban archipelago. Forests were seen as no more than lumber to build sugar mills, firewood to fuel them, and sources of stunningly fertile soil, thanks to the rich organic matter that remained after the thick tropical forests were cleared.

The system of cutting and burning in order to establish sugar plantations and build mills had been practiced since the beginning of the Cuban sugar industry, around 1600, but the absolute right over forests granted to private landowners, who owned most of the island, created an unprecedented situation: the possibility of exercising this right with no consideration other than their own benefit, to which could be added the desire for their nation to belong to that select group of countries considered "civilized." In the past, the growth of the sugar industry had had to wait until land was cleared by the Royal Forest Reserves (Cortes del Rey), the service charged with harvesting lumber for the Havana shipyard and sending wood to the metropole.

From early on, sugar production around Havana spurred diverse conflicts over the use and exploitation of forests. But only after the English took the city in 1762 did bureaucrats in the royal navy begin to see the industry as the greatest danger to the future of shipbuilding on the island. In 1772 lengthy confrontations began between two very different views of forest exploitation. For those in the navy, lumber was the primary material needed to build a powerful naval force capable of defending the empire's strategic interests, and thus they sought to control the use of forests, and in a way to promote their preservation. For the criollo landowners and the sugar planters in particular, the most important concern was the commercial value of sugar and other produce of the colony; they were only interested in forests as sources of lumber to build mills, of firewood, and (after their destruction) of richly fertile soil.

This book is primarily concerned with the impact of the latter conception of how forest resources should be exploited, studying sugar's historical relationship to forests since the early nineteenth century, when the island became the principal supplier to Europe and the United States. Not that, since Spanish colonization, the sugar industry had been the only cause of deforestation, but it certainly became the most important one, both because of its direct impact and because of the type of society that took shape amid its splendor. For more than a century, the burning desire to produce sugar, which seized the economic and political sectors that controlled the exploitation of national resources in Cuba, was fed largely by its centuries-old trees. Although the environmental consequences quickly became evident, nothing could stop clear-cutting of land for sugarcane until the damage had been done.

In 1927 Ramiro Guerra y Sánchez published his well-known *Azúcar y población en las Antillas* (Sugar and Population in the Caribbean), in which he denounced the grave economic, social, and political consequences of the arrival, during the Cuban Republic's early years, of sugar plantations controlled by U.S. capitalists in the provinces of Camagüey and Oriente. He established a parallel with the much earlier experiences of neighboring Caribbean islands, colonies or former colonies of England, France, and Holland that had been the world's primary sugar exporters from the mid-seventeenth century until the end of the eighteenth, to the point that they became known as the Sugar Islands.

As a result of this, Guerra decried, a land-exploitation (or latifundista) regime had been imposed that divided the population into two groups: "a small number of dependents of capitalism, who lead and administer the cultivation of sugarcane and the making and shipping of sugar, and the mass of wage workers of the race [*de la raza*] who are most urgently compelled by necessity to agree to a minimal daily wage and to tolerate the lowest standard of living."[1] This system, which had been sustained with African slavery, had brought to the island an inevitable social and political decadence as the sugar plantation owners completed their occupation of available land. Guerra mentions in particular the case of Barbados (400 km²), whose history reproduced in miniature and in a short period the same process that occurred in the rest of the Caribbean islands and that continued to evolve "in lengths of time directly proportional to the surface area of each one." In the case of Cuba, the largest island (110,992 km²), the absorption of the entire territory by the plantation owners took longer.[2] But sugar's conquest of hundreds of thousands of acres in recent years led Guerra to predict that in twenty years, unless steps were taken to prevent it, sugar would dominate more than four-fifths of the country.

Guerra's view, however, turns out to be problematic because it could lead us to idealize the situation in Cuba prior to the arrival of the large U.S.-owned sugar plantations at the beginning of the twentieth century. There are various differences between Cuba and other sugar-producing islands in the Caribbean but also many similar processes that affected lands invaded by sugar at different times. One aspect that could be compared and that Guerra did not take into account was the environmental impact of the spread of the sugar plantations. sugar plants spread= enviro impact

The role of the growing sugar industry in the disappearance of forests was first mentioned in the nineteenth century. These writings tended to emphasize the effects of sugar's dependence on clear-cutting rather than those of sugar itself, which after all was seen as the main road to civilization and progress. In general the writers denounced other causes with greater vigor, such as the legal or clandestine lumber trade, the building of fences with boards, and the increasing use of land for grazing. Despite this, as sugar conquered new territory, Cubans became aware that their country could end up like the Sugar Islands, which were almost entirely deforested in the rush to replace Haiti as the world's principal supplier of sugar.

It would have been difficult to imagine, given the evolution of sugar cultivation since the end of the eighteenth century, that in less than a century and a half Cuba would be stripped of its vast forests. What made the Cuban case unique was the scale of the space conquered, a result of the simultaneous arrival of the sugar industry and the industrial era, which brought increased demand and the use of steam power. As in other lands, sugar production in Cuba was sustained by excellent natural conditions and by the importation of African slaves. It also was favored by factors such as the structure of property ownership and the configuration of colonial society. But although markets were opened after the drop in Haiti's production and Spain's adoption of free trade reforms, the number of these markets was limited.

What most characterizes the Cuban case is the constant growth in the scale of production throughout the nineteenth century and into the early years of the twentieth. An estate with available woodlands was thus guaranteed, since the plantation owner could thus obtain the highest production while minimizing labor costs, without the use of more or less expensive agricultural techniques and with an abundance of lumber and firewood. In a certain sense the nineteenth-century Cuban sugar industry and even, in a more general sense, the system of plantation slavery could be considered as early examples of the industrial conception of the use of natural resources, or at least as transitional phases between sedentary farming and industrial agriculture.[3] Of course, these changes were part of the great transformation taking place in the traditional agriculture of the Spanish metropole and of Europe generally.[4] They were also part of the development of economies based on specialization in certain agricultural or mineral products destined for export, grown primarily in the colonies, whose role was to furnish the industrializing urban centers of the Old World and the United States with raw materials and food.[5]

Generally speaking, little was done to replace the valuable resources offered by the forests, at least not until the early days of mechanization. In this new phase, forests had a more limited importance in providing fuel and building materials, but they maintained their decisive role as suppliers of the soil nutrients necessary to obtain the highest agricultural yields. New means of transportation, such as trains and steamships, were decisive in making accessible resources from the most distant areas, including those goods imported from abroad. In this sense the production of sugar in Cuba is an interesting case of the shift from an advanced organic economy to one based on the use of fossil fuels. From the mid-nineteenth century, these combustibles became increasingly important for the island's sugar plantations. Nevertheless, conquering new areas covered with forest entailed the large-scale consumption of organically based materials and energy based on growth guidelines typical of an economy based on the use of fossil fuels.[6]

In this book we will consider in general terms the interaction between sugar and the Cuban forests from its beginning around 1600 until its essential culmination in the mid-1920s. The first half of this period we will approach primarily as an antecedent that helps us understand many later events and the increasing environmental transformation. Taking as a symbolic point of departure the year 1772, we can discern five phases, subdivided by milestones in sugar's relationship to forests and in the relationship between nature and society generally in Cuban history. At the same time we will trace some general lines for a future history of the forests or, perhaps better, of their disappearance. As early as 1918 the engineer Juan Antonio Cosculluela noted in one of his reflections on this process that "to write the history of the Cuban woodlands is to outline the course of their destruction, carried out in a short time."[7]

This study will take as a spatial frame of reference the concept of physiconatural regions rather than socioeconomic ones, although of course it will complement this with the information available on the different administrative sectors.[8] In its conquest of physical space, sugar production occupied the territories most likely to bring profits, particularly plains and moderately hilly regions (about 75% of the island). Seen from this perspective, each period in sugar's expansion corresponds to the occupation of different natural regions, on a scale proportional to the increasing productive capacity of the mills. Of course, this cannot be seen in absolute terms but only as a way of identifying the moments when sugar became the central element in the economic and social configuration of these regions.

As we consider the main theme, we will approach other aspects, including the system that guided the supplying of lumber for shipbuilding until the end of the eighteenth century, the process by which a modern forestry administration was established, and the efforts of legislators and others to raise awareness about the environmental and economic consequences of deforestation. In addition to evaluating the influence of the island's socioeconomic evolution and dominant ideologies on attitudes toward the environment, my aim here is to stress the importance of forests in the formation of the Cuban nation, rather than to consider them as a mere backdrop that is spoken of nostalgically. In a certain sense this book is an homage to the silent importance of forests in Cuban history, in which we see reflected many of the warnings of contemporaries about the dangers of the landscape's accelerated transformation, itself a sign that these dangers were not a remote possibility but rather a reality to which the main beneficiaries of commercial agriculture paid scant attention.

The way natural resources were used in Cuba, which placed the production of sugar for export at its center, no doubt had a profound impact on the country's ecosystems and living conditions. Their exploitation began very early, thanks to the use of slave labor and the accumulation of wealth by landowners and bureaucrats in Havana, who benefited from their city's being a port of call for the Spanish royal fleet. It was natural that the most powerful in a small population, people with abundant land and available forests, would chose a crop like sugarcane, which would bring enough profits to purchase the consumer goods to which the colonizers were accustomed. And yet it was not until the drop in Haiti's production and the arrival of the Industrial Revolution that the dynamics of relationships with foreign markets, complemented by the triumph of economic liberalism, became powerful enough to devour rapidly the many resources sheltered by the island's forests. This allowed Cuba to attain a somewhat privileged position among colonial or peripheral regions producing food and raw materials, but the splendor of sugar's glory years could not outstrip its high human and environmental costs. It cannot be ignored that the way Cuba became the world's principal exporter of sugar inflicted great damage on the environment and became a permanent mortgage on the island's future, in not simply environmental but also economic, social, and political terms.

1

The Omnipresent
Forest and the Beginnings
of the Sugar Industry

Cuban Forests on the
Arrival of the Europeans

When Christopher Columbus and his retinue landed on the coast of Cuba in 1492, the landscape they found was that of an almost entirely wooded island. During his first voyage, the Admiral described valleys and mountains "full of tall, cool trees that it was a glory to see," landscapes in which one saw "everything full of palm trees and groves," and "great and marvelous pinewoods" from which one could build as many ships as one desired.[1] And although these descriptions were only of the eastern portion of the north-central coast, the first chroniclers' impressions of the rest of the island were no different. The most famous account is by Bartolomé de Las Casas, who affirmed that all was "flat land full of woods and glades" and that one could walk for 300 leagues and remain under the trees.[2]

The debate over Cuba's "original" vegetation, and in particular that which existed when the Spaniards arrived, has engaged botanists, geographers, and historians. As early as the nineteenth century different accounts appeared of the characteristics of the island's landscape before 1492. After visiting Havana twice during the first five years of the nineteenth century and traveling through part of the island's west, the German scholar Alexander von Humboldt argued that "the entire island was in its origin a forest of pines and wild lemon and orange trees."[3] Three decades later, the renowned Spanish naturalist Ramón de La Sagra, with more evidence, claimed that most of Cuba had been covered "with a corpulent arboreal vegetation, one thick and even denser for the climbing and parasitical plants that filled the gaps between trees' trunks and branches," in a proportion far greater than the herbaceous vegetation of the savannas.[4] The savannas' existence prior to the conquest and the Caribbean origin of this word are prominent topics in discussions about the natural or cultural origin of the Cuban savannas.[5]

To say that the island was covered with forests is not to say that its vegetation was in a pristine state when the Old World colonizers first landed. How could we believe such a claim if we take into account the different estimates that place Cuba's fifteenth-century population at between 100,000 and 200,000 people, most of them living in communities of farmers and potters whose ancestors had first arrived on the island about a millennium before? These groups used wood in various ways and practiced agriculture by clear-cutting—felling and burning a given section of woodland—a method that was transferred to new territories when the land became covered with weeds or when its productivity declined. In the most densely populated areas this technique had direct consequences for the land's transformation, ones that recent studies have found to be more important than usually acknowledged, reaching a point such that clear-cutting "appears to have played a role in the emergence of some areas of savanna."[6]

Columbus records this influence at various points — for example, on November 27, when he mentions that among the mountains of Baracoa he observed "much smoke and great settlements, and fields well tilled." Similarly, on December 3 he climbed to a mountaintop and found it "all flat and sowed with many things of the earth . . . and in the middle of it was a great settlement." Even so, neither the areas under cultivation nor the greater or lesser use of lumber diminished in any way the predominant image of a nature prodigious in trees and forests, with a diversity of fruit and flowers, a great variety of brightly colored birds that amazed with their songs, and traversed by rivers whose waters were transparently clear.[7]

In any case, any impact on the original forest area that could be attributed to the indigenous Cubans would be very limited, especially with regard to the Neolithic communities of farmers and potters in the center-eastern half of the island. The western half, by contrast, was peopled at the time of the Europeans' arrival by late Mesolithic communities that lived fundamentally from fishing, hunting, and gathering, although they also practiced in less advanced forms both agriculture by clear-cutting and woodworking.[8] In general, as David Watts notes for the entire Caribbean area, the indigenous communities of Cuba developed complex socioeconomic systems that allowed them to live "in harmony with their physical and biological environment, preserving its innate resource potential."[9] ✳

In the 1920s, Hugh Bennett and Robert Allison of the United States carried out the first general study of Cuban soils. Their research led them to conclude that a third of the island had once been covered by natural savannas, the result of insufficient drainage in areas where the soil could not be penetrated by water or tree roots and that therefore were subject to periodic flooding.[10] The 1943 census categorized 46 percent of the nation's territory as destroyed forests (replaced by fields used for crops or livestock or that simply lay fallow), 18 percent as still existing forests, 9 percent as mangrove swamps and keys, 4 percent as pinewoods, and 23 percent as savannas, wet schlerophyllous low forests (*charrascales*), and "naturally uncovered" terrain.[11]

In 1943 also, an article by the German geographer Leo Waibel became one of the most important contributions to the debate over Cuba's original vegetation.[12] Waibel studied the island's toponymy to see whether he could confirm the claim by Bartolomé de Las Casas that one could cross the island and never leave the shade of trees. He consulted cartographic works from the early twentieth century and works by famous geographers and botanists beginning the century before. He concluded that forests had originally covered two-thirds of the island (hardwood, 68,500 km², or 60%; pine, 4,500 km², or 4%), a proportion that rose to four-fifths if one included so-called park vegetation (17,000 km², or 16%). He estimated the natural savanna areas (which he determined based on soils, not climate) at 13,000 square kilometers (11%). The rest of the island had been swamps (6%), keys (3%), and thickets of thorn bushes (1%). Waibel pointed out that many of the toponyms, such as those including the words *sabana, sabanilla, sabanita, sao,* and *ciego,* had been devised for areas where savannas were rare in order to draw attention to them.[13]

In 1984 Waibel's article was published in Spanish together with one by Ricardo Herrera, "El origen de las sabanas cubanas" (The Origin of the Cuban Savannas).[14] Herrera followed Waibel's approach and compared his own findings with those of field studies and historical research. He took as his point of departure several works on the presence of savannas in Cuba until the nineteenth century and reconstructed maps of *hatos* (cattle ranches) and *corrales* (hog farms) conceded (*mercedados*) by the authorities.[15] Although he generally agreed with Waibel, Herrera argued that Waibel, like other botanists and historians, mistakenly took literally Las Casas's claim that it was possible to walk, as he had, for 300 leagues without leaving the shade of trees. Herrera believed the area originally covered by savannas to be larger, in keeping with the findings of scholars such as Bennett, Allison, or Earl Smith, also of the United States, who in 1953 claimed the area originally covered by forests to be only 60 percent.[16]

Other more or less recent research argues that the forested area was much larger. In the early 1970s the dasonomist Eliseo Matos calculated that when the Spaniards arrived forests covered 90 percent of Cuba's territory.[17] In 1989, the *Nuevo atlas nacional de Cuba* summarized the different positions, noting that the proportion of vegetation taken up by forests in the sixteenth century was between 70 and 80 percent according to some authors and between 90 and 95 percent according to others. The *Nuevo atlas* seems to agree more with the latter when it affirms that the predominant vegetation was of semideciduous and evergreen forests, whereas "the gramineous vegetation, known as the savanna, was no doubt relatively reduced and may have alternated with some types of forests, influenced by the soil or micro-topographical conditions."[18]

This criterion is expressed by map 1.1, which depicts the island's vegetation at the beginning of the sixteenth century.[19] Its creator, Enrique del Risco Rodríguez, bases his conclusions on the remains of still existing vegetation and its relationship with the soil, geology, relief, and climate, criteria given in greater detail in a book on the Cuban forests that he published in 1995.[20] He questions the conclusions of authors like Bennett and Allison for not taking sufficiently into account the ability of trees to form types of forests in soils with deficient drainage, in his opinion "sufficiently demonstrated in the case of semicaducifolious forests with fluctuating humidity and in the case of marshes."[21] He also criticizes Waibel's toponymy-based study for concluding that some sites probably had been savannas when their conditions indicate they were covered with trees. Nonetheless, del Risco agrees that the references to the term "savanna" in the earliest historical documents by themselves indicate the savannas' exceptional nature. In his opinion, the savannas did not account for more than 3 to 6 percent of the Cuban archipelago. He concludes that at the time of the conquest forests of different types covered between 88 and 92 percent of Cuba's territory. Of this area, 75 to 80 percent was tropical forest, with the rest pinewoods and more or less short forests. ⁊ৎ - 80 ৵-

Map 1 indicates that the predominant types of forests were the semide-ciduous (or semicaducifolious) and the evergreen (or subperennifolious).[22] The former were more abundant and were mainly found in the plains and the rolling hills of the island's west and center, areas with generally good natural soil drainage. Many of this region's trees (from 40 to 65%) lost their leaves during the dry season, which is considered an adaptation to the trop-ical climate, with three to six dry, relatively cool months and between 1,250 and 1,600 millimeters of rain a year. The forests were also found in the cen-ter east, in areas with similar topography but less rain (1,000 to 1,200 mm of rain a year) and somewhat higher temperatures, which led to smaller leaves. These forests present an arboreal stratum with two substrata and a few emergent trees. The higher substratum, dependent on the fertility and humidity of the soil, reaches a height of 20 to 25 meters and includes species such as the cedar, Cuban or Caribbean mahogany, jocuma, jobo, and sabicú or jigüe. In the lower substratum are found the frijolillo or jurabaina, Cay-man oak, male and female guara, lancewood, and yaití. Emergent trees in this type of forest include the ceiba, almácigo, and royal palm. Finally, at the bush stratum important plants include palo de caja and ingenio torchwood, as well as herbs, epiphytes, and many lianas.

Semicaducifolious forests include the coastal and subcoastal varieties as well as those with fluctuating humidity. The first are shorter with two arboreal substrata, one 5 to 10 meters high and the other 10 to 12 meters high, with about 40 percent of their trees losing their leaves because of the five- to six-month dry season and an annual rainfall of between 1,000 and 1,200 millimeters. These forests are found on high coasts, especially in the center west. The first substratum has species such as the júcaro, almácigo, roble de olor, abey, and guaiacum; the second includes coastal ateje, thorny júcaro, aceitunillo, coastal carbonero, wild avocado (aguacate cimarrón), and guano campeche.

The semicaducifolious forests with fluctuating humidity are home to about 50 percent of the caducifolious species. These forests stay quite humid during the rainy season and very dry during the dry season, so the

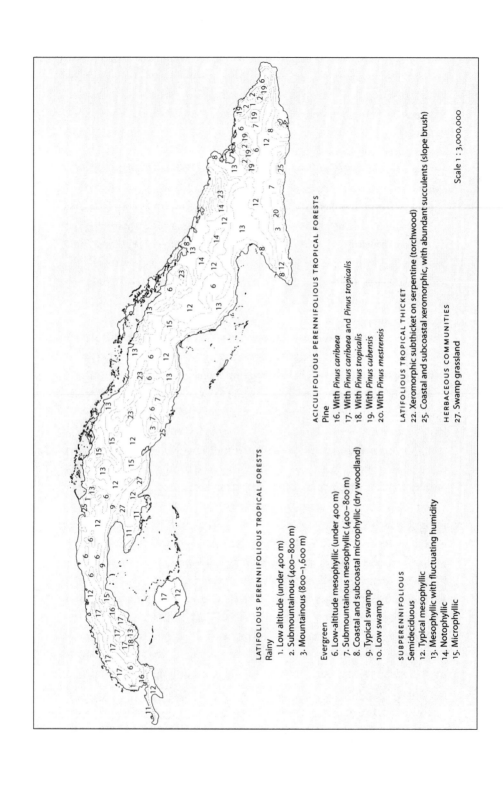

LATIFOLIOUS PERENNIFOLIOUS TROPICAL FORESTS

Rainy

1. Low altitude (under 400 m)
2. Submountainous (400–800 m)
3. Mountainous (800–1,600 m)

Evergreen

6. Low-altitude mesophyllic (under 400 m)
7. Submountainous mesophyllic (400–800 m)
8. Coastal and subcoastal microphyllic (dry woodland)
9. Typical swamp
10. Low swamp

SUBPERENNIFOLIOUS

Semideciduous

12. Typical mesophyllic
13. Mesophyllic with fluctuating humidity
14. Notophyllic
15. Microphyllic

ACICULIFOLIOUS PERENNIFOLIOUS TROPICAL FORESTS

Pine

16. With *Pinus caribaea*
17. With *Pinus caribaea* and *Pinus tropicalis*
18. With *Pinus tropicalis*
19. With *Pinus cubensis*
20. With *Pinus mestrensis*

LATIFOLIOUS TROPICAL THICKET

22. Xeromorphic subthicket on serpentine (torchwood)
25. Coastal and subcoastal xeromorphic, with abundant succulents (slope brush)

HERBACEOUS COMMUNITIES

27. Swamp grassland

Scale 1 : 3,000,000

plants that live there must be resistant to such shifts (a three- to six-month dry season and between 1,000 and 1,600 mm of rain a year). They have a single arboreal stratum that reaches 15 meters in height, with representative species including black júcaro, majagua, majagua de Cuba, red ateje, Cuban mahogany, roble de yugo, gray palm (palma cana), ácana or jaimiqui, yamaquey, ocuje, and yarey. They also have a bush stratum and a herbaceous stratum with little species variety. These forests occupy extensive areas in the island's flat zones, in regions like the plains of Cauto and the coastal plains of Holguín, north and south of Camagüey and Ciego de Avila, north of Las Villas, north and south of Matanzas, and south of Havana and Pinar del Río. humid→ rainy , dry→ dry

Evergreen and subperennifolious forests also have two arboreal substrata and some emergent trees, but fewer than 30 percent of their trees lose their leaves at some point during the year. These forests include bush and herbaceous strata, although less dense, as well as epiphytes and lianas. They are conditioned by a tropical climate with one or two dry months during the winter and between 1,600 and 2,000 millimeters of rainfall a year. The first substratum reaches a height of between 20 and 25 meters and includes species such as aguacatillo, quiebrahacha, majagua, ocuje, dágame, cedar, bayúa, native walnut (nogal del país), and yamao or yamagua. In the second substratum appear lancewood, female and white guara, levisa, and vigueta naranjo. The prominent emergent tree of these forests is the ceiba. In their original distribution, these forests covered significant stretches of the plains, although they also exist in the foothills (*zonas de premontaña*) and lower mountains.

The types of trees I have mentioned predominated in many of the best soils and flatlands. This fact and their abundance in precious woods and lumber explain their almost total destruction to satisfy the growing desire for cropland and wood for diverse uses. These vegetal formations were prevalent in physico-natural regions invaded by the sugar industry throughout its career in Cuba (see map 1.2).[23] What most interests us about these natural regions is their plains and heights that extend from the far

---

MAP 1.1. Estimate of Original Vegetation, Sixteenth Century

Source: Map by Enrique del Risco Rodríguez, in Academia de Ciencias de Cuba, *Nuevo atlas nacional de Cuba* (Havana: Instituto de Geografía [Academia de Ciencias de Cuba] and Instituto Geográfico Nacional [Spain], 1989).

Note: Only geographic categories most pertinent to our discussion are listed here.

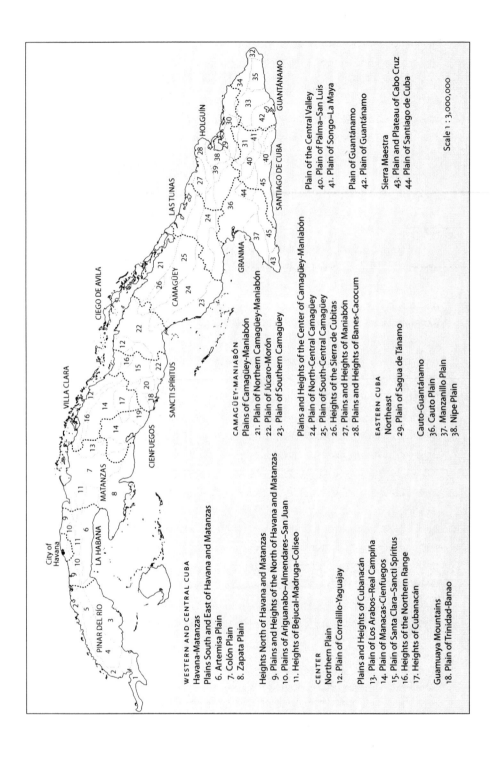

WESTERN AND CENTRAL CUBA

Havana–Matanzas

Plains South and East of Havana and Matanzas
6. Artemisa Plain
7. Colón Plain
8. Zapata Plain

Heights North of Havana and Matanzas
9. Plains and Heights of the North of Havana and Matanzas
10. Plains of Ariguanabo–Almendares–San Juan
11. Heights of Bejucal-Madruga-Coliseo

CENTER

Northern Plain
12. Plain of Corralillo-Yaguajay

Plains and Heights of Cubanacán
13. Plain of Los Arabos–Real Campiña
14. Plain of Manacas-Cienfuegos
15. Plain of Santa Clara–Sancti Spíritus
16. Heights of the Northern Range
17. Heights of Cubanacán

Guamuaya Mountains
18. Plain of Trinidad-Banao

CAMAGÜEY-MANIABÓN

Plains of Camagüey-Maniabón
21. Plain of Northern Camagüey-Maniabón
22. Plain of Júcaro-Morón
23. Plain of Southern Camagüey

Plains and Heights of the Center of Camagüey-Maniabón
24. Plain of North-Central Camagüey
25. Plain of South-Central Camagüey
26. Heights of the Sierra de Cubitas
27. Plains and Heights of Maniabón
28. Plains and Heights of Banes-Cacocum

EASTERN CUBA

Northeast
29. Plain of Sagua de Tánamo

Cauto-Guantánamo
36. Cauto Plain
37. Manzanillo Plain
38. Nipe Plain

Plain of the Central Valley
40. Plain of Palma–San Luis
41. Plain of Songo–La Maya

Plain of Guantánamo
42. Plain of Guantánamo

Sierra Maestra
43. Plain and Plateau of Cabo Cruz
44. Plain of Santiago de Cuba

Scale 1 : 3,000,000

west of the current (politico-administrative) province of Havana to the far east of the current province of Camagüey — that is, the districts of Havana-Matanzas, Centro, and Camagüey-Maniabón from the physico-geographic subprovince Plains and Heights of Western and Central Cuba, with their corresponding subdistricts and regions and a flat or rolling topography. I will also mention some of the natural regions of the East Cuba subprovince, significant portions of which were taken over by sugar beginning in the late nineteenth century.[24]

On the margins of a general characterization of the different areas, I will place greater emphasis on certain natural regions as examples of each phase of sugar's expansion. Taking physico-natural regionalization into account contributes to our understanding of the impact of sugar's advance and of the different edaphic, climactic, topographic, and hydrographic circumstances (among others) to which agribusiness had to adapt and that may have contributed to its success. Map 1.3 shows the fertility and potential agricultural use of the soils and gives an idea of their productive qualities, although it should be noted that the map's delimitations correspond not to homogeneous areas but to ones formed by a mosaic of soils intermixed in different proportions.

Colonization of the Island and Its Forests to 1772

The colonization of Cuba began in 1510, with three hundred Europeans under the command of Governor (Adelantado) Diego Velázquez. Between 1511 and 1515 the first seven cities were established: Baracoa (1511–12), Bayamo (1513), Trinidad, Sancti Spíritus, and Puerto Príncipe (1514), and Santiago de Cuba and Havana (1515). Remedios was established some time later (the town of San Juan de los Remedios de la Sabana del Cayo was founded in 1578, although the settlement of Santa Cruz de la Sabana del Cayo had existed there since 1515). From this point until the middle of the eighteenth century, most of the new settlements were established in the historic region of Havana. Many of the others were founded in Nueva Filipinas (Pinar del

MAP 1.2. Natural Regions of Cuba and Current Provinces

Source: J. M. Rodríguez and M. A. González, "Map of Physico-geographical Regionalization," in Academia de Ciencias de Cuba, *Nuevo atlas nacional de Cuba* (Havana: Instituto de Geografía [Academia de Ciencias de Cuba] and Instituto Geográfico Nacional [Spain], 1989).

Note: Only regions most pertinent to our discussion are listed here.

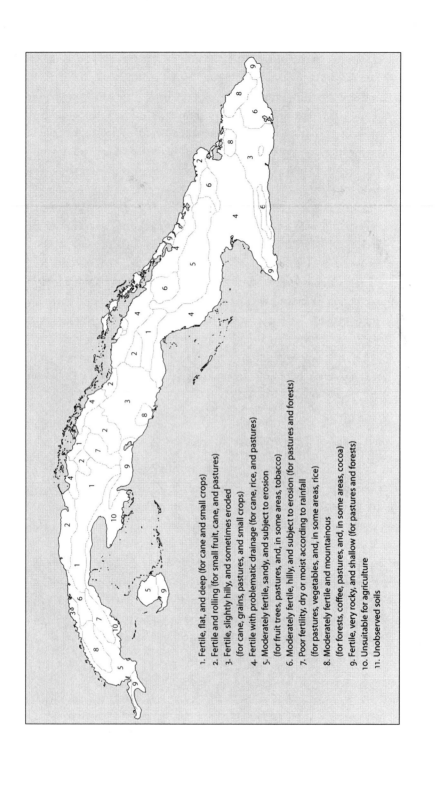

1. Fertile, flat, and deep (for cane and small crops)
2. Fertile and rolling (for small fruit, cane, and pastures)
3. Fertile, slightly hilly, and sometimes eroded (for cane, grains, pastures, and small crops)
4. Fertile with problematic drainage (for cane, rice, and pastures)
5. Moderately fertile, sandy, and subject to erosion (for fruit trees, pastures, and, in some areas, tobacco)
6. Moderately fertile, hilly, and subject to erosion (for pastures and forests)
7. Poor fertility, dry or moist according to rainfall (for pastures, vegetables, and, in some areas, rice)
8. Moderately fertile and mountainous (for forests, coffee, pastures, and, in some areas, cocoa)
9. Fertile, very rocky, and shallow (for pastures and forests)
10. Unsuitable for agriculture
11. Unobserved soils

Río), Santa Clara, and Holguín. The conquest of territories on the American continent led to the exodus of many of the first colonizers, while the shrinking of indigenous communities was accelerated by physical violence, enslavement, and European diseases. In the second half of the seventeenth century the principal economic activity of the island's scant population was raising livestock. Generally speaking, the first centuries of European colonization had a limited impact on the forests, although the latter were increasingly exploited for varying ends.[25]

Beginning in the early sixteenth century, the town councils of the first cities began to distribute lands through the system of *mercedes*, in the form of vast properties that later became known as *hatos* and *corrales*.[26] In 1574 the Ordinances of Cáceres established the legal framework of this distribution of large estates destined for livestock and of small farms for crops.[27] The concession of land by municipalities fundamentally continued until a royal edict of November 23, 1729, eliminated this municipal privilege, which according to several authors had no parallel in the rest of the Spanish Empire.[28]

The "ideal" dimensions of these haciendas for raising livestock, formalized by measures taken in 1579, give an idea of the disproportion between their size and the relatively small population of the time. The *hatos* had a circumference of 2 Cuban leagues (resulting in an area of 1,680 caballerías, or 22,512 hectares), while for the *corrales* this dimension was 1 Cuban league (an area of 420 caballerías, or 5,628 hectares; see figure 1.1).[29] The distributed lands constituted the majority of the island's territory, and only in Oriente did large spaces remain that had not been conceded. Because of the peculiar circular form of the parcels, except in the eastern zones, and the absence of boundaries, haciendas frequently overlay each other, resulting in lengthy legal fights over title. Licenses to establish small farms at first included the lands closest to villages, such as the *ejidos* (common lands). With time small farms (estancias) also appeared in the spaces, known as *realengos* (royal possessions), between the circular haciendas, as well as within the haciendas themselves, as in the case of the *ingenios*[30] or the tobacco plantations that followed riverbeds.

MAP 1.3. Agricultural Use of Soils

Source: Instituto de Geografía de la Academia de Ciencias de Cuba and Instituto de Geografía de la Academia de Ciencias de la U.R.S.S., *Atlas Nacional de Cuba* (Havana, 1970).

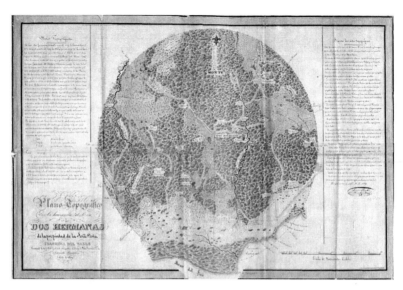

FIGURE 1.1. Francisco Lavallée, "Representation of the Dos Hermanas *Hato* in the South of the Current Province of Ciego de Avila, in 1839."

(Archivo de Agrimensores Serafín Sánchez Govín, Fundación Antonio Núñez Jiménez de la Naturaleza y el Hombre [Havana], box 176)

The concession of land did not confer full property rights. The *merced* rather transmitted a right of use of the land and its natural products, with certain associated obligations such as supplying meat to villages within a hacienda's jurisdiction. It was this characteristic that later allowed town councils to grant new licenses within the haciendas as a way to overcome the apparent shortage of land.[31] Furthermore, if usufruct of land was granted, one would have to consider as a separate category woodlands, streams, and pastures, which were considered communal property following the Castilian tradition that colonists brought with them to the Americas.

Thanks to the sparse population of the island, however, these restrictions had little impact during the first phase of colonization, although lawsuits defending communal property or assets in areas near the main towns quickly became common.[32] For more than two centuries the large livestock ranches that encompassed almost the entire island had relatively little impact on the landscape, in part because of the kind of livestock husbandry that was practiced. Far from conflicting with the *hatos* and *corrales*, the vast forests were one of their fundamental components. Hogs were predominantly raised within these forests, on whose fruit they fed. In these early years, cattle were raised on *hatos* generally composed of larger forests mixed with savannas, whether of natural origin or cleared by the ranchers (*hateros*). The custom was to fell a certain portion of woodland for pastures, a practice that had to be repeated rather frequently owing to the latter's diminishing quality and the rapid proliferation of weeds and secondary vegetation. But the forest also had the important function of providing food during the dry season. Between October and March, when the grass in the pastures thinned, the livestock stayed in the wooded areas of the haciendas and ate shoots and fruit on the ground, branches within their reach, and reeds.

The dominant image in contemporary accounts is that of a territory covered with forests, despite the latter's reduction for different reasons. In 1544, for example, the bishop Fray Diego Sarmiento affirmed, during a tour of the island, that if the Indians were left free, most of Cuba's cities would be depopulated and "there will only be this town [Bayamo] and Havana, and the island left impassable due to the thick woodlands that will swallow the roads."[33] Two centuries later Nicolás Joseph de Ribera wrote that all "is covered with thickets and evergreen forests that make it quite lovely," although he also mentioned that "in parts there are many savannas, which are bountiful pastures that produce much feed for livestock." His description includes many other images of a scarcely modified environment: "Its forests are made more beautiful by parakeets and parrots, in extreme abundance, by macaws, whose chicks are quite flavorful, by royal woodpeckers, tocoloros, and infinitely more brilliant and rare feathers and colors." The island was full of royal palms and wild dogs that lived free in the forests, "where, if no meat is to be had, there are plentiful fruit for them to nourish themselves and be independent," with vast, "most beautiful" forests in which precious woods "abound wherever one likes." Elsewhere Ribera notes that "even for the building of Warships this Island may be the best suited on the Globe; it is entirely covered with a continuous forest of precious woods."[34]

It did not take long for this abundance to awaken the interest of the Crown. Felipe II, for instance, mentioned it in several letters dated between 1578 and 1588, discussing the use of Cuban precious woods such as ebony, mahogany, ácana, and quiebrahacha in the construction of the monastery of San Lorenzo el Real (El Escorial).[35] It was also common for such woods to be harvested by smugglers or pirates in the service of other European powers. English and French inhabitants of much smaller neighboring islands found in Cuban forests a reserve of precious woods lacking in their own territories. As Manuel Moreno Fraginals noted, "Before sugar, before tobacco, before livestock, precious woods were the very symbol of the Far Antilles."[36]

The attention that the metropole paid to the Cuban forests resulted above all from the strategic importance given to shipbuilding, central to many of the measures adopted during the seventeenth and eighteenth centuries relative to the colony's rich forests. No other use of Cuban woods, such as for the gun carriages of artillery pieces, required so large an infrastructure or so copious and regular a supply. The support of shipbuilding on the island began in 1518 with a royal decree that authorized Cuba's inhabitants to equip ships with guns in order to discover and conquer islands or territories. Although vessels were built in different locations, Havana and its surrounding area quickly became the center of this industry.

The city's status, beginning in 1561, as a port of call for the fleet stimulated commercial, agricultural, and livestock activities unavailable to other towns, many of which had to depend on smuggling. The development of a service economy favored the distribution of lands by the city council, so that the number of *hatos* and *corrales* conceded increased from 28 between 1550 and 1567 to 148 between 1567 and 1578.[37] Thus almost all the available territory between Cape San Antonio and the borders of lands conceded by towns in the center of the island was distributed. The strategic location of Havana also led to the building of military fortifications that sheltered the city from incursions by pirates and privateers. All this favored the growth of Havana's population at a rate faster than that of other urban centers.

Havana's importance relative to other Cuban cities and regions became increasingly established, so it is not surprising that the natural landscapes of the Havana region were also transformed at a far more rapid pace.[38] With the exception of a small portion of its northern and southern coasts, areas of tropical thickets and swamp vegetation, the region was covered with hardwood forests. In the colony's first centuries, these landscapes were significantly affected by the felling of trees for shipbuilding and by the radial expansion of agriculture, particularly of cash crops. The area most affected until 1772 was, generally speaking, that of the zones closest to the natural region of Plains and Heights of the North of Havana and Matanzas, that of Plains of Ariguanabo–Almendares–San Juan, and, to a lesser degree, that of Heights of Bejucal-Madruga-Coliseo.

The city of Havana is located in the first of these natural regions, which extends from east to west for about 165 kilometers, with a width of from 3 to

12 kilometers and an area of 2,025 square kilometers. The land, generally undulating and fertile, is traversed by many rivers, including the Almendares, the San Juan, and the Bucaranao, the majority of them small. The region of Plains of Ariguanabo–Almendares–San Juan extends for 120 kilometers, with an average width of 15 kilometers and an area of 1,913 square kilometers. Its land is considered fertile, with remarkable subterranean drainage. The part of the Mayabeque that crosses the region is one of its few rivers of any importance.

The impact of the first European settlements on the wooded areas was felt early in this zone. On November 12, 1550, the city council found it necessary to promulgate what Leví Marrero has called Cuba's first conservationist regulation. It prohibited blacks from cutting mahogany and cedar — wood that the slaves used to build troughs (or flat-bottomed boats) and other rudimentary items — in a radius of 2 leagues (8.5 km). The ordinance established a penalty of ten days in the stocks and three hundred lashes for the slave who violated it, as well as a fine of twenty gold pesos for the master if the slave acted under his or her orders. The measure's goal was to ensure a sufficient supply of wood for the Catholic Church and for houses in the city.[39]

During the sixteenth century the Havana city council adopted other measures to curtail deforestation. For example, in 1552 it sought to restrain shipmasters and other "outsiders" (*forasteros*) from cutting trees and taking the wood to Castile to sell or use for building. In 1557 Governor Francisco Carreño complained to the council that the chaotic felling of trees was forcing inhabitants to travel 2 or 3 leagues to find wood. To remedy this, he asked the council to establish a municipal woodland. The council agreed that within a radius of 1 league no one could fell trees for any reason; nor would any farmland be conceded there, the aim being to ensure a supply of trees for lumber and firewood.[40]

But the greatest demand for wood resulted from Havana's transformation into a center of shipbuilding, considered to be Cuba's primary industry. The first galleon was listed in the registry of Seville's Casa de Contratación (chamber of commerce) in 1551. In the second half of the sixteenth century small and large galleons as well as frigates were built in Havana.[41] Pedro Menéndez de Avilés (governor from 1568 to 1573) claimed in a 1568 letter to the Council of the Indies that he had built in Havana six ships as excellent as those in Biscay. This expansion was related to the effort, led by the governor, to conquer Florida. One of the governor's subordinates, Lieutenant Pedro Menéndez Márquez, became one of the foremost shipbuilders.[42]

After two decades of inactivity, Havana's shipyards returned to work thanks to a royal decree of March 2, 1617, which mandated the establishment of an arsenal. In 1619 the management of the shipyards was entrusted to Captain Juan Pérez de Oporto, who faced a formidable legal battle when livestock ranchers tried to prevent him from felling trees in estates closest to the shipyard.[43] In 1622 and 1624, Laws 13 and 15, Title 17, Book 4, in the *Recopilación de las leyes de los reinos de las Indias* (Code of Laws of the Realms of the Indies) sought to stimulate and protect shipbuilding.[44] This legislation prohibited the felling of cedar, mahogany, and oak for 10 leagues to the east and west of the city (or 42.4 km in either direction).[45]

Ovidio Ortega Pereyra notes that "military shipbuilding in the seventeenth century was sporadic, in accord with metropolitan needs, which were in decline." He also observes that when speaking of shipbuilding prior to 1747 one should think only in terms of careenage, or "low-lying areas at any point on the coast or along a river where there is sufficient shelter and abundant wood in the vicinity."[46]

A royal decree of October 27, 1713, again ordered construction of the arsenal, which began in 1722. Two years later, the captain of the arsenal, Juan de Acosta, launched a fifty-cannon ship and with it Havana's renascent shipbuilding career. In the arsenal, located beside the Real Fuerza castle, twenty-two ships of the line, six frigates, and three packet boats were built before it was deactivated in 1747. The enterprise was financed by revenue from Mexico and, beginning in 1740, with capital from the Havana Company of Commerce, which was allowed to build its ships in the royal shipyards.

In the midst of this flowering of the industry, an area of 335 meters along the ramparts inside the bay was reserved for a new arsenal. The project was led by Lorenzo Montalvo, first Count de Macuriges, who inaugurated it in 1748. From this time until 1761 fifteen vessels were completed, including eight ships of the line. The industry was stimulated by the determination of the new Bourbon dynasty to reaffirm the empire's naval power. The Havana shipyard became one of the principal suppliers of the royal navy, created in 1714.[47] Various authors have noted Havana's importance, considering it to be Spain's main shipyard not simply in the Americas but also in the empire as a whole at different points in the eighteenth century.[48] Such efforts required a great amount of wood. In 1717 woodlands in the metropole began to be harvested for shipbuilding, and in 1723 areas near the coasts were first explored with the aim of exploiting their timber. Finally, in January 1748 the ordinances were promulgated to conserve and increase the woodlands of the navy, which was given control of wooded areas for 25 leagues from the coasts and navigable rivers. This represented an area estimated at between half and two-thirds of Spain's woodlands.[49] The new system created a kind of monopoly over these forests, which were placed under the jurisdiction of the navy quartermasters general of the maritime departments of Cartagena, Cadiz, and Ferrol.[50]

Although they were not the metropole's first regulations that sought to protect shipbuilding by curbing the exploitation of woodlands, the 1748 ordinances did represent a turning point. The Cuban case was no different; Law 13 from 1622, in the *Recopilación*, could even be considered a significant precedent. In same year, 1748, the Marquis de La Ensenada informed the captain general Francisco Cagigal y de La Vega that the latter's edict of August 20, 1747, which reaffirmed and amplified the reservation of the best wood for shipbuilding and the development of woodlands for this purpose, had been approved. For Marrero this legislation updated, "in the strictly local sense," the dispositions contained in the *Recopilación*.[51]

Cagigal y de La Vega's edict sought to remedy the fact that, after several years of uninterrupted construction at the arsenal, shipbuilders had to travel increasing distances to find wood. The counsel of knowledgeable people had led him to conclude that the number of trees needed for ships was declining as this timber was put to "less recommendable" uses. Much of the woodlands in the vicinity had been "cleared and uselessly burned with the opening of many sites of mills and small farms." For this reason, it seemed necessary to increase the area reserved for the navy and the number of species that could be felled only with a license. The latter now included sabicú, chicharrón, yaba, ocuje, guaiacum, and the three species of oak. The newly restricted territories included "all the coast on both seas for forty leagues windward and leeward of this port for a distance of six leagues inland from the northern coast and twenty from the southern one beginning at the anchorage of Batabanó, with no distance indicated, because in terms of distance what is important is to conserve all the [wood] that exists in the narrow width of the island."[52]

For common usage other trees were allowed, including baría, ácana, frijolillo, vigueta, jaimiqui, and quiebrahacha. One of the most important articles stipulated that no land could be cleared for mills or cultivation without a license, so that it could be ordered that "when trees [had to] be felled or cleared for the planting of cane or other crops, and in areas where trees

[had] been or [were] being cut for firewood," no tree reserved for the navy, "whether grown or newly planted," would be cut but rather would be "left standing so that it [did] not prejudice the cultivation and so that it [could] be found when ready to be harvested." Violation of this regulation was punishable by a fine of 100 ducats. A person who cut down a tree was also required to plant "four cuttings from the same tree around its trunk," and it was forbidden to fell any cedar three-quarters of whose bark could not be cleanly removed or to cut down a palm tree, "since its fruit is suitable for feeding pigs, and its branches useful for diverse purposes." Various stipulations specifically concerned the exploitation of forests by the navy, with the general restriction that "in those places reserved for the usage of the King, no other person may fell trees in any manner."[53]

The felling of timber to supply the Havana shipyard and the metropole spread to various points on the island, but it was much more intense in the center-western part. Beginning in the seventeenth century, the preferred area for harvesting wood was the northern coast, especially in those places where rivers such as the Almendares, or the Zanja Real aquaduct, or bays like those of Cabañas, Mariel, and Bahía Honda could be used for transporting the lumber. During the 1760s the supply came principally through contracts signed with individual property owners, who allowed their woodlands to be cleared. In the east, in the area of Matanzas, these sites included the so-called *montes*, or haciendas, of La Palma, San Andrés, and El Acana, whose timber was sent down the Canimar River. In the southwest, they included the haciendas of Anafe, San Pedro, Guayabal, and Ariguanabo, whose timber was sent to the wharf at Baracoa on the northern coast. In 1770 a contract was signed with Francisco Franquiz that would encompass "all the *montes* along the Cuyaguateje and Guadiana rivers, their surroundings and those on the southern coast, from the mouth of this river to the Batabanó."[54] Other sites farther from the capital where timber was harvested for the navy during the seventeenth century and the first half of the eighteenth were in the areas of Trinidad, Sancti Spíritus, and around the Sagua la Grande and Sagua la Chica rivers, in the vicinity of Remedios.

Few practical details are known about how timber was harvested and removed to supply the shipyards in Havana and in Spain.[55] What is certain is that this was an important productive activity that required considerable labor, some of it specialized. Without a doubt it had an impact both in its exploitation of forests and in its creation of a certain infrastructure: pastures for the oxen, roads for the hauling of lumber, and hamlets or villages for employees and slaves. It likewise stimulated the coastal traffic between different territories on the island and the port in Havana.

The Initial Advance of Sugar
in the Havana Region, 1600–1771

Sugarcane, originally from New Guinea, was one of the earliest goods traded between Europe and the East. Grown in tropical and semitropical climates, cane is associated with different processes of conquest and colonization.[56] In the fifteenth century Portugal and Spain took sugar to the Atlantic islands of Madeira, São Tomé, Cape Verde, and the Canaries.[57] Columbus himself introduced cane to the New World during his second voyage, although the sugar trade began in Hispaniola around 1517, promoted by individual property owners and with the support of the Crown through decrees and loans designed to encourage it.

As Hispaniola developed its sugar industry in the second half of the sixteenth century, Cuba remained on the margins of a colonial system based on the exploitation of cash crops. Several of the first cities, including Bayamo and Santiago de Cuba, became the sites of sugar plantations toward the end of the sixteenth century, but these never attained the importance that those around the Havana port did very quickly. No other city had so many of the assets needed to undertake an industry whose success depended first and foremost on the ability to ship abroad. Since the crop was first introduced, most of the varieties of cane grown in Cuba have belonged to the species *Saccharum officinarum* L. It grows very well in dry conditions and has high ecological plasticity. It uses solar energy efficiently. When favored by the humid subtropical climate, it responds well to the photoperiodicity of short days during the phase of flowering and maturation (the winter or dry season, from November to April), when there are fewer daylight hours, moderate temperatures, and low-intensity light. The rainy season, from April to October, with long days, high temperatures, and high humidity, influences its development and growth (see figure 1.2).[58]

In 1595 two events led to the birth of the Cuban sugar industry: Felipe II authorized Gómez Reynell of Portugal to introduce black slaves into the Indies, and a royal decree, on December 30, extended to Cuba the advantages granted to mill owners in Hispaniola, that is, "that the lands, slaves, animals, machines, tools, etc., of mills may not be seized for reason of debt, whether totally or partially."[59] Another milestone was the arrival in Havana

FIGURE 1.2.

Growth of sugarcane during the rainy and dry seasons.

(Franklin S. Earle, *El cultivo de la caña de azúcar en las Antillas* [Havana: Germán Kali Works, Imprenta La Prueba, n.d.], 73)

royal loan
to support
sugar

in 1602 of a royal loan solicited by some of the city's inhabitants in order to promote sugar.[60] Among the peculiarities of Havana's first sugar plantations was the use of water power, although in general, given the limited flow of the region's rivers, this source of energy to crush cane was eventually exhausted.

From 1602 to the 1670s Habaneros became increasingly enthusiastic about sugar. An analysis of the requests for concessions before the city council reveals that between 1599 and 1699 a total of 204 were granted for the building of sugar mills (170 on small farms [estancias] and 30 within *hatos* and *corrales*), although fewer than half of these mills were actually built.[61] In the seventeenth century, the number of mills in the Havana area fluctuated around 80, most of them founded in the 1650s and 1660s.[62] Beginning in the 1670s, however, the industry fell into a prolonged crisis brought about by several factors, including the rise of the Caribbean plantation colonies, whose model of exploitation promoted significant growth in the sugar industry through the massive importation of slaves and through improved commerce with their metropoles.

sugar →
bc slaves

In a letter of July 14, 1690, Governor Severino de Manzaneda and the city council informed the court of the Habaneros' worry about the possible collapse of the tobacco and sugar industries, which the city saw as its only sources of wealth.[63] After a devastating hurricane hit the west of the island in September 1692, the city council noted that "of seventy mills only thirty remain operational."[64] The crisis lasted until the 1720s. The installation of the new Bourbon dynasty in 1713 and several of its initial decrees, such as the one that same year contracting the English South Sea Company to introduce slaves and the one four years later proclaiming a state tobacco monopoly, created new conditions. Their effects, however, were not immediate. In 1737 the Havana city council could still write to the king about "the miserable state to which this city has fallen, and which contaminates the entire island, with the imminent danger that the colony will be extinguished entirely due to the decline of the sugar and tobacco trades."[65] decline of trade

The creation of Havana's Royal Company of Commerce in 1739 impelled the sugar industry's gradual reemergence. The agent of Havana City Hall, Martín de Aróstegui, obtained in Madrid the support necessary to take this step. One of the first measures that sugar's promoters requested, and which the Council of the Indies granted, was the freeing of Havana sugar from all levies when it entered Spain. This stimulated a rebirth of the industry, also promoted by the introduction of slaves by the Company of Commerce. One of the company's members claimed that "between 1741 and 1747 thirty large mills were built in the vicinity of Havana, and during these years many woodlands were cleared to make room for cane plantations."[66] In 1750, a company lawyer and officer, Bernardo de Urritia y Matos, faced with the possibility that the headquarters would move to Seville or Cadiz, argued that the 62 mills in the Havana jurisdiction could produce up to 93,000 exportable arrobas and that other jurisdictions could not produce as much because their mills had smaller capacities but that combined they could produce as much as Havana. In both cases, "given that the territories are good, different crops will prosper conforming with their production and their possession of slaves."[67] A year later Governor Cagigal y de La Vega offered higher figures: 81 mills in the Havana region producing more than 250,000 arrobas.[68]

A book of charges for the 5 percent tax on the mills' production in the years 1759, 1760, and 1761 shows 88 mills and 350,515 arrobas for the first year, 93 and 280,359 for the second, and 97 and 367,752 for the third. The majority did not produce 8,000 arrobas, but 12 surpassed this figure, including the mill of Nuestra Señora de Loreto y San Nicolás, owned by Ignacio Peñalver in the Guanabacoa region, which produced 14,923 arrobas in 1761.[69] Joseph de Ribera argued in 1756 that sugar had great potential

free from levies

in Cuba: "Sugar is another extremely important sector that competes with tobacco and whose trade could flourish throughout the World. The only Cuban sugar that is shipped to Spain is that made in the territory near Havana . . . but not even the thousandth part of the land suited to this crop is planted with cane. It is clear that if the cultivation were developed here, the crop would abound proportionately, and foreigners would quickly lose the trade they do in Europe with their own sugar."[70]

It is important that we take into account the vision of these men who speak from the middle of the eighteenth century before we verify the traditional landmarks used to explain the development of sugar on the island. At the least, surpassing the production of other territories did not seem impossible to them. And the fact is that none of the other principal Caribbean sugar islands could compare with Cuba in the natural conditions they offered the industry, in terms of either total land area or topography. The most important recent studies of the development of Cuban sugar in the eighteenth century tend to reaffirm the preponderance of internal factors, although with their corresponding insertion into the development of the international sugar market.

The capacity of the Havana Company of Commerce was called into in question in 1759 when Governor Cagigal y de La Vega was compelled to authorize the shipping of sugar in freighted ships, which for Moreno Fraginals shows that the company had "ceased to be an instrument capable of channeling the irrepressible growth of sugar." Two years later, the city was taken by the English. Aside from its specific consequences, such as the increased importation of slaves and the establishment of contacts with the thirteen North American colonies, this event no doubt catalyzed the reforms taken later by Carlos III and his ministers with respect to their American colonies. Finally, the eleven-month English occupation "accelerated the transition to the plantation."[71]

After Spain recovered Havana in 1763, Cuba became a laboratory for important reforms in how the metropole related to its American possessions. With this object in mind, Count de Ricla and Alejandro O'Reilly traveled to the island to take charge of its administration. Under their government, in the opinion of Allan James Kuethe, the foundation was laid for a lasting transformation. Kuethe also notes that at the same time (between 1763 and 1764) a council of ministers was organized in the court, meeting every Thursday to analyze the progress of reforms in Cuba and the possibility of extending them to the rest of the empire.[72] Notable among the measures adopted are the establishment of the first quartermaster corps, the freedom to set up distilleries, the initiation of weekly mail service with the metropole, and the increase in tariffs for foreign sugar imported into Spain. It should also be noted that the expansion of sugar around Havana contributed to the freeing of trade in the empire. In 1765, Cadiz's port monopoly was ended, opening direct trade between nine ports on the peninsula and five in the Caribbean. This was the first step in a process that culminated in the promulgation, on October 12, 1778, of the regulations and tariffs for free trade between Spain and the Indies, which established thirteen ports in the metropole and twenty-two in the colonies, three of them in Cuba.

Havana Mills until 1771: Fertile Clearings, Abundant Lumber and Firewood

Compared with the voluminous information available for other Caribbean sugar islands, relatively little is known about the characteristics of Cuban sugar mills before the mid-1700s.[73] Among the reasons for this are the smaller size of the Cuban industry and the little need for innovation given Cuba's considerable advantage in terms of land area. Formulating a prototype of Havana-area mills prior to the mid-eighteenth century from the fragmentary documentation is thus difficult. In the first place, one would have to differentiate between the units used before the 1740s and those that appear afterward. Nonetheless, for both periods the average land area for the mills can be situated between 20 and 30 caballerías. For instance, the data in the thirteen petitions for concessions of mill sites submitted in the seventeenth century for Guanabacoa region, located southeast of Havana Bay, show an average of 23.7 caballerías.[74]

The data available for the eighteenth century are not much different. Fe Iglesias García estimates a size of 24.9 caballerías per property for the first half of the century, while Mercedes García Rodríguez gives a figure of 26.8 caballerías for the entire century and argues that woodland terrain was more abundant than cultivable land.[75] Moreno Fraginals offers the lowest average figure: between 10 and 12 caballerías for Havana mills until 1762.[76] Guanabacoa, with a sample of twelve mills between 1725 and 1753, had an average of 31 caballerías.

In fact, before establishing a figure for the total area under cultivation, we need to take into account the correlation between open land and woodland. In the former were established the mill, slave cabins, gardens, and *conucos* (areas set aside for slaves' subsistence crops). The latter was used for lumber and especially firewood, the only combustible then used to boil and evaporate cane juice. The total amount of land devoted to sugarcane in the Havana region in the mid-1700s was not much different from that of other Caribbean islands. According to David Watts, the "idealized plantation" that predominated in Cuba during this period, following the model of Jean-Baptiste Labat until 1724, had about 61 hectares devoted to cane, or about 4.55 caballerías for properties with an average of 120 slaves.[77] In the mid-1700s, only a few mills in the Havana area had this much labor. For the previous century, Marrero gives an average of 20 slaves per property in Cuba, while in Barbados the average was 40 when the sugar trade began in the middle of the century.[78]

Since the average number of slaves was smaller in Havana plantations, we can conclude that the amount of land in sugarcane was similar or inferior to that indicated by Labat. In Caribbean plantation colonies, improvements in the cultivation methods and technical innovations had to be implemented early to offset the land's decreasing fertility and the diminishing yields.[79] In Havana and Cuba generally, in contrast, the most common solution was simply to abandon the properties and look for new land, whether because of a shortage of firewood or because of the loss of fertility. Which of these factors was determinant? The available information does not point to a categorical response, but the evidence suggests that the "transhumant," traveling, or mobile nature of Cuban mills in these first centuries may have largely been the result of the woodlands being used up.[80]

In areas where the soil was adequately fertile, new cane plantations gradually replaced old ones as farmers sought to keep up with evolving methods of processing. Insufficient forests worried planters primarily because the latter needed large amounts of lumber to build the various components of the mill. There were three basic units, built with different woods: the *casa de molienda*, where the crusher (*trapiche*) was set up in order to extract the cane juice; the *casa de calderas*, where it was cooked; and the *casa de purga*, where the production cycle ended with separation of the sugar from the molasses. Large parts like the crusher were made from the hardest woods, like sabicú and chicharrón. Smaller parts and tools were usually made from cedar. Often these had to be replaced after a short time. Containers, which at least until the last third of the eighteenth century were made of cedar, also required a lot of wood, as did the houses, cabins, and other buildings of people who worked on the site. Finally, wood was needed to build carts and other vehicles necessary for agricultural operations and the transport of sugar to the coasts, rivers, and port of Havana.

Woods had to be sorted by quality. For firewood, the best-quality ones, which came from the forests' first or second substratum, were used first, followed by others in the same substrata and in the bushes. Consumption of these was increased by the so-called Spanish system, or *tren*,[81] for cooking the cane juice. It consisted of lighting a separate fire under each kettle or boiler, requiring an enormous amount of wood to keep all the fires lit during the entire fabrication process (*zafra*).[82] This was a basic difference between milling in Cuba and on other Caribbean islands, where the scarcity of wood led millers to use alternative combustibles like cane pulp.

Not surprisingly, the sugar industry became one of the main sources of conflict with respect to the use of forests around Havana in the seventeenth century. For Julio Le Riverend, this reflected the "contradiction between the commercial livestock farming and agriculture, on the one hand, and communal and state use of forests, on the other."[83] In his opinion, beginning in the 1630s and 1640s, the development of sugar was at the center of the conflict. Le Riverend points out that the city council customarily defended mill owners' requests for forests despite protests from owners of the *corrales* closest to the city, who argued that the timber should be reserved for communal use or set aside for shipbuilding. At the end of the 1640s, as part of a large-scale offensive against the heavy use of firewood by the mills, the council forbade the latter from taking wood from reserved forests.[84]

Similarly, Marrero notes that forests were getting more and more distant from the urban center because of the insatiable need for firewood, "which razed the low woodlands and residual timber in a wide area around the Factory."[85] Another problem was that many small farms intended for subsistence crops began planting cane for processing in nearby *trapiches* (mills powered by oxen) and *ingenios* (mills that used waterpower).[86] The scarcity of staple foods attracted the attention of the city council, which attempted to require farmers to abandon cane for the public good. One means for reducing the effects of the preference for cane was the May 1653 legislation requiring mill owners to plant cassava to supply Havana.

Also central to the conflict were the so-called *montes vedados* (private woodlands preserves), which surrounded the city for 1 league to the east and west and were part of its defensive system. Sugar played its part in this conflict. In 1670 Governor Francisco Rodríguez Ledesma complained that two mills had been allowed to locate in this area and consumed more than

mill preserved in area

thirty thousand loads of firewood, as well as four or five small farms that were like fruit orchards "from which there is no benefit whatsoever in addition to the firewood they steal from the woodland." He proposed that the mills be dismantled, with the owners given four times more property 8 or 10 leagues from the city, and that a person be charged with caring for these woodlands and given a seat next to the mayors during public ceremonies. The court prohibited the cutting of any tree, ordering that the woodland be allowed to grow and that the farms within it be dismantled[87] in the interest of the city's security and defense. In short, it ruled, "the public good [must be preferred] to the private."[88]

For several centuries the arrival of sugar in the new territories was an attractive force because of its economic advantages for property owners and the rest of the inhabitants, who saw it as a surer means to meet their daily needs. In contrast, it became a focal point of conflict over the exploitation of natural resources and in this sense was perhaps the principal motive for confrontation between public and private interest. This pattern expanded in the early days in a radial movement out from the port of Havana and by the mid-1700s encompassed a considerable area compared with other regions of the island, although still tiny compared with the island's total area.

Geography of Sugar and Transformation of Havana's Space

The first *trapiches* and *ingenios* were built in areas closest to the port, sites originally considered to be common lands or fields for planting. The sugar plantations were concentrated in three zones: one to the northeast centered on the town of Guanabacoa, 2 leagues to the south of Havana, extending north to Cojímar and south to Santa María del Rosario; a second to the south, also 2 leagues distant, in the area known as Nacimiento de la Chorrera (or Source of the Chorrera, the Chorrera being today the Almendares River), extending to the *corrales* of Calabazar to the west and Jiaraco to the east; and a third between 1 and 3 leagues west-southwest of the city, in the area of the villages of Puentes Grandes and Jesús del Monte, extending to Marianao and Luyanó. More distant plantations were scattered around rivers and the coast — in Guanabo to the east, for example, and Jaimanitas to the west — since waterways facilitated the transport of sugar.

All these facilities were located within the 8-league limit that since the mid-seventeenth century had been set aside for communal use of woodlands, waterways, and pastures, not to mention being within the zone reserved to supply the shipyards. In fact, this did not prevent the sugar planters and mill owners from occupying the same space, a tendency that continued in the first half of the eighteenth century.[89] Bishop Pedro Morell de Santa Cruz gave a detailed idea of the distribution of *ingenios* following his travels on the island between 1754 and 1757. Most of the mills were within the ecclesiastical boundaries of the Havana area: Guanabacoa had 24, Calvario and Managua each had 12, and San Felipe y Santiago (Bejucal) had 10. Farther to the west but still within the Havana region were the *ingenios* of Quemados (5), Cano (20), and Guanajay (1). To the east, Río Blanco had 2 (see figure 1.3).[90]

The bishop's account indicates that at the end of the 1750s most Havana *ingenios* were located within 8 leagues of the port. The ones farthest away were those in Santiago de las Vegas and Managua, 5 leagues from the harbor. Within 5 or 6 leagues of the capital, deforestation had transformed remarkably the former landscape of semicaducifolious forest. After visiting the three *ingenios* seized from the Jesuit order after its expulsion from the island in 1767, Inspector Manuel Becerra Betancourt of the Temporalities Committee and Leandro Luis Jorge, overseer of the Río Blanco *ingenio*, wrote, "We climbed the hill they call the Nazarene, and we saw from its top the two coasts, both North and South, from which one can infer the destruction of the thick forest and of the woodlands that had covered this panorama."[91]

The case of Guanabacoa is typical of sugar's expansion during this whole first period. The *ingenios* were concentrated in the environs of the village, which had been created in the 1550s to bring together the Indians who roamed through the woodlands of the region.[92] Its location, 2 leagues from Havana, quickly made it attractive to European settlers and a prized territory for those petitioning the city council to found small farms. Of the *trapiches* and *ingenios* that benefited from the 1602 loan, at least four were found in this area. Radiating out from this nucleus, *ingenios* appeared in the *corrales* closest to it: Bacuranao, Cabezadas de Bucaranao, Bajurayabo, Guanabo (upper and lower), Jiraco, Río Piedras, and Jiquiabo. From 1620 to 1700 we find twenty-eight requests for concessions to found sugar estates in this region, although not all of these were actually created.[93]

With the industry's rebirth in the 1740s and 1750s, Guanabacoa reaffirmed its position as the leading site for plantations. As the areas farthest from the village became increasingly settled, their importance grew parallel to that

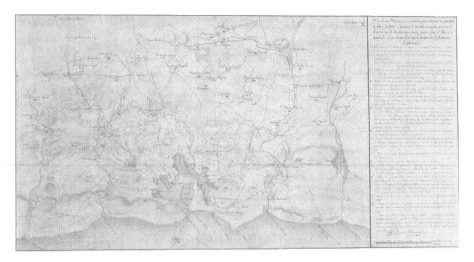

FIGURE 1.3. Area occupied by *ingenios* around the port of Havana in 1771.

(Instituto de Historia y Cultura Militar, Centro Geográfico del Ejército, *Cartografía y relaciones históricas de Ultramar*, vol. 9, *Grandes y Pequeñas Antillas*, part 1 [Madrid: Ministerio de Defensa, 1999])

of sugar in their jurisdiction. In 1659 its town council was created, and, in response to a request first made in 1696, Guanabacoa was declared a town (*villa*) by royal decrees of July 3, 1733, and August 14, 1743. During Bishop Morell's pastoral visit, it stood out as the leading sugar zone, fourteen *ingenios* having been built after the recent delimitation and sale of former *corrales*.[94] Some of these were the largest of their era, with more than one hundred slaves and an annual production of between 10,000 and 15,000 arrobas of sugar, a figure much higher than average at the time. In 1778 the new areas where sugar production was concentrated were between 2 and 4 leagues from the town, like the farm at San Jerónimo, in Río Piedras, a former *corral* 4 leagues from the Havana port that had eleven *ingenios*.[95]

Sugar's advance and the concomitant deforestation of these territories had adverse consequences for the Indians of Guanabacoa, who little by little were stripped of the lands and woodlands that they had been granted in the region. A royal decree of January 27, 1632, attempted to contain their displacement:

Natives, descendants of the former inhabitants of this island, are so impoverished by the bad neighborliness of the Havana inhabitants, who, being more powerful have entered into the boundaries of their town with the approval of the City Council, which has entrusted to them the lands of the Indians in order to set up *ingenios* and small farms on all sides of this town, hardly leaving the Indians with a way out, or woodlands to cut firewood, or earth to make into pitchers and pots, their ordinary trade.[96]

Under the influence of cash crops, the agrarian structure began to be modified in the mid-1600s. Around 1751 the *corrales* of the Guanabacoa area were made up mostly of the sixteen that had been dismantled by that date.[97] The revalorization of these lands by the sugar industry and the latter's economic benefits led even livestock farmers to consider subdividing their estates so that more *ingenios* could be built. The irruption of *ingenios* transformed the way natural resources were exploited as no economic activity had before. The tobacco farms were small and preferably located near riverbanks, allowing them to coexist with *hatos* and *corrales*. The selectiveness of woodcutting kept it from radically transforming the territories in which it was practiced. In contrast, the making of sugar resulted in an unprecedented alteration of the landscape, for both economic and ecological reasons. ~~tabacco: near riverbanks~~

As the sugar industry expanded, so did the local power wielded by the mill owners. Le Riverend notes that the decisions of the Havana city council gradually lost the sugar-related contradictions that had characterized them in the seventeenth century. Although this may be related to the crisis that lasted until the 1730s, he argues that the main reason lies in livestock farmers' interest in sugar production, as well as in more general motivations of agrarian policy.[98] In any case, it does not appear that early phenomena, such as the scarcity of subsistence foods, the increasing shortage of firewood and lumber, or the deviation of productive force toward sugar production, were overcome. ~~deforestation~~

The most important environmental effect was undoubtedly deforestation. Around the mid-eighteenth century, this phenomenon was most pronounced within 5 or 6 leagues of the port, but this does not mean more distant territories were free from it. We see a much more complex picture when we examine other specific consequences of deforestation up to this time, since the area of sugar's influence was so small in comparison with the forests that spread over the length and breadth of the island. The slow pace of sugar's expansion allowed the areas first occupied and then abandoned to become used for the cultivation of the "lesser fruit" or as *potreros*,[99] a new, intensive variety of livestock husbandry. This limited the impact when land was abandoned after being deforested and impoverished by several years of cultivation. Nevertheless, symptoms of soil erosion probably appeared early, especially on mountain slopes, together with the proliferation of invasive and plants and a certain contamination of rivers and streams.[100]

The disappearance of the forests was also said to have military consequences, as in the case of the *montes vedados*. In 1689 Governor Antonio de Viana Hinojosa complained to the court about the attitude of Lieutenant General Francisco Manuel Roa, who was related to one of the most important families in Havana. The governor had prohibited them from cutting firewood in these woodlands, to which they reacted by claiming that he would thereby "destroy their sugar mill for not having other firewood . . . than that of this woodland."[101] Two years later Governor Severino de Manzaneda lamented that much wood had been taken from the woodland that stretched from the Morro to the mouth of the Cojímar River for different individual factories. His concern was that "if the cutting is continued it will be a great prejudice because if the enemy were to land in Matanzas and drive his artillery onto the highest mountain of the woodland, which abuts the canal leading to the port, he would train his batteries on the Morro. . . . This would endanger it, and the Fuerza Vieja, the Punta, and the city would simultaneously suffer from the superiority afforded by the dominance of the woodland."[102] This warning seems a premonition of what happened later when the English took Havana.

The conflicts over use of the *montes vedados* and other communal resources and the initial struggle between livestock farming and sugar would lose force and validity before the transformations brought about by the sugar industry. But this does not mean that the way was left open for sugar plantations to expand, impelled by the ambition of mill owners and people who aspired to be mill owners. Beginning in the mid-eighteenth century, the center of the dispute over the exploitation of woodlands shifted almost entirely to sugar's competition with the equally powerful industry of Havana shipbuilding.

This was nothing new, but never before had the two sectors been so close to a direct confrontation. Internally, there was no more powerful obstacle to the growth of sugar than the legislation that privileged the Havana shipyard and the shipyards of the metropole in supply of wood, especially during the second half of the eighteenth century. And little wonder, since what was at issue was not limiting the common good of the colony's inhabitants but calling into question the strategic importance of a powerful naval force to the maintenance of the empire. In this sense, the inevitable clash between sugar plantation owners and civil servants of the navy is a fundamental element in deepening our understanding of the profound economic, social, and ecological changes that occurred as Cuba's plantation economy took off.

clash b/w sugar /navy

Shipbuilding and the Sugar Industry, 1772–1791

The Growth of Sugar in Havana: Geographic Expansion

Spain's reforms of its colonial system, begun after it signed a peace treaty with the British in 1763, stimulated sugar production in the Havana region. The number and size of *ingenios* in the area increased significantly, and in the 1790s the slave revolt in Haiti allowed the Cuban sugar industry to make its great leap forward. Nevertheless, during the final third of the eighteenth century, even after the Haitian Revolution, the industry's growth was not a straight and unimpeded line. Its progress was largely dependent on the Royal Forest Reserves (the service that could monopolize the logging of woodlands for shipbuilding), within a conception of the exploitation of forest resources that privileged the empire's strategic need for a powerful navy, one of whose bulwarks was the Havana shipyard.

As Manuel Moreno Fraginals has observed, direct contact with the English "rooted in the island the concept of the British colonial plantation," although the latter "was not foreign to the Havana oligarchy."[1] In his famous "Discurso sobre la agricultura en La Habana y medios de fomentarla" (Discourse on Agriculture in Havana and How to Promote It; 1792), Francisco de Arango y Parreño, promoter and ideologue of the great leap in the sugar industry, identified this event as "Havana's true period of resurrection. . . . With their blacks and their free trade, the British did more in a year than we had done in the previous sixty."[2]

After the English occupation of Havana, Cuba became a kind of proving ground for the intensification of Bourbon reforms of Spain's colonial system, most illustriously during the reign of Carlos III (1759–88). As part of the program of the Count de Ricla's government after recovering the city, the Count de O'Reilly was commissioned to travel the island as a *visitador general*. His recommendations, which included increasing the supply of workers and freer trade, had a direct impact on the 1795 decree that ended the monopoly of Cadiz's port and on the order that Cuba abolish taxes on the import of slaves. Shortly thereafter other measures favorable to the expansion of commercial agriculture were adopted, including the ones that established the first quartermaster corps in Havana, increased levies on the importation of foreign sugar into the metropole, and reduced taxes (in the regulations of 1788) on free trade between Spain and the Indies in various products, including sugar.[3]

But the possibilities for growth within the imperial framework were limited, as evidenced by the roots of the independence struggles of the thirteen British colonies in North America (1776–83). In 1779 Spain declared war on Great Britain, leading to shortages of and high prices for slaves and tools in Havana and, as a result, diminished sugar production. The artificial increase in prices thanks to the arrival in the city of the Spanish army gave sugar producers renewed incentive. The links between Havana planters and the slave traders and businessmen of the North American colonies, which had already existed illegally, were reinforced in those years, revealing their importance to both parties.

The suspension of this trade at the end of the war provoked a crisis in the sugar sector.[4] As Ramiro Guerra y Sánchez has shown, 600,000 to 800,000 arrobas of sugar were produced each year in Cuba, while consumption in the metropole was only 500,000 arrobas.[5] In 1787, the customs treasurer Antonio de La Paz suggested as his only proposition for developing the colony's sugar industry "export[ing] the island's products to the United States in exchange for flour, wood, and comestibles." For sugar producers, finc a permanent foreign outlet was an essential demand.[6]

The relative crisis in the industry neither impeded its growth nor diminished the Havana oligarchy's interest in sugar. On February 6, 1789, Arango y Parreño, as an agent of Havana City Hall before the court, asked the highest authorities to free Cuba's trade in slaves. At the end of this same month, the petition was agreed to for an initial period of two years, which to a certain degree was indicative of the Crown's support for the development of the sugar industry. This backing, however, continued to be contingent on there being no impact on Havana shipbuilding or on the shipment of wood to shipyards in Spain.

The interest of the two industries in woodlands became increasingly impossible to reconcile, although the sugar producers generally continued to have secondary status. This situation began to change at the end of 1791, when the revolution broke out in Haiti, which had been supplying about 50 percent of the world's sugar market. With the Haitian Revolution, Moreno Fraginals notes, "sugar fever swept the entire world . . . but Cuba was the only one able to realize, in a short time, the enormous leap in sugar production."[7] While the French and British sugar colonies in the Caribbean were practically at their production limits, Cuban plantations occupied a small portion of the island's territory.

That November, when news reached Madrid of the Haitian Revolution, Arango y Parreño sent a letter to Carlos IV, thereby obtaining a two-year extension for the free trade in slaves. Shortly thereafter, on January 24, 1792, the Havana representative presented his "Discurso sobre la agricultura," considered to be a sort of program for the consolidation of a Cuban plantation economy, with the sugar mills as its primary engine. Arango y Parreño's goal was not only to take advantage of the situation created by the collapse of production in Santo Domingo but also for Cuba to attain "a degree of power and wealth able to sustain competition, even when your competitor revives."[8] To accomplish this, Arango y Parreño discussed the handicaps faced by sugar production in Cuba compared with that in neighboring colonies, as well as what he saw as the essential remedies. Some of his proposals were quickly accepted: that same year sugar, tobacco, cotton, coffee, and indigo were exempted from all sales taxes and tithes for a decade.

These new incentives broadened the support for an industry that in thirty years had experienced remarkable growth. The number of *ingenios* in the Havana region increased from 102 in 1771, to 168 in 1778, to 237 in 1792.[9] From 1786 to 1789 the number of *cajas* (crates)[10] of sugar loaded onto ships in the port of Havana increased by 6,420, and between 1789 and 1791 the increase was 15,287.[11] This required more land and woodland, in addition to the expansion of existing plantations. Areas where *ingenios* had first been concentrated, such Guanabacoa and Bejucal, were already in decline. The former, which between 1754 and 1757 had 24 *ingenios*, had 22 in 1778 and 20 in 1792, although at the same time the amount of land per mill increased; the 20 *ingenios* and 2 *trapiches* that existed in 1801, which had an average area of 31 caballerías in the mid-1700s, increased that figure to 38.4 caballerías by the beginning of the new century.[12] Similarly, the average number of slaves per estate increased from 30 to 40 in 1762 to about 70 three decades later.[13]

Augmenting productive capacity entailed the conquest of new territories for sugar. To the south of the city are productive zones centered in the towns of Cano and Managua. The first, 4 leagues to the southwest, increased the number of its *ingenios* from 20 at the time of Bishop Pedro Morell de Santa Cruz's visit (1754–57), to 26 in 1771, to 41 in 1792. The second, to the south and with 12 installations at the middle of the century, had 31 by 1778 and 32 in 1792. To the east-southeast of the city, in an area centered in San Antonio del Río Blanco, at 12 leagues from Havana and 3 from the anchorages of Jaruco and Santa Cruz, the number of *ingenios* increased from 6 in 1771, to 20 in 1778, to 45 in 1792. Finally, to the west and centered in Guanajay, 12 leagues from Havana and 2 from the Mariel wharf, the number increased from 1 in the mid-1750s to 28 by 1792.[14]

These figures show that during this period settlement increased to the east and west, in the natural regions of Plains and Heights of the North of Havana and Matanzas and of Plains of Ariguanabo–Almendares–San Juan. If in midcentury the area where sugar plantations were concentrated extended 6 to 8 leagues on either side of the port, by 1792 this area extended out 14 to 16 leagues. This zone facilitated the transport of produce to the Havana port. To the extreme east of both regions began the settlement of the Bay of Matanzas.

To the south the distance was less, 6 to 8 leagues, although Artemisa Plain was not without *ingenios*. The first foundations in this area began to appear before 1792. In Güines, 15 leagues to the southeast, there were three mills in 1778 and eight in 1792.[15] Another eight *ingenios* that existed then on the southern plains were located along the road from Havana to Batabanó.[16] The distribution of mills was influenced by the increasing cost of transport as one established farther and farther from the port. Nevertheless, one must also take into account that in the last third of the eighteenth century two of the main Royal Forest Reserves occupied much of the Artemisa Plain: these were centered in the estates of Casiguas (to the east) and Alquízar (to the west).

Prior to 1792, the majority of *ingenios* were located in areas much of whose best wood had been harvested for shipbuilding. The most convincing proof of this is the slow pace of (at least formal) dismantling during this period. For example, the 1796 proceedings of the Royal Consulate of Agriculture, Industry, and Commerce of Havana affirmed: "Until 1796 the part of our woodlands devoted to cultivation around the capital has extended south to Managua and Bejucal, east to Guanabo and La Pita, and west to Baracoa, that is, an area no more than five leagues around."[17] Sugar had begun to invade more distant terrains, but most of the cane fields were within 6 to 8 leagues of the Havana port. Those farthest away were near the northern coast, in zones where the felling of trees had been historically more common, whether or not their haciendas had been formally dismantled.

It is no accident that the Royal Forest Reserves were seen as a great obstacle to the growth of the sugar industry: in addition to depriving sugar planters of some of the best wood for their estates' diverse needs, the *cortes* (logging operations) impeded development of plantations before woodlands were logged by the navy. Nor is it by chance that navy bureaucrats saw the sugar trade as the greatest threat to shipbuilding on the island — owing not simply to competition for the use of the abundant lumber but also to the fact that planting cane fields eliminated the possibility of woodlands' regenerating. The characteristics of the sugar industry at the time, specifically its need for lumber, firewood, and fertile soil, were sufficient justification for these fears.

Mills in Havana and Matanzas between 1772 and 1815

Until 1815 at least, changes in the way sugar was made were mostly quantitative, allowing us to treat the phase from 1772 to then as a unit. Sources offer different estimates of the types of *ingenios* at the time. One possible point of departure is the thesis presented in 1793 by José Ricardo O'Farrill to the Patriotic Society of Havana on how cane was grown and its juice extracted. His prototype was an *ingenio* on 30 caballerías of land, with 100 black slaves, 40 pairs of oxen, 30 mules, and 10 boilers, producing 10,000 arrobas a year.[18]

A few years later, in 1800, the civil servant Antonio del Valle Hernández estimated that a properly furnished mill estate would cover 30 caballerías, although *ingenios* existed, "if few, that have a personnel of up to three hundred slaves," and "the most formidable harvest that has been seen with this number of hands is forty-two to forty-five thousand arrobas."[19] Alexander von Humboldt reproduced these maximum figures when he described plantations able to produce 32,000 to 40,000 arrobas, with 300 slaves on 50 caballerías, half in cane and half in vegetables and pastures.[20] For his part the bishop Juan José Díaz de Espada, in his report "Diezmos reservados" (Reserved Tithes; 1804), noted that according to municipal ordinance an *ingenio* should be on at least 40 caballerías, 30 in cane and 10 in pastures and subsistence crops, and that they should have about 50 slaves.[21] In Güines, for example, the 26 *ingenios* in production in 1800 averaged 34.15 caballerías and 75 slaves. In Guanabacoa, the 20 *ingenios* averaged 98 slaves.[22]

The typical *ingenio* in those days must have been closer to the size described by O'Farrill.[23] In the first two decades of the nineteenth century plantations were not much different from those that existed at the end of the eighteenth. Ramón de La Sagra reckoned in the early 1830s that to produce a thousand *cajas* (16,000 arrobas) one needed 30 caballerías of land, 6 of them devoted to cane, and a crew of 90 slaves.[24] This period witnessed a notable increase in production per *ingenio*, perhaps owing in part to the more intense exploitation of the workforce in the new plantation phase of the sugar economy. If in the mid-eighteenth century the average harvest produced 100 arrobas per slave, in the early nineteenth, according to Humboldt, it produced between 106 and 133; by 1831, according to La Sagra, this number had risen to 178. Arango y Parreño, in his notes on Humboldt's book on Cuba, claims that new *ingenios* in Matanzas could produce, with 150 or 160 slaves, 32,000 arrobas of sugar, or 200 to 213 per slave.[25]

Far more than to technological advances, this increase was due to the high output of the traditional system of planting cane in cleared woodland. Valle Hernández explained this in 1800: "Among the French, production is regulated at 60 @ [arrobas] of sugar per head of negro; in Jamaica, this figure increases to 70 @ of broken or unrefined sugar. Here a producing *ingenio* that does not yield 100 @ of brown and unrefined sugar per negro is considered to be of quite inferior quality, since the best yield up to 160 and 180." The main reason for this was that Cuba, the largest of the Antilles, had an immense virgin territory, new, fertile lands where more cane could be obtained with fewer hands through the "rustic, but economical and appropriate, method that is profitably used." Valle Hernández congratulated himself on the advantageous position of Cuban producers. After affirming that the French colonies were ruined and that only Jamaica prospered, mostly thanks to coffee, he pointed out, "But the same is not true of the windward British islands, where the sugar sector is collapsing due to the sterility of the soil, since on most of them sugar is pressed only every other year." In other words, "None of the Antilles . . . possesses to the eminent degree that this island does the foundations of true greatness."[26] A greatness that depended above all, one could say, on its enormous forests.

THE TRADITIONAL SYSTEM OF CULTIVATION

O'Farrill's 1793 thesis offers an idea of the method of cultivation that had prevailed since the beginning of the Cuban sugar industry. When seeking to establish an *ingenio*, one chose "a suitable terrain" for growing cane, preferably one that had "a black, loose, light topsoil . . . and where at a depth of more or less one vara another soil is found, somewhat clayey, which is commonly termed yellow mud." Also usable were terrains with coffee-colored (*mulata*), or brownish, topsoil, "loose like the one formerly mentioned and with the same mud at a lesser depth; because it is rarer in the windward part, it appears to be more greatly esteemed." Other varieties of soil were occupied to a lesser degree.[27] This is in keeping with the distinction made at the time between two large groups: black or dark soils and red, vermillion, or coffee-colored ones. Valle Hernández noted that the soils of the island were of varying quality and that the former type was thought best for cane because it better retained moisture, although many *ingenios* were found on the latter type of soil.[28] Humboldt echoed this distinction recognized by farmers and observed "that they are often mixed, like the squares on a checkerboard."[29]

In reality the sugar planters had to adapt to the conditions of their chosen location. In this sense, the preference for black earth is relative; it is no accident that when the time came to settle the Artemisa Plain, where red soils predominate, their quality began to be more highly esteemed, as exemplified by Antonio de Morejón y Gato in 1797.[30] But the most common point of reference, more than an understanding of the soil, was the existing vegetation. Humboldt wrote on this subject: "What is most common[ly understood] is that the lemon tree and orange tree do not mix; and after clearing the terrain with fire, the new settlers determine the quality of the soil by the groups of social plants with which it is covered, and they prefer land with orange trees to land that produces the small lemon tree."[31] This intuitive practice led to frequent misunderstandings about the chosen site.

What is most important to keep in mind is that these sites were almost always covered predominantly with woodlands. Natural savannas, in addition to being rare in the Havana region, were not considered conducive to planting; nor were artificial ones cleared for livestock, since these areas quickly covered over with grasses and weeds. Their only usefulness was as pasture for oxen, mules, and horses, and this only at first because with time pastureland could grow at the expense of dismantled cane fields. During the initial phase of clearing and burning land for cane fields, O'Farrill said, "They do not pull up the trunks or separate fallen trees that are too thick and of useless wood; they only remove the larger branches, because the rest of the tree, in addition to being very difficult to drag away, can eventually make the cane plants in its vicinity more robust and fecund with its rotten remains."[32] This practice guaranteed high yields, independent of the soil's natural fertility.

Once the terrain was "clean," the cane was sowed in rows half a vara apart, 6 to 7 inches deep, 9 inches wide, and of a length dependent on the number of slaves working the fields. The sewing was done during the rainy season, between May and December, preferably in the first four months and as soon as possible after the land had been cleared, before the grasses could invade, sapping the soil of fertility and suffocating the young cane plants. For this reason, the fields had to be weeded two or three times as the cane grew. Some farmers harvested a crop of rice one year before beginning to grow cane, but O'Farrill opposed the practice, believing that "it prejudices the increase and duration of the cane, since this first fruit and the grass that occupies the land in the period between the harvest of one crop and the sewing of the other wastes part of the earth's fertility."[33] It was also customary to intersperse cane with corn, another practice that came under criticism with time.

The remains of trees, which fertilized the land, largely determined how long a cane field could produce. According to O'Farrill, cane could typically be cut for twenty years without the field needing to be sowed again, even longer in the best soils. Humboldt agreed that cane carefully planted in virgin soil could last for twenty or thirty years and offered as an example a field that in 1804 had been producing for forty-five years.[34] In this period, after the crop had been harvested, the husks left on the ground were burned with the goal of enriching the soil, but this had to be done before new plants could be damaged. Each year yield dropped an additional 5 percent relative to the first crop, until the fields had to be sowed again. This life span could be shortened by accidents like fires in the cane fields, the destruction of young plants by poor handling of carts, and by insect infestations. The field was resowed following the same method every three years or less. In some cases plows were used, but O'Farrill argued that experience on the island had shown that the use of plows reduced the time before a new sowing was necessary.

In general this is the cultivation system that had predominated since the seventeenth century. The abundance of woodlands and the relatively small size of the cane fields favored the custom of sowing in cleared forest, a guarantee of high yields. Land that had been resowed, in contrast, offered marginal production while the time of the farms' dismantling approached. The larger size of the estates and of the cane fields beginning in the mid-eighteenth century led some to seek improvements in agricultural techniques that would extend the life of the fields. This trend was encouraged by the arrival of Haitian immigrants experienced in growing cane in soil that had been farmed for many years.

The most important effort was the use of irrigation to alleviate the effects of the dry season. Introducing it in the Havana region was limited by the lack of large rivers. Only in the area crossed by the Mayabeque and the two Güines rivers did these efforts meet some success, as we see from proceedings from 1798 (one of whose signers was O'Farrill) on improvements in *ingenios.*

> It is clear that irrigation can only be applied in plains favored by nature, like the Güines tobacco plantation; and no one denies its usefulness in general, but there is no lack of farmers who doubt its benefit in old and used soils; alleging that in this plain despite irrigation the vegetation is much weaker, and the cane will have to be resowed every two or three years, whereas in good, unirrigated land we have vigorous stands of cane that are fifty or sixty years old.[35]

Another example of planters' increasing interest in agricultural improvements was the introduction of so-called Otahití cane, which began to be used along with iron *trapiches* in the 1790s. The Royal Consulate of Agriculture, Industry, and Commerce promoted this variety because of its greater size and robustness, which allowed it to produce more juice and pulp. Moreno Fraginals notes that it was not generally used in the fields of Havana and Matanzas until the 1820s, and even then it far from displaced creole cane. The tendency was to plant both, thereby taking advantage of the different times of maturity to increase the quantity of cane.[36]

The degree to which new agricultural techniques were applied depended largely on the region where the plantations were located. For instance, the growth of sugar in the last third of the eighteenth century was related to the occupation of the regions Heights of the North of Havana and Matanzas and Heights of Bejucal-Magruda-Coliseo. Valle Hernández referred to *ingenios* in the highest parts of the mountain range. O'Farrill, for his part, prized the relative equilibrium of temperature in broken soils that were not in the highest hills, which led the cane juice also to be more constant. For higher elevations he recommended an earlier harvest to reduce the effects of a harsh drought. In lowlands and plains abundant precipitation could cause cane to waste or rot.[37]

Little is known of the agricultural techniques used at the time to adapt to the topography. When fields were sowed on slopes, precautions had to be taken against erosion. Drainage was another factor that had to be accounted for in the red plains of Havana and Matanzas (predominantly subterranean), as did the distinction between black and red soils.[38] But any intrinsic quality of the terrain could be concealed by woodlands. On these the traditional system of cultivation depended, and it played a leading role in their destruction. But it was not the only cause. The use of wood to build mills and as fuel long seconded this ancestral need to ensure higher yields by clear-cutting and burning.

WO IN TB *INGENIOS*

Since the seventeenth century, the established practice for sugarcane farmers arriving at a site was to begin by clearing the woodland, sowing the first cane fields, and simultaneously or afterward building the processing facilities. This allowed pressing to begin immediately; if the mill was not built immediately, the option remained of processing the cane at neighboring farms. The slow advance of sugar and the small size of Havana *ingenios* into the mid-eighteenth century led to a certain self-sufficiency in wood. But with the plantations' increasing size and number beginning in the 1740s, assuring supply from one's own land became more difficult.

On the one hand, there might not be enough wood within the dismantled estate or hacienda where the *ingenio* had been established to meet all the latter's needs. On the other, the urgent necessity for new lands for sugar endangered the system of forest exploitation established for shipbuilding. Seeking to remedy this, navy officials were able to impose greater and greater restrictions on sugar planters. The goal was not simply to limit the use of wood for construction but also to slow the dismantlements before it was too late. According to the interests of both parties, woodlands became ships or *ingenios*, especially because the industries used several of the same species of trees.

The use of woods in the *ingenios* and the way they were obtained is an aspect of this history about which little is known. From what O'Farrill says about tree trunks being left on the ground when they were considered useless, we can infer that those needed to build the facilities of the *ingenios* were removed. Even when the Royal Forest Reserves went through first, there always remained some trees that could be used for lumber, although these were considered to be of inferior quality or for other, more specific needs. When the plantation's land could not supply the wood required, farmers were forced to ask the navy for it or to cut it clandestinely.

The three main buildings of the *ingenio* — the *casa de molienda* (pressing house), *casa de calderas* (boiler house), and *casa de purga* (purging house, where the sugar was separated from the molasses) — were constructed with lumber from the island. Among the most commonly used woods was cedar, although the arrangement of the mill's buildings and the type of woods employed varied depending on the period and other circumstances, such as regulations against using certain species of trees. In 1793 O'Farrill wrote that the pressing house "was erected entirely from quiebrahacha" and that it was composed of three parts: one for the crushers, 34 varas long (28.8 meters), divided by a wall 2.5 varas high; another for the boilers, 14 varas long (11.8 meters), divided by a wall 6.25 varas high; and another for the furnaces, 10 varas long. The purging house he mentioned separately, "encircled with rubblework and the main part held up by supports of quiebrahacha," with an approximate length of 80 varas and a width of 26 varas (67.8 meters x 22 meters).[39]

To the core of the mill complex were added several associated buildings of varying size that increased the consumption of wood, such as the living quarters, the pulp house (*casa de bagazo*), cabins, a chapel, stills, lime furnaces, and tile works. In a 1784 letter to the king, a number of Havana mill owners argued, "With cedar we make the ties, roofing, sheds or garrets, conduits [*canoas*][40] or receptacles for molasses, and a multitude of other pieces of the substantial crushing, purging, and drying houses." Following cedar in order of preference was sabicú, whose hardness made it useful, along with chicharrón, for "the mills or *trapiches*, robust machines which press the cane, powered by four pairs of oxen that drive its arms, or springs, rendering up to the last drop of its juice." The mill owners predicted that their industry would be threatened if the prohibitions were continued on the use of cedar, without peer for resilience "in the construction of such costly buildings," and of sabicú, since both woods were needed "to build new *ingenios* or to repair ones already established" (see figure 2.1).[41]

The alarm was due to successive restrictions on the use of these and other woods, even within haciendas that already had been dismantled. Theoretically, the legislation of 1622 and 1748 had set them aside for the navy; but either these regulations were not followed in practice, or new refinements were required. In fact, my choice of 1772 as the starting date in the title of this chapter is due to the prohibition in that year of the use of cedar for making sugar containers, crates (*cajas*) with a capacity of about 16 arrobas. Nevertheless, the savings in wood that would result were not a sufficient argument in themselves. This is why the promoter of this measure, navy commander Juan Bautista Bonet, argued that cedar could be done without in many of its applications, concluding that "it is not absolutely necessary in all the different parts used in building an *ingenio*, which is the only important use of it in the countryside, and which has consumed more than is invested in one hundred warships."[42]

For roofing Bonet suggested vigueta wood as a substitute, and for taps (*llaves*) 18 to 20 varas long and at least 0.66 vara thick he recommended guajani, baría, ocuje, guaguasi, jocuma, and other hardwoods. He was motivated by having seen "cedar used in crushing and purging houses and each one needing twenty trees of this size, as many beams of seventy- and eighty-canon ships have been lamentably consumed in each house." He thought the same woods could replace cedar in the stirrups and yokes of *trapiches*. He also called for building the mills' partitions out of rubblework, which offered the advantage of not being as susceptible to fire and moisture as cedar, as well as being easy to construct owing to the existence in the mills of lime furnaces with brickworks. According to Bonet, his efforts were not in vain: "Today after my repeated efforts at persuasion one can see the wisdom of some individuals who create farms using no other woods than these."[43]

These points about the unnecessary uses of cedar in *ingenios* were taken

FIGURE 2.1. Vertical wood *trapiche*.
(*Censo de la República de Cuba, 1919* [Havana: Maza, Arroyo y Caso, n.d.])

up by navy commander Francisco de Borja, Marquis de Camachos. In September 1783 Borja proposed a new method for the conservation of woodlands, decreeing that no cedar or other construction lumber be used for fences, braces, entresols, or flat roofs, all of which could be made instead with more durable woods such as ácana and jocuma. Instead of planters' cutting 16- and 18-foot lengths of cedar, "which make excellent ship beams," Borja suggested reserving smaller trees with the 8 or 9 varas needed in an *ingenio*. As for the use of sabicú in *trapiche* sets, he said: "There is a tree of twelve or more varas; an individual cuts it down when a much smaller one, of four to six varas, would serve, and the King loses an excellent keel." In another letter, of February 1784, Borja argued that mills should be forbidden from stocking more spare wood than necessary for a repair, since he had found that some had up to six *trapiche* sets for one that was in use.[44] Nevertheless, his main concern was avoiding the advance of dismantlements ahead of the Royal Forest Reserves: "If this dismantlement happens in a bountiful hacienda from which the wood has not yet been taken, the King will lose in ashes the equivalent of four or five ships."[45]

In the following years, different proposals were devised to save the shipyard's supply of wood, increasingly threatened by the growth of the sugar industry. Under Borja's orders, an April 1784 decree prohibited the use of cedar for the making of taps, supports, beams, and tie beams. An exception was made for taps in crushing houses if other wood of their dimension (16 to 18 varas) could not be found; cedar could then be requested from reserved woodlands. Cedar was permitted, however, for roofing boards, molding, ogees, paneling, ridge poles, rafters, and other relatively small pieces for which it was absolutely indispensable, although "no more spare wood than for one repair is allowed."[46]

A detailed regulation on the use of woods was promulgated on December 11, 1789. Several of its articles referred specifically to the sugar industry. Article 5 prohibited the requesting or granting of more wood than was needed for buildings and machines. Article 6 reiterated the woods reserved since 1622 and 1748: "Cedar may only be used in the countryside for roofing board, flooring, doors, windows, ogees, vats, rafters, troughs, molding, and household furniture, for the last of which mahogany may also be used. And as concerns crushers [trapiches], benches, stools, frames, pivot joints, conduits, and all types of flywheels [voladoras], sabicú and chicharrón will also be provided." Article 14 allowed ingenios to keep twice as much wood as they would need for repairs. Article 22 announced the reduction of tariffs on iron pounders and crushers coming from Biscay, a measure that had been proposed by the Havana Wood Committee (Junta de Maderas) following a request from a mill owner: "the object being to provide with this material pieces that must be of hardwood, and are fashioned from sabicú and chicharrón, two species that he assures are not among the most abundant on this island, and are quite useful for the keels of all kinds of boats, but much of which is used each year in said ingenios."[47]

All of this means that the sugar industry had to adapt to conditions imposed by the navy, although it does not mean that mill owners stopped secretly cutting cedars and other forbidden trees. Above all it shows that sugar was entering with all its transformative power into the zone occupied by the Royal Forest Reserves. Sugar's peak in the 1790s multiplied the need for lumber by people interested in starting ingenios, and the navy found itself drowning in requests for licenses (see table 2.1). The royal navy had plenty of reasons to fear that the results would be detrimental to the future of Havana shipbuilding. "More ingenios, fewer ships" was an elementary conclusion.

The ships of the Spanish Armada have been called a "floating forest." This image could also be applied to Havana's ingenios, not on the ocean but on

TABLE 2.1. Different Types of Lumber from Reserved Woodlands
Conceded by the Navy for *Ingenios* and Country Estates, 1785–1800

Type of Wood and Use	Jan. 1, 1785– Feb. 13, 1789	Feb. 14, 1789– Oct. 31, 1800
Cedar logs	5,197	57,191
Cedar taps	106	1,365
Cedar soleplates and decks	126	1,452
Cedar tie beams	257	3,050
Cedar conduits and beads	131	1,524
Sabicú and chicharrón logs	119	935
Trapiche sets	200	989
Pounders	12	143
Benches and stools	55	408
Carts and handcarts	259	7,310
Ocuje trees	29	2,146
Mahogany trees	25	342
Jocuma trees	179	1,370
Acana trees	16	1,739

Source: AGI, Ultramar 9, "Relación de las maderas de construcción de todas clases que de los montes reservados a la Marina en esta Isla de Cuba para la fábrica de bajeles, se han concedido por la Comandancia General a los particulares Hacendados."

a sea of cane. In 1802 the Wood Committee appointed one representative of the sugar planters and another from the navy to indicate jointly which terrains could furnish the Havana jurisdiction with wood. The two men acknowledged that "the buildings and machines necessary for making sugar are of much greater size than those of any other type of agricultural establishment even beyond the island." The need did not end with construction because the difficulty and force of the work done in the *ingenios* meant that many wooden tools wore out and were rarely usable for more than one harvest (*zafra*). In addition, many carts were needed: "It is incredible how many the *ingenios* use, and how many break each year: suffice it to say that all the cane must be transported in them from the fields to the crushing house; firewood, all the tools, and everything an *ingenio* needs [are] carried in carts; many also haul the sugar and molasses: in a word, one can say that land, cane, blacks, oxen, and carts go together when it comes to putting together an *ingenio*."[48]

For an estimate of the amount of wood generally used in the construction of an *ingenio* we can consult a 1784 paper by Alférez de Navío Nicolás del Villa, who reckoned that one could not be built with fewer than 500 to 600 trees.[49] In the early nineteenth century, Arango y Parreño gave another figure based on a review of haciendas put up for public sale in 1779 and singling out those that produced the most trees: Corral Feo and Crucecitas, to the east of the port, with 3,450 and 3,100 pieces of more than 14 inches in diameter, respectively. After assigning to each another two-thirds above these amounts, he figured that 10,918 trees, as an average, could be extracted from each.

Of the 8 leagues, or a bit more than 832 caballerías, that the two together theoretically covered, Arango y Parreño said only half were suitable for *ingenios*, a quarter for coffee plantations, and the rest, of inferior quality, for small farms (*sitios*) and livestock farms (*potreros*). Four large and six medium-size *ingenios* would fit on the first 416 caballerías. He had used 2,000 lengths of useful wood, or about 1,200 trees, for his large *ingenio* La Ninfa. The four large *ingenios* thus needed no fewer than 4,800 trees together, while the six remaining ones required at least 800, totaling another 4,800 trees.[50]

The intention of Arango y Parreño was to show that not even the estates with the most wood had enough to supply their sugar plantations. Such was the case of La Ninfa, on 61 caballerías of land, since in addition to timber cut under the terms of its permit, it took more "in its shadow." Despite having been the first to set up at one end of the Mayabeque *hato* (cattle ranch), which the Royal Forest Reserves never reached, it was unable to get all the wood it needed on the estate's 14 leagues, as can be seen from its requests to supply itself from the neighboring Barbudo, Omoa, Gabriel, and Guanamón farms. In any case, Arango y Parreño congratulated himself for still having on his plantation 35 caballerías of thick woodland, "with several good trunks of small dimension," and for not being too far from virgin forest, at only 14 leagues. But the experience of the sugar planters was not very reassuring: "We are all beginning to pay four [probably pesos] for a length that later costs us ten or twelve, and we all end up not leaving in our properties' forests a single tree of any significance."[51]

During the last third of the eighteenth century the lumber shortage was felt most acutely in areas closest to Havana, which led to reforms concerning the building of *ingenios*. Rubblework began to replace posts and boards, which made the services of bricklayers increasingly costly.[52] Nevertheless, this was still a relatively rare phenomenon. Referring to the new mills and the reforms impelled by Haitian immigrants, the authors of a report to the Royal Consulate wrote in 1798: "It should be added that these devices have brought equally recommendable changes to the construction of rural mills, building them out of rubblework instead of on posts, laying them out in a more reduced and less costly manner without sacrificing necessary breathing room; roofs are covered with a flat tile that, thanks to its lightness, does not require such strong joints, managing in this way to save as much wood as possible."[53]

For many years, Cuban wood continued to be an important element in the building of *ingenios*. At the beginning of the nineteenth century, abundant woodlands remained on the frontier of sugar's expansion, so that innovation was undertaken only in the earliest-settled areas or by those owners who could afford the luxury of experimentation. It was more "economical" to clear forests and put cane fields in their place, using the wood to build the mill quickly. Finally, there was the imperious need to keep a reserve of woodland to feed the fires under the boilers during the harvest.

FUEL: FORESTS INTO FIREWOOD

The great consumption of firewood was a prime cause of the dismantlement of *ingenios* into the mid-eighteenth century. It could even be called the prime cause owing to the relatively small land area of the cane plantations compared with their need for fuel. This began to change as the area under cultivation increased, although not enough to change this panorama completely. Unlike the clearing done to open land for cane fields, which could go twenty years without being resowed, and logging to build the houses of the *ingenio*, wood as fuel needed to be cut every year.

Much evidence exists suggesting that a shortage of woodlands was the main reason for the dismantlement and mobile nature of sugar plantations. A contract signed in November 1772 to import Louisiana cypress into Havana for building sugar crates (*cajas*) warned, "If the *ingenios* multiply normally, or if some accident of fire, or lack of woodlands, should require some to be dismantled, the number of crates ordered will increase or decrease (not in a number so serious as to alter this contract), advising New Orleans each year." Three years later, the then captain general of the island, the Marquis de La Torre, noted with respect to *ingenios*: "Although before they required at least thirty caballerías of land, today, with the use of reverberatory furnaces, which avoid the former great consumption of firewood, much less is sufficient."[54]

Nevertheless, at first these pulp furnaces were used on only the few *inge-nios* already affected by the shortage of firewood, or they were used no more than marginally given firewood's superiority as fuel and its abundance in new areas of expansion. At the end of the eighteenth century, at the height of the sugar boom, this issue was seen as one of the most urgent problems. In his 1772 "Discurso sobre la agricultura," Arango y Parreño included among the handicaps suffered by sugar production in Havana compared with that in foreign Caribbean colonies the fact that an *ingenio* lasted only sixty years "at the most, the time of the lands' youth and luxuriance," after which it was abandoned, being considered no longer useful for this purpose. He then pointed out that in these mills reverberatory furnaces were used, allow-ing them to reduce their immense consumption of firewood, "sufficing for them dry cane pulp: when in Havana it is still undecided whether these reverberatory furnaces are more suitable than using up a ninth of the crops' worth by cutting and uprooting a whole woodland full of trees for each harvest."[55]

The lack of interest in burning pulp originated in the abundance of forests to supply the plantations, but it was also due to practical reasons. O'Farrill argued in 1793 that few harvesters used reverberatory furnaces or the French sugar kettle battery (*tren*) for four reasons: (1) they could not be sure the bricklayer would build the furnace properly, a doubt justified by the variety of furnaces already constructed; (2) in rainy years the pulp got wet and had to be dried in the sun, compromising the continuation of the harvest and processing, since what was stored in the pulp houses was not enough; (3) in new *ingenios*, "since it was necessary to cut the woodland to increase the planting of cane, this firewood is used"; and (4) the pulp pro-duced in the processing of sugar and the slight amount of supplementary firewood did not suffice to finish the harvest, so that reverberatory furnaces were "frequently established in *ingenios* that have no woodlands at all, or in those that have them quite a distance away."[56]

O'Farrill and the other two signers of the 1798 proceedings of the Royal Consulate of Agriculture, Industry, and Commerce on new developments in *ingenios* wrote that in those formerly located near the Chorrera (today the Almendares) River "the agriculture was so depressed that [these farms] were soon abandoned, either because the owners, not knowing how to save firewood by using reverberatory furnaces, found themselves obligated by the lack of woodlands to dismantle their estates, or because, as their lands gained value with the increase in population, they found more profit in parceling it out than in continuing without aid the cultivation of a crop of little value." These were the antecedents of the use of waterpower, which then implanted itself in the Güines region. Nevertheless, O'Farrill and his colleagues found more important the new methods for saving fuel in the boiler houses, "through the use of reverberatory furnaces, which at the same time heat several boilers, while formerly each boiler had its own furnace."[57]

> This point is of such a nature that it will influence the fortune, size, and life span of *ingenios*, which, since those of this type will not need woodlands, can be located in any cleared place, even if this is close to a town, limiting itself of course to the amount of land that is indispensable for mills and cane fields, with the result that not every *ingenio* will need twenty or thirty caballerías of land for the sole purpose of reserving the woodlands for firewood, nor will estates exhaust their woodlands and have to be dismantled.[58]

In 1800 Antonio del Valle Hernández admitted that the variety of forms of reverberatory furnaces was a shortcoming and that no theory had been devised for their construction, but he argued that they were nonetheless "an extremely useful invention because, there being many old *ingenios* that find themselves forced to use reverberatory furnaces, the latter will be improved daily."[59] This confirmed that innovation was paramount in deforested areas and that firewood was the fuel par excellence of most of the new *ingenios* being established on the wooded frontier.[60]

Estimates differ on the amount of firewood consumed on Havana *ingenios* at the end of the eighteenth century. In a 1796 thesis on conservation of the island's forests, O'Farrill calculated that every year 2 flat leagues of woodlands, or 268 caballerías, were annihilated for firewood. This represented an average of 0.75 caballería on each of the 217 *ingenios* and 61 sites for *ingenios* then being developed. A similar quantity of woodland was destroyed for the consumption of villages, livestock farms, and small farms.[61] This figure is about half the one offered by Moreno Fraginals, who claims that at this time 500 caballerías (6,710 hectares) of woodland were felled annually as firewood for *ingenios*. The difference may be depend on the type of *ingenio* being used as a referent, although we must keep in mind that during the sugar boom the need for firewood from woodlands multiplied.[62]

In the part devoted to the fuel used by the Cuban *ingenios* of 1800–1860, Moreno Fraginals gives several of the figures used at the time on the quantity of firewood necessary for a harvest and how much could be provided by

1 caballería of forest. Based on the data of the sugar technician José Ignacio Echegoyen, he notes that between the late eighteenth century and the early nineteenth, the Spanish boiler system was estimated to produce 57.5 to 80 kilograms of sugar for each tarea of firewood, while with the same amount of wood *ingenios* that used reverberatory furnaces produced 150 kilograms of sugar.[63] These numbers were used by Humboldt, who observed, "As the island has been depopulated of trees, due to the excess of terrain that has been cleared, *ingenios* have begun to want for fuel."[64]

Humboldt argued that Cuban producers had always used some pulp to revive a fire but that it was only after the arrival of the Santo Domingo emigrants that they tried to burn only pulp. Humboldt was probably alarmed by the destruction of forests that the *ingenios* caused and thus wanted to find a solution, despite his short stay. During his travels through the Güines region, but especially in Río Blanco, where sugar had a longer history, he experimented with "the use of many new buildings, with the goal of reducing consumption of fuel, surrounding the hearth with substances that transmit heat poorly, and finding a way for slaves to suffer less when they stir the fire."[65]

Linked to the quantity of sugar produced per tarea of firewood was another fundamental question: How much firewood was produced by the forests used to feed the furnaces? The answer depends on the type of forests occupied by the sugar industry at different times and on their degree of anthropization (impact on them of humans as environmental agents). For Moreno Fraginals, the late eighteenth-century estimates show that a caballería of good woodland should provide 2,750 tareas of firewood. He then gives the calculations of Alvaro Reynoso from the early 1860s, that is, between 2,430 and 2,592 tareas, and concludes with treatises that find an average of 1,000 tareas per caballería.[66] If we use a mean of 2,500 tareas of firewood in 1 caballería and the estimate of 5 arrobas of sugar obtained per tarea through the old system of furnaces (the Spanish sugar kettle battery), we arrive at 12,500 arrobas of sugar produced per caballería cleared for firewood, which is approximately the average capacity of *ingenios* during the period. Obviously, farms able to produce more than 30,000 arrobas per harvest used much more wood or adopted measures to reduce their consumption. The solution for large-scale mills of the early nineteenth century was to install so-called mixed sugar kettle batteries (which combined firewood and pulp), allowing them to burn just over 1 caballería per harvest.[67]

Which firewood was burned depended on several factors, including the type of forest on each estate, prohibitions on felling certain trees, or the industry's degree of technological development. Humboldt notes that orange and lemon trees were used. According to Reynoso years later, planters preferred to burn in their boiler houses trunks that were not too thick. About the preparation of fuel he wrote, "Firewood that is less thick is stacked near the sugar kettle batteries, and that of larger dimension is piled next to the machine."[68] Another document from the steam era mentions species that provided good "local firewood" and which ones should not be used. In the first category it included lancewood, baría, guásima, levisa, raya lengua, jaguar, and ramón; in the second it placed jagüey, almácigo, jobo, yagruma, and the like.[69]

This account helps explain why the navy feared sugar's advance. Not only were the best woods for shipbuilding used instead to build *ingenios*, but some that could be substituted were burned to heat the boilers. Thus was the cycle of the forests' destruction closed under the impulse of the sugar industry. With good reason, the royal navy did everything in its power to stop or contain the sugar boom. The shipbuilding and sugar industries had two irreconcilable conceptions of how the forests should be exploited. This does not mean that for the former the protection of forests was an end in itself, but shipbuilders did see woodlands as a resource that, if exploited in a reasonably orderly manner, could regenerate itself. The period from the late eighteenth century to 1815 was marked by this conflict of interests over exploitation and colonial politics, the economy, and the natural environment. For this reason, when we speak of sugar's impact on the forests, we must mention the long struggle that pitted sugar against Havana's prominent role in the shipbuilding of the Spanish Empire.

Shipbuilding and the Royal Forest Reserves

The inauguration of the new shipyard in 1748 signaled the flourishing of Havana shipbuilding that had begun in the 1730s. The boom was interrupted only briefly by the destruction of these facilities by the British, but once the city was retaken, rebuilding began quickly. The project was once again entrusted to Lorenzo Montalvo, and in 1765 two eighty-canon ships and one schooner were put to sea.[70] For the next three decades the Havana shipbuilding industry was in full splendor.

Table 2.2 shows the growth in the construction of different types of vessels between 1765 and 1796 compared with building between 1724 and

TABLE 2.2. Shipbuilding in Havana, 1724–1796

Type of Vessel	1724–47	1748–61	1765–84	1785–96	Total
3-bridge ship	—	—	1	5	6
Ship of the line[a]	22	8	11	4	45
Frigate[b]	6	2	7	7	22
Packet boat	3	1	3	—	7
Brigantine[c]	—	3	5	2	10
Schooner	—	1	12	—	13
Pontoon	—	—	2	2	4
Fishing barge	—	—	2	4	6
Total	31	15	43	24	113
Yearly average	1.34	1.25	2.26	2.18	1.57

Source: "Corte de Maderas, Artículo 5°," in Anales de la Junta de Fomento (Havana, 1851), 4:27–37.
[a] Ships of the line had 50–80 cannons.
[b] Frigates had 22–50 cannons.
[c] Brigantines had fewer than 22 cannons.

1761 (the latter period is broken into 1724–47 and 1748–61 to show the effects of the new shipyard completed in 1748). The former period not only confirmed the Havana shipyard's important role in Spanish naval power but also showed that Cuban woods were a possible palliative for the metropole's declining forests. Ships built in the Havana port were considered to be among the highest quality owing to resistance of the woods from which they were built. These ships were reputed to last twice as long as their European rivals. One of these Havana vessels was the ship of the line completed in 1769, with four bridges and, when first put to sea, 112 cannons (it would eventually have 136). It was christened *Santísima Trinidad* and in its time was considered the finest warship in the royal Spanish Armada and the world (see figure 2.2).

Havana's significance to Spanish naval power had been confirmed after the inauguration of the shipyard in 1748, when the Windward Armada, which until then had been headquartered in Veracruz, was permanently moved there. The same year saw the constitution of the Navy Post, which until 1767 was headed by squadron commanders or captains of individual ships sailing to America. After 1767 the General Navy Command of the Port of Havana, the Island of Cuba, the Windward Islands, and the West Indies was permanently established.

FIGURE 2.2. The *Santísima Trinidad*, built in the Havana shipyard and completed in 1769 by Alejo Berlinguero de La Marca y Gallego (1750–1810).

(Museo Naval de Madrid, Watercolor Collection)

In order to develop the empire's naval force, the Crown gave the royal armada vast privileges.[71] Faced with the diminishing reserves of woodlands in the region closest to the port, navy commanders were able to increase restrictions on forest exploitation in the interest of shipbuilding and shipments to Spain. One of the ways they did this was by extending their sphere of action to include all forests on the island, except those estates intended to supply towns, an indication of metropolitan support for the role of Havana and the colony in the development of naval power.

To understand the constant conflicts between the navy, on the one hand, and sugar planters and the Captaincy General, on the other, we must study the system implemented for the exploitation of lumber destined for the Havana shipyard: the Royal Forest Reserves. Unlike shipbuilding at the arsenal, which has received significant attention, the way the shipyard was supplied with lumber has been little studied. From the point of view of the relationship to the environment, however, it is key to evaluating the differences between sugar's evolution until the late eighteenth century and that which began then.

The earliest efforts to organize the cutting of wood in the interests of shipbuilding date from the seventeenth century, but it was in the eighteenth that this was organized under the direct control of the navy. It appears that until the 1760s a system of registries or contracts prevailed through which individuals were supplied with wood. These agreements could cover the felling, working, hauling, and transport of the wood to the port of Havana or only the last two of these activities. Beginning in the 1760s, however, these services came under a "regime of administration" through which the navy took over all of their phases. The position of director of the Royal Forest Reserves was created, a civil service post whose holder was specifically charged with everything entailed in the exploitation of woodlands. It is no accident that before the earliest treatises on sugar cultivation were published, there appeared a detailed instruction on this position that could be considered one of Cuba's first scientific publications and that was a model for the use of forests in other territories of the Americas.[72]

The first *cortes* overseen by the navy during the last third of the eighteenth century were established during Juan Bautista Bonet's years as commander of the navy. In accordance with the established system, a suitable estate was chosen for the royal livestock farms or meadows (*potreros o dehesas del Rey*), water supply, and haulage. From these estates, which gave their name to the *corte* as a whole, neighboring estates were logged. In keeping with Bonet's renewed efforts to guarantee a supply of wood for the shipyard, the *cortes* of Alquízar, Casiguas, Matanzas, and San Juan de los Remedios operated from the 1770s to the 1790s (see figure 2.3).[73]

The *corte* of Alquízar (or San Antonio) encompassed a region that had already supplied the shipbuilding industry, but around 1770 it was once again

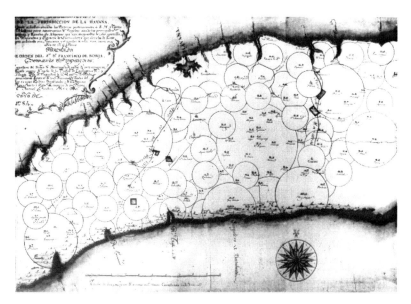

FIGURE 2.3. *Hatos* and *corrales* and Royal Forest Reserves of Alquízar and Casiguas in the Havana area in 1784.

("Plan of the Jurisdiction of Havana Where Are Located the Potreros Belonging to H.M. and Logging Sites for the Construction of Vessels," British Museum [London], add. 17645a)

in shape to furnish a large amount of wood. Its center was the Alquízar estate on the Artemisa Plain, 9 leagues south-southwest of the Havana port. In addition to having good pastures for ox teams, it was considered, despite the distance, to be an easy haul. The wood was dragged 5 or 6 leagues to the bank or woodpile (*tumbadero*) of the Almendares River, down which one floated for 3 leagues until beaching a quarter of a league from the arsenal. The *corte* of Alquízar had many cedars and other useful trees. When felling was suspended in 1795, at least twenty estates in its vicinity had been logged; they received permission to dismantle it between 1788 and 1797.

The *corte* of Casiguas was 10 leagues south-southeast of the port, extending another 2 leagues in this direction (and up to 14 in 1790), and was centered on the estate of the same name. Most of its land was on the center-eastern portion of the Artemisa Plain. The haul from there was somewhat more difficult than that from Alquízar, including several slopes on the 5 to 6 leagues between it and the mouth of the Jaruco River, where boats came to load the wood. It had several livestock farms overseen by the navy and many sabicú, mahogany, and cedar trees. By the end of the eighteenth century no fewer than nine estates within its borders had been logged. These were dismantled between 1791 and 1797.

The *corte* of Matanzas, bordered the bay and estate of the same name, lay between 20 and 22 leagues east of Havana. This was an area where there had been *cortes* at different times. During the last third of the eighteenth century, the largest were those of San José and of San Andrés (or San Juan). They were graced with good conditions for the transport of wood on the Canimar and San Juan rivers, although the haul over land was rather long, 9 leagues for San José and 11 for San Andrés by the end of the century. Both featured *potreros del Rey* for oxen and were rich in mahogany, sabicú, and cedar. By January 1792 eighteen estates in these territories had been dismantled after their trees were cut for shipbuilding (see figure 2.4).

Another important *corte* was located in the center of the island, in the area of the former town (*villa*) of San Juan de los Remedios, or El Cayo. It was 80 leagues from Havana with abundant woodlands near the sea and in flatlands, which made hauling quite easy to the landings of the Sagua la Chica and Sagua la Grande rivers. In the 1780s it was called "the most abundant in woods of all kinds, and quite especially those for construction, as experience has shown."[74] By the end of the eighteenth century it had been somewhat abandoned because of its distance from Havana, although wood destined for the arsenal was still taken from it. Unlike the other three areas where Royal Forest Reserves were located, San Juan de los Remedios was not subject to the pressure of dismantlements. The ship captain Félix de Estrada, charged by Commander Bonet with reconnoitering the island's woodlands between 1773 and 1775, reported that, during his tour of about 20 leagues windward and leeward of the town of Remedios, he did not find, unlike in other regions, vast swaths of land burned, since most of its estates were *corrales* (hog farms). He did find, however, great disorder in the individually owned sawmills, of which he counted eighteen to twenty in the town. He also called attention to the respectable citizens who had workers harvest beehives (which often required felling the trees in which they were located) and to the use of cedar for fences, despite the ban on this practice.[75]

The exploration of the island's woodlands was customary in the second half of the eighteenth century. Two modes of reconnaissance merged in these years. One originated on the island as a responsibility of the Navy Command; the other was promoted from the metropole and was linked to broader purposes, including military-strategic and scientific ones, as well as

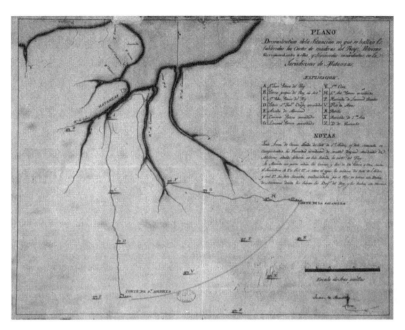

FIGURE 2.4. Map of the Royal Forest Reserves in Matanzas.
(Archivo General de Indias [Santo Domingo], 638)

the interest in developing new towns.[76] Sometimes the two modes fused, as in the "secret" expedition of the sailor Ventura Barcáiztegui, which sought to map eastern Cuba and identify its water resources.[77] A similar mission was that led by the chief engineer Miguel de La Puente, accompanied by his brother Juan de La Puente and other subordinates experienced in the exploitation of the island's forest resources. They calculated that the woodlands of the southeastern coast, from Cabo Cruz to Miasí, contained no fewer than 5 million cubic cubits of wood. In addition, reconnoitering of other points along the coast, with navigable rivers and immense woodlands in their vicinities, like the bays of Jagua, Guantánamo, Nuevitas, and Nipe, encouraged the hope that the exploitation of such significant forest wealth would allow Spain's woodlands to "rest" for a hundred years.

These missions had major significance for the understanding of Cuba's woodlands, since they provided information necessary to comprehend the true state of forests. For example, Estrada explained to Bonet that during his journeys through the interior of the Havana jurisdiction in 1772 he found, within a periphery of 14 to 16 leagues, "much destruction in the woodlands of trees cut for the *ingenios*, most lamentable being the construction materials that are lost in the large branches of the cedars."[78] Evidence of this type led the navy to extend its privileges to the entire island.

In their repeated efforts in this regard, the navy's civil servants, who were charged with ensuring that the Cuban forests could help compensate the declining ones in Spain, were not motivated by a simple desire for power. Their action was rooted largely in a fear that this policy would fail as a result of other economic activities. In other jurisdictions the sugar industry's growth did not present as great a danger as in Havana, but it was best to take precautions, especially because most of the island had not been within the scope of the Royal Forest Reserves and had to be preserved for the day when it would need to be logged for shipbuilding.

Conflicts over the Granting of Woodcutting Licenses, 1772–1783

In the strengthening of the navy's privileges over the Cuban forests, two basic phases can be distinguished: one from 1772 to 1783, dominated by limitation of the use of certain woods, and another from 1784 to 1790, when the center of attention, while not ignoring the previous era's restrictions, shifted to the topic of dismantlements. As a point of departure, we can take the royal decree of May 23, 1772, requested by navy commander Juan Bautista Bonet to ban the use of cedar in making sugar crates. Since his arrival on the island six months earlier, Bonet had made great efforts to guarantee the supply of wood to the Havana shipyard so that lumber could be sent to Spain. In his opinion, the 1767, 1769, and 1771 measures to restrict the use of cedar and other lumber were insufficient or had not been put in practice.[79] The May 1772 order decreed the formation of a committee with the highest authorities in the colonial administration; they could hear mill owners and agree to ban cedar containers and provide another wood for the product.[80]

In the meetings, mill owners insisted on the necessity of having a wood similar to cedar before enacting the ban, and they noted the failure of efforts to find a substitute. Finally, all agreed to investigate the practicality of having wood shipped from New Orleans, in accordance with the proposal made in 1770 by businessmen in that city to supply Havana's sugar planters with crates. Shortly after the Marquis de La Torre wrote to the Louisiana governor about this matter, two offers were received in Havana to supply the Cubans with cypress pieces for crates. The lowest bid, and the one chosen, was that of Santiago Foutant (11 reales per cypress piece). On November 26, 1772, a large group of mill owners or their representatives meeting in the town hall accepted the contract, although with some conditions. Under its terms, they were to receive approximately 49,730 cypress pieces annually, the amount the mills then needed.[81]

In parallel fashion, another very important discussion emerged about how to grant licenses for the use of wood in construction. It seems that the Count de Macuriges, quartermaster general of the navy, usually granted the permits, although rightfully it was the captain general who should give his assent. The Marquis de La Torre proposed modifying this practice. In September 1772 Macuriges lamented that, because of this pretension, in the future one "could not proceed under one's own authority, nor be informed of those matters in which one exercises it."[82] This was the prelude to a direct confrontation that would later occur between the Marquis de La Torre and Bonet, both of whom managed to tolerate their differences for a time.[83]

At the end of 1774 and the beginning of 1775, however, the apparent harmony in the granting of licenses came to an end. The detonator was the seizure decreed by Bonet of wood cut without his license by the Marquis de Jústiz de Santa Ana and the Count de Jibacoa, at a time when this lumber was urgently needed for the careenage of three ships. The reaction of the Marquis de La Torre was swift. From then on the two leaders were locked in a perpetual struggle to control the granting of logging licenses. In addition to exchanging letters defending their irreconcilable points of view, the two men took their positions to the court in search of a resolution in their favor.

Bonet was of the opinion that the preservation of the forests was his responsibility, with the power to allow individuals to cut wood and ensure that those under the authority of the Royal Forest Reserves strictly abided by it. He found it scandalous that Jústiz de Santa Ana and Jibacoa should continue to sell cedar when other residents, including "those most recommendable," did not dare cut a length without the required license, "even for the most urgent and essential needs of their estates." His alarm was all the greater because the estates on which Jústiz de Santa Ana and Jibacoa cut wood lay within the Royal Forest Reserves of Matanzas. Despite the services to the monarch that the two men claimed to be rendering, one could not ignore "the need to cut off the disorder with which, using two sawmills almost equal to that of the Arsenal, these two houses have been destroying the woodlands of this Jurisdiction for more than forty-five years."[84] The governor also complained that until now no licenses had been granted to individuals without previously informing him, and no objections had been raised to the confiscations "until the complaints and protests of Sres. Jústiz and Jibacoa determined your servant to contest these claims."[85]

Beyond the case of wood confiscated from two powerful landowners, the subject of the granting of licenses to cut wood centered efforts to delimit and defend mutually questioned authority. The controversy came to a head when the captain general issued his edict of March 7, 1776, preceded by a royal order addressed to both civil servants that the woodlands destined for the use of the public and of the shipyard be separated. The two men interpreted this text differently.[86] Bonet, asked to choose the woodlands necessary for the shipyard, concluded that all those of the island were, since in his opinion the estates around the port of Havana were sufficient for the public.

Obviously, neither the landowners nor the captain general would accept this. With his March 1776 edict, the Marquis de La Torre sought to clarify his interpretation of the royal orders. In a conciliatory preamble, he wrote that without a "quick and effective remedy," in a few years no woodlands would remain, or they would be at a distance that would render shipbuilding so costly as to be impractical. He therefore ordered that nowhere on the island, without permission of the government, could one fell mahogany, cedar, oak, sabicú, yaba, chicharrón, ocuje, or guaiacum. Similarly, those owners who obtained permission must "plant indispensably for each tree they render useless four cuttings from the same tree beside its former trunk."[87]

Bonet and La Torre once again submitted their points of view to the court. Meanwhile, La Torre continued granting licenses for estates owned by the public, but he soon found this to be insufficient. On July 1, 1776, La Torre wrote Bonet that the estate owners had "begun to repeat appeals detailing the difficulties they find acquiring wood in the designated locations." Fearing that the complaints would increase, he requested of Bonet a remedy that would allow residents (vecinos)[88] to obtain the wood necessary for the "maintenance or expansion of the mills on their estates," for their own good and for that of the state (La Torre claimed), "which has an interest that harvests increase of the estimable fruit produced by these lands, which until now have remained nearly uncultivated."

Shortly thereafter La Torre sent a long letter to José de Gálvez, minister of the Indies, on his continual conflicts with Bonet. In addition to expressing his disapproval of the latter's choice of woodlands and accusing him of "ambition to wield superiority over the residents and to restrict the authority of the Government that he so seeks to emulate," La Torre argued for his viewpoint on the subject of the woodlands. Although the estates designated in 1767 were still sufficient for the needs of the city, the same was not true for the country estates, which used more wood. In further agreement with the estate owners, he argued that the wood from New Orleans not only was more expensive (11 reales per container rather than the 7 or 8 previously paid for cedar crates) but also rotted easily and soon had to be replaced.[89]

Worst of all, in La Torre's judgment, was that all this was occurring "in a country that abounds in fine woods, perhaps more than any other in the world." He supported this opinion with the argument that lands with few cedars again "became fecund." In effect, residents were being told "that they must not use an ax on their property, which is condemned to being forest in perpetuity, without thinking of making any other use of it than for grazing, since on this island there are no lands that are not covered thickly with trees." The letter thus went to the heart of the conflict, that is, the rapid agrarian transformation being undergone by the territories closest to the port of Havana. About this La Torre argued, "The knowledge of wood is not so narrowly limited here as it is in Spain, nor is it simply reduced to granting licenses to fell trees when individuals need wood; annexed to this is the grave care in dismantling Estates, which here means reducing them to arable land, since this transformation can only be brought about by cutting down and annihilating trees, with which the entire surface of the island is covered."[90]

The captain general also countered Bonet's claims that La Torre's authority was "limited by the walls of the plaza, since eight or ten leagues from it the forests begin." Bonet's choice of woodlands not only left the old difficulties standing but also revived pretensions that people who lived on the island must obey the navy commander "in all that concerns wood, in other words in the greater and main part of their affairs."[91] The provisional decision to grant licenses alone was supported by the Crown, providing that they were given with care not to prejudice "the preferential effort to conserve wood useful to the making of vessels, in conformance with the Royal Order of February 29."[92] La Torre, who had reached the end of his term, was also informed that his successor would be given instructions, by the order of November 1776, to avoid any future conflict on authority over forests.[93]

In June 1777 the new captain general, Diego José Navarro, took office. By the end of the year he established a mechanism for reconciling the interests of the navy and the estate owners: the Havana Wood Committee. The objective was to agree on how to grant licenses, and who should do this, so that residents and estate owners could harvest wood "without experiencing the delays undergone thus far because of the differences that have occurred." Each member of the committee explained his concerns, and it was finally agreed that the governor "shall grant licenses or permits himself and without any intervention from the Navy . . . in the woodlands designated for supplying the public . . . , reserving the rest for the making of the vessels of the King." A truce was thus agreed to, after which the governor suspended the meetings so that "time and events may fully instruct the points that should be considered and on which agreement much be reached."[94]

The next sessions of the Wood Committee were held during four days in February 1779. At the first meeting Navarro presented a report with several points that should be dealt with in order to reach an agreement. The board agreed to name three experts to reconnoiter exhaustively the woodlands destined for the public, determining their size, their distance from the city and the landing, and the number, quantity, and type of trees they contained. In their deliberations, committee members proposed several rules for the use of trees. The first established that in woodlands intended for residents and estate owners in Havana and its jurisdiction, "for the building of houses and furniture, for *ingenios*, their apparatuses and machines, as for the cultivation of fields," the governor would be the one authorized to grant licenses; if there was insufficient wood in these woodlands, or if they were too distant, one could request a license from the navy commander. The fourth provision determined that, since suppliers were not the appropriate way to furnish wood to the public, each resident was free "to cut, work, and haul wood for himself or to sell" but with the obligation to bring to the city all large branches that could be used for shipbuilding. The sixth provision granted those landowners who had obtained permission to subdivide their land the right to use the lumber produced in clearing, "without any other resident being able to remove it without his consent and previous permission of the Government."

One very important question was what stance to take when a resident asked permission "to clear a portion of terrain to set up an *ingenio*, to grow livestock feed or cultivate fields, when this land is located in woodlands reserved for construction." Could a license to dismantle be granted "to the owner of a livestock estate virgin of trees useful for shipbuilding"? If so, under what conditions could this wood be used, and who would have the power to sanction violators? The committee members decided to request the opinion of the *asesores* (advisors to the court), "since this is a point of law rather than of governance." Those consulted included the *auditores* (judge advocates) of war and the navy and the adviser to the royal treasury, who were asked to submit their opinions in writing because their points of view disagreed.

Ignacio Ponce de León y Maroto, judge advocate of the navy, presented a report in which he not only defended its primordial rights but also articulated interesting economic and ecological opinions. He began by specifying the type of activities engaged in by *hatos* and *corrales* in order to show that most of their properties were covered with woodlands. The latter, he said, naturally produced cedar, mahogany, sabicú, chicharrón, and yaba, which were the woods necessary for shipbuilding and ones that continuously multiplied, although over the course of many years. Logging them, furthermore, did no harm to the estates, since their fruit was not the kind eaten by livestock.

Ponce de León y Maroto claimed that the king and the vassal were "partners in the domain of the Estates, the former in the woodlands and the latter on the terrain." Without going into whether the property owner had the right to vary the use assigned when the land was conceded to him, "with manifest prejudice toward he who conceded it," Ponce de León y Maroto argued that for the moment no permits should be granted for the dismantlement of estates with wood useful to shipbuilding. Experience had shown that shade made planting crops useless and that "to open up the countryside, one needs fire, which destroys all the lumber still standing."

The objection that this opinion was against the interests of the population was dispelled, in Ponce de León y Maroto's view, because dismantlements were permitted not out of a need for arable land (of which there was plenty on estates already dismantled) "but out of [concern for] the harm to neighbors." Individual interest, moreover, "can never prevail over the interest of the state." In this sense the conservation of trees producing construction lumber not only strengthened the Havana arsenal, it also preserved material for arsenals in Spain. The former's continued presence was in the interest of "the whole of the Island," since shipbuilding guaranteed entry to the site, which in the future could be larger and where now "more than six hundred people live, including carpenters, caulkers, blacksmiths, and their families."

Ponce de León y Maroto concluded that the estate owners thought only of subdividing their lands to enrich themselves. The establishment of logging sites for the king required considerable expense for ox teams, tools, and leveling of terrain for hauling, so one "should not burden the Royal Treasury just to suit this individual, with most of the expenditures being lost." According to his calculations, in eight to twelve years the *cortes* would be withdrawn from the estates located within 12 to 14 leagues of the city. He also noted that the raising of livestock "was increasingly lacking." In the case these arguments were not sufficient, Ponce de León y Maroto wrote, prior to dismantlement the king should be able to buy the land in question "for the price of the most recent acquisition, or for the value in the current tax assessment." This would create a "sure defense of lands for cultivation and livestock; the motive for dismantlement would disappear; and the abundance of lumber would be secured in perpetuity."[95]

The report by Diego Moya de Colón, adviser to the royal treasury, generally agreed with these points. Moya de Colón first observed that the committee had not adopted the solution decreed years before by the Count de Macuriges regarding the dismantlement of the Melena *corral*, "allowing it but requiring the owners of the land to maintain its wood that is useful for construction." To the Wood Committee's query he replied categorically that lands with virgin woodlands could not be dismantled "because this would be contrary to the Dominion that the King indisputably has in them, and that His Majesty has in all times reserved." In addition to the laws of the Indies, Moya de Colón mentioned the rulings of the island's governments: "If the estate owner claims to be able to use the lands because they are his, this motive is insufficient to deprive His Majesty of the same freedom with respect to the timber in his Dominion." In general he was more exhaustive than Ponce de León y Maroto in outlining the legal precedents that supported his viewpoint, showing that the beneficiaries of "land concessions were not given dominion for time immemorial . . . but only have use, for which they have populated them with livestock; and in spite of this right timber may be felled for ships."[96]

Moya de Colón concluded that his argument implied two basic points, without intending to contest the authority of the city and town councils. The first was that when the object of the land concession — the raising of livestock — was concluded, so was the concession itself. Thus, when the estates were allowed to be dismantled and converted into arable land, "this cannot prejudice the right to their timber of the very sovereign who grants the right, but rather should provide the effects of this new favor, with the usefulness and benefit of the Majesty that enacts it." The second implication was that estate owners should not feel delayed or harmed by having to wait for the Royal Forest Reserves to use the trees on their land, since "the highly increased advantages given to them by subdivision compensate, excessively, any delay." To support this he noted that in the ten years preceding February 1, 1775, thirty-one *corrales* had been dismantled, which, when one counted also those already dismantled, showed that "the city is not wanting for arable land"; far from it, many of these estates had not been able to find buyers for all their subdivisions. "For all these reasons," Moya de Colón concluded, "I believe that preference must be given to the need the King always has to build vessels for his Armada. As a result, when an Estate with virgin woodlands is dismantled, the Navy must immediately and without delay be allowed to clear it, felling and removing the trees it requires. To the extent practical, one can then proceed to subdivide, alienate, and cultivate the land, unless permission [to dismantle] is obtained from the King."[97]

The third of the experts consulted, war judge advocate Félix del Rey, argued for the opposite position. For him, it was undeniable that the discoverers, settlers, buyers, and legitimate leaseholders of the lands held "full and true dominion in them."[98] The dominion of the landowners and of the king "in the plants useful to shipbuilding" constituted a sort of contract of fellowship "though which no fellow may deprive another of the use of the common thing." For this reason, he thought it evident that to prevent property owners from "converting it into an object of agriculture is to do them a well-known injustice." The very Law 13, Title 17, Book 4, of the *Recopilación de las leyes de los reinos de las Indias* (Code of Laws of the Realms of the Indies) served as proof, since it reserved for the king only mahogany, cedar, and oak trees, so that all other species could be felled "without offense to the Law." He acknowledged, however, that it would be nearly impossible to leave the reserved trees standing because of hurricanes and especially fires set to clear land for crops.

Del Rey's report sought to demonstrate the landowners' full property rights. As for the supposed increase in value resulting from dismantlement, he claimed this was an imaginary advantage. He estimated that at least a third of the 421 caballerías in a *corral* were rocky and prone to flooding, so that only 280 could be sold, in addition to which experience had shown that it took fifteen to twenty years to complete the process of subdivision.[99] His determination was that if in the terrain to be cleared there was wood useful to shipbuilding, an amount of time "in no way causing distress, but rather quite ample" should be allowed for all this lumber to be harvested. Similarly, if dismantlement was requested for an estate through which the Royal Forest Reserves had not passed, this would be announced four to six years in advance so that the navy could take the useful wood, after which period "it would be within the power of the Owner of the land to subdivide and dismantle it, so long as the excepted species are left standing."

As we can see, all these reports did was arm the contending sides with legal arguments. The members of the Wood Committee confessed the impossibility of reconciling the motives that had led them to seek the reports and agreed, "by common opinion," to submit the documents and other agreements and rules adopted to the court so it could resolve the matter according to its judgment. The committee also named a commission charged with determining whether the woodlands destined for the public remained sufficient.

In October 1779 the committee met for the final time under the direction of Diego José Navarro. On this occasion the state of the estates destined for public use was shown, and new rules were adopted for their exploitation. The captain general reported to José de Gálvez, minister of the Indies, in accordance with the royal order of November 20, 1776, that the circumstances in which the matter of the forests stood when he arrived in Havana "classed it among those most needful of rules to order its direction, which has fluctuated due to the perturbation produced by the lack of agreement between the Government and the Navy." His intention was "to calm the disputes and determine a method that is tranquil and free of fault." Nonetheless, the disagreement among the experts consulted, which caused "perplexity among the Committee," caused him "to submit this doubt to His Majesty so that, having better considered the grounds of these opinions, Royal Resolve may descend."[100]

From this point the center of discussion definitively became the dismantlements. The future of shipbuilding, threatened by the rapid advance of the sugar industry in the Havana region, largely depended on how the wooded estates were divided. It was clear that the struggle between the royal navy and the sugar planters would not end. The question was which side would receive royal backing. And in this case the scales tilted in favor of the navy. In a letter addressed to Bonet on June 24, 1779, apparently without the character of a royal order, the king expressed his agreement with the opinions offered by Ponce de León y Maroto and Moya de Colón, that is, that dismantlements of wooded estates should not be authorized without the reasons being reported to the king so that he might give his approval.

Control of the Dismantlement
Process by the Navy, 1784–1791

In 1783, the conflict between the Navy Command and the Captaincy General over forests erupted again, this time provoked by the former's refusal to allow use of dismantlement licenses granted under the rules agreed to in October 1779. This led the Wood Committee to begin meeting again on September 3. After exchanging opinions and reading the three experts' reports and agreements from 1779, the board members agreed to await the decision of the Crown. They therefore resolved to suspend the issuing of dismantlement licenses, "since His Majesty urgently needs as much wood as possible for the building of vessels made here and for shipment to Spain."[101]

Two days later, navy commander Francisco de Borja wrote a statement explaining how he believed woodlands should be preserved to supply the Havana arsenal and the arsenals in Spain without depriving the public of material needed for its mills and for agriculture. He began by saying that the island's woodlands abounded in cedar, mahogany, sabicú, chicharrón, yaba, ocuje, baría, and some oak and guaiacum, woods that could be available forever if consumed methodically, while "if the opposite is done, they will quickly be exhausted." He insisted, therefore, that for the moment, dismantlement permits issued without the knowledge of the navy should not take effect. They were unnecessary, since closer to the city were thousands of treeless caballerías that were lying fallow for want of farmers; in addition, "the same Estates have Savannas, and other land, whose use would not hinder agriculture." In his view, the pretext of dismantlement had no other purpose than to allow a landowner to "destroy the King's woodlands and enrich himself with their timber."[102]

Borja also requested the renewal of the ban on burning woodlands on estates, "to prevent fire from spreading," as well as restriction of the use of cedar. As sources for the public he recommended only the woodlands closest to the coast. And since individuals used only lengths of wood, he asked that licenses include the condition that loggers work the larger branches and take them to the arsenal, where they would be paid the wood's "just value." Estate owners closer to the woodlands of the navy than to public ones could use trees that, "not being of the most valuable for construction, [remedy] necessity without prejudicing the Service." Another condition was that, in order to avoid confusion, no lengths could be removed without being marked by the navy. Similarly, Borja proposed two types of licenses for public woodlands: the first for felling and working timber and the second for removing it. This measure and the presence of wardens would "lessen the abuse and disorder of exceeding permits, of removing eight hundred under cover of having been permitted to remove eighty."[103]

The next February, in another written statement, Borja again insisted on the need to strengthen measures to guarantee the supply of wood to the Havana arsenal. He remarked that since he took command of the navy, the conservation of woodlands had been one of his chief concerns. Given the repeated requests by individuals wanting wood for their mills after dismantlement licenses had been suspended at his request, Borja took a tour of the Royal Forest Reserves that confirmed his misgivings: with the cedar used in five *ingenios* and the discarded large branches, two ships of the line could be built, and this did not take into account the hardwood used in *trapiches*, textile mills, and conduits. And yet for these uses cedar was not indispensable, as it was for roofing boards, molding, ogees, vats, ridge poles, rafters, and "other small items."[104]

The new rules would provide the public with the cedar, sabicú, and chicharrón it needed from the Royal Forest Reserves providing that this wood was marked to ensure "that the permit was not exceeded." The designer would appear with his carpenters to ascertain that tie ends and curves were not lost, since private individuals took only "straight trunks of the trees." This procedure would be followed in the most distant estates, while residents of the city and its environs would be directed to woodlands near the coast, with the obligation that for each straight trunk harvested they bring two figured ones to the arsenal, "satisfying the King's share." For other needs, the resolution of the Crown with respect to dismantlements would be awaited, with the proviso that these should never be allowed before the navy had removed the lumber from the estates.

Borja also believed it indispensable that agreement be reached on how to supply inhabitants of towns in the island's interior, where the disorder was so great that he had seen "beautiful lengths of wood being used as fencing for cockfights," large houses that instead of walls had cedar panels, and much of this and other woods "lost . . . without being put to any use." As in Havana, only straight trunks from these woodlands were used. Finally, he asked for an exemplary punishment of the practice of felling trees to collect honey from beehives. All of this showed the "little appreciation of lumber."[105]

The *ingenio* owners collectively rejected Borja's proposals. Seventeen of them signed a statement in which they expressed "imponderable pain" at the injury to their estates and predicted the latter's "total extermination" if the owners were not freed to use cedar and sabicú, "as abundant on this island as they are absolutely necessary to build new *Ingenios*, and to continually rebuild those already constructed." They also alleged that the public woodlands were not useful to them because their cedar and sabicú had already been logged and because they were too far away, which compelled the mill owners to "pay exorbitant amounts for hauling over more or less thirty leagues" of roads in terrible condition. Most of these sites, the owners claimed, had been maintained for many years by the Royal Forest Reserves and abandoned when considered to have no more wood useful for shipbuilding.[106]

The sugar producers' statement also argued that when estates were subdivided for agriculture permission was granted to "clear forests, cut trees, and transform them into ashes, because no one would buy [the lands] if they were prevented from clearing them, plowing them, and fertilizing them with seeds." They also denied that trees needed for shipbuilding could become extinct, indicating that the experience of travelers and sailors testified to the existence of forests "so florid and abundant that in hundreds of years they could not be used up, even if [ships] were built with them most actively." Among other examples, the estate owners asked when the newly exploited woodlands of Alquízar and Casiguas would be exhausted and when the end would be seen of "those grown by nature and still virgin" on the edges of the island's many bays. In short, "in many centuries of incessant application, and bringing many Ships into the world each year, in the shipyards of Europe as in our own, the island's timber would not be exhausted."[107]

The sugar producers stated that they would be content to use the trees in woodlands subdivided for cultivation and the wood discarded in the *cortes*. They attributed the behavior of the navy commander to the "influence of his subordinates, to whom he confides the direction of these matters, and according to whose opinions he conducts himself."[108] Nevertheless, when the Wood Committee met on February 27 and March 3 and 17 to study Borja's proposals, it accepted them with slight variations. On April 19 an edict by Captain General Luis de Unzaga y Amezaga announced the new rules. Among the innovations was the indication of estates that would supply the public: the windward haciendas included Las Pozas, Sierra Morena, Juanillas, and Limones; those leeward were Río de Puercos, Buenavista, San Marcos, and La Vega. The new rules also specified how villages of the interior would be supplied: from one of the estates closest to each in the southern part of the island and with the permission of the lieutenant governors.

The mill owners did not give up. In July the city council named two commissioners to write a statement to the court "in order to free this public from the grave oppression by the Commander General of the Navy in the provision of wood." In the preamble of the letter, addressed to Gálvez, the minister of the Indies, the writers warned of the handicap that the population and agriculture would suffer if the system being pursued by the navy were continued, since the latter intended to "extend its jurisdiction to include all of the Island's territory, so that of the great number of estates of which it is composed, the Government can allow the public to cut down trees in no more than thirty, and then only pending provisions . . . so long-winded and irrelevant that for the slightest reason one's property may be seized."[109] Despite these efforts, the desire to guarantee the supply of wood for the Havana arsenal and for shipments to Spain continued to prevail. After consultations by the Counsel of the Indies, the attorneys general of New Spain and of Peru (Fiscales de Nueva España y del Perú), and the Committee of State, a royal order was finally decreed on October 4, 1784. It maintained the disposition of Law 13, Title 17, Book 4, of the *Recopilación* and the order of April 8, 1748. Trees not reserved would be "available to the Government for public use, and the other purposes of the population, agriculture, and commerce . . . so that each leader [would grant] the respective licenses." In addition, the king ordered the naming of "twelve wardens of the woodlands who will be subject to the satisfaction of both parties."[110]

As for the "agitated and unresolved point in Havana of whether individual landowners may break up wooded lands and make them into plantations," it was established that licenses would be requested of the Wood Commission, which would decide by majority vote whether the estate was located "in terrain included within the area indicated for the Navy." When woods reserved for public works and the common good were needed, these would also be requested of the commission, "but if the resolution is adopted by majority vote, it is the Navy Commander who issues the licenses in conformance with the agreement." The royal order expressed confidence that the captain general and the navy commander would proceed "with perfect concord and harmony," seeing shipbuilding, on the one hand, and the island's population, agriculture, and commerce, on the other, as "equally important and worthy of attention."[111] This satisfied the navy's aspiration to intervene directly in the granting of dismantlement licenses in territories with reserved timber.

It was not clear, however, that the navy would realize its hopes to stop the process of dismantlements, since it needed a majority of votes on a Wood Committee whose members were not all inclined to its viewpoint, quite the contrary. The next step in securing dominion over the forests was precisely to control as completely as possible the granting of licenses to dismantle estates. The man charged with doing this was not a navy commander but the director of the Royal Forest Reserves, José Manuel de Villena, who had served in this post since the early 1780s. With time his power over the exploitation of forests for shipbuilding became so great that he locked in frequent conflicts with navy general commanders Francisco Javier de Morales and Juan de Araoz, who saw their responsibilities in this area diminished. However one may read these events, the undeniable result was the strengthening of the navy's monopoly over the forests, up to its final consequences.

In July 1787 Villena proposed new methods for the development of forests, which essentially differed little from previous proposals.[112] Among these was the granting of reserved woods to individuals for the uses indicated in the edict of April 19, 1784, with the addition of cedar for conduits, mahogany for furniture, and sabicú and chicharrón for *trapiches* and carts. Those who had such timber on their own lands were allowed to use it, even if the large branches were lost, and those who did not have such woods could request them from the Royal Forest Reserves. As for the supplying of the city and villages in the countryside, Villena's only significant innovation was an increased rigor in the application of fines and penalties. He did, however, oppose the creation of the twelve warden positions foreseen in the royal order of October 4, 1784, considering these insufficient to keep watch over the whole island.[113]

Villena concluded his proposal by insisting that all the woodlands on the island be reserved for shipbuilding, all those indicated in the 1748 edict being nearly exhausted. This also would legally end two practices that entailed great losses for the state: the frequent burnings of forest "to enlarge savannas for livestock grazing" and the felling of trees to harvest honey from beehives. With respect to dismantlements, he was of the same opinion as other civil servants in the navy: if there were already dismantled estates with much unpopulated land, why did new ones have to be permitted? But nothing in his "new rules" was as new as the proposal he submitted with them that he be made a member of the Wood Committee.

This desire deepened the tension that already existed between Villena and the navy commanders. For example, Juan de Araoz reported, in response to a royal order of April 8, 1788, that the disagreement with his predecessor "flowed from Villena's wanting the General's [i.e., Araoz's] independence in putting officers in the logging sites, and captains of the boats that led them to the Arsenal, replacing all of them in time." Nevertheless, it was the woodlands director whose position was strengthened when he was authorized to travel to Spain to discuss the woodlands and shipbuilding face to face with officials there. In the metropole the inspector general of the arsenals, in a communiqué of October 17, 1788, qualified his work as "meticulous and useful." The inspector general argued that "even when these appropriate responsibilities exceed constant use, the latter should be abolished and the former placed in one who has particular knowledge of these matters, without the essence of this mandate compromising the office of the Commander General of the Navy and the resolutions of the Committee."[114]

In keeping with this support, the royal order of February 15, 1789, was issued. Its preamble acknowledged the shortcomings of the order of October 4, 1784, on the division of the jurisdiction over woodlands between the Captaincy General and the navy command, offering as an example of this the fact that the twelve wardens had not yet been named. It thus resolved that the Wood Committee should propose "the means that best will achieve the development of the population without destroying the woods used in shipbuilding, and the way to keep watch over the woodlands at the least cost possible." To this end the order named Villena a member of the committee "so that his knowledge of these matters, his zeal and love in the service of His Majesty, assist that of the Committee, which will hear his reflections with the utmost attention." In case of disagreement, each member would submit his written vote through the channels established for the Indies, "and while His Majesty resolves the matter definitively . . . the Committee will grant dismantlements of Estates, in one Jurisdiction as in another if the aforementioned Villena, who is charged with the direction of woodlands, their logging, working, hauling, and transport, does not identify handicaps prejudicial to the service."[115]

The results of these new sessions in Havana of the Wood Committee were communicated in August by the governor and interim captain general Domingo Cabello de Robles. In general these proposed rules were consistent with those articulated by Villena, except that they provided for a veto suspending estate dismantlement. These precedents underlay the royal order of December 11, 1789, published in Havana on March 8, 1790, through an edict by Cabello de Robles. Several of its measures repeated those articulated in previous years, but others were made explicit for the first time. Among the latter were prohibitions on cutting trees to harvest beehives and their wax or to make fences, a stipulation that logging for export be supervised, and a reduction in entry tariffs for iron from Biscay. Also very important was the formal elimination of the boundaries established in 1748 (and ratified in 1784) delimiting the territory reserved for the Royal Forest Reserves. In the future the arsenal would harvest lumber "where it is deemed most useful by officers of the Navy."[116]

These royal measures supporting Villena's desire to put woodland matters under his direction led to the navy commander and other members of the committee being for the first time on the same side, if only in the most circumstantial way. Disagreements eventually led Villena to tender his resignation, "no longer being able to resist Araoz's personal animosity nor the machinations he threatens." He specified later that his resignation should be accepted if Araoz was not replaced at the command of the navy, "good harmony" having become "quite impossible . . . given the state that disagreements have reached."[117] His resignation, however, was not accepted. A royal order of September 11, 1790, directed the Havana Wood Committee to "proceed in these matters in conformance with the opinion of Villena, whose intelligence in them, and his noted zeal, leave no room for doubt."[118]

The broad authority given to the director of the Royal Forest Reserves and the detailed regulations of 1789 were the culmination of the navy's efforts to control, to the maximum degree possible, the exploitation of the island's forests. During the same years, large-scale projects were undertaken to ship wood to arsenals in Spain, also under Villena's orders.[119] The monopoly the navy had enjoyed since the sixteenth century on the best woods in the Havana area not only was extended to the entire island but also would now be led by a civil servant whose specific mission was to guide logging and to supervise the pace of dismantlements. Despite the Crown's support for his management, Villena transferred to Spain. Before leaving he gave instructions to his successor, the frigate captain Pedro Acevedo.

Under the latter's direct supervision, and with the support of Araoz, the system established in the early 1790s lasted for a few more years. It was the last attempt to save shipbuilding in Havana, which coincidentally was undertaken at the outset of a period when circumstances for Cuban sugar had never been more favorable.

The Struggle over Private Ownership of Forests, 1792–1815

*The Sugar Boom and the
Occupation of the Artemisa Plain*

The collapse of the French colony in Haiti allowed Havana's sugar and plantation economy to take off definitively after several decades of increasing production. The coincidence of this event with the dawn of the Industrial Revolution, which led to increased demand for raw materials and foodstuffs, technological advances, and the liberalization of commerce, allowed nineteenth-century Cuba to remake itself into one of the primary producers of "fruits of the colonies." Land- and *ingenio* owners, seeking to take over the role of the neighboring former colony and consolidate their economic position and political influence, won the backing of the highest colonial authorities. They began to realize their ambitions as never before, and among these aspirations was, of course, reaching a definitive and profitable solution to the contested issue of the forests.

Among the measures Francisco de Arango y Parreño advocated in his

"Discurso sobre la agricultura en La Habana y medios de fomentarla" (Discourse on Agriculture in Havana and How to Promote It) were a sharp increase in the import of black slaves and in foreign trade, the application of technical and scientific knowledge, and the creation of a credit fund with revenue from the farmers themselves. In one way or another most of these measures sought by Havana landowners were enacted. The free selling of slaves, decreed in 1789, was extended until the formal abolition of the trade in 1817. The liberalization of trade generally took longer, but it was finally established in 1818. Nevertheless, beginning in 1792 and 1793, because of the war with revolutionary France, a series of licenses had been granted for trade with neutral countries, which stimulated exchange with the United States.[1] This was a significant development because Spain did not have a market capable of absorbing the constant increase in Cuban production; nor did it have a refining industry or a large enough merchant marine.

In 1792 sugar, tobacco, coffee, and indigo were exempted from all sales taxes and tithes for ten years, and imported tools and utensils were also freed from tariffs. Four years later the establishment of refineries was authorized, and tariffs on the export of *aguardiente* and rum to other ports in the Americas and in Europe were eliminated. The trend toward granting privileges to sugar and plantation interests continued throughout these years. For example, a royal decree of April 4, 1804, excepted new *ingenios* from paying the tithe and froze the rate old *ingenios* were assessed at one based on that year's production.

Two fundamental players in this process were the Royal Patriotic Society of Friends of the Country and the Royal Consulate of Agriculture, Industry, and Commerce of Havana, corporations founded in 1793 and 1795, respectively.[2] Through these organizations, Havana's oligarchy and intellectuals united the defense of their class interests in order to modernize the colony and develop it economically. In these two groups scientific trips were organized and financed, and papers on various subjects of economic, scientific, or moral interest were debated and published. Both were responsible for the proliferation of innovations in the sugar industry, favored by the arrival on the island of many technicians from Haiti.

Thanks to the circumstances created by the drop in Haitian production, new *ingenios* multiplied in the Havana region, in the areas around the port of Matanzas and the Trinidad area on the southern coast. According to the 1792 census, 245 *ingenios* existed that year on the farms of Havana and

Matanzas, 140 more than at the beginning of the 1770s. Eight years later, in 1800, the number of sugar plantations in the same region was 350, and another 50 were being developed.[3] The average number of new plantations founded each year had increased from 5 to 20. In 1820, there were 625 plantations in a provincial district that extended to Santa Clara (which had 14) and Trinidad (which had 77). In the same zone there were 779 coffee plantations, also representative of the triumph of this economic system.[4]

The rise in the number of *ingenios* and in their productive capacity spurred a constant increase in sugar production and exports. Between 1786 and 1791, with the price at 12 to 16 reales per arroba, 425,775 crates of sugar left the port of Havana. Between 1792 and 1797, with the price at 16 to 20 reales per arroba in the first three years and 26 to 30 reales in the last two (the increase due to the complete loss of the Haitian harvest in 1794), 573,330 crates were exported.[5] Although prices dropped, sugar production continued to increase: in 1796, for instance, 120,375 crates were shipped, with that number rising to 165,602 in 1799.

Production kept rising despite the relative crisis in the industry caused by the Napoleonic wars and the blockade of England, one of Cuba's primary markets. According to Rafael A. Cowley, exports in the first decade of the nineteenth century were 207,696 crates a year, while during the preceding decade the annual average was 110,091.[6] The most critical moment was around 1807, when prices dropped between 3 and 7 reales. That year the captain general asked the Royal Consulate whether it was true that new *ingenios* were no longer being founded and whether the oldest ones were being dismantled. Diego José Sedano replied for the Royal Consulate that after the Haitian Revolution the value of Cuban sugar increased more than 100 percent, which "excited an effort and an emulation in founding *ingenios*," so that "in something like three or four years the sugar void left by the revolution had been nearly filled." When the high profits disappeared, they were replaced by "an almost universal repentance and an overwhelming dismay." Sedano even predicted "greater dejection closer to home," since the sector offered only "current bankruptcies and terrible prospects."[7]

This is one of the first warnings that the dominance of cash crops was making the colony increasingly vulnerable to the vagaries of the market. In the report Sedano warned, "Here . . . what is necessary has been neglected in favor of what is useful; I mean, there is a preference for growing produce for export, and even the primary necessities of life are brought from abroad."[8] This same reasoning was used by Bishop Espada in opposing the royal decree of April 4, 1804, in particular and the exemption of cash crops from tariffs in general.[9] Counter to the vision of slaveholding planters, the bishop imagined a country with nine million inhabitants, most of them free laborers and farmers of widely varied crops. The plausibility of Sedano's and Espada's concerns is shown by the similar views expressed by Alexander von Humboldt in his book on Cuba when he warned about the lack of subsistence crops that characterized many of the tropical regions owing to "the imprudent activity of Europeans, which has turned the order of nature on its head."[10]

This critique of the imbalances generated by the plantation economy and their impact on the island's economy, society, and politics foreshadowed what would later be known as the choice between "big Cuba" and "little Cuba," that is, between the dominance of monoculture through a system of slaveholding plantations, on the one hand, and diversification of production, small farms, and free workers, on the other. In this context, the royal navy may have been the force best able to challenge the planters' growing power. Although the navy had a very specific interest in exploiting the island's timber, it is not surprising that its agents sometimes echoed these alternative conceptions of a Cuba not dominated by the limitless extension of commercial agriculture.

It would be a mistake to consider the navy as simply an obstacle without taking into account the validity of its arguments in its lengthy conflicts with the estate owners. It is not coincidental that Bishop Espada, unlike the planters, saw the regulation of woodlands and lumber as adequate. Nevertheless, little could be done by people who argued for a diversified agriculture and a means of peopling the island other than the massive importation of slaves, especially as Cuba consolidated its position as supplier of the world's sugar market. Between 1810 and 1815 the price of sugar in Havana rose from 16 to 20 reales per arroba, thanks in part to the reestablishment of trade with North America.[11]

Part of the sugar boom of those years can be explained by the conquest of still wooded land in the natural regions where sugar had been most solidly established since the early seventeenth century, such as the Plains and Heights of the North of Havana and Matanzas to the east and west. To the east, around Río Blanco and Jaruco, the number of *ingenios* increased from 6 in 1771, to 20 in 1778, 45 in 1792, 73 in 1796, and 133 in 1820.[12] Around the port of Matanzas the number rose from 8 in 1792, to 27 in 1796, and

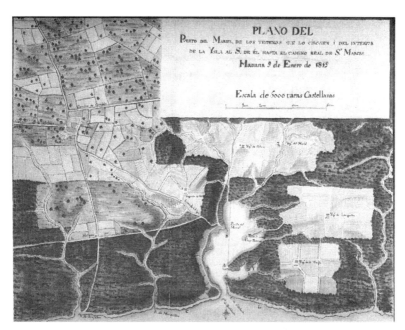

FIGURE 3.1. Forests and *ingenios* in the area of Mariel-Guanajay.

(Instituto de Historia y Cultura Militar, Centro Geográfico del Ejército, *Cartografía y relaciones históricas de Ultramar*, vol. 9, *Grandes y Pequeñas Antillas*, part 1 [Madrid: Ministerio de Defensa, 1999])

95 in 1820.[13] To the west, *ingenios* were founded around Mariel Bay and to the south of it. Similarly, the eastern and western extremes of the Plains of Ariguanabo–Almendares–San Juan region were settled (see figure 3.1).

But the period from 1792 to 1815 was characterized above all by the settlement of the Artemisa Plain, which includes all the southern part of the Havana territory to the northern edge of the western swamp of Zapata. This area covers about 2,925 square kilometers. Also known as the red plain of Havana-Matanzas because of its red, fertile soil, it has a fundamentally subterranean drainage. This natural backdrop was one of two areas of expansion noted by Juan Pérez de La Riva in 1796 statistics: one to the north, with 141 *ingenios*, from Santiago de las Vegas to Jaruco and Matanzas; the other to the south, with 164 *ingenios* and centers in Guanajay and Güines.[14] A precursor to the conquest of the southern Havana plains, the subdivision of the Managua *corral* (hog farm) in the 1770s and 1780s to establish *ingenios*, together with those established around the urban centers of Santiago de las Vegas and Bejucal, was followed by continued expansion south to Batabanó (44 *ingenios* in 1796), southeast to Güines, and southwest to Quivicán, Güira de Melena, and Alquízar. In the western half of the plain expansion began in the area of El Cano and Mariel. In 1820 two of the most important sugar areas were Guanajay and Güines, with 122 and 78 *ingenios*, respectively, maximal figures that represent the end of the settling of the Artemisa Plain.[15]

The case of Güines shows how rapidly sugar emerged in this new period. By around 1730, in the Güines *corral*, a small nucleus of farmers had settled along the river. In 1775, the Marquis de La Torre noted, "On this island there is no piece of land more healthy, fertile, and lovely, with a broad plain, abundant water, and recommendable quality of produce." On October 30, 1779, the Crown bestowed "the grace to found it as a town [*villa*]."[16] Nevertheless, its location 15 leagues from the port kept it out of sugar's ambit, with only 8 small *ingenios* in 1792. This situation quickly changed. By 1800 the area had 26 *ingenios*, of which 15 had been *sitios* (small farms) three years before, in addition to 20 developing *sitios de ingenio*, of which 6 ground their cane in other *ingenios*.[17]

Later in the nineteenth century, the increasing number of *ingenios* in this jurisdiction was driven by the movement of industry to the east. In 1835, when it was recorded that there were 25 *ingenios* in Güines-Catalina established before 1804 and 5 after, Guara, to the west of the town, had 6 old and 5 new *ingenios*, while Pipián, Nueva Paz, and Madruga, to the east, had 8 old and 15 new ones. That year some of the old farms in the western part of Güines were included in Macurijes, which is shown to have 95 *ingenios* founded between 1804 and 1835 and only 8 established before then. What is certain is that the number of *ingenios* in Güines was far from what had been predicted shortly before the definitive emergence of sugar by the estate owner Nicolás Calvo, who dreamed of a region "of cane fields prepared for irrigation and water mills short distances apart, a broad plain with three hundred *ingenios*."[18] In this sense, we could say that the navy officials and others who argued for a more intensive settlement of the land were correct when they noted the difference between real and potential occupation of dismantled estates in the areas of Royal Forest Reserves, claiming that this showed that new dismantlement licenses were unnecessary. This is borne out by 1797 statistics tabulated by the wardens to demonstrate that much available land existed (see table 3.1).

TABLE 3.1. Difference in Caballerías Dismantled and Occupied
by Type of Farm in Royal Forest Reserves, ca. 1797

Royal Forest Reserve	Estates/ Caballerías Dismantled	Farms Created/Caballerías			Potential Farms		
		Ingenios	Potreros	Sitios	Ingenios	Potreros	Sitios
Alquízar	20/8,440	18/594	9/90	48/240	138	9	639
Casiguas	9/3,376	6/198		1/5	60	20	239
Matanzas	18/5,064	48/1,584	18/180	443/2,215	70	30	509

Source: AGI, Ultramar 9, Pedro Acevedo, Havana, February 28, 1797.
Note: The average land area was 33 caballerías per *ingenio*, 10 per *potrero*, and 5 per *sitio*, with an average of 100, 10, and 12 slaves, respectively. More than a third of inhabitants were estimated to be free and included landowners, clergy, civil and military officers, colonists, "free wage workers," artisans, and their families.

After 1797 more *ingenios* and other farms were established in areas formerly occupied by Royal Forest Reserves, without the land use's becoming as intensive as desired by the navy, Bishop Espada, or Nicolás Calvo. In truth, the estates already dismantled were insufficient for the sugar planters, especially now that they hoped to take over the void left by Haiti. Various explanations can be given for this, including the transition in those years from small *ingenios* to much larger plantations worked by slaves. The sugar plantations needed more land for cane and more wood for mills, carts, tools, and fuel. At the same time, the planters, wanting to seize the opportunity created by the Haitian Revolution to expand their plantations, were not prepared to wait until the Royal Forest Reserves had passed through to get their dismantlement permits. The conflict with the navy quickly reignited.

This battle against the limits placed on the exploitation of Cuba's forests in the interests of shipbuilding became central to the changes occurring in the island's agricultural structure and to the triumph of plantationist views and liberalism in the colony's economic sphere. By further exploring the debates between the two camps, we can better understand the great economic and ideological transformation then taking place in the way Cubans interacted with nature.

The Estate Owners' Counteroffensive:
Preparation of Their Arguments

As the 1790s began, Cuba faced a fundamental conflict: on the one hand, the navy's privilege over the forests had been strengthened; on the other, the world political and economic situation gave the island's sugar planters unprecedented motivation to expand. The problem of authority over and exploitation of the forests was among the first to surface, as well as being among the most difficult to resolve, owing to the competing interests.[19] Beginning in 1794 at least, numerous attempts at dismantlement were vetoed by the Havana Wood Committee. That year Pedro Acevedo, having toured seven estates that requested this authorization, told the committee's November 22 meeting that permission could be granted only in three cases, "since they do not have timber involved in the building of Vessels." The others, in contrast, "should not be dismantled so long as their many thousands of cubic cubits of good wood have not been used."[20]

The royal logging operation (*corte*) of Casiguas was then harvesting in the area, specifically in the Pipián estate, from which it would continue on to the three others (Cayajavo, Gabriel, and San José de Arroyo Barbudo) whose dismantlement petitions Acevedo had recommended rejecting. To this end, livestock farms (*potreros*) were developed, and a 9-league road was opened "to send the lumber to the Riverside." For Acevedo, it was clear that if the dismantlement requests were granted, the *corte* would have to be suspended, which he found entirely unnecessary, since the property owners "currently have sufficient land to set up their establishments without prejudicing the greater service of the King." He reminded the Wood Committee of the planned establishment of *cortes* in Cuba's forests to supply the three departments of the navy in Spain.[21]

Reaction was swift: the syndic procurator general of the community, Josef de Coca, also a member of the Wood Committee, opposed Acevedo's recommendation. Given the irreconcilable disagreement and in keeping with royal decree, each party presented arguments that would be transmitted to the court. Acevedo reiterated that harm would come from dismantling estates abundant in lumber.[22] The need for the *cortes* to hire staff to "assist in clearing the woodland surrounding the lumber" created a high cost, with "the near certainty that it will be of no use, inasmuch as the loss of the other plants with which [the tree] was born gradually destroys it."[23]

Josef de Coca, in contrast, demonstrated the usefulness of the dismantlements for the Crown, the public, the private citizens, and the church, sufficient reason to "incline the piety of the King" in his favor.[24] As for the harms noted by the committee's "reluctant members," very slight in his opinion, Coca claimed that on *sitios de ingenio* woodlands were never entirely cleared, "rather they are preserved," and that the island was "quite abundant in timber, and in addition to their being no announced shortage of it, the fact remains that land is required for its growth and development." The councillor Miguel García Barreras voted in Coca's favor, arguing that the needs of inhabitants could be reconciled with those of the royal service if dismantlements were permitted with the condition that trees reserved for the navy be left standing.[25]

Once again the committee was divided, and the different arguments were taken to the court for resolution. And again the ruling favored the navy. In August 1796 the royal order of December 10, 1795, was read before the Wood Committee ordering it to bear in mind "the arguments made by the Director of the Forest Reserves in his opinion . . . and proceed in the future with due caution in granting said licenses." With this support, Acevedo recommended granting eight dismantlement requests that had been pending since May 1795 and opposed only one, "on account of its virgin woodlands, full of abundant and precious trees." The committee members agreed, with the exception of Captain General Luis de Las Casas, who abstained, considering the motion "inconducive."

Despite the Crown's support, navy officials were aware that their position was in danger. Struggles with estate owners over dismantlements were becoming increasingly frequent as the sugar trade became increasingly prosperous. In this context, navy general commander Juan de Araoz decided to write the court through channels reserved for the navy.[26] His goal was to inform his superiors, "for the notice of the King," of the formation in Havana of "a strong and respectable faction seeking to propose to HM [His Majesty] the means and advantages of invalidating all the well-considered and certainly wise Royal resolutions from time immemorial to the present with respect to these woodlands." He noted that the previous night the Government Committee of the Consulate had attempted "to compile and compose a great report to HM on this matter, misrepresenting and giving different meaning to the very long-standing custom and ownership of HM." Charged with this mission were the syndic Francisco de Arango y Parreño and the estate owner, and colonel of the cavalry militias, José Ricardo O'Farrill, to whom the governor made available his secretariat and the papers of the

Wood Committee "in order that they may extract and take from them all the appropriate data."

Araoz was not surprised by the attitude of Las Casas and recalled the latter's previous abstentions on opinions of the director of the Royal Forest Reserves. He also mentioned the direct conflict of interest of Arango y Parreño, the owner of estates whose dismantlement was vetoed, a situation that "does not please the members of the Wood Committee; and there are also two Councillors, and the Syndic Procurator, who own Estates inappropriate for dismantlement because of their virgin timber." In support of his warning, Araoz included statistics on agriculture and population in the jurisdiction of Matanzas and asked that before any decision "a visit be made there" by José Manuel de Villena, "whose knowledge of these woodlands, whose zeal and love of service, will inspire the royal will of HM to dispatch said Royal Order of February 15, 1789."

On October 22, 1796, O'Farrill read to the Economic Society his report on a paper by Father Manuel Gil, written for the Patriotic Society of Seville, that discussed a proposed woodlands ordinance.[27] The object was to analyze its merits and ideas "adaptable to the country"; from the beginning the focus is clearly the latter. O'Farrill asked, first, if Cuba needed to seek the replenishment and conservation of its woodlands; second, if, this being true, which methods should be adopted; and, third, what benefits could be expected. In answer to the first question, he argued that the island's lack of population and produce was not due to its woodlands. This could be shown by the practice on large livestock farms of burning woodlands for pasture and by the fact that an *ingenio* destroyed in each year's harvest 2 flat leagues of woodland, to which could be added the amount of wood consumed by towns, livestock farms (*potreros*), small farms (*sitios*), and estates, "which probably cut down half as much."[28]

Taking into account "the woodlands' relationship with our life and its comforts," O'Farrill wondered how one could be "so unconcerned with their conservation and increase." Without restricting or preventing clearing for agriculture and pastures, he therefore considered it appropriate to reserve a few "for growing trees." Best suited for this purpose would be the woods already missed in Havana, "from whose surrounding area they have disappeared, leaving the communal lands [*ejidos*] without a single tree." To accomplish this a higher order would be necessary, since neither the population nor agriculture would progress to the degree desired if their access to wood was made difficult. O'Farrill warned: "Let us not be insensitive to the clearing and almost universal ruin to which they are subject in our hope that their lack will be filled by other means of equal or greater usefulness. Although their use for fire can be substituted for with coal, when the latter can be found in this country, wood still has an infinite number of uses for which there is no equivalent material."[29]

Another incentive to conserve Cuba's forests, O'Farrill noted, was the decline of those in Spain. Among other measures, without neglecting "the respectable right of property" and the conciliation of individual sacrifice and public utility, he proposed a definitive ban on burning woodlands to open savannas or increase those already opened in estates located up to 5 leagues from coasts with wharves and from navigable rivers; a requirement that in rural districts 1 caballería of trees be planted for every 40 caballerías of open land, with the cost paid by the residents; and the reserving by town councils of part of communal lands for this purpose, with fences put up or ditches dug by them, or through the purchase of lands "at a proportionate distance." Among other proposals were one to create a prize, with public funds, for the inhabitant who on 1 caballería of land would raise "the greatest number of trees useful for mills . . . provided that they be more than two thousand and that they be at least twelve years old, vigorous, and healthy" and another to plant useful trees along roads and the borders of properties.

Estate owners, O'Farrill recommended, should "strive" to plant twenty or thirty trees of construction timber each year, in banana fields or "in woodlands farthest from the mills[,] . . . areas that they believe they will not soon clear or use to plant cane." Through such measures the landowners would obtain forests "that will perpetually sustain their *ingenios*" and "absolute dominion over the trees that they conserve or grow on their lands." So that these regulations, inspired by Father Gil's paper, would not be wasted, O'Farrill added rules such as ones prohibiting the tying of animals to tree trunks or close to saplings or young trees and requiring the planting of shoots from seed and not from branches. He concluded this part by noting that in climates like Cuba's woodlands could be used for half as long as in Europe.

Up to this point there is little or no hint of dissension with the views of the navy, which only becomes perceptible when O'Farrill argues for the estate owners' absolute ownership (*dominio*) of construction timber on their property. Nevertheless, the true nucleus of his argument is left for the end:

To the above I would only add that to preserve this growing population and its countryside from the miserable state of lacking, within a few years, in lumber useful for mills, etc., I believe it necessary to represent to YM that Royal Forest Reserves should be diminished or suspended in the area within twenty-five leagues of the city, and placed instead along the most convenient coast, as much because it is in YM's interest to have so many bountiful estates, and the convenient supplying of towns, as for the savings that would result for the Royal Treasury, due to the difference in cost between hauling the lumber from Casiguas and Matanzas over land and transporting it by sea.

O'Farrill assured his audience that this transfer would not lead to losses for the royal treasury, since the mills, lands, and livestock farms could be sold at a profit, while the oxen, tools, and workers could be transported. And without the restrictions on wood reserved for construction, "various branches would be developed, as well as estates more active than current ones, producing more profits for the King." In conclusion O'Farrill summarized the multiple benefits of forests: supplying tools for agriculture, "fertility to the countryside due to the rains they attract, and freshness to the environment due to the excess transpiration of trees that can cool living creatures and moderate the aridness of the soil during dry seasons." Like Gil's paper, O'Farrill's essay suggested establishing a chair of agriculture to give theoretical and practical instruction to young people, as well as creating schools of agriculture in the principal towns of districts, under the direction of the Economic Society and financed through tithes.

O'Farrill's essay was published as a pamphlet by the Economic Society and distributed with the February 9, 1797, edition of the *Papel periódico de La Havana*. Pedro Acevedo, a subscriber, reacted quickly after receiving his copy.[30] No one better than he could understand O'Farrill's fundamental meaning, and therefore, in his response, Acevedo went directly to the topic of the Royal Forest Reserves, "about which the author, with decided partiality, has dragged out his argument in order to dispatch with them." Acevedo countered that in reality what was sought was "the supplying of lumber to estate owners who need it on the farms that they have established or plan to establish." For Acevedo, "nothing would be further from benefiting the public and agriculture than withdrawing the Royal Forest Reserves from woodlands where they are established and into which they are penetrating." If this happened, it would be seen that "dismantlement serves only to keep fallow and sterile land classified as arable."

Acevedo's rejoinder attacked O'Farrill directly. He asked ironically whether, if the Casiguas *corte* withdrew, O'Farrill would refrain from dismantling his Cayajabos estate, "so that the neighbors and the public might freely benefit from the abundant and fine lumber that it contains." In addition to arguing that estates' woodlands could be thinned without the land losing value, Acevedo discussed the opening of roads and the maintenance of "clearing and hauling from the estates until the labors of Agriculture are about to begin." He asked whether this could be expected from the estate owners, given their self-interest and behavior, and he included the Royal Forest Reserve statistics mentioned above, which showed the great difference between dismantled properties and land that remained uncultivated. After explaining the great difficulties that would be entailed in moving the Royal Forest Reserves to other regions, Acevedo concluded that it would be best to conserve the forests and distribute lands "with prudent economy" rather than being "dependent on the goodwill of venal men, who because of their particular and poorly understood self-interest dismantle and clear leagues of terrain." His condemnation of this system included a clear warning about the effects of commercial agriculture: "I cannot understand how the dismantlement of Woodlands, work that takes time and the zeal of the Government, can be combined with the destruction and replacement of many fields that is sought through it: how can one seek the ruin of trees that need centuries to become useful?"

The causes of agriculture's "languor," in Acevedo's opinion, did not lie in restrictions on the use of wood; on the contrary, its use would be affected in the future under the system sought by the estate owners. Finally, he considered O'Farrill's affirmation that cedar resin could be considered analogous to the sealing wax "with which the bee varnishes the vessel before beginning its work" to be cynical. A March 1796 report had opposed the beekeepers' proposal — through Las Casas — to use cedar, an idea that would become another front on which the navy was attacked.[31]

Two other essential topics in the discussion about forests, lumber, and dismantlements would be debated in 1797 and 1798. One was the scarcity and high price of lumber in Havana, and the other was the causes of the presumed decline of the island's livestock sector. The first was the subject of a February 1797 report to the Royal Consulate by the lumber merchant Tomás de Piña.[32] Seeing the "wise" measures taken by the government and the Wood Committee to be in error, Piña sought to show why the price of lumber, especially cedar, had risen. Among the culprits he identified were the obligation to take two large branches to the arsenal for each length cut, a practice that led to great waste; the reselling of lumber on the La Luz wharf, which was intended for forest products; and the lack of lumber in the public woodlands, in his judgment "the main reason for the high price of cedar." Aggravating factors were the ban on sawing on the coast, since a ship that could carry sawed boards worth 1,500 pesos could only transport unsawed lengths worth 1,000 pesos, and the need for permits to build vessels on the coast, in order to more easily load lumber, save money on hauling, and avoid (in part) having to buy boats from foreigners, "as is occurring."

In order to conserve the woodlands, Piña asked that the ban on cutting cedar braces in *potreros* be reinstated and that wardens be hired, with sufficient salaries to avoid fraud. Where the navy's loggers had passed, he believed it "quite useful to allow, even before a resident requests permission," the use of the many logs and pieces not considered useful for the navy's purposes. To this point no hidden motives could be suspected, but Piña had not yet raised the subject of *ingenios*. After mentioning the authorizations granted for their development, he wrote, "In keeping with the same royal intentions, it would be appropriate to indemnify the founders [of *ingenios*] for the grave harm to which they are subject due to . . . the formalities established for permits that they are given for lumber indispensable for such operations." In short, Piña pointed out, the wardens' inspections took "many days and even months to carry out, because in addition to there being . . . many [*ingenios*] in all directions . . . it is impossible for the [wardens] to dispatch with so many rituals with the necessary speed." He suggested therefore that permits be granted without time limit or other hindrance, since any fraud would be limited to the cutting of a length here and there for "use on the same farm."

This paper was read during the Royal Consulate's November 1, 1797, session by Piña, who made the clarifications requested of him. In response to the syndic's proposal that the paper be formalized as an official record, the consulate members agreed unanimously to forward it to City Hall, since the latter was responsible for "determining the necessity of public expenditure" and with the goal of "proceeding jointly with the city in this matter." The consulate also requested the relevant measures and orders in the files of the Captaincy General. The city council's reply arrived in less than a week. The councillors agreed that in recent times lumber had been less and less available and more and more expensive, "with the difference from previous periods that then the public could be supplied at moderate prices, with less prejudice to the woodlands and the Royal Service's important concerns for the construction of vessels."

Before evaluating Piña's paper, the council referred to its earlier agreement with respect to the complaint by Councillor Francisco Peñalver that Acevedo had insulted him when he requested a permit to cut one hundred lengths of lumber for the building of public baths. Peñalver related that he had been "thrown out shamefully . . . without being heard or greeted other than with contempt after being kept waiting for a long time like the most despicable man in town . . . and not as a Commissioner of the City Council . . . dressed in his uniform." The councillors thought it pertinent to include this fact and express "the Board's desires to root out such pernicious abuse, which exposes the honor of an entire body to the arrogance of an individual."[33]

The council proposed that an impartial person certify the possibility of taking the two additional required pieces to the arsenal, in which case a certification could be sent to the district captain; it also expressed its feeling that, without forgoing paid wardens, it would be better "to carry out a scrupulous inventory of all the cedars now existing in said environs and to mark them as is done in Europe." It also repeated the need to allow new estates for the public and thus to preserve young cedars. Finally, the councillors said they knew "from experience the delays and prejudice imposed by the rituals observed in granting licenses to cut cedar and similar woods needed to build sugar-making *ingenios* and other public buildings." To make even clearer the point of view of a body composed of many of the most prominent sugar planters, they concluded: "Above all every effort should be made that farmers are not distracted from their main tasks and to facilitate the development of their estates, of such great interest to the State, so long as it is not proved that they abuse the licenses they have been granted."

The incident between Peñalver and Acevedo well illustrates the tension between the parties involved in the woodlands conflict. It is not at all strange to find it in the proceedings we are discussing, to which was added another report in May 1798, when Piña consulted Luis Guerra, Francisco Escovedo, and José Patricio Prendis, "the most important men doing business in lumber with the public." The three agreed that before 1779 an 18- to 19-inch length of cedar sold for 8 to 9 reales, during the war with revolutionary France for 12 to 14 reales, after the war for 10 to 12 reales, and after 1791 for 4.5 to 5 pesos. Guerra said he did not know the reason for this increase, which had led him to quit the business. Escovedo observed that since the felling of trees was prohibited, "effects were felt contrary to abundance and equity of prices." Prendis went furthest in denouncing the extortion of lumber vendors by navy officials.[34]

The other major theme of debate in 1797 was introduced by Acevedo during the May meeting of the Wood Committee as a means to restrain the pace of dismantlements. After setting forth the results of a tour of several haciendas that had requested dismantlement permits, Acevedo reflected on the need for the conservation and stimulation of livestock farming. He believed that this sector was in a notable decline that would only worsen, since "no end can be seen to the occupation and cultivation of dismantled lands by colonists who on their small farms equal or surpass the yields of the respective estates." On the committee's instructions, the captain general wrote City Hall on May 31 to request a report.

After taking several sessions to study the matter, the city council replied that dismantlements caused no harm to the livestock sector but rather had quite the contrary effect. The commissioners noted that although in the near term there would be no more "small herds that equal or surpass the yields," the *sitios* and estancias on which foreign breeds were raised would "advantageously" fill the gap.[35] As an alternative the board proposed fencing off dismantled estates, at least where they bordered livestock farms, which might help retain the avalanche of petitions. The syndic added that there would be no meat shortage if herds grew "on the innumerable Estates in the interior of the island that are almost unpopulated." Elsewhere the commissioners made this observation about the transformation of Cuban agriculture: "The true wealth of a State does not consist in a few of its members being powerful and rich and the rest beggars, but rather in everyone having enough to live on, and in opulence resulting from the assemblage or union of all."

The syndic supplemented the report with a statement by Councillor and Treasurer General José Armenteros, who had referred to the subject of livestock at a previous council meeting and whom the syndic had asked to commit these thoughts to paper. Armenteros's detailed report left no doubt about his position: "No one can doubt that dismantlements have increased and improved the important livestock sectors, and all forms of agriculture; that they have benefited commerce and even contributed to the increase in population that one sees in this City." His recommendation therefore was that "in general dismantlements should be permitted to the point that the estate owners and farmers deem useful."

The judgment of City Hall was "that in no way should the dismantlement of Estates be suspended, and the measures set forth should be taken to prevent the harms that until now have been experienced by farmers and ranchers." The proceedings were forwarded to the judge advocate general, who recommended that no limit be placed on dismantlements "because if they are useful to individuals, they cannot be less so for the State." He also agreed that they should not be authorized without the condition that the land be enclosed with stones, "fenced with stakes or living plants," since this would keep livestock from being harassed and "promote the universally recommended system of enclosing all kinds of possessions."

The City Hall report was read at the Wood Committee's meeting on May 5, 1798. The quartermaster general commented that if livestock farming was neglected "it would come to pass that meat would become so scarce that the poor and numerous part of the population will have difficulty affording it," especially in time of war. For this reason, a new report was requested that, "taking into account as exactly as possible both wooded estates and land under cultivation, will show the influence that dismantlement of Estates may have on the raising of livestock, since it appears that the report of said Capitulary Body did not incorporate this important goal in all its parts."

The subsequent reply, dated May 28, reiterated the points of the previous one. Nevertheless, it admitted that cases might exist in which it would appropriate for the government to moderate dismantlements. It therefore recommended that petitions include data like the distance from the city, land area, types of terrain (whether open or wooded), the purposes to which it could be put with the most usefulness for all, and location of docks, with the goal of determining fully what the land "yields in its current state, and what it is capable of if converted into another state." The city councillors insisted, finally, that dismantlements should be allowed not simply in case of necessity "but also because of their usefulness to the raising of livestock itself, as to the highly important sector of agriculture and to the prosperity of the State."

The Havana Consulate's Communiqués to the Court: The Turning Point

On May 22, 1798, the consulate's long-awaited paper against the navy's woodlands monopoly was sent to the court.[36] Until now little had been achieved by timid and isolated protests against the increasingly strict regulation of forest exploitation and estate dismantlement. Nevertheless, circumstances had changed since the 1789 regulation, and a frontal assault could be made on the navy's venerable privileges over Havana's forests.

The report's authors began by noting that if political complaints were validated by the opinion of the patient, they would have appealed to the king much sooner but that they had preferred not to follow "the blind impulse of a public that in the vehemence of its shouts and protests showed its partiality." They had thus waited more than a year since the intention was first expressed by the consulate's members. Their strategy was first to examine the effects of the existing woodlands regime, considering two questions: (1) whether the public could obtain lumber at a feasible and just price, and (2) whether by conserving lumber the momentum of agriculture on the island was slowed, "or simply in this Jurisdiction [of Havana]."

With respect to the first question, the consulate followed the results of the proceedings opened by Tomás de Piña's paper, concluding that "although this country is the most agricultural one in our Americas, and thus the one that most needs a convenient and inexpensive supply of the appropriate woods, it is also the country that obtains them at the greatest difficulty and cost." With respect to the second question, despite royal orders that the public be given "as much land as it demands or needs for cultivation," quite the contrary occurred. The reason was that the Wood Committee, charged with "such a sacred principle," had been powerless to act since 1789, able to follow no other rule than the opinion of the woodlands director.

Despite these evils, every effort had been made to avoid "the great mortification of appealing to the throne with demands and complaints" through the study of three topics: (1) the dismantlement of livestock estates and permission to split them into farmland, (2) the supply of lumber for use in the countryside and the city, and (3) the construction and careening of private vessels. On the first, the consulate referred to the request for permission to dismantle three estates linked to other property after the death of their owner, Manuela Meyreles, estates represented by Arango y Parreño. The proceedings begun because of the impossibility of continuing the raising of livestock included a map and the testimony of twenty-two witnesses who certified that they neither could raise livestock nor had lumber for shipbuilding. Nevertheless, they waited seventeen months without a reply, during which time the Wood Committee met only three times, without accepting the presence of the consulate syndic, who had offered to join them and answer any questions.[37]

For the consulate, there was no benefit to the king in "repressing the rapid, promising progress of agriculture in the Jurisdiction of Havana." On the contrary, even the "whims, caprices, and abuses" that might be committed against trees in the interest of agriculture should be discounted because agriculture is "worth more than the miserable conservation of twenty, of one hundred thousand cedars." Along the same lines, a key element in the estate owners' argument appeared: comparison with the British model as an example of the benefits of economic liberalism. Following this criterion, "the intelligent Britons," "masters of the Navy and of Public Economy," had colonies in North America with much lumber "and never did it occur to them to conserve [trees] through prejudice to, complaints against, or even dependence on free agriculture."

The report opposed the procedure of soliciting licenses because this only served "to compel the unfortunate petitioner to travel sixteen or more leagues to deliver a request that one can delay in answering as long as one likes." The consulate members rejected having to depend on the report of the subinspector of woodlands, who, "without any reconnaissance [of the site] or site plans, determines from a corner of his house whether the wood requested is much or little." There remained the formality of presenting the request to the Royal Forest Reserves official responsible for the estate "so that he may reconnoiter and mark, and exercise an insulting jurisdiction." The only precaution that seemed rational to the authors of the consulate's report was that of assuring that no prohibited use was made of precious woods, something that should be observed during construction, not in the forests. Similarly, they denounced the obligation to take large branches to the arsenal, the exhaustion of public woodlands, and the ban against sawing on the coast.

Another object of complaint was the ban on the building and careening of vessels by individuals, which, if lifted, could reduce the price of boats. Such authorization had been requested in Matanzas and in other smaller ports on the island. But the navy commander, "in audience with the Director of Woodlands," replied that although he was not opposed to such work being done in the smaller ports along both coasts, he refused it "entirely" for the port of Matanzas and allowed careening only in Havana. In the opinion of the consulate, this was the same as a complete refusal, since these ports were the places "where the other aid that building requires could be obtained." In this respect the benefits of private property were once again invoked: "The waste and excess that are almost irremediable in employees of the Royal Navy never are found in the individual builder, who calculates and inspects everything."

The root of these evils was the woodlands' dependence on the actions of a single man, "who, without any interest in the public good . . . [,] is quite particular about upholding his code and the supposed benefit of shipbuilding." At the moment when the island's agriculture "was going to take flight," "the bloodiest disputes [took place] over the Woodlands Jurisdiction," and "the deadly idea of the Wood Committee" was born. But the consulate members reserved their worst opinion "for the memorable era of don José de Villena, who, seeing the Ministries of the Navy and of the Treasury of the Indies in the person of Sr. don Antonio Valdés, promised great benefits for the Royal Armada and obtained the Royal Order of February 15, 1789." Thus the island found itself "suddenly" with a regime of regulation that was "arbitrary and oppressive, dependent essentially on the terrible Jurisdiction that the subinspector exercises behind the back of the Commander of the Navy."[38]

According to the consulate's report, from the beginning the "full weight of this dictatorship" was felt, which ignored "the instructions of YM that cultivation should be, if not preferred, at least carefully attended to." In contrast, the Wood Committee only spoke of benefits for shipbuilding, under the pretext that the king had absolute dominion over the forests. The delicate discussion of property rights was more daring than ever, although without questioning the Crown's right to harvest reserved woods. The idea was that the Laws of the Indies, on which the navy was founded, favored estate owners "because [the laws'] prohibition was limited to a given terrain and certain kinds of wood."

Finally, the report sought to demonstrate that "the monopoly" on lumber did not even benefit shipbuilding. The wood in the arsenal cost the king 5 pesos per cubic cubit, whereas individuals were offering it for 3; buying pastures, oxen, and other provisions from the Royal Forest Reserves was similarly disadvantageous. Nor did the current system lead to faster shipbuilding, "as one becomes convinced knowing that of the 113 ships of all sizes that have been built to date in this port, only 17 were constructed under the current regulations." The members of the consulate wondered whether, rather than the Royal Forest Reserves' costly system of prohibitions, fines, and restrictions, it would not be better for the trade in lumber to be completely free. With respect to the conservation of woodlands, they argued that their disappearance was improbable, a "vain and unwise fear that, in exchange for preserving the woodlands for a remote future time," would deprive all "of the innumerable and convenient benefits offered to the Royal Navy, merchant shipping, commerce, and, finally, sacred agriculture by the system of absolute freedom."

After this argument for the free exploitation of forests, the consulate's members sought to show that their intention was not to request "insinuated freedom" but rather to present "a very important question, and very worthy of consideration by YM." They specifically requested that motions again be approved by a plurality of votes in the Wood Committee, where the consulate would have at least one member, and that meetings be held at least once a month. Old ambitions, such as the removal of the Royal Forest Reserves to other zones and that logging not be permitted on estates without the permission of the owners, were withdrawn. The consulate also offered that the navy be allowed to maintain its control over the rest of the island and that restrictions on the use of wood be kept, so that no one could believe that the estate owners sought "the ruin of the forests."

A few days later, on May 31, 1798, a second report was sent to the metropole with statistical evidence of the gradual rise in the price of lumber since 1784.[39] After the two documents arrived, it was determined that testimony was needed from two residents of the court who had served as Cuba's captain general: the Count de Espeleta (1785–90) and Luis de Las Casas (1790–96). After examining the documents and with "practical knowledge of the locality," the two men gave full support to the consulate's arguments. They began their testimony by recalling Las Casas's proposal from May 1798, in response to a request for permission to buy lands in Cuba, that woodlands intended for logging be marked off so that the rest of the woodlands could be freely used by the landowners. The principles on which this previous report was based were reiterated: "It is in fact a truth proven by centuries of experience that civil societies have prospered to the extent that individuals were free to use their property. The interest of societies is simply the sum of the assembled interests of their members."

Espeleta's and Las Casas's estimates showed that the fear that landowners would end up with all the woodlands on the island was "morally impossible, as can be seen from the natural order of things," in addition to the island's being "covered, for three hundred leagues, with woodlands and forests of an inexhaustible fertility." The former captains general reckoned that if "a prodigious competition among farmers" occurred, the time would come when the low prices of agricultural products would lessen the appeal of clearing land, and owners therefore would return to planting trees for sale as lumber to shipbuilders. Espeleta and Las Casas offered an idyllic view of the free play of supply and demand as the mechanism regulating the forests' existence: "There will always be powerful stimuli balancing the interest in wiping out woodlands with the interest in conserving them."[40]

Before concluding, Espeleta and Las Casas took care to show their agreement with the consulate about the model offered by "the policy of the English, our enemies and rivals in the Gulf of Mexico." The proof of its efficacy was that in Jamaica, which did not have woodlands as prolific as Cuba's, the English, through absolute freedom of logging, achieved "the development of not only their Royal navy and merchant marine, but also of agriculture in this flourishing colony." They noted that they made this observation not out of the Anglomania suffered by some Spanish politicians but rather in "conformance with the localities" and above all because "this simply consecrates the great foundation and eternal principle of property." Finally, they recommended a return to the status quo prior to the 1789 regulation, or at least that the Wood Committee be restored to its status before that date. They also asked that the committee meet twice a month, and they supported the incorporation of two members from the consulate, in case the "system of freedom with the restriction proposed for Cuba's wood" was not agreed to. If these recommendations were not found to be suitable, the consulate's proposal should be followed and a commission should be named that would propose regulations "able to reconcile the interests of YM with those of these faithful colonists."

In the end, the measures of the Havana consulate, the support of the two former captains general, and the transformations taking place in the Havana countryside led to the royal decree of February 14, 1800, which began to tip the scales in favor of the estate owners.[41] After consulting the Council of the Indies, the attorney general, and the treasury, the court decided to create in Havana a special committee composed of the captain general, the quartermaster general, the navy commander, the hydraulic engineer, "two estate owners with theoretical and practical knowledge of agriculture," and the consulate syndic and two of its members, as well as the syndic procurator and a councillor from City Hall. Its objective would be to fashion rules for "the due and most convenient supplying of lumber for the building of ships for my Royal Armada" without the prejudice that "arbitrary indication and felling of timber" might cause for estate owners, agriculture, and commerce. Not only did the estate owners win more seats on the committee, but they also obtained the exclusion of the director of the Royal Forest Reserves. In addition, they realized their old ambition of having estates within 30 leagues of the coast declared free for agriculture, given the "excessive" number of forests on the island where logging could be performed. The deliberations of this committee would be forwarded to the court so that the latter could take the steps it found most advantageous.

The Wood Committee and the Subject of Dismantlement

The arrival in Havana of the royal decree of February 14, 1800, seems to have taken officials of the royal navy by surprise. On June 10 the captain general, the Marquis de Someruelos, informed Araoz of the king's decision and asked Araoz to choose either Thursday or Saturday morning as the time for the meetings of the new committee. Less than a month later Araoz sent a letter to the court through the channel reserved for the navy. In it he repeated his earlier warnings and, in particular, expressed surprise that the woodlands director was not included, especially since on various occasions the Crown had declined to reassign him.[42] After indicating his confusion at not having received the royal decree through this same channel, as was customary, he announced that he would attend meetings of the committee.

Now it was the navy that found itself at a disadvantage. Given the new membership of the Wood Committee, it would not be easy to make up the lost ground: in addition to Someruelos, Araoz, and the quartermaster general, the committee now included, from the consulate, Arango y Parreño, the Marquis de Monte Hermoso, and Count de O'Reilly; from City Hall, the councillor Francisco Peñalver and the syndic procurator Andrés de Jáuregui; and the estate owners the Count de Zaldivar and Bonifacio Duarte. The navy's other representative was Miguel de La Puente, who had replaced Honorato Bouyón as director of navy engineers.[43] During the first meeting, on September 11, 1801, Someruelos ruled that, since the business at hand "required, due its gravity, the most careful consideration," copies of the documents would be distributed to the panel members so each could respond with a written opinion.

Araoz was the first to have his opinion ready, a long and meticulous report dated December 31 based on his thirteen-year experience in his post and supported by data and "bona fide [*de hecho y derecho*]" knowledge from Acevedo and the navy general adviser.[44] Seeking to answer the answer the consulate and the former captains general point by point, Araoz included thorough documentation of the conflicts with estate owners and statistics on such matters as the amount of lumber conceded in the navy's woodlands and in those destined for the public, as well as on dismantlement licenses and the Royal Forest Reserves.

On June 3, 1802, treasury superintendent Luis de Vigurí presented his report, beginning by saying that by now few people were ignorant of the great benefits brought about by the exercise of respective freedom.[45] In keeping with his support of the estate owners, he included a few "notable words" that the king supposedly had addressed to him when Vigurí left Madrid to assume his post in Cuba: "Bring happiness to those vassals, who merit all my consideration. Increase agriculture and population, and clear all the woodlands if necessary." Did this conversation actually occur? It is impossible to know, but the remarks seem odd, at the very least, coming from a king who had sanctioned the controversial woodlands measures of 1789.

Naturally all the members present, except the two from the navy, agreed with Vigurí. The same day, Someruelos referred to various matters that should be debated and decided in the coming meetings. Since there were no royal dispositions with respect to the plan for choosing woodlands for the navy, the committee's agenda included selecting the estates for this purpose and giving landowners the right to allow or refuse logging but not to have lumber shipped abroad.[46] The next week the committee decided to excerpt from Araoz's report its essential points (given its length), a task that La Puente and Jáuregui were asked to carry out quickly, since it already had been delayed by the war.

Beginning on June 18 the committee met every Thursday for several weeks. The first of the questions taken up was that of dominion over and ownership of Cuba's lands and woodlands. Araoz reiterated his position that the king had direct dominion and that the estate owners simply enjoyed usufruct of the property.[47] He also questioned the supposed benefits of the right to private property, calling this a strange argument:

It is [strange], because . . . it ignores the inviolable principle of the conservation of pastures and woodlands, recommended in sacred and profane History; it does not account for the fact that the economy of these is so nonexistent in agriculture, population, and commerce that without [forests] these cannot exist; that to achieve this conservation the abuses and freedom of men must be repressed . . . because not everyone maintains the prudence and moderation required by the common good and of men in particular.

After further comment on the matter, the committee agreed unanimously not to go into the question of dominion over the woodlands but rather to submit the arguments to the Council of the Indies. As far as the supposed shortcomings of the existing regulations, the navy commander's strategy was to show that the shortage of land was an illusion. He noted that from January 1787 to May 1798 the dismantlement of thirty-six *corrales* and five *hatos* had been authorized in the Havana jurisdiction, a total of 184 leagues (19,360 caballerías), which in 1798 nevertheless "were almost as uncultivated and wooded as . . . when the dismantlement began." Other committee members replied that none of the dismantled estates were sufficiently large and that each estate included much inferior or unproductive land.

The next meeting focused on the effects on the supply of meat to the city and on the scarcity and high price of lumber. Araoz opposed all the remedies suggested by the consulate, since "far from contributing to conservation, they would quickly destroy the luxuriant woodlands of this colony." He repeated that "the individual will never take anything into account other than his private interest, which must be silent when faced with the general interest." As supporting evidence, he mentioned seven logging licenses granted to Arango y Parreño, "freely and in timely fashion," for his La Ninfa *ingenio*, and he invited him to give examples of vexation, insult, or ill treatment by Araoz's employees. Arango y Parreño admitted that he had always received from the navy commander "the most convincing proof of his courtesy" but that the complaints "expressly excluded all personal aspects and only concerned the matter as seen abstractly," which he felt was how the committee should examine it. Here a rarely used perspective was introduced: Should the committee treat equally estate owners from the coast and those from the interior, those who could not sell on the black market with those who could, "those who live in cultivated jurisdictions and those who live in the wilderness"?

Another day was spent on the exhaustion of public woodlands and the ban on sawing in the countryside. To disprove the supposed shortness of supply, Araoz noted that in barely ten years (up to 1798) the government had granted 132 permits to city residents to introduce, from estates and for public supply, the "prodigious number" of 28,798 trees, which of course did not include those sold on the black market.[48] In his opinion, therefore, the short supply and high price of lumber could be attributed to the wars of that time and to the logging operations' increasing distance from the city.

At their August 5 meeting, members debated the effects of the existing regulations for shipbuilding itself. Araoz observed that despite the greater distance over which lumber had to be hauled, a keel cost as much or perhaps less than it had during the time of the Count de Macuriges, the period that estate owners always took as a reference. The average number of ships built per year had increased, despite it "having been necessary to suspend construction." Although the other members granted these points, it still seemed irrational to them that they should be penalized by not being allowed to profit from "the immense and useless forests of unpopulated areas." Nor did they find it reasonable that estates should be designated to supply the city when the same was not done "with privileged attention to the inhabitants of the countryside." Save Araoz, all agreed that new areas should be designated "that, separated from the Royal logging operations and under judicious and prudent rules, will serve to meet all [rural and urban] needs." This task was assigned to Jáuregui and La Puente, who were asked to report back in two weeks.

The two men presented their recommendations on schedule at the August 26 meeting.[49] They examined two principal questions: how much wood did urban and rural areas in the Havana jurisdiction, including Matanzas, consume, and where could this wood be obtained. They began with the urban areas, that is, the capital and eight other cities and towns.[50] They noted the capital's progress in the past fifteen years, during which many houses were built, although many more were still needed. In addition, although most houses previously were small, the wealthy now undertook "works of a size and elegance nearly unknown here." Other towns of the jurisdiction also were beginning to feel the influence of prosperous trade and the colony's development.[51]

To measure rural needs, Jáuregui and La Puente began with the registration figures for 1800, according to which the jurisdiction had 300 active *ingenios* and another 50 in the process of creation. In addition to sugar, coffee was grown, a crop that had great potential to expand given its exemption from tariffs. There were 70 to 80 coffee plantations, most of them in the process of creation, and they needed a large amount of wood for their offices, machines, and tools. The jurisdiction also had 5,700 livestock farms and small farms (*potreros, sitios y estancias*), according to 1796 figures, "and

FIGURE 3.2. Traditional cart for hauling sugarcane.

(Josiah T. Crawley, "El cultivo de la caña de azúcar en Cuba," *Boletín de la Estación Experimental Agronómica* [Havana], no. 35 [1917]: 83)

all of them need more or less lumber for their buildings, agricultural implements, and furniture of whatever size they can afford" (see figure 3.2).

In addressing where wood could be obtained, Jáuregui and La Puente said that one line could be drawn from Puerto Escondido and another from Mariel showing "that all the Island's territory between them has been dismantled." Moreover, from Puerto Escondido along the coast to beyond Matanzas, at a depth inland of 6 or 8 leagues, and from Mariel to Bahía Honda at a similar distance, the terrains had been dismantled and were now under cultivation. The current location of the Royal Forest Reserves showed this most clearly: the Matanzas logging operation hauled lumber 8 leagues or more to that port, the one at Casiguas hauled 12 leagues to the port in Jaruco, and the Alquízar operation, restarted because of the war, hauled no fewer than 16 leagues to the Havana shipyard.

Up to this point Jáuregui and La Puente coauthored their report, but La Puente, not having "sufficient knowledge of a country in which he has just arrived," excused himself from discussion of the territorial limits within which the urban and rural populations could be supplied with wood. Jáuregui made the provisional proposal that "the territory could be sufficient that lies from three leagues east of Matanzas to as many west of Bahía Honda, because although along the north coast the depth of land inland is quite shallow, between these two points some wood nonetheless may be obtained." Before concluding, Jáuregui and La Puente made two observations about the purchase of lumber from the United States: (1) that without this source the consumption of Cuban lumber would have been greater; and (2) that the price was quite favorable, despite commissions, freight and insurance costs, profits, and royal tariffs.

For several weeks each side kept firmly to its traditional focus. Little was left to do before the respective positions could be sent to the court. On September 2 discussion concluded on the consulate's report and Araoz's response. Before the meeting adjourned, Arango y Parreño, the consulate syndic, asked the navy for an estimate of the cost of moving royal logging operations. A week later navy commander Araoz presented a map of the operation in Matanzas to show the great expense and time entailed in getting it started.

On December 1, 1802, the consulate syndic presented his opinion, key to the decisions of the new Wood Committee.[52] He began by refuting Araoz's claim about the disadvantages and cost of moving the Royal Forest Reserves. He described the felling and hauling of timber, the "least costly and simplest" of agricultural operations, whose expense was amply offset by the fact that a distant and uncultivated caballería cost one-sixth to one-quarter as much as one that had been cleared for farming.[53] He gave examples such as that of the Bay of Jagua, where in eighty or ninety years one could not expect the communities to grow to a point where they would harm the forests, and the region from Cape Cruz to Jagua, "perhaps the most fertile on our Island." He offered more detailed calculations of the need for lumber in the Havana jurisdiction, whose population and agriculture "need in their current state not thirty but fifty leagues both windward and leeward." He therefore wondered whether the king preferred "to build a ship and leave us without houses in which to labor and with which to form cities." Similarly, he asked, "Are there minds in which the idea fits that the King would think for a second of keeping woodlands where one could create a fertile and handsome garden?"

Regarding the shipment of lumber to Spain, Arango y Parreño argued that Cuba's wood was more expensive to the king than wood from the peninsula, and he noted that not even the English and the French, "who understand so much about economics," had ever thought of using trees in the Americas to supply their arsenals in Europe. But Arango y Parreño's intention was not to be this daring; he simply wanted to dispel the fear that the changes proposed by the estate owners could cause "shortages of the lumber from our forests that the metropole has asked for or may ask for." Before detailing his specific recommendations, he argued that the existing regulations did not help conserve woodlands or benefit the rural economy. In his opinion no article met the goal that on every estate, "and especially on those needing buildings as large as do the estates on this Island, terrain should be set aside for growing trees." On the contrary, this eliminated all interest in conserving them. As a remedy Arango y Parreño proposed twelve measures, which can be summarized as follows:

- 1 and 2: Removal of the Royal Forest Reserves to at least 40 kilometers from Havana, not suddenly but in such a way that the king's interest would not be harmed, and at the Wood Committee's expense.
- 3, 4, 5, and 6: Multiplication of royal logging operations near the coasts and large towns to avoid the theft of lumber by foreigners. Where no large town was expected to emerge for one hundred years, reconnoitering of the woodlands and marking of useful trees, with the obligation for the landowners of caring for them and making them available at the navy's request. Every five years the woodlands would be inspected, according to terms defined by the committee, which would be charged with establishing penalties for offenses or carelessness by the estate owners. In exchange the latter would be ensured that only officers of the king could enter their forests and take unmarked wood without permission.
- 7, 8, and 9: Annulment of the designation of territories to supply the towns of the jurisdiction of Havana, which would be supplied by landowners with respect to unmarked trees and through the introduction of foreign lumber exchanged for molasses, liquors, and other articles. The rules on use of precious woods would remain, with an increase in penalties, with enforcement the responsibility of the navy. The consulate would award "a large prize for the essay that proposed the best methods for developing good lumber without impeding the progress of agriculture."

- 10 and 11: If it became necessary to dismantle an estate with marked trees, permission would be requested of the Wood Committee, showing how dismantlement could be combined with the goal of providing the king with trees. For Havana estates without marked trees, the committee would evaluate the usefulness of dismantlement, hearing the subinspector of woodlands before issuing an opinion.
- 12: The Wood Committee would be composed of the governor, the navy commander, the quartermaster general, the hydraulic engineer, the subinspector of woodlands, the syndic of the city council, the syndic of the consulate, and two respectable estate owners elected annually by plurality vote. Meetings would be held monthly, with extraordinary sessions as needed.

Clearly the primary goal was to remove the Royal Forest Reserves from the ambit of sugar's expansion and toward this end use the enormous potential of other regions, where the urgency of liberty was less, to supply shipbuilding. The offer, however, was quite suspect. If *ingenios* kept being created at the current pace, it was not clear that territory beyond the 40-league limit would remain unoccupied by agriculture one hundred years later. As was to be expected, Arango y Parreño's proposal became the standard of the majority group on the Wood Committee, which ratified it, adding only small details, such as Jáuregui's proposal that the lieutenant governors and town halls testify for the interior of the island, or Peñalver's suggestion that two councillors be added as committee members.

Only Araoz and La Puente voted against the measures. The former argued for the unmodified observation of the 1789 regulations and for the Woodlands Committee's jurisdiction over dismantlements, with the woodlands director given a suspensive veto or resolution by the Crown in cases when the committee could not agree. Araoz suggested that after a dismantlement license was granted a three-year delay be observed so that trees unneeded for construction could be harvested and that solid fences be required around the edge of properties. He also shared the idea of buying 80 to 100 leagues of land abundant in timber, with easy terrain for hauling, and keeping them as a preserve or under lease. Finally he insisted that the king's civil ownership of lumber in Cuba's forests be maintained.

La Puente, the director of navy engineers, introduced interesting elements into the debate.[54] The first was the island's colonial condition and its location as brakes on the consulate's ambitions. "Liberty . . . [,] so attractive and innocent on the Peninsula, is not practicable here, because it would benefit the individual to the known detriment of the entire nation and its interests." In addition, Cuban trees differed from Europe's oaks, cork trees, holm oaks, chestnuts, walnuts, and hazelnuts, whose fruit accounted for most of their owners' income. In La Puente's judgment, the navy's logging was not the only reason for the scarcity and high price of "types of wood that it does not use," which he attributed largely to "immense" harvesting for shipment abroad and to increasing daily wages and salaries, rents, and costs for fuel as well as all commercial articles in the past ten years, to the increasing luxury of life in Havana and the disproportionate distribution of the island's population: "Nearly three hundred leagues long, the island has only been settled in a few areas, concentrating people in such a way that the largest and best part of the Island has been veritably abandoned. This has produced a peculiar hypocrisy in the members of the political body, which are completely disfigured in proportion with the whole. The head is gigantic, but the arms and muscles are completely emaciated, and lack the strength necessary to minister to the body's needs."

La Puente indicated that it would be necessary to reduce the number of inhabitants in cities like Havana, Santiago de Cuba, Puerto Príncipe, and Bayamo and offer incentives, in the form of freedoms and exemptions, to settlement in deserted areas of the coast. This would lessen urban needs and rural consumption by not grouping rural establishments around a few cities. Towns could thus diminish their "immense number of destitute persons that the luxury and disproportionate nature of current cities have attracted to live off the leftovers of about a hundred powerful men, to the notable and true detriment of agriculture." Nevertheless, he recognized that these measures, the most effective and sure, as well as the only ones to address the root of the problem, would take a great deal of time, while what was being sought was "a quick remedy."

As a more immediate strategy, La Puente proposed that in each town the rights to the stock of needed lumber be sold at public auction to an estate owner "of means and integrity." This system would not apply to residents of the countryside, because of the increased risk of embezzlement, but they would be asked to "bear a small inconvenience." The current regime could be modified in various ways, such as not having to appeal for licenses to the "superior judge of the woodlands" but rather only to his subordinates, in order to avoid delays. In sum, he proposed that the rules be "those necessary to ensure that all the timber cut in our woodlands be invested to the benefit of the natives." In this way the goal of the royal edict of February 14, 1800, would be achieved: "The public [sector] will provide a useful [*interesante*] branch of administration, and the individual will enjoy all the healthy liberty that wise administration allows, without detriment to the common or general good."

La Puente reasoned that a minority of woodland trees were straight and thus were useful for civilian purposes, while the majority could be used only in shipbuilding. He thus believed that the jurisdictions should be indivisible and that "the primary and unique authority over woodlands should reside exclusively in the Navy." Long experience with this system in Europe had shown, in his opinion, the need for "a barrier against all impulses of ambition and usury." Obviously, the navy was not prepared to relinquish its control over Cuba's forests.[55]

Before concluding, he offered three very important observations. First, he noted that a shortage of trees could lead to diminished seasonal rainfall and that this should be a primary consideration in deciding whether to clear more terrain. After observing that in heavily wooded regions clouds condensed more easily, he warned that around Havana, "according to natives, dry [seasons] seem to predominate." Second, he argued that no crop should be favored over another but all should be protected equally.[56] Third, he noted that the committee dealt only with dismantlements, "that is, with enriching one individual with only one measure, but what effect on the public does this measure have?" He noted that farmers "already cannot find land to work that is not burdened with such an exorbitant levy [*canon*]."

The committee's labors on the subject of dismantlements ended with the opinion submitted by Someruelos, who since the beginning had made clear his full support of the estate owners.[57] He based his position on answers to two questions. First, what did the king gain when land whose woodlands had not been harvested for shipbuilding was left unfarmed? Second, did the current regulations allow the navy to obtain the lumber it needed at a reasonable price? In other words, he framed the matter in strictly economic terms. He gave the example of a *corral* for which a twenty-five-year delay was observed before dismantlement, so that trees useful for shipbuilding could be harvested. With this wood a seventy-canon ship (27,000 cubic cubits of lumber) could be built, at a cost of 135,000 pesos for felling and hauling. But the loss occasioned by not permitting the dismantlement immediately was 5 million pesos, enough to build or buy twenty-five ships.

On the second question he supported Arango y Parreño's arguments, finding them "rational and well founded" and considering it an obligation to his conscience "to beseech the King to annul . . . all these useless regulations, which prejudice his Royal Treasury and oppress, molest, and afflict exceedingly his faithful vassals." As for the fear that the forests would be exhausted, he argued that only a small part of the island's 1 million caballerías had been reconnoitered, which had enough timber to build eighteen thousand seventy-canon ships. He proposed, among other things, that all regulations on lumber be annulled except for the limitations on its use in construction; that all Cubans be allowed to farm their land and cut down trees for allowed uses without need for a permit; that all navy officials employed in "areas outside their profession" be returned to service on warships; that felling and hauling be contractable with individuals; that all forest wardens and overseers be dismissed; and that all the Royal Forest Reserves' slaves and impressed laborers be taken to the shipyard, "where they will be much more useful under the immediate supervision of the Chief of the Navy." If these requests could not be granted, he asked that at least the 30 leagues around Havana be withdrawn from the Royal Forest Reserves.

On these points we can assume Someruelos's desire to limit the navy's influence. In addition to these proposals, he argued that the committee should include, instead of two estate owners, two councillors named annually and that in the cities of Santiago de Cuba, Trinidad, and Puerto Príncipe wood committees subordinate to the one in Havana be established. This marked the end of the deliberations on the royal order of February 14, 1800, and all that remained was to submit the differing positions to the Council of the Indies.

Araoz lost no time seeking to make up lost ground. In August 1802, while the Wood Committee was meeting in Havana to discuss dismantlements, he sent a letter to Manuel Godoy repeating his view that the consulate was forming a bloc against the navy, with Arango y Parreño at its head. He argued that the majority of committee members were estate owners, and he insisted on the harm that resulted from the exclusion of the woodlands director. Given that the meetings were about to end, he suggested that the royal decree of May 1, 1802, issued for peninsular Spain, be applied to Cuba; it gave "to the Navy all-embracing jurisdiction over the administration and management of its woodlands." The petition responded to "the just motives there detailed, which are virtually the same as occur on this Island with respect to its woodlands and trees."

The suspicions expressed to the "Generalísimo de Mar y Tierra" (High General of Sea and Land) were fully confirmed, and in his final report to Madrid about the committee's conclusions with respect to dismantlements he insisted on the need to enlighten the Council of the Indies.[58] Araoz also denounced the fact that he had not been provided with Arango y Parreño's opinion, on the pretext that everything would be sent to the council.[59] Another indication he noted of the strong bias against the navy was the fact that the consulate syndic, without being "either the first or last member of the Committee," had begun the submission of opinions with his essay, "thus betraying the order observed by all magistratures and political bodies." In his opinion, Arango y Parreño did this to "bias the opinions of the others and make them into followers, as in fact happened . . . and this will always occur as long as they are made up mostly of Estate Owners such as the Syndic, who aspire to no other end than independence and absolute freedom in the use of the woodlands, preferring their own convenience to that of the State."

Araoz attributed the consulate's resolutions to the "presumptuous resentfulness in the judgments of Syndic Arango," who had been denied dismantlement permits for his Majanas and San Marcos estates and who initially had not been admitted to the committee. Araoz then cited several points in his opinion, with the goal of convincing his readers of the falseness of the "damages claimed by the Consulate Committee in order to amend legislation whose origin goes back centuries," so that, "amounting to no other end than impugning [sindicar] such high principles as irrelevant, they should be not only scorned but withdrawn." As a more delicate point he reposed the problem of civil property, introduced by Arango y Parreño, in the discussion of which "his followers dared not formulate an opinion, the Body fleeing the difficulty." Finally, he stressed the importance of the woodlands director and of woodlands inspections.

What happened from then until the early 1810s is unclear in the archives. It is uncertain whether the Woodlands Committee returned to its former membership, but it is clear that dismantlement permits continued being subject to the ruling of the woodlands director. Until 1809 at least, documents appear in which he grants or rejects such applications. It appears that pending the response of the Council of the Indies, the navy essentially maintained control of the exploitation of forests. An October 25, 1803, report by Acevedo, about a petition to use cedar in Remedios, reflects this:

The most proper and particular knowledge of this matter seems to me to be rather that of the General Command of the Navy, which YM has charged with the conservation of woodlands and with the use of the Island's timber (excepting the eight estates destined for the public), than that of the Committee, which you have charged only with the dismantlement of terrains when this is necessary for agriculture and does not prejudice the raising of livestock, and when the above-mentioned party [the king and his navy] has harvested the abundant timber.[60]

The Wood Committee remained focused during these years on requests for dismantlement permits, the arguments for and against which remained invariable. For example, in his opinion on five petitions that same October 25, 1803, Acevedo opposed those of the La Sierra *corral* and its windward annexes, Santo Domingo and La Pendejera, because they had "many pieces of woodland abundant in cedar, mahogany, sabicú, and yaba." Also in 1803 new estates that formerly had been destined for the same end were designated for Havana's use, four west and four east of the port.

Among the subjects that the committee dealt with beyond the Havana jurisdiction was the sugar boom. In December 1804 the lieutenant governor of Trinidad, Alfonso de Vianas, reported that several estates "were being dismantled visibly because due to arbitrariness each landowner cultivates the lands he desires, converting estates destined for the raising of livestock into *potreros*, small farms, and *ingenios*." To check this disorder the committee passed the edict of March 7, 1803, which required the demolition of houses built on these estates; nevertheless, new construction sites opened every day. One was an *ingenio* "contracted without the necessary formalities"; since it was now ready to begin making sugar, to prohibit this would ruin its owner, "resulting in a greater harm than the one we sought to avoid." From Havana Acevedo recalled that woodlands could not be cleared to establish *ingenios*, *sitios*, or other rural farms without appealing to the Wood Committee.[61]

Another debate had to do with the disadvantages of the designation of the Yayabo River, on the Guantánamo coast, for the public supply of Santiago de Cuba. The Santiago council argued that its city did not receive the benefits that Havana did from the shipyard and from royal logging operations, "in which so many men are employed daily." The council also noted Habaneros' access to lumber granted by the navy, while the residents of Santiago had such great need for posts as a result of earthquakes and the arrival of more than twenty-five thousand immigrants after the Haitian Revolution. La Puente replied that the governor and the judge of the navy for that district would choose the most suitable estates. The Santiagueros hoped for more, however. In accordance with their council's resolution of November 28, 1803, they asked the Havana Wood Committee to

> be so kind as to as to grant us the lumber necessary to continue [operation of] private and public mills in the vicinity, designating for this purpose the woodlands ten or twelve leagues windward of this port and as many leagues leeward, with just consideration of the fact that the five or six leagues closest to this city are today quite exhausted because the population has been using them since the area was settled . . . and because within these five or six leagues are located almost all the sugar *ingenios*, two towns, . . . many tobacco plantations, and all the other fields of produce for daily consumption.[62]

This petition shows that pressure on the forests was not experienced only in the Havana jurisdiction. In different towns on the island and their rural estates a significant increase could be observed in the consumption of lumber to the extent that *hatos* and *corrales* were transformed into *ingenios*, *potreros*, and other small farms. In other regions old problems such as those of fences, beehives, and the use of fire to clear savannas for livestock persisted and even became more acute. But nowhere could deforestation compare with that in the Havana area. The common image of the island as a whole was not very different from the one people held in the mid-eighteenth century. In 1794 the first archbishop of Santiago de Cuba, Joaquín de Ozés y Alzúa, wrote: "If we except the fourteen to sixteen leagues around Havana and a few other stretches of land, like in Villa Clara, a town dedicated to agriculture, others with many *ingenios*, and livestock pastures, cleared lands called savannas, all the rest is dense forest."[63]

To the above should be added the removal of lumber that was either clandestine or authorized (in exchange for slaves). In July 1804 Araoz demanded the suspension of the permit granted in 1790 for the sale of cedar and mahogany to foreign colonies, which had led to serious conflicts between the grantees and estate owners.[64] Araoz consulted the frigate captain José del Río, commissioned to map the southern coast, about this trade, then concluded that it was best not to tempt black marketeers and that given the abundance of slaves and of agricultural tools, the concession should be suspended for ten years or the wood should be brought first to Havana in case it was needed by the arsenal or the residents.[65] The court chose the second option in its order of October 15, 1804, which shows that the navy still had influence on the subject of forests.

As we have seen, this does not mean that the advance of commercial agriculture in the Havana territories was slowed. In an 1809 report on how to revive shipbuilding, a new navy commander, Juan María de Villavicencio, noted that timber was now 30 to 40 leagues from the city and that, since the beginning of his command in 1805, 33,387 lengths of cedar, mahogany, and other lumber reserved for mills and rural use had been conceded in this jurisdiction alone, without counting the many thousands of pieces removed from estates destined for the public.[66] As usual, these figures were employed to show that there was no reason to revoke the existing woodlands legislation. And in fact, despite the time that had passed since the Wood Committee concluded its deliberations on dismantlements, the awaited royal resolution that would favor the position of the estate owners still had not arrived. It would not be until 1812, and the transformations impelled by the Cortes of Cádiz, that the scales would tip definitively in favor of individual interests.

Individuals' Right to Clear Forests

The restrictions on the exploitation of Spain's forests in favor of the navy, especially the effects of the Woodlands Ordinance of 1748, were one of the topics that captured the attention of the Cortes of Cádiz.[67] The obstacles and disadvantages created by excessive regulation, the extensive bureaucracy needed to put it into practice, and the counterproductive effects for the conservation of forests were the customary arguments of many Enlightenment Spaniards in favor of liberalism.[68] A paradigmatic, frequently cited example is the *Informe sobre la ley agraria* (Report on the Agrarian Law; 1795) by Gaspar Melchor de Jovellanos, which proposes the elimination of all the navy's privileges, the annulment of all the ordinances, and complete freedom for individuals to exploit and trade in lumber as a means to return forests to their former density and reduce the price of wood products.

These theories had been adopted by the Havana estate owners and their supporters — in Cádiz the time was coming to make them law. The minister of the navy, José Vázquez de Figueroa, opened debate on the topic on October 5, 1811, and was also the first to attack the existing ordinances, a sign of the change in the wind. Finally, on January 14, 1812, a decree was promulgated to, as its first article puts it, "abolish and annul in all their parts all the laws and ordinances on woodlands and fields for cultivation as concerns those owned by individuals, and as a result owners now have complete and absolute freedom to do in them what suits them best." Article 2 gave owners "equal freedom to fell trees and sell their lumber to whom they like," while Article 4 eliminated the entire bureaucratic apparatus on which the navy's privileges over forests rested.

One of the Cuban deputies in Cádiz, representing Havana, was Andrés de Jáuregui. It seems odd that he did not participate in the initial debates over the abolition of the woodlands ordinances, based on his experience in Cuba. But a few months later he was requested to intervene on the matter, together with the deputy from Santiago de Cuba, Juan Bernardo O'Gavan. The request was motivated by the tension created in Cuba when news arrived of the royal decree on woodlands and fields under cultivation; on the Wood Committee, the commander of naval engineers, Diego de Parra, expressed reservations and asked that before the decree was established the committee discuss "the delicate point of how to save, without prejudicing the same liberty of woodlands, the peaceful portion in which the King has been able to use trees since the most remote times."[69]

The Havana estate owners were immediately suspicious and told the representatives in Cádiz that this new attack was intended to "keep things in the state that they have been and expose us again to the hindrances and difficulties against which we have been struggling now for twelve years running." They cited Vázquez de Figueroa's reference to Cuba and protested that it would be a crime "to seek now to except [the island], reviving reasons that have been buried by the Decree of the Cortes." Forgoing the caution of previous eras, they wrote, "No one in the world except the Commanders of the Navy of this port has spoken nor could speak of this dominion of the sovereign over our woodlands, which was eliminated by the absolute ability to concede [lands] given to the town halls of the Indies." Moreover, the fact that the proceedings on the creation of the Wood Committee in 1800 had been misplaced in the government secretariat should not prevent the island's representatives from "making . . . the most vigorous appeals in the Cortes over the steps taken by the Navy." They promised the representatives all their support, as well as "the assistance of the finest jurists in this city in determining whether it would be appropriate to go directly to the question of dominion over the land."

The consulate called the conduct of the island's government contradictory, since, on the one hand, it implemented the decree and, on the other, it prevented the order from taking full effect by accepting reservations that left it pending. It was the first time in many years that a captain general supported the navy's claims. In truth the situation was more complicated, since the highest authority in the colony was also the head of the Department of the Navy, both posts occupied by Juan Ruiz de Apodaca, Count of Venadito, between 1812 and 1816. This may be why the letter to the representatives in Cádiz ended in an alarmist fashion: "It is evident as a result that we are compelled to use our last resort to counter in the national Congress the blow that is being prepared to disable Congress's rights, since we know that the government itself leaves the actions of the Wood Committee up to the Regency of the Kingdom."

The deputies' offensive began with a letter to the Regency in which they expressed amazement at what was happening in Havana. Among other issues, they denounced the fact that neither the Town Hall nor the consulate had been informed of this important decree, leading the deputies to demand, "with the utmost energy," the implementation of such a definitive measure. They also invoked laws that established penalties for civil servants who did not immediately implement orders and decrees of the Cortes. The Regency decided to forward the proceedings to the Council of State, although, as José Piqueras Arenas has indicated, the Regency supported a royalist interpretation.[70] Disagreeing with this action, Jáuregui and O'Gavan took the floor at the Cortes session of October 9, 1812. The preamble of their statement began as follows: "Lord, one of the most beneficial laws that YM has granted . . . has suffered a rigorous contradiction in Havana by those who feed on abuses that YM thought you had cut off at the root." After reviewing what had occurred, the deputies accused the navy of wanting to maintain, through judicial appeals, "the monstrous monopoly on lumber."

The island's deputies received the support of Spain's liberal leaders. Manuel García Herreros proposed that all civil servants who contributed to the decree's not being enforced in Havana be dismissed from their posts, a motion that was approved by the majority. The controversy also led another deputy, José Castelló, to move that a commission be named "that will ensure the prompt enactment of the decrees of HM." This was also approved. What was at stake was the "sacred" right of property championed by Spain's first bourgeois revolution. Finally, the chamber approved the proposal of the deputy José Canga Argüelles that the proceedings be forwarded to the commission on agriculture, where the issue was never taken up.

Apodaca replied from Havana that enactment of the decree had been prepared by the Wood Committee at its meeting of June 22, 1812. To confirm this he noted an act of the city council that expressed "the astonishment caused us by the mistaken news that Deputies of the Cortes received about what happened here with respect to said decree." In another letter of April 1813 Apodaca urged that a trusted person be sent to the customs office of the port of Havana or that certification be requested of its administrator, "since, this sugar harvest being the first since publication [of the decree], much of the crop is being packed in cedar crates, whose use was previously prohibited."[71]

When Fernando VII ascended to the throne in March 1814, the 1812 measures regarding woodlands and fields under cultivation were abolished. The royal order of September 1814 reestablished the status quo of 1808 with respect to communal woodlands and state-owned property "comprehended [de la comprensión de] by the Navy." This followed "the need to provide quick relief for the wrongs suffered by the State due to the scandalous clearing, burning, and destruction of all kinds experienced in the woodlands of the Kingdom." This change did not affect privately owned woodlands, although the exemption was "without prejudice to what YM may later determine is appropriate."[72]

The change had no effect on Cuba, since on June 11, 1815, the Council of the Indies produced an extensive report on the history of the conflicts between Havana estate owners and the navy. It was several years late. In 1804 Someruelos had submitted the results of the Wood Committee's debates on dismantlements. The subject was not taken up again for a decade after the General Accounting Office issued its August 1805 opinion. The chief accountant found that Arango y Parreño's opinion best combined the interests of agriculture, commerce, and the navy, although he offered small modifications of the freedom to clear land so that individual interest, which had stimulated the progress of the first two areas, would "not degenerate into abuses prejudicial to the person involved as well as to the public."[73]

In its report, the Council of the Indies briefly reviewed what had happened between 1622 and 1789, then compared the existing regulations with those suggested by Arango y Parreño in his 1802 opinion. The former, the council found, fulfilled none of the criteria that rules of this kind should meet: "Prohibitions, hindrances, usurpation, impositions, costs, delays, aggravations for the public, and unlimited authority for the Navy are the exclusive contents of this regulation." The results of this were "discouragement, abandonment, shortages, high costs, and many other ills, including the decline of the Navy itself." In contrast, Arango y Parreño's proposal "at first glance brings together precision, equity, simplicity, impartiality," intended to "reconcile the rights of the property owner with the immediate goals of this regulation."

As for the royal patrimony's supposed dominion over Cuba's forests, the council called this a "wretched appeal," since "the compiled laws as well as many other sovereign decisions leave not the slightest doubt that the rightful possessors of land are its true masters."[74] In Spain, where woodlands ordinances and regulations included private landowners, the laws' drafters did not mean "that the Crown had in [the regulations] the common dominion that is wrongly confused with the eminent right that it exercises in this manner and others." Among other grounds the council members acknowledged that woodlands were commonly owned so long as they were not divided or sold, but in Cuba, "except for those pieces of woodlands assigned to the use of towns (of which there are none . . .), all the others have been sold or are being sold without any reservation when they are registered." For this reason the 1789 regulation "operates exclusively in woodlands that are privately owned."

According to the Council of the Indies, the regulation had not resulted in the benefits sought when Carlos IV approved it. Arango y Parreño's proposal, in contrast, "was recommendable in its own right" and was "authorized by the vote of intelligent and impartial persons." The council's conclusion on the long debates between the navy and the Havana estate owners was also based on the "axioms of good economy," in other words, "that luminous principle, well known and developed since the last century, which deposits and ensures the wealth and prosperity of nations in the use of property rights and in the stimulation of individual interest, decides the matter definitively. No rules, no authority, no vigilance can replace the action of a man interested in his own benefit."[75]

To support these claims the council cited opinions expressed by members of the Economic Society of Madrid about woodlands ordinances in Spain and their negative impact on property owners.[76] According to members of the society, the formalities and hindrances in Cuba, such as the obligation to deliver two curved pieces to the arsenal and the suspensive veto on the Wood Committee, were even greater. Finally, the Council of the Indies' report repeated the belief that the risk that free harvesting would exhaust Cuba's woodlands was remote, since "the small population compared with the immensity of the prodigiously stocked woodlands hardly allows one to conceive of this possibility." The council advised that efforts to address the problem take into account the Cádiz measures and the royal order of September 13, 1814, with respect to private woodlands. If with time the expected results were not produced, the regulations proposed by Arango y Parreño would enable "the opportune remedy."

A little more than two months later an end was finally brought to the conflict over Cuba's forests. On August 30, 1815, the king put his seal on the royal edict giving private property owners the perpetual right to fell their trees with complete freedom. The text left not the slightest doubt that the estate owners were definitive victors in their long battle against the navy's centuries-old privileges.

> (1) Are abolished and annulled in all their parts all the laws and ordinances on woodlands and fields for cultivation as they concern those owned by individuals (whether their titles are possessed through distribution, sale, or arbitration), and as a result owners are completely and absolutely free to do in them what suits them best . . . ; (2) Although on this Island there do not seem to be any woodlands set aside for the common use of towns, some may exist that belong to my royal crown, . . . with respect to which the general rules dictated on this point will be observed; (3) Landowners will be free to fell their trees and sell their lumber . . . ; (4) Fields destined for cultivation are declared reserved and sealed off in perpetuity . . . , remaining open to royal roads, and to passages or rights of way, cattle tracks, and watering holes, as well as to hunting and fishing.[77]

The fifth and final point ordered the formation of a new Havana Wood Committee composed of the captain general, the navy commander, the quartermaster general, the hydraulic engineer, the subinspector of woodlands, the syndics of the city and of the consulate, and two estate owners named by the committee. Its goal would be to observe the effects of the royal decree and inform the king "at whatever time of matters that it . . . considers worthy of my royal notice with the appropriate reports." The navy's defeat was as absolute as the rights granted to private citizens over trees. This was the triumph of individual freedom as economic leveler, mindful in theory not only of material gain but also of resource conservation.[78] Nevertheless, it was also obvious that the fears expressed by the navy were not inspired only by its indisputable eagerness to control the exploitation of for-

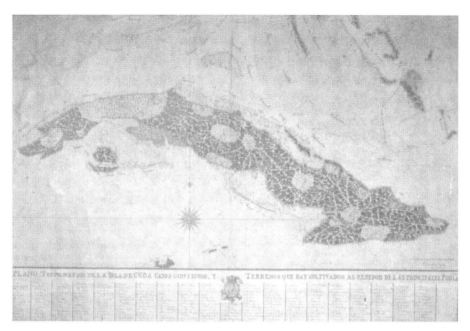

FIGURE 3.3. Forests and cultivated terrain in 1816
according to the representation of Honorato Bouyón.
(Museo Naval, maps 17-D-9 [Madrid])

ests. The environmental implications of sugar's advance were too evident to
be ignored, as the estate owners themselves occasionally acknowledged. But
the benefits for the royal treasury of the growing plantation sugar system
were also too great to be outweighed by the controversy over woodlands
dominion. While Havana shipbuilding had fallen into bankruptcy in 1796,
the sugar industry was ever more prosperous. Climatological and ecological factors had little influence on an island whose territory still was mostly
covered with forests (see figure 3.3).

The royal decree of August 30, 1815, was published in the *Diario del Gobierno de La Habana* (Daily of the Havana Government) on February 7, 1816.
In accordance with Article 5, on May 7 Captain General Apodaca convened
a meeting of the new Wood Committee at the government house. The officials designated by the decree, all of whom were present, unanimously
elected the Count de Zaldivar and José Ignacio Echegoyen as the two estate
owners who would join them. It is worth noting that in a report on the
committee Apodaca referred to the order as the "method that should be

observed in the conservation of said woodlands and trees."[79] For one of the members, the subinspector of woodlands Pedro Acevedo, that day was a severe setback after so many years leading the Royal Forest Reserves.

The jubilation of the estate owners was such that a few days after the decree was published in Havana they wrote the attorney general requesting permission to print and distribute additional copies: "This wise providence, which the Consulate considers of utmost importance for the progress and development of agriculture and the development of that highly interesting part of HM's domains, should be extended to and propagated on the Penin-sula." They suggested accomplishing this through their agent (*apoderado*), who would distribute the decree to all the consulates. On August 2, 1819, the attorney general replied that the Havana consulate was "entirely free to have [the royal decree] published" and delivered to "those [consulates] of the Peninsula and America as well as other Corporations and individuals that seem appropriate," without approval being required of the Council of the Indies.[80] It is not known whether the estate owners carried out this plan, but it clearly reflects the newfound sense of freedom of Cuba's sugar barons.[81]

Sugar and the Absolute Freedom to Clear Forests, 1815–1876

*First Golden Age of Cuban Sugar:
Semimechanized and Mechanized*
Ingenios

The royal edict of August 30, 1815, left the expanding sugar industry completely free to invade Cuba's wooded areas. Until the 1790s *ingenios* generally kept behind the front lines of the Royal Forest Reserves and thus affected forests that already had been harvested for shipbuilding and other uses. The Cuban sugar boom spurred by the Haitian Revolution forever upset this relative order. Dismantled estates were soon considered insufficient, leading Havana's large-scale landowners to focus on obtaining a 30- to 40-league area where a blossoming plantation system could enjoy complete freedom.

It is clear that at the rate at which sugar cultivation was growing in the 1790s it would soon run out of room. The Royal Consulate of Agriculture,

Industry, and Commerce of Havana therefore sought the enforcement of the measures approved by the Cortes of Cádiz on woodlands and cultivated fields. At stake was the future of the industry, one of whose pillars was the occupation of virgin territories, where clearing left such fertile soil. To limit sugar to a fixed area would require a different conception of agriculture, one based on small farms using more intensive methods of cultivation, as well as the creation of reserves of firewood and lumber and even a free workforce, for which the island was unprepared, at least in the short term. The same conditions were required as in other Caribbean plantation colonies, as well as in Brazil and other areas dedicated to supplying the European metropoles with raw materials and foods: slave labor as a source of rapid enrichment, resulting from a rapacious worldview with respect to human beings and the environment.[1]

The period from 1815 to 1876 in Cuba is one of the best examples of a relationship with the environment based on a combination of slavery, economic liberalism, and early mechanization in the Industrial Revolution.[2] In their struggle with the navy the estate owners had claimed that no one could care for forests better than landowners; now they had a chance to prove it, all the more so because most of the island's territory belonged to them. Any attempt to bring order to the exploitation of the colony's forests thus found itself limited by the defense of the "sacred" right of property, definitively sanctioned by the royal edict of July 16, 1818, which recognized the town councils' land concessions up to 1729 as legitimate titles of ownership (dominio).[3]

Favorable internal conditions, the free foreign trade granted by the royal decree of February 18, 1818, and the massive arrival of slaves combined with excellent market circumstances and the introduction of Industrial Age technological advances to promote the longest-lasting sugar boom in Cuban history.[4] Production increased from 45,396 metric tons in 1815 to 750,062 metric tons in 1875. Cuban sugar represented between 13 and 20 percent of world production in the 1820s and 1830s. From 1840 to 1876 this figure rarely slipped below 20 percent, and between 1850 and 1870 it was never less than 24 percent, reaching as high as 31.15 percent in 1855. It maintained this position despite the success of beet sugar, which rose from 1.82 percent of world sugar production in 1830 to 43.26 percent in 1875. Moderating the impact of beet sugar's popularity was the consolidation of the North American market as a destination for Cuban sugar.[5]

This increase in production resulted from the multiplication of sugar farms and of their capacity, while the center of the slave-plantation system moved from the Havana area to the east, occupying natural regions in which cane had not yet been grown (see table 4.1). The 1815–76 period saw the conquest of the Colón Plain region and of the plains of the Central District, specifically the western half of the Plain of Corralillo-Yaguajay and the Heights of the Northern Range, as well as the Plain of Manacas-Cienfuegos and part of the Los Arabos–Real Campiña and Santa Clara–Sancti Spíritus plains. These regions, and to a lesser extent those that had been longer occupied, were the stage for changes in the industry springing from the introduction of steam engines into mills and of railroads as a means of transporting sugar. Although *ingenios* existed in other areas, their smaller numbers and less powerful technologies made their impact on the environment relatively less.

The first attempts to use steam to power a *trapiche* were made in 1797, but it was not until 1819 that an entire harvest was successfully done, at the Cambre *ingenio* in the jurisdiction of Güines. This innovation, and the generalized use of Jamaican sugar kettle batteries (*trenes*) in boiler houses, led to the semimechanized *ingenio*, as Manuel Moreno Fraginals has termed it. The introduction of steam power led to a qualitative leap beyond the traditional means of making sugar, despite the fact that its initial success lay not so much in a greater milling capacity (between 6 and 12 horsepower) as in savings in oxen and slaves during processing.[6]

Steam's impact on the environment, however, was characterized first by an increased need for fuel and later by an expansion of the surface area of the cane fields. The 1827 census reported that 26 *ingenios* in Havana and Matanzas were using steam engines. The 1846 census found that in the same territories 251 *ingenios* (out of a total of 735) were now using them. Many of these steam-powered *ingenios* were located in Matanzas (52 *ingenios* out of 152) and in Cárdenas (115 out of 199), where more fuel and virgin land were available.[7]

Carlos Rebello's 1860 statistics show significant differences between the *ingenios* of the center west and those of the center east of the island in their use of steam. The Western Department had 829 *ingenios* that used steam (or 77.4%) and 231 powered by oxen (22.3%), while in the Eastern Department there were 120 of the former (40%) and 178 of the latter (59.4%). Although the average area, 44.6 caballerías, was slightly higher for sugar plantations in Puerto Príncipe, Nuevitas, and jurisdictions of Oriente, the average area planted with cane was barely 5 caballerías. In the west and center the average

TABLE 4.1. *Ingenios* in Western and Central Cuba, 1820–1877

Zone	1820	1827	1846	1860	1877
Havana[a]	439	338	384	228[d]	115
Matanzas[b]	95	204	351	442	517
Centre[c]	91	127	321	395	326
Total	625	669	1,056	1,065	958

Sources: Census of 1827 and 1846; Carlos Rebello, *Estados de la producción azucarera de la Isla de Cuba* (Havana: Intendencia del Ejército y Hacienda, 1860); *Revista económica*, May 15, 1878.
[a]The current province of Havana and part of Pinar del Río.
[b]Roughly the current province of Matanzas. The figure for 1827 includes 93 *ingenios* in development.
[c]The current provinces of Villa Clara, Cienfuegos, and Sancti Spíritus.
[d]This includes Güines and the *partido* (district) of Alacranes, whose 41 *ingenios* were reclassified in Matanzas. It does not include the *ingenios* of Puerto Príncipe and Nuevitas when they appear in the Central Department.

total area was 43.3 caballerías, with 18 in cane, indicative of a greater impact, in terms of both land under cultivation and consumption of firewood.[8]

This situation intensified with the introduction for boiler houses of the *trenes al vacío* (vacuum-heating technologies), which, although they used less fuel than the Jamaican sugar kettle batteries, required more caballerías of cane per plantation. The arrival of these new machines in 1842 (the first being used in Wenceslao de Villaurruitia's *ingenio*, La Mella, in Limonar, Matanzas), with their innovative system for evaporating and concentrating sugarcane juice, signaled the birth of the mechanized *ingenio*. At the time José Luis Casaseca, the Spanish chemist and director of Havana's Institute for Chemical Research, referred to this event as the Cuban Industrial Revolution.[9]

The 64 mechanized *ingenios* in 1860 were about 5 percent of Cuba's sugar plantations, but their production was 15 percent of the total. Their average capacity was about 1,176 metric tons, while that of the semimechanized *ingenios* (67.5% of all *ingenios* on the island) was 411 metric tons, and that of animal-powered *ingenios* (27.3% of Cuban *ingenios*) was 49 metric tons. At the time the greatest concentration of the new type of mill was in the jurisdiction of Colón, which had 28, which explains the greater average area of its *ingenios* (54 caballerías) and especially of its cane fields (27.3 caballerías). The 126 *ingenios* in Colón were 9.2 percent of those in Cuba, all categories combined, but they produced 22.6 percent of crates of sugar and 11.2 percent of the casks. The greatest contribution was made by the mechanized *ingenios*, prominent among which were several sketched and described in *Los ingenios* by Justo Germán Cantero (12 of the 25 were mechanized, with an average area of 86 caballerías, 37 of them in cane). Their productive potential resulted from a substantial increase in the use of steam power, in some cases with nearly 500-horsepower machines (from 50 to 100 horsepower in those moving the *trapiches* and between 350 and 400 in the *trenes al vacío*).[10] As Dale Tomich has noted, this new type of sugar mill reconfigured the technical and spatial organization of the industry compared with its traditional forms during the early nineteenth century (see figure 4.1).[11]

The great impact of these technological advances on forests was not offset by the decreased consumption of firewood resulting from the use of cane pulp and fossil fuels. Semimechanized and mechanized *ingenios*, of much greater size than the traditional animal-powered mills and run by several hundred slaves, continued to require large amounts of wood, as is demonstrated by the fact that many of the largest ones included a carpenter's shop with a steam-powered saw. Beginning in the 1820s the old vertical crushers, made of wood, were gradually replaced with horizontal crushers, made of iron, while in building the use of other construction materials and lower-grade, imported lumber increased. Still, these savings could indicate that many of the best Cuban woods ended up in furnaces to produce steam or on fields to fertilize the soil.

Deforestation occurred in every region of the island, for different reasons, but nowhere to the extent it did around the slave plantations, as we can observe by comparing the census of 1846 with that of 1862. Although sixteen years is a short time to discern the full magnitude of the impact on the environment, the differences in these three departments are clear. In the Western Department, forests accounted for 27.8 percent of the territory in 1846 and 16 percent in 1862. In the Central Department, which during this period saw the sugar industry expand significantly around Cienfuegos and Sagua la Grande, the wooded area decreased from 59.3 percent to 41 percent. In contrast, in the Eastern Department, the decline was just from 65.4 percent to 59.3 percent. Despite the differences in classification criteria and in recorded area, these figures give us an idea of the intense process of savannization that was taking place in regions occupied by slave plantations.[12]

According to the census figures, the island's forested area decreased from 409,825 caballerías in 1846 to 250,845 in 1862, although again the difference

FIGURE 4.1. The Purísima Concepción *ingenio* (Echeverría), in Guamutas, jurisdiction of Cárdenas. Lithograph by Eduardo Laplante.

(Justo G. Cantero, *Los ingenios: Colección de vistas de los principales ingenios de azúcar de la isla de Cuba* [Havana: Litográfica Luis Marquier], 1857)

in total caballerías recorded must be taken into account. The first figure is not very different from that offered in 1831 by Ramón de La Sagra in his first work on Cuba, in which he noted 430,247 caballerías of uninhabited woodland and 9,734 of fields and woodlands included in coffee plantations and *ingenios*.[13]

A decade and a half later the Spanish naturalist Miguel Rodríguez Ferrer compared the 1846 and 1862 figures in order to demonstrate the alarming shrinkage of Cuba's forests. His *Naturaleza y civilización de la grandiosa Isla de Cuba* (Nature and Civilization of the Magnificent Island of Cuba; 1876), the fruit of his years of residency on the island, argued that the deforestation was the result of causes he classified as ordinary, normal, and extraordinary. In the first category he included rural practices that had existed since the conquest, ones due to the itinerant nature of Cuban agriculture:

> When the land has been purged or its substance and salt consumed, the pasture, coffee plantation, or *ingenio* is moved farther along, always

with an eye to the remains of cleared and burned woodland. The system, therefore, could not be simpler: collect the first fruits of the soil for several years, then abandon it for other land in order to receive the latter's extraordinary product with equal ease, and without the need to plow the soil or improve it with any fertilizer. . . . No preaching against individual convenience can compete with such immediate profit, no matter how harmful the latter is for the community and no matter the consequences for the climate and the forest of the worst-possible system.[14]

It is difficult to determine precisely how much forest disappeared between 1815 and 1876. Based on the above census figures, 158,980 caballerías would have vanished in only sixteen years, which seems an exaggeration. Our uncertainty grows if we take into account the 1861 statistics that Jacobo de La Pezuela cites in his *Diccionnario*, which give a figure of 466,331 caballerías of woodland for the entire island.[15] Puerto Príncipe and Oriente, beyond the limits of the plantation economy, account for 82 percent (382,845 caballerías) of this total. In the hope of contrasting more precise data we could take the calculations of Eliseo Matos, who denotes three stages in the 1828–77 period, during which 175,487 caballerías (2,352,539 hectares) of woodland disappeared, or 35.1 percent of the initial area (dropping from 560,284 to 384,797 caballerías).[16]

Given the nearly 60,000 caballerías occupied by *ingenios* in 1860 and the fact that *ingenios* in the first half of the nineteenth century had a life span of between thirty and forty years, we could assume that no less than half this area was directly affected by sugar during this period. The amount could even be greater if we take into account that midcentury sugar-industry tracts estimated that more than 1,000 caballerías were cleared each year to fuel the *ingenios*. The figure given by Emilio Santos in "Costumbres cubanas" (Cuban Customs; published in 1871 in the Madrid journal *Revista forestal*) speaks for itself: each year, he estimated, 70,480 hectares (5,259 caballerías) of woodland were felled.[17]

In addition to the sugar industry's impact on wooded areas, we must not forget the plantations' stimulus of other economic activities that required forest resources, such as firewood, charcoal, railroads crossties, and transport of lumber. Another category would have to account for the export lumber industry itself, which grew significantly after 1815. Not all the responsibility for the rapid deforestation can be attributed to the measures taken that year, but granting individuals full property rights over forests helped consolidate an attitude toward the environment as a means to individual economic benefit, with no thought of the common good (as the former rules put it) or of foresighted ecological values. Thoughtful voices warned of the dangers of this approach, but they were scarcely heard by property owners and businessmen ready to extract the colony's natural resources to enrich themselves as quickly as possible.

The Arrival of the Railroad
and Expansion to the East

The lack of good transportation infrastructure was one of the major obstacles to sugar's expansion. For the Havana area, the proximity of the northern coast and its excellent port influenced the siting of plantations, but as this region filled, new farms began to locate farther away. According to Moreno Fraginals, the lack of roads was the principal impediment faced by large-scale manufacturing, although the passage through an area of the Royal Forest Reserves indicated the existence of a certain infrastructure. During the sugar boom of the late eighteenth century the idea of building a canal from Güines, which in 1767 had been suggested for the transport of lumber to the Havana shipyard, was taken up again, but despite direct support this time from plantation owners it was never built.[18]

In the end it was decided to repair old and build new cart tracks linking the new producing areas with shipping ports or with docks on navigable rivers. It is significant that once the freedom to cut down forests was granted, many of the new *ingenios* were established toward the north of the Colón Plain, which previously had been under the jurisdiction of the navy (see figure 4.2). But during the second half of the 1830s the former limitations to transport began to disappear thanks to the arrival of the railroad, which, for Moreno Fraginals, was "the primary element of the Industrial Revolution, completely transforming Cuban conditions of production."[19] Cuba thus became one of the first countries to enjoy this means of transportation, ten years before its metropole.[20]

The first line extended south from the port of Havana, first to Bejucal in November 1837 and on to Güines the following year. The Compañía de Caminos de Hierro de La Habana (Havana Railroads Company) then extended its lines west to Guanajay, south to Batabanó, and from Güines east to Unión de Reyes. In these cases the railroad traversed regions where the plantations' heyday had passed, but in other new sugar areas it arrived

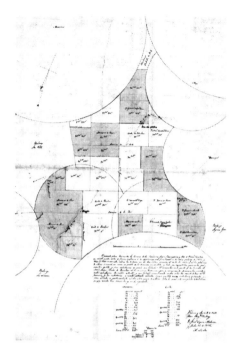

FIGURE 4.2.

Subdivision of the haciendas of Banagüises, Jigue, and Río Piedras, south of Cárdenas, to develop *ingenios*.

(Fondo Archivo de Agrimensores Serafín Sánchez Govín, Fundación Antonio Núñez Jiménez de la Naturaleza y el Hombre [Havana], 244)

nearly or at the same time as the *ingenios,* steam engines, or, later, *trenes al vacío.* During this period the principal inhabited natural regions of Havana-Matanzas where sugar had taken root were furrowed with railroads. In 1840 construction began on a line from the port of Matanzas southeast to Limonar and Coliseo (completed in 1848) and another that reached Cidra, Sabanilla (both in 1845), and Unión de Reyes (in 1849), where it met the line coming from Güines before continuing east toward Isabel, in the *partido* (district) of Macuriges (see figure 4.3).

The most representative case of the relationship between the railroad and sugar's development was the occupation of the natural region of Colón Plain, the center of Cuban sugar production between the 1830s and 1860s. These railroads were made even more important by the region's slight number of rivers and by a topography subject to flooding during the rainy season. Here the second line on the island was built: the Ferrocarril de Cárdenas (Cardenas Railroad), begun in December 1838. Heading south, it reached Bemba (today Jovellanos) two years later, then continued on to the southwest toward Navajas (which it reached in 1844) and southeast toward Macagua, with stations along the way in Nueva Bermeja (today Colón) and

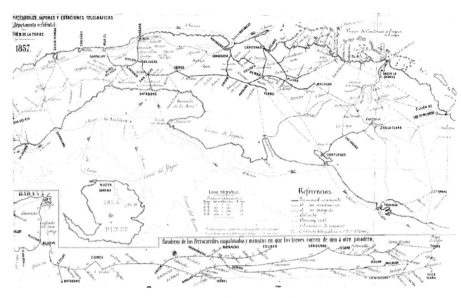

FIGURE 4.3. José María de La Torre, "Railroads, Steamers, and Telegraph Stations in the Western Department," 1857.

(Fondo Archivo de Agrimensores Serafín Sánchez Govín, Fundación Antonio Núñez Jiménez de la Naturaleza y el Hombre [Havana], box 41)

Agüica (where it arrived in 1851). In 1841, a few kilometers east of Cárdenas, the Ferrocarril de Júcaro appeared, heading southeast from Júcaro to Sabanilla de la Palma, Altamisal, and Banaguises (which it reached in 1844). The two railroad companies reached an agreement in 1853 that led to their merger in 1857 as the Ferrocarriles de Cárdenas y Júcaro (see figure 4.4).[21]

The other regions that symbolize sugar's implantation from the 1840s to the 1870s had their own railroads. Plain of Manacas-Cienfuegos was traversed by the Cienfuegos to Villa Clara railroad, whose construction began in 1847. It first reached Palmira (1851) and Cruces (1853). Plain of Corralillo-Yaguajay was home to two small and two larger railroad companies. The first were those of Carahatas and Mallorquín-Las Pozas, begun in 1855 and 1856. Of the latter two the largest was the Ferrocarril de Sagua la Grande, whose construction began in 1855 and which in 1860 reached Cruces, where it met the Cienfuegos line. An eastward spur was completed to Cifuentes in 1858, serving the *ingenios* of the Calabazar de Sagua area. Another railroad in this region linked Caibarién and Remedios in 1851, later continuing west to Tabaguayabon.

FIGURE 4.4. Railroads and *ingenios* in the area of Matanzas and Cárdenas.

(Manuel José Carrera y Heredia, *Informe general presentado a la Junta Directiva del ferrocarril de La Sabanilla, con el proyecto de prolongación de su camino hasta Navajas y el plan de entroncamiento con los ferrocarriles de La Habana y Matanzas* [Matanzas: Imprenta de Gobierno y Real Marina, 1846])

The railroads accelerated the settlement of areas farther from the coast and had a dual impact on the environment. First, in the early years of the sugar industry's development, they facilitated the extraction of forest products, as can be seen from the cargo they transported, in which the importance of the regions' lumber declined.[22] Second, the railroads supplied plantations with foreign wood and fuels, which partially offset the disappearing local forests.

The close connection with the sugar industry's development was not the only way the railroads impacted forests. In the early years the only fuel the locomotives used was firewood, from the forests either of the island or of the United States. For example, in 1839, the administrator of the Havana Railroads Company, given the great consumption of firewood and the danger of his firm's being short of fuel, proposed contracts that would establish a mix of U.S. firewood (hard and difficult to burn) with domestic wood, at a rate of 1,100 cords of each per year, enough to fuel three or four engines a day.[23]

In 1853 the same company requested that foreign lumber be included in the permit previously granted to import coal, free of all tariffs and notwithstanding a ship's flag or origin. It warned that if this authorization was not granted, the railroads would be "in danger of death in a not very distant future," since only the Cárdenas and Júcaro companies offered "ample dividends." Unlike the steam engines in *ingenios* and ships, which could use coal, locomotives required firewood or coke, which were widely used in Europe but whose cost and transport rendered them inaccessible. The administrator explained that firewood was one of the most important needs of railroad companies, which could never be obtained in sufficient quantity and sometimes had to be purchased at exorbitant cost to avoid interruptions in service, prices that could continue to rise as supplies diminished. To give the request more weight he also expressed interest in the healthiness of the island's climate, "which can certainly lose much given the rapidity with which our forests are being cut down and eradicated." The Development Committee supported the petition, counter to the opinion of the administrator of royal naval revenue, who argued that coal was not a product native to Cuba. The supporters of the petition argued that "for firewood to become a native product it would be important to promote logging, although this is a grave and significant evil, so the Deputy Syndic does not believe this to be a logical and profitable measure. On the contrary, he believes it would be disastrous, because given the use of this fuel its rapid and immediate exhaustion can be predicted, with obvious harm to these companies and to the country."[24]

Eventually most railroad companies stopped using firewood, although some continued to use it exclusively or in combination with other fuels into the 1880s and 1890s. But firewood was not the railroads' only direct use of Cuba's forests. In fact, when lines were extended to new points, the estate owners who would benefit ceded wood or established contracts to furnish different needs, particularly crossties (*traviesas*). An active coastal shipping of the latter can be noted from different points on the island to areas where the railroad was expanding, although crossties were also imported from the United States. Esteban Pichardo Tapia's *Diccionario provincial casi-razonado de vozes y frases cubanas* (Quasi-Reasoned Provincial Dictionary of Cuban Words and Expressions) defines *atravesaño*, synonym of *traviesa*, as "in railroads, the pieces perpendicular to the two parallel Bars of the road, placed at an interval of one vara [0.84 meters] or less, and for which are preferred native hardwoods, such as quiebrahacha, júcaro, etc."[25] For many years some of the island's best woods were used for this purpose.[26]

Transformation of Northern Las Villas: Part One

The expansion of sugar toward the plains and heights of the north of the former province of Las Villas,[27] in the center of the island, is symbolic of the environment's transformation from the beginning of the steam age. By studying sugar's implantation in this area we can appreciate the movement of cane cultivation and the production of sugar through a single natural region as the latter's natural resources (at the time essentially its abundant forests) were exhausted. This first part focuses on the western half of the physico-natural regions of the Plain of Corralillo-Yaguajay and the Heights of the Northern Range, where the jurisdiction of Sagua la Grande was established in the mid-nineteenth century. The growth of Sagua la Grande coincided with the generalization of semimechanized *ingenios* and the first use of mechanized ones (see figure 4.5).

The Plain of Corralillo-Yaguajay is bordered to the west by the Colón Plain and to the south by the Heights of the Northern Range, part of the Plains and Heights of Cubanacán subdistrict. It is made up of flat land 220 kilometers long and between 3 and 30 kilometers wide. Its 3,150 square kilometers are hydrologically quite active, with important rivers such as the Sagua la Grande, Sagua la Chica, and northern Jatibonico. The 1,125 square kilometers of the long and narrow Heights of the Northern Range extend parallel to the south of the northern plain. From its elevations flow the rivers that cross both regions. The soils of these territories in northern Las Villas are considered deep and fertile, but some of them had problems of surface drainage.

When the Europeans arrived, this area was covered with semicaducifolious forest, much of it with fluctuating humidity, as well as a smaller proportion of subperennifolious forests. Their abundance and frequent harvesting beginning in 1492 made them among the most famous wooded areas on the island. In his account of the passage of the Narváez colonizing expedition through Carahatas, Bartolomé de Las Casas wrote that everyone in the party was amazed by the abundance of fruit, cassava, fish, and birds given to them; in fifteen days his companions ate the incredible quantity of ten thousand parrots.[28] It is also commonly claimed that wood from these

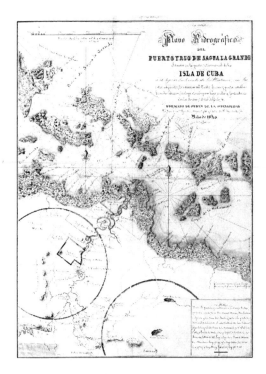

FIGURE 4.5.

First *ingenios* along the Sagua la Grande River.

(Francisco Lavallée, "Hydrographic Plan of the Sagua la Grande River and Port," Mapoteca, Archivo Nacional de Cuba [Havana])

forests was used to build El Escorial castle in Spain. Until the end of the nineteenth century forests and hog farms were the principal economic activities of the region, whose lumbering, centered in Remedios, supplied the shipyards in Havana.

The jurisdiction of Sagua la Grande was established in 1845 on lands extending to the Sierra Morena River, on the border of the jurisdiction of Cárdenas, up to the Granadillo or Caunao estuary. It was bordered to the south by the jurisdictions of Cienfuegos and Santa Clara. In the nineteenth century it was composed of seven *partidos*. On the northern edge, from east to west, were the coastal *partidos* of Rancho Veloz, Quemado de Güines, Sagua la Grande (initially Jumagua), and Calabazar de Sagua. To the south, also from east to west, were Alvarez (later known as Ceja de Pablo), the circumscription (*colonia*) of Santo Domingo (initially part of the *partido* of Yabú), and Amaro (later Cifuentes) (see figure 4.6).

The geographic center of these lands is the powerful Sagua la Grande, the largest river on Cuba's northern coast. Its presence and that of the Sagua la Chica facilitated the transport of lumber to the coast, as indicated by

FIGURE 4.6. Sketch of the jurisdiction of the Government Lieutenancy of Sagua la Grande in the mid-1900s.

(Archivo Nacional de Cuba [Havana], Gobierno General, file 334, no. 16062)

reports from the 1770s and 1780s, which called Remedios the most abundant logging operation in lumber of all kinds, although it was eventually abandoned because of its distance from Havana. Antonio Alcover y Beltrán notes that in 1780 an individual was authorized to establish a logging operation on the Jumagua farm and that families were brought from Florida to populate a town at a point on the river that, owing to the latter's sinuous course, lay 27 kilometers from the coast. Farmers and farmworkers began to settle here. According to Alcover y Beltrán, in 1792 the community was composed of rustic dwellings of prisoners and their guardians, who sent lumber to the Havana shipyard. Other sources tell of unsuccessful attempts to increase the population prior to 1812.

The royal edict of August 30, 1815, according to Alcover y Beltrán, gave "the stimulus of our countryside's development" by which "the impediments were removed." Most of all, it offered speculators a "rich mine," since "the abundance and excellent quality of the lumber found in the woodlands will find certain use." Several businesses were established to exploit the forests, including the business of Francisco Ponce de León in 1812. In 1819 Tomás Romay wrote that the Sagua lands were of the highest quality, their forests thick with cedar, mahogany, ácana, and other useful and precious woods; at its dock schooners and smaller boats arrived to take to Havana "the finest woods for its buildings and households and can also furnish it with fire-wood, charcoal, and other articles."[29]

Sugar arrived in 1835 with the subdivision of several farms along the river. Here a criollo and three U.S. citizens founded the first *ingenios*. Four years later Idelfonso Vivanco visited this region and wrote a report whose title, "Sagua la Grande," might lead one to think that he would write about its lumber. But no: "As soon as one reaches the end of the mangrove — that is, the great belt that separates sea from terra firma — one begins to see on both shores of the river cane fields and the mills of *ingenios*, amid nearly all of which stands out the steam engine that is the agent used for milling."[30] Vivanco showed enthusiasm for the rapid development of the past three to four years, although obstacles remained, including the need to shorten shipping time with canals, improve the port, and establish a railroad to Villa Clara. He noted that only unrefined sugar was made here, which from the beginning distinguished this region closely linked to export to the United States.

By the early 1840s there were already twenty-six *ingenios* along the banks of the river, as well as livestock farms (*potreros*), tobacco plantations, and small farms (*sitios y estancias de labor*). The land was thought to be extraor-dinarily fertile, especially for cane, which grew in a manner "that seems incredible," with very high yield. Planters claimed to get 7,000 or 8,000 arrobas of sugar per caballería. For example, Jorge Bartlet's *ingenio*, on only 3 caballerías, produced more than 23,000 arrobas, an average of 5,353 arro-bas of refined sugar per caballería, a yield much higher than was custom-ary at the time, while on the Drake *ingenio* cane grew 8 varas (6.7 meters) high.[31] Two decades later Ramón de La Sagra, although not confirming this size, reiterated the great fertility of the Sagua area, "where cane reaches a prodigious height and thickness." He also observed that along the banks of the river there formerly had been tobacco plantations that the river flooded, until the *ingenios* displaced them; the fertile alluvial soils occupied a band 20 cordeles (100 paces) wide, "after which one finds clay soils, exceedingly compact and difficult to work."[32]

In 1844 an article on Sagua la Grande appeared in the *Memorias* of the Economic Society. "It is extremely agreeable to travel the river at milling time," the author wrote, "observing the glow of the *ingenios'* smokestacks along the shore; the dark and steaming plumes reflected in its waters." The author also noted that sugarcane here "has a stunning yield." But despite the continuous clearing of forests in the *partido*, there still existed "an infinite quantity of lumber suitable for construction and ornament." As for game, hutia[33] were so abundant "that many small farms sustain their slaves partly with them."[34] In 1844 as well, a Sagua customs office was established for exports, and the following year it became an independent jurisdiction, including part of the territories that had previously belonged to Villa Clara.

This division left Villa Clara without egress to the sea, which led to a petition that Villa Clara not be left "a strange jurisdiction" without a port. The complainants argued that the progress of Cienfuegos, to the south, and Sagua la Grande, to the north, reduced Villa Clara to a paltry radius, stripped of its richest and most fertile lands. They claimed that the seven *partidos* transferred to the new deputy government of Sagua were "those that possessed ports and harbors . . . leaving to this villa those farthest from the sea and least wooded." Most of the *ingenios* also were left out of the old jurisdiction, a situation worsened by livestock farming's loss of workers to more productive industries such as sugar refining. The requested solution was that the Granadillo estuary, east of the Sagua la Grande River, be made into Villa Clara's natural port. Combined with this measure and the "highly economic" system adopted in the sugar industry, the petition declared, "the thickness of their inexhaustible forests [would] make these enterprises so lucrative and so easy to undertake, that it is certain and can be said without fear that the latter would multiply infinitely, making this town an opulent city."[35]

In 1850 the deputy government of Sagua la Grande had forty-one *ingenios* in the coastal *partidos* and thirty-three in the interior.[36] Influencing this distribution was the proximity of docks and the later the Carahatas and Mallorquín–Las Pozas railroads. But by the end of the decade the Ferrocarril de Sagua contributed to the settlement of the interior. In 1858 the local daily announced that a branch from Sitio Grande to Cifuentes would soon open, which would transport the produce of the fertile and productive region. Another line was evoked that would connect with the Cienfuegos railroad. The newspaper reported that, in addition to having less arid land than that of the route originally proposed, the new one would also encompass "more producing farms and more wooded land that could accommodate an even greater number [of farms], whose opening and development is destined to occur quite soon."[37]

The nineteenth-century statistics are very limited in their ability to quantify the vanishing of Sagua's forests, among other reasons because they do not cover precisely the same territory. Table 4.2 shows the land distribution in the different areas envisioned as part of the jurisdiction between 1846 and 1899. What is most obvious is that while the amount of forest declines abruptly, a nearly equal proportion of pasture and arid land increases. In contrast, the amount of land under cultivation does not change significantly. The greatest reduction of forest area occurred after 1862. At this time La Pezuela wrote that clearing and logging occurred with the same "prodigality and waste" in Sagua la Grande as on the rest of the island, although Sagua still had woodlands with abundant precious wood and lumber, such as cedar, mahogany, guaiacum, ebony, and granadillo.[38]

Between Rebello's statistics for 1860 and the statistics for 1877, the number of *ingenios* in the jurisdiction increased from 119 to 156 — that is, 37 new farms in that period, although the number must be greater because in 1877 nearly 70 *ingenios* appeared that had not been recorded in 1860. For example, Alcover y Beltrán gives a figure for 1871 of 165 *ingenios*, not counting those in development. During this time the *ingenios* grew in average size, from 44.4 to 55.2 caballerías, and the average area in cane increased from 13.4 to 18.8 caballerías.[39] This was influenced both by the technological modernization of some *ingenios* and by the need to intensify land use during the Ten Years' War.

In the early years of plantation expansion the exploitation of forests in these areas intensified. When the increasing disappearance of Cuba's woodlands was denounced in the *Diario de la Marina* in 1845, Sagua was cited as an example. Much of the wood that was cut in its extensive and still virgin woodlands was entirely wasted: "They cut lengths and take them to the river, keeping them in the water until the river rises and then sending them downstream to where they are loaded for shipment here [Havana] or to foreign nations." The unintended result was that, "if the river does not rise sufficiently, as has happened due to lack of rain in recent years, they are rotted by the dissolving action of the water . . . or become useless for construction."[40] Only a quarter of the lumber was used, the rest being "lost due to the absurd method used to extract it."

The occupation of woodlands by the sugar and forest-product industries

TABLE 4.2. Evolution of Land Use in Sagua la Grande, 1846–1899

Year	Area in Caballerías	Area under Cultivation (%)	Ingenios	Forest (%)	Arid Land (%)	Natural Pasture (%)	Artificial Pasture (%)
1846	19,595	1,124 (5.7)	59	17,386 (88.7)		1,015 (5.2)	70 (0.4)
1850	21,874	2,993 (13.7)	60	12,032 (55)	2,349 (10.7)	3,809 (17.4)	693 (3.2)
1862	24,498	2,160 (8.8)	125	11,023 (45)	7,486 (30.6)	3,221 (13.1)	608 (2.5)
1899	16,364	2,398 (10.9)[a]	73[b]	3,163 (19.3)	3,290 (20.1)	8,123 (49.6)	

Sources: Census of 1846 and 1862. For 1850: ANC, GG, file 334/16062; for 1895 and 1899: *Memoria del año fiscal de 1899 a 1900*.
[a] This is the figure for land under cultivation in 1895. The cultivated area in 1899 is not representative because of the recent three years of war (1895–98).
[b] The census mentions a quantity for 1899 of 79 *colonias*, 42 of which were in Rancho Veloz. For the same year, a figure is given of 6,218 caballerías in sugar farms and plantations.

continued in Sagua la Grande as long as forests remained. Statistics for the jurisdiction of the district seat in 1888 indicated the existence of twenty-one *ingenios* on 1,474 caballerías, an average of 70.2 caballerías per farm, divided into 17.7 for cane, 25 for pastures, 13.6 fallow, and 13 in woodlands. In other words, while the total average area had increased by 20 caballerías, that of cane remained stable relative to the 1877 averages.[41] These figures seem to indicate a certain eagerness to increase the land area of *ingenios*. In fact, amid the crisis of those years, some lamented the inability of many Sagua estate owners to modernize, putting them in danger of irreparable harm "if they are not favored by an exceptional fertility of the land or a just as exceptional price of sugar."[42]

As deforestation advanced, intrinsic limitations of the jurisdiction's soils for cane cultivation became clear. Drainage and canal systems were built to moderate the effects of excessive humidity. In the twentieth century Hugh Bennett and Robert Allison, writing about the soils of the coastal plain of Cárdenas and Caibarién and the hilly terrain of Sagua-Caibarién, indicated poor cane yields for nearly the entire area, owing to such factors as impermeable subsoil, salinity, and the rapid invasion of weeds.[43] Similarly, the arrival of sugar had effects not directly derived from deforestation, such as contamination of the Sagua la Grande River, leading to numerous protests by residents of the district seat.[44] As for direct consequences, one could investigate deforestation's role in the increasingly violent floods suffered by the city. After discussing the catastrophic floods of 1904 and 1906 and the economic depression that affected the region, Alcover y Beltrán lamented: "In its countryside that once boasted dozens of *ingenios* and in its lands . . . that yielded the most beautiful cane that any region had produced, nothing of this can be seen today."[45] The same could be said of many parts of the island that fell into decadence after the ephemeral years of sugar's splendor.

The Mirror of the Sugar Islands and Havana: Voices of Warning

The increasing number of *ingenios* in a growing radius around Havana in the last third of the eighteenth century and the beginning of the nineteenth led some to question the impact on forests. In their arguments, navy officials noted not only the shortage of wood but other consequences such as decreasing rainfall and the decline of livestock farming. They also defended a view of agriculture and population different from that implied by the advance of a plantation economy. The most forward-thinking estate owners also noted the adverse effects that rapid deforestation of the island could entail. The fundamental difference was how the two groups thought the problem should be confronted. According to the navy, greater measures were needed to guarantee the conservation of forests as an asset of the community and the state. For estate owners and their advocates, private interest was the best means to ensure this objective; the state should limit itself to offering landowners and municipalities incentives for reforestation.

Each of these perspectives had advantages and limitations. Clearly, a command centralized in the navy and the colonial government would have difficulty controlling the exploitation of forests on an island still largely covered with forest. Critics of such a system argued that restrictions led private citizens to lose interest in conserving trees and inspired fraud and much waste of wood. The proposal to allow unregulated logging in a given area, with the rest of the territory under the control of the navy, was an intermediate and temporary solution. How would commercial agriculture be developed once the 30 leagues around Havana were settled? The effects of the royal edict of August 30, 1815, removed all doubt. Cuba's forests went from a system of more or less rigorous control to one of no control other than landowner interest.

The defects of the former system had already been revealed, and the time was coming to test how effective the latter would be. While municipal property was almost nonexistent on the island and that of the state remained to be determined, the owners of traditional estates, the primary form of land ownership in Cuba, had a free hand to do whatever they liked with the land. In this way the advance of slave plantations toward the east simply amplified what had already occurred around Havana. Now everything was happening at once: intensive exploitation of wood and other forest products, opening of large spaces for cultivation, and an expansion of lesser crops to feed the towns. This great economic transformation brought changes in the landscape that did not go unnoticed.[46] Voices of alarm were frequently raised, regardless of birthplace (Cuba or Spain) or political affiliation. There were certainly differences in focus: one view proposed an exploitation of forests more rational in its implications for the development of sugar plantations, with no limits placed on individual property; the other argued for state intervention in control of forest exploitation, including privately owned woodlands. With different emphases, these views reflected the growing anxiety about the negative implications of accelerated deforestation.

EMPHASIS ON THE PROBLEM OF FUEL

Much of the criticism of Cuba's rapid deforestation pointed to the consequences of the same process on the so-called Sugar Islands. Since the eighteenth century, these much smaller Caribbean neighbors had been suffering the effects of deforestation, which motivated the implementation of technological innovations and methods of cultivation to avoid the use of firewood and prolong the land's fertility.[47] At the beginning of the 1790s available land remained in Haiti, left aside by the revolution, and in the interior of Jamaica, but the latter case, on the largest of the Caribbean's non-Spanish islands, showed the enormous opening for Cuba's sugar boom. The Havana-Matanzas district by itself, predominantly flat and still with wooded areas at the end of the eighteenth century, had a surface area of 12,783 square kilometers, while the entire area of Jamaica, much more mountainous, was 11,424 square kilometers.[48]

With the advance of the plantations, the landscapes of Cuba's natural regions underwent the same radical transformation that had occurred earlier on other Caribbean islands. Other sugar- and coffee-producing regions, such as those in Brazil, experienced similar environmental effects of forest destruction, soil exhaustion, and loss of biodiversity, but because of their distance or their continental size, they were less often compared.[49] Journeys made to Jamaica beginning in the late eighteenth century seem to indicate that Cuban sugar planters found neighboring islands a useful mirror in which to see themselves, not only to solve problems such as the shortage of firewood and loss of fertility but also to warn about the impact of commercial agriculture on the environment. In their 1828 report on their trip, Ramón de Arozarena and Pedro Bauduy note: "The forests are entirely destroyed; the rains are much rarer than before; and, to close the catalog of its bad qualities, no country has rougher terrain or smaller valleys."[50]

Such reports sought not only to show these dangers but also to indicate what methods were used in Jamaica to eliminate dependence on firewood and to maintain the productivity of lands that resembled Cuba's and were "worn out by nearly two hundred years of farming." On this same journey the authors took a closer example when they passed through the town of Trinidad, in the center south of Cuba, where the estate owners "had been compelled to reduce the use of fuel, because if they had not they would have been forced to abandon the growing of cane, the whole country being entirely deforested and the soil being so arid that not even the *brusca* can be used." By "the *brusca*" they meant the use in nine *ingenios* of furnaces that burned cane pulp instead of firewood, although in the thirty-five others, which still had woodlands, "the old method" continued to be used. In mentioning these examples, the authors had Havana producers in mind: "For more than two centuries we have been making sugar with a method more complicated than our neighbors'; to make two thousand crates [*cajas*] of it, we burn two thousand tareas [7,200–8,600 cubic meters] of firewood, and in this manner we destroy our forests and send away the rains that the forests bring and that are so necessary in the tropics; we also rid ourselves of our crops due to our extraordinary caprice of not wanting to use fertilizers."

Two years later Alejandro Oliván arrived at similar conclusions after his journey to Jamaica, England, France, Belgium, and Holland, also for the Royal Consulate of Agriculture, Industry, and Commerce of Havana.[51] These warnings, however, came late in the Havana region's oldest plantation areas, which themselves had become a mirror. In 1828 José Antonio Saco recalled the 1796 predictions of José Ricardo O'Farrill that the forests would soon be pushed back 40 leagues from the city. Saco then affirmed:

"Painful experience has borne out this sad prophecy." He argued that this should serve as warning to the residents of the interior and that policing regulations should be effected for when raisers of livestock became farmers, so that "the catastrophe now affecting many estate owners will never be repeated."[52]

The emphasis on the problem of fuel was not fortuitous: by the mid-nineteenth century it was one of the arguments brandished by the most forward-thinking estate owners, scientists, and intellectuals who argued for a system of cultivation that would not depend exclusively on occupying virgin territory. Saco explained that despite the savings resulting from the use of cane pulp in the new sugar kettle batteries, the use of firewood had increased because of the rising number of *ingenios* and the enormous consumption of firewood by steam engines. He saw this consumption as responsible for the slow application of these machines on *ingenios*.

In 1843, at the request of the Economic Society, the Count de Mopox y de Jaruco wrote his essay "Ruina de nuestros preciosos montes: Necesidad de reponerlos" (The Ruin of Our Precious Woodlands: The Need to Restore Them). In his opinion the dearth of lumber for urban and rural construction, the diminishing supply of fuel — when sugar, the principal source of wealth, "requires a violent action of fire" — and the railroads were enough to "draw the attention of everyone who looks with interest on the destiny of this island." Although some of these needs could be met with wood from North America and coal, he warned that the effects on weather remained a danger, since rains would pass over the "long and narrow" island without nourishing the fields and then "the land[,] . . . deprived of coolness and shade, will become arid savanna, and the proverbial fertility of Cuba will be replaced by the sterility of African plains." These effects could be noted in regions where agriculture had been established the longest: "Both coffee plantations and *ingenios* that we see dismantled and the complaints we hear voiced about scant harvests should warn us of the changes in and deterioration of our fields, to which we should put a prompt end."[53]

As a remedy the count suggested a large-scale system of crop rotation. When cane and coffee were moved to new areas "whose coolness and fertility allow them to compete with foreign [crops]," the forests and livestock farming, "which have been vanishing before these two main branches of our economy, will be reborn behind them, and may regenerate the impoverished soil." Rocky terrain and bare hills abandoned by planters could be covered with forests more suited to the location: "and perhaps experience will prove that many impoverished fields around the capital would yield abundant resources if converted to the old forests." For *ingenios* he recommended distributing 30 to 40 caballerías in the three or four blocks and, after fifteen years of good cane yields, making each into forests for thirty or forty-five years to furnish lumber and firewood and allow the tired land to recover.[54]

Three years later another interesting essay appeared, this one by the estate owner José Pizarro y Gardín on fuel in *ingenios*. His goal was to reduce the consumption of firewood on the many farms "that in the end fail for lack of wooded areas."[55] His point of departure was a belief that this shortage was a fatal illness, since the so-called exhaustion of land had as many possible cures as in Europe and other parts of the Americas. Based on the existence at the time of fourteen hundred *ingenios* and the felling at every harvest of 1 caballería per farm on average for firewood and 2 caballerías for charcoal and other needs, he estimated that 4,200 caballerías of forest were cleared on the island each year. This led to a decline in yields as a result of drought and to deterioration of the most costly and productive farms as a result of the vanishing of their forests and the dependence on foreign fuel for their furnaces.

Pizarro y Gardín suggested reserving 1 or 2 caballerías for royal palms, so that the *pencas de guano* and *yaguas* that fell from the trees would provide enough fuel for a normal harvest and feed (with *palmiche*) an increased number of pigs.[56] Once established, the palm grove would provide annual fruit that would need only be gathered and stored. This would allow estate owners who no longer had forests to save the expense of buying firewood from their neighbors, since none remained on farms "in full force of production." Aware that attempts to create forests artificially had failed, Pizarro y Gardín assured his readers that palm trees could save many of the island's forests.

Sugar industry tracts from this period nearly always referred to the problem of fuel. In 1832 Alejandro Dumont proposed planting on each *ingenio* 4 caballerías of forest divided into eight sections. After the half caballería corresponding to each cane harvest was cut down, tree seeds and saplings would be sown, with brush and weeds removed to ensure the trees' growth. As each section of forest was cleared, 500 to 600 trees should be reserved per caballería for lumber. If this system had been adopted before, "we would not have seen so many beautiful farms abandoned for want of fuel," and "firewood and lumber would have been sufficient to guarantee the survival of the *ingenios* for many centuries."[57] In 1836 Andrés de Zayas wrote that this was the most important of topics because the clearing of woodlands had ruined many farms with excellent land and location. He recommended planting in the farms' worst land varieties of trees that were resistant and grew rapidly, such as guásimas, paraísos, and guavas.[58]

In 1857 José Montalvo y Castillo argued that the destruction of forests showed that *ingenios* had not yet been perfected, despite the fact that coal and steam were already used in furnaces. In his opinion, this matter was the most important to resolve, since "in fuel is wealth."[59] Another sugar tract, from 1862, found that *ingenios* with steam engines and Jamaican sugar kettle batteries (which produced most of the island's sugar) and a production capacity of six thousand crates consumed about 1,500 tareas of firewood a year. The author arrived at this figure by estimating that 1 or 1.5 caballerías of forest were needed per *ingenio*. If after being cleared this land was planted with cane, "as is generally done, within a few years the woodland is exhausted and as a result one is left without fuel." He proposed creating a continuous woodland of 24 caballerías, divided into 3-caballería sections, that would be logged every eight years, so that they would continue to produce firewood for "an incalculable time, with no more than twenty-four caballerías, which today's system clears within sixteen years."[60]

If we compare the surface area of firewood reserves recommended by Dumont in 1832 with that of three decades later, we can deduce a greater impact on forests, which occurred despite the use of cane pulp and the granting of free importation of coal, no matter under which flag or of which origin. A petition written in 1847 by the estate owner Francisco Diago to the Development Committee requested this authorization as a means to solve the grave fuel problem and promote the conservation of forests. In his opinion what was at stake was the "truly very near" future of "all the island's industries, whether agricultural or manufacturing, and especially those involved in urban construction, shipbuilding, and railroads."[61]

Diago warned that if Cubans continued the "reckless clearing of forest, thus far undertaken with most deplorable lack of foresight," the current generation's grandchildren would experience "the double calamity of shortages of fuel and scarcity of water." He based this conclusion on the unanimity among meteorologists that forests had "a powerful impact on atmospheric movement and the ability to provoke and regulate rainfall." He cited the observations about rivers and lakes of the Americas and Asia by Alexander von Humboldt, Charles Marie de La Condamine, and Jean-

Baptiste Boussingault, who noted a reduction in flowing waters as a result of deforestation. But one need not go abroad: on the island was irrefutable confirmation of this truth:

> The waters of the Güines River, which in the past century fulfilled all the needs of the industry and agriculture of the *partido*, have gradually diminished as the woodlands have retreated, and one often sees the local estate owners fighting over now insufficient water to drive their *trapiches* and to irrigate their fields, despite having eliminated in recent years some of their water-driven mills. It is furthermore the common opinion of the most long-standing inhabitants of this district that the river's level has dropped one vara in the past fifty years.[62]

In the twentieth century the engineer Juan A. Cosculluela claimed that the clearing of woodlands in the Mayabeque Basin increased the violence of the river's flooding upstream. Not that there were no floods when the river's banks and tributaries were surrounded by old forests, but he argued that radical changes in the former conditions worsened this problem in Güines.[63] And this was not the only effect of the arrival of the slave plantations. During his journey through this area in the 1830s the Spanish traveler Jacinto de Salas y Quiroga, in crossing with a friend the broad fields sown "some with coffee, some with banana trees, most with cane," was surprised to observe "the sepulchral silence that reigned everywhere; rare were the birds that crossed the sky or perched in the trees." Pages later he wrote, "The sky seemed uninhabited, but the land no less so."[64]

EMPHASIS ON THE EXHAUSTION OF THE SOIL

The use of cane pulp and customs exemptions on the import of coal reduced the clearing of forests to fuel the steam engines and boilers of the *ingenios*. This does not mean, however, that sugar had less impact on woodlands. The need for larger cane fields led to more clearing to open fertile land, as well as the more rapid wearing out of land occupied by sugar, with implications for the environment as serious as the old problem of fuel.

Although it was not a new concern, we could say that beginning in the mid-nineteenth century the so-called exhaustion of land began to be the main reason for alarm.[65] The work of the Count de Pozos Dulces for reform of the cultivation system is one of the primary examples of this transition. He preached the substitution of extensive, migratory, or transhumant farming, which exhausted and sterilized the soil, with intensive farming, and in general with a forward-looking agriculture less vulnerable to fluctuations in yield. He demonstrated that the best *ingenios* and tobacco plantations had been located near the capital, while finding new ones now required "traversing wide spaces . . . toward Vuelta Arriba or Vuelta Abajo [districts in Pinar del Río Province], whose separation by territories that today are completely sterile and exhausted is the best refutation of the system that claims to be able to forgo fertilizers." Each new railroad revealed the need to "chase after treasures already used up in the space passed through."[66]

Increased milling capacity led to greater impact on the environment and eventually on the life span of the farms themselves. This is what José Jacinto de Frías y Jacott, brother of the Count de Pozos Dulces, referred to in 1851 when he wrote of "monster *Ingenios*" like those being established in the Banagüises area.[67] These farms could produce as much in a harvest as three good *ingenios* of the more traditional variety. Despite their economies of scale in workers, wages, and construction, Frías y Jacott saw a great disadvantage in the amount of land required to "maintain the cultivated area sufficient for the great production sought and expected, considering invariable the system of planting in new land and abandoning exhausted cane fields, and entirely forgoing any procedures to improve the crop and the land." He wondered what would be the fate of these colossal edifices, costly sugar kettle batteries and magnificent steam engines, huge cabins and railroads to transport cane and sugar, when the land wore out and yielded not ten thousand crates but five thousand: "What will be done with this vast terrain, which, although it has produced mountains of gold, will become sterile and without forests, and in which will stand out like ancient ruins the remains of the costly mills?" (see figures 4.7 and 4.8).[68]

This situation helped impel agrarian reform; proposals were made to replace slave with free labor, to develop small-scale ownership of property and crop diversity, and to separate agriculture from milling on sugar plantations. To these ends the Economic Society's journal, *Memorias*, publicized technological innovations useful to producers, as well as the experience of other estates on the island. Among the issues to which it drew attention was the need to drain soil and control weeds. It also promoted the plowing of fields that had been used for several years and the use of green and mineral fertilizers.[69] It often recommended using cane pulp to revive soil, as a more practical use for pulp than as fuel. Nevertheless, all this remained in the realm of good intentions or small-scale application in an agricultural landscape still largely dominated by the eagerness to plant in virgin fields.

FIGURE 4.7. Boiler house of the Santa Rosa *ingenio*, in the
jurisdiction of Matanzas. Lithograph by Eduardo Laplante.

(Justo G. Cantero, *Los ingenios: Colección de vistas de los principales ingenios
de azúcar de la isla de Cuba* [Havana: Litográfica Luis Marquier, 1857])

The greatest exponent of efforts to improve cane cultivation was Alvaro
Reynoso, particularly in his *Ensayo sobre el cultivo de la caña de azúcar*
(Essay on the Growing of Sugarcane), first published in Havana in 1862.
His principal objective was to overcome the idea that clearing and burning
was the only way to produce high yields and to revive declining production
on an old *ingenio*. Although he acknowledged the great fertility of cleared
fields, he argued instead for an improved agriculture, since after a few years
these new fields lost their productivity and "cane planted in them languishes
proportionally to the impoverishment of the soil."[70] Reynoso warned that
the ephemeral fertility of cleared land was due above all to the amount of
organic matter that remained on the ground, which could conceal soil inapt
for cane cultivation.

Improved agriculture did not simply mean obtaining excess fertilizers,
such as one did through clearing and burning; it also entailed bringing together the factors that determined the "law of land fertility," taking into
account that soils were the products of different conditions. The idea was to
produce a sort of *artificial clearing*, one more permanent, productive, and

FIGURE 4.8.
Plan of the Recompensa
ingenio, area of Colón,
province of Matanzas,
1879.

(Fondo Archivo de
Agrimensores Serafín
Sánchez Govín, Fundación
Antonio Núñez Jiménez de
la Naturaleza y el Hombre
[Havana], box 135)

economical than the clearings where fertility was often short lived. Reynoso recommended, for instance, working land free of tree trunks, which could be plowed and which would "produce beneficial results with certainty and without the farmer's finding himself subject to the disastrous fluctuations in yield that today compromise his fortunes." Similarly he argued for the consideration of "general and local obstacles such as weather and hygienic circumstances occasioned by the clearing of woodlands."[71]

Reynoso's proposals gave birth to a system of cane cultivation that bore his name. It stressed the use of fertilizers, irrigation, distance between plants, care of plantations, size of *guardarrayas*,[72] intercalated crops, and other details that should be part of a scientific agriculture. In his studies Reynoso began with the conviction that Cuba's deforestation had changed its climatological conditions. In *Apuntes acerca de varios cultivos cubanos* (Notes on Several Cuban Crops; 1867), he wrote: "For the past few years our production has been disrupted, compromised, continually threatened, and frequently annihilated by a cause . . . that, in our opinion, will lead us to ruin: the lack of rain and the carelessness with which we fail to seek water for our plants."[73]

Count de Pozos Dulces wrote the foreword for several of Reynoso's books, since they gave key support for the reforms he advocated, counter to the common belief that the difficulties in sugar production resulted from a shortage of workers and that only slaves could do agricultural work. Reynoso and Pozos Dulces were leading critics of Cuba's dominant farming system and of its consequences for the country's agricultural progress. Their positions thus can be distinguished from those adopted at the same time by Spanish scientists like La Sagra and Rodríguez Ferrer, for whom the need to protect woodlands was more emphatic and not just because of forests' relationship to agriculture. This difference had to do partly with the old debate about who should be responsible for the conservation of forests, individual landowners or the colonial administration. In general, estate owners and criollo intellectuals opposed state intervention. For example, in his 1843 essay mentioned above, Count de Mopox y de Jaruco argued that "the less direct intervention by the public authority the better."[74]

The arguments of the Spanish naturalists were closer to the old position of navy officials and advocates of government invention. Beginning in 1831 La Sagra denounced the felling, when woodlands were cleared, of all kinds of trees: "robust ácana and mahogany, thick cedar and sabicú, ancient chicharrón and guaiacum." The same thing happened when forests were cut down for firewood and to make charcoal, leading to the disappearance of "the most costly trees, which cannot be recovered in four generations." As a result of this destructive clearing and the prevailing careless system, "lands once bountiful and lush [became] sterile, scorched plains." Valuable farms were abandoned for lack of fuel and the cost of materials to establish new ones increased. If this situation continued, La Sagra warned,

> temperatures will rise and rain become scarce around the cities; the beneficial and abundant dew, which during the dry season helps replace rainfall, will disappear; . . . and plants and animals [will be] condemned to extinction between November and March, and in the hot months the vivifying breeze of the forests and balmy scent of forest flowers will no longer be perceptible. Finally, where trees are annihilated a scene of solitude and death will replace the joyful spectacle of a youthful and wild nature, which repaid a thousandfold the efforts of well-managed industry.[75]

On this occasion La Sagra briefly recalled how the royal edict of August 30, 1815, had come to be promulgated, following the "just demands" of the

Havana estate owners. Three decades later he wrote a more detailed reevaluation of these long-standing conflicts and argued that individual freedom must be subordinated to the public good. This change of attitude was fed by his impressions during a new journey through the island in late 1859 and early 1860. About Cárdenas, for instance, he wrote: "It produces the immense harvests of the richest sugar regions on the island of Cuba, where during my former residency there had been virgin forests. . . . From then until now, what change, what progress, what advances in agriculture, in population, and in the intellectual culture of these districts, which could hardly be numbered."[76] Nevertheless, he also noted the increasing unlicensed felling of trees in areas "that after the seductive sight of rich gardens offered sad, barren, and lonely panoramas." The reason for this was that the basis for the great reform, "which should ground agriculture and rural industry in fecund and foresighted principles," continued to be neglected. In La Sagra's opinion, this could not be blamed on individuals but required government intervention, since it was time to implement a "foresighted farming."[77]

Among the consequences of the disappearance of forests La Sagra again mentioned the vast stretches of abandoned land, the shortage of lumber, and the exorbitant price of charcoal. In particular, he noted the imbalance that would soon emerge in the country "between artificial vegetation, resulting from the progress of agriculture, and forest vegetation, carelessly destroyed." To remedy this Cuba would require "the active, simultaneous, collective, and impartial cooperation . . . of men of science, men of wealth and of the government. Everyone will be needed." This group would be charged with carrying out reforms, since only it could bring together the necessary data, determine the advantages for local communities and collective interests, "look to the present and the future in order to promote the community's interests, without being misled by any individual passion[,] . . . without being dominated by any selfish calculation." As a first step he recommended determining the island's forest wealth scientifically and drafting a cadastral map.[78]

A few years later Rodríguez Ferrer insisted on the need for the government to intervene to protect forest resources. His *Naturaleza y civilización de la grandiosa Isla de Cuba* includes two chapters on "forest studies."[79] The first is a historical account of the vanishing of the forests, one of whose principal causes, he argued, was the freedom given private citizens to cut down trees on their property.[80] In addition to traditional contributing factors to deforestation, such as the clearing of fields for farming, the development of pastures, fenced areas, and commerce, woodlands were now threatened by railroads, which allowed lumber to be transported greater distances at less cost. As an example of increasing deforestation he noted that from Sagua la Grande and Remedios on the northern coast and from Cienfuegos on the southern coast "one already finds cleared areas, despite the fact that the island of Cuba is most fertile in trees precisely at these points."[81]

This was also the time of the war for independence, which began in 1868. Rodríguez Ferrer wrote of the narrow road from Júcaro to Morón, 56 kilometers long, that "a five-hundred-meter-wide swath has been cut through the forests, with forts built in sight of each other and with a fence the entire length of the road." Nature was transforming into brush and thickets what had been roads, green pastures, and bountiful cane fields, so that the affected region regressed "to an almost wild state in both society and nature."[82]

It is clear that Rodríguez Ferrer and La Sagra were apprised of advances in forest science and the management of state woodlands in Spain. Neither suggested an absolute ban on felling privately owned forests, but they did advocate some type of regulation. Other contemporaries agreed on the need for urgent measures, including Vicente Vásquez Quiepo in his *Informe fiscal* and the French naturalist Arthur Morelet, who during his visit to Cuba in 1847 gave a letter to the Havana Economic Society in which he wrote: "The traveler who tours the island of Cuba, and especially the area around Havana, is amazed by the bareness of the land, which rarely offers shelter from the heat of the sun. And yet this countryside was once covered with forests that agriculture is causing to disappear, with the remains increasingly lost each day."[83]

The most energetic demands for control of forest exploitation again came from the navy. Articles in its official daily frequently noted the intense deforestation taking place and its economic, military, and environmental consequences. La Sagra and Rodríguez Ferrer both used this forum to publicize their views. We could say that the *Diario de la Marina* and the *Memorias de la Sociedad Económica de La Habana* represented two different conceptions of how to approach the forest problem. Although they agreed on the need to rein in uncontrolled deforestation, they diverged on what posture to take with respect to the old polemic over the ownership of forests.

During the 1840s, when there was an obvious crisis in the supply of fuel and wood, a consensus emerged on the need to take action of some kind. But the issue of ownership of the forests continued to feed suspicions. In 1846 members of the Economic Society's Agriculture Section discussed the need to avoid the total destruction of forests with "some law that regulates and methodizes [logging], to free us from the total lack with which charcoal, steam power, railroads, and cane cultivation threaten us." Nevertheless, the writers did not intend "in any way to attack property, which requires such respect," but rather to call for the reestablishment of "the thick and useful forests that make up the excellence of our countryside."[84]

A few years later, in seven articles published between 1850 and 1851, the History Section brought back to light documents from the old conflict between Havana estate owners and the navy. The goal was to show "the onerous situation to which our grandfathers found themselves reduced in order to use the forests on their property." The final article described the situation in the years following the disappearance of "hindrances to the free development of agriculture, leaving way for others no less grave and important." It listed the causes of the accelerated deforestation since 1812, including the legal and illegal trade in lumber, coastal shipping for mills and construction on the island, and "the indiscriminate clearing to develop gigantic new sugar-making *ingenios* and the enormous amount of fuel consumed by steam engines, whose number continues to increase." Unfortunately, the article noted, selfishness was the invariable guiding principle, all observations about the ill consequences of the forests' destruction were met with smiles of disdain, and scientific papers were quickly forgotten.[85]

But these assessments, far from implying an inclination "to advocate measures of violent prohibition," sought to head off any suspicion of such intentions: "We know that forests are the exclusive property of those who justly own them, that [the owners] may do with them what they like, and that any restrictive measure would cut off the rapid and extraordinary expansion currently experienced by the country's agriculture." It was therefore urgent to find effective measures "to lead the nation's opinion on the path of the public good and the future destiny of this island." The goal was not to come up with particular legislation "to restrain the abuse of the woodlands we have left." But if the "horrific dilapidation" continued for another century so impelled by agriculture, "what could result from such a system except ruin, the complete devastation of our woodlands and all the consequences this situation entails?" Finally, the article's author sought to make clear the healthy doctrine that "man does not live only for the few days during which he plays his role; posterity may also require of him a severe accounting for the evil he has done or allowed to happen to those assets he has denied to his descendants."[86]

The Business of Exporting and Importing Lumber

The freedom of private citizens to cut down their forests gave an immediate boost to the trade in precious woods and in lumber. Freed from the former obstacles to forest exploitation, estate owners now had a source of rapid income and a way to pay for their great investments in sugar. Similarly, those outside the plantation system could lease or sell land to people or businesses selling lumber, firewood, or charcoal. During the nineteenth century and early twentieth, Cuba exported a significant amount of precious wood, although at the same time it imported much wood from the United States. This apparent contradiction was one of the arguments frequently raised against the accelerating disappearance of Cuban forests.

The harvesting of trees that began in 1815 around the Bay of Jagua is a good example of this new phase. Before the nineteenth century the southern coast had been the scene of a notable black-market wood trade with Jamaica. When the Royal Consulate of Agriculture, Industry, and Commerce and the navy discussed moving the Royal Forest Reserves or establishing new towns in the interior, the Jagua area was always mentioned as one of the best options. Navy officials noted its excellent conditions for a shipyard, an idea that Honorato Bouyón advocated in 1818, arguing that wood could be stored quickly and at less than half the cost as in Havana or in Spain "because of the abundance of lumber in the area, with which [ships] can easily be built along its more than two hundred leagues of windward coast, covered with virgin forest."[87]

No shipyard was ever built in the Bay of Jagua, but a town was established there. Lieutenant Colonel of the Infantry Louis de Clouet, of French origin, proposed to his superiors in January 1819 that a colony be founded there. A few months later Clouet, Captain General José Cienfuegos, and Quartermaster General Alejandro Ramírez formalized a contract to establish forty-six settlers from Bordeaux, who would be the initial nucleus of what became the colony of Fernandina de Jagua and, in 1829, the town of Cienfuegos. From the beginning the wood trade was a source of conflict. In 1826 Clouet petitioned for the prohibition from this port of wood bound overseas. One of the first inhabitants' economic resources was the sale for export of cedar cleared from their lands and those of surrounding estates; if a stop was not put to this, the immediate area soon would be without wood. This traffic, Clouet argued, threatened the area with shortages of an item of prime necessity, "due to the extraordinary consumption of it by *ingenios* and other agricultural establishments," as well as for shipbuilding "that H M [His Majesty] wants to establish here."[88]

As proof he asserted that at that moment English ships from Jamaica were anchored in the harbor waiting to take on loads of cedar bought by an agent the English had in the colony for this purpose. The price at which the pieces were being sold — 7 pesos — was considered very low, so that "the inhabitants make no more than the tiny share left after dividing with the trees' owner and his workers, almost nothing compared to the considerable profit made by the buyer." The treasury was also harmed, since the tax assessed was proportionately small; also compromised was the agriculture of the emerging town, "whose colonists, rather than developing [the economy], as they should by obligation, devote themselves to and distract themselves with things that produce nothing for them"; and estate owners were deprived of trees indispensable for their mills, as were the king and the state. Clouet said he did not know if the traders had authorization to export the cedar, but in any case he recommended that "its removal not be permitted except in boards or planks of a kind not to exceed three inches [in width]."[89]

The response from Havana, however, was that it would not be proper "to deprive the colonists of those means of subsistence allotted to them, all the more so for an article free [to be cut and used] on the rest of the island."[90] And even though removing the cedar in sawn pieces would be advantageous, it was felt that the conditions for this ideal did not exist. The matter was discussed by the island's Population Committee, which requested a report so that it could take the appropriate measures. The reply from Jagua indicated that in 1825, 1826, and 1827, 36 ships left the port loaded with cedar, mahogany, and guaiacum, including 22 boats from Great Britain, 11 from the United States, and 3 from the Netherlands. Although the pieces generally were straight, many came from curved trees that had been cut, and roots and branches were left in the woodlands, to be burned or left to rot "because they have no use except in shipbuilding, which does not exist in this port." In addition, "since the [granting of] complete freedom . . . in the cutting and use of wood," the area's estates had built their fences from the cedars on their land: "They cut the trunks for this purpose in pieces three to four varas long, then slice these into planks." This use of wood increased as a result of the division of estates into smaller farms (*potreros, estancias y sitios*), as a result of which, the report concluded, there was "good reason to fear that this District may experience what has occurred in that of Havana, where this kind of wood can no longer be found except at such great distances that the wood might as well be completely absent, so great are its transport costs for those who need it."[91]

In 1836 officials in Cienfuegos again insisted that the "undue commerce . . . in cedar and mahogany" threatened to "destroy completely a genus so necessary for this colony." They attributed this danger to the fact that "the immediate convenience of merchants makes them indifferent to the inevitable consequences of absolute lack [of wood], which is already experienced in an eight- or even ten-league radius around the town." At a time when sugar plantations were beginning to be established in the region, it was extremely important to restrain the increasing outflow of wood overseas and to other points on the island. Six *ingenios* were then in development, and inhabitants of Trinidad and other localities were buying land "that finds itself in incompetent hands which seek only to exploit natural production while ignoring industrial production." The Cienfuegos leaders feared that shortages of wood would lead many entrepreneurs to abandon such efforts, since they would be unable to find "sufficient lumber for their workshops." But the response from Havana was the same, accepting only the suggestion to increase "somewhat the tax that is assessed."[92]

The trade in wood through the Cienfuegos Bay increased as the land in the region was occupied by sugar. From 1825 to 1829, 62 ships sailed from the port with a capacity of 6,741 metric tons; from 1830 to 1834 the number of ships dropped to 54, but they had a greater total capacity (6,815 metric tons); and from 1835 to 1839, 87 ships carried wood, with a total capacity of 11,147 metric tons — in other words, a total of 1,337,333 cubic feet of wood in fifteen years.[93] This was one of the examples used by Commander General of the Navy José Primo de Rivera in 1845 and 1846 to request an absolute ban on the exportation of wood. This amount was enough for thirty forty-four-cannon frigates (each 44,000 ft^3) and did not include the enormous waste of curved pieces.[94] The fruit of these efforts was the decision by the island's Superior Authorities Committee, on June 21, 1845, to prohibit the export of wood through bays, beaches, and coves not authorized to engage in foreign trade. This was insufficient for the navy commander, however, as was putting a heavy tax on the export of wood.

Primo de Rivera argued that there were no longer trees appropriate for building materials within 3 leagues of bays such as those of Mariel, Bahía Honda, Matanzas, San Juan de los Remedios, Nipe, Guantánamo, Jagua, and others that had been full "of virgin woodlands until recently." If efforts were not made to conserve and increase these forests, lumber would be lacking in the places most in need of it; there would also be effects such as drought and shortages of wood "at a time when the number of steam engines on land and sea is increasing so rapidly, many of them sustained exclusively with firewood." As a result, he felt trade in wood with foreigners was inappropriate: "Its scant usefulness for the country in no way compensates the wealth that is taken from it, whose concession only benefits those who increase the power of their navies and merchant marines." As this was happening, from the beginning of the century to 1841 "the best-provisioned cash boxes on the island" bought ships abroad worth 4 million pesos, "it being well worth noting that none of them was larger than a corvette or lasted six years, as a result of the simplicity of their construction." As further reason he observed that shipments of wood to Spain's arsenals could no longer be made because of the artificial raising of prices by foreign firms.[95]

The limits on the wood trade agreed to by the Superior Authorities Committee apparently did not have much impact. An 1846 article in the *Diario de la Marina*, based on an analysis of Cuba's balance of trade between 1841 and 1845, insisted that some obstacle should be placed on this commerce "because, thanks to the freedom introduced a few years ago, these lush forests, pride and source of wealth of the Queen of the Antilles, are disappearing." In addition to the considerable increase in exports of cedar and mahogany, the author of the article claimed that the same thing was happening with other woods that were not recorded, such as fustete, guaiacum, lancewood, and granadillo.[96] Five years later in the *Memorias de la Sociedad Económica* the same tendency was confirmed in the export of mahogany and cedar from 1849 to 1850. For this reason the article supported the ban on export through unauthorized ports, the root of the illicit trade, "a very different thing from the free permission to dispose of forests in the undefined use of property and for the benefit of the major crops that constitute our country's agricultural wealth."[97]

In 1849 the director of the *Diario de la Marina* engaged Rodríguez Ferrer to write an in-depth article on the destruction of the forests. In it the naturalist listed several causes that he would explore further in *Naturaleza y civilización de la grandiosa Isla de Cuba* (1876). He divided these into causes that brought no good to the country — outdated agricultural methods, poor division of lands and "the evil of jointly owned estates," and the distance and uncertainty of state-owned property as well as the ease with which they were made available for clearing — and those that could have some positive consequences, "although disproportional and quite ephemeral," including landowners' speculation with the wood of their forests and the "increasing consumption by railroads and *ingenio* machinery, whose daily feeding would no doubt astound us if we endeavored to calculate it." The first led to clandestine logging as well as to "the annihilation, burning, or rotting of what should have value on the market or, being conserved, bring to the country the benefit of rain." As for the railroads and *ingenios*, he pleaded for caution, but with the right of the civil service to enlighten landowners about their suitability and to promote replanting. Specifically, he recommended setting up sawmills in the countryside, as well as "economical furnaces and charcoal, paraíso trees and wild cane" in order to "diminish the impact of steam engines on forests and timber."[98]

Rodríguez Ferrer referred especially to the removal of wood by foreigners that resulted from uncertainty about state-owned property and speculation by landowners. He gave several examples for the western area of the island, such as the destruction in the colony of Moa "of the wealth of abundant ebony by the Americans" and the logging in Cabo Cruz paid for by the English, who were "disposing of all the sabicú whose trunks are at least eight inches high and eight varas wide for twelve and sixteen pesos." In the same region was the port of Manzanillo, which from the opening of its customs house in August 1827 to September 1847 exported, among other woods, 282,813 varas of mahogany, 245,335 varas of cedar, 219,209 quintals of fustete, and 27,617 of granadillo. As for fustete, a forest tree used for ink and which was already rare throughout the island, Rodríguez Ferrer was informed by a merchant in Guantánamo that "from the year 1825 to 1840 three thousand tons a year had been shipped from this one port . . . [and] sold in Santiago de Cuba for twenty to twenty-one pesos."[99]

Rodríguez Ferrer also deplored the disappearance of pinewoods, which affected civil construction and the turpentine and tar industries. In his travels through the island he also noted "the evils caused by drought," which "already have changed even the intertropical physiognomy of many locations." Faced with such an alarming situation, he proposed requiring the planting of mango trees, especially in the mountains. Although mango wood had no value, the trees provided food for animals, as well as cool shade in very degraded and sterile areas. In a commentary that followed the naturalist's article, the director of *Diario de la Marina*, Araujo de Lira, was harshly critical of landowners for their carelessness: "They have neither seen nor want to see . . . and since it is said that they in fact have the right to dispose of their property, after they are warned, they will have to race to the precipice and bury themselves there. At last they will have been landowners!"[100]

The 1815 agreement limiting foreign trade in precious woods to authorized ports remained in effect with the proviso in 1846 that transport of these woods would be tolerated on rafts towed by domestic and foreign boats, whose mother ship had to remain in an authorized port as security. According to Félix Erenchún's *Anales de la Isla de Cuba*, in the mid-1850s there were 73 wood-trading firms in the country, 43 in the eastern half and 30 in the western. But while the west had 21 warehouses for lumber and boards, none were recorded for the east. A similar statistic is the 25 sawmills on the island, 18 steam-powered ones and 4 ordinary ones in the west and only 3 ordinary sawmills in the east.[101] About the wood trade, Rodríguez Ferrer affirmed that "during my many years of residence in Puerto Príncipe, I met a number of foreigners who lived there as representatives of different foreign companies and firms with no other mission than to buy caballerías of woodlands to cut down and harvest."[102]

The town of Santa Cruz, on the southern coast of the jurisdiction of the same name, was one of the most active centers for the wood export trade. In 1850 the port captain ordered that tree trunks left on the beach be collected and their owners store them in more appropriate places. His decree was supported by the fact that the beach was in the navy's jurisdiction, but it provoked immediate protest, "since it will entirely paralyze the only trade that now exists." The captain's measure clashed with the residents' desire for exemptions similar to those in ports that had been important sites in the wood trade, such as Nuevitas and Cienfuegos. To the complaint submitted to the Colonization Protection Committee, the navy official replied that he could not agree to "there being, between the fury of the sea and the houses, projectiles that could obstruct them after a few hours of bad weather." As wood arrived in the port, he said, it should be loaded for shipment abroad, "since this is most appropriate to avoid for the owners the mishaps caused by inclement weather."[103] In 1856 one of the businesses cited in the proceedings, the Compañía del Comercio de Manzanillo, requested permission to load in the coves of Júcaro and Vertientes wood that had been extracted from the vicinity, owing to the "prejudice incurred by having to transport them to the ports of Trinidad and Santa Cruz, thirty leagues distant."[104]

Around these coves is the port of Tunas de Zaza, regarding which a new debate emerged about forest conservation. In November 1857 the German Friedrich Naumann, a resident of and businessman in Sancti Spíritus, petitioned for permission to remove wood that he had brought to this location when he learned that it would become an authorized export site. Given the delay in putting this authorization into effect, Naumann requested that following the unloading in Matanzas of the brigantine *Gazelle* the ship "be permitted to proceed and enter in ballast . . . to confirm the loading of the wood."[105] In January 1858 he again petitioned for the same vessel and for one *Margarita*, which was leaving Bremen, Germany, bound directly for the port of Zaza. The administrator of terrestrial income ruled that the exception could be made for one occasion, on the condition that the ships formalize their registry in Trinidad.

The administrator of marine income opposed this solution, however, as did the Accounting Office, which furthermore proposed "the absolute ban on extracting shipbuilding lumber that produces the ships found on this island." It based this opinion on the principle that all nations "maintain their integrity and are respected because of their Navy," which would be threatened "if the petty interest of individuals consummated the acceler-ated eradication of Cuba's woodlands." It was essential that "the wood not be removed . . . , [to the point that we reach] the lamentable extreme of see-ing houses and roofs far from the capital made from foreign wood that is expensive and not durable."[106] If the removal of precious wood could not be banned, the Accounting Office asked that it at least be heavily taxed.

The Superintendence of the Treasury took a different posture, recalling that in 1815 an end had been put to the authority the navy had enjoyed "since time immemorial" to prevent logging, and on this matter it requested a report from the attorney general. In his reply, the latter acknowledged that the navy was at the vanguard of "national enhancement," but he observed that although forest conservation was essential this did not mean landown-ers should be obstructed in their right "to dispose of their forests freely, according to Article 3 of the Royal Edict of 1815, whose sovereign precept so favors them that it denies the State the right to purchase [*tanteo*]." In addi-tion to favoring livestock farming over tobacco and other crops, "because of the pastures and shade," the reservation for the navy was incompatible "with the sacred right of property, or with the desirable development of woodlands and fields." If privately owned woodland areas were necessary for shipbuilding, the state could always forcibly seize the land, but this was unnecessary because "the coastlines, including high tide and twenty varas more of sea room, have ample precious woods." State-owned lands "could remain under the exclusive dominion of the State" and, with an ordinance "adapted to the country's circumstances . . . and thanks to a good regime of cutting and clearing, reproduction would continue infallibly given the fertility of the island's soils and forests will become eternal, without the slightest difficulty."[107]

Naumann's petition was finally resolved by the opening of the port of Zaza. But the general question remained of the appropriateness of current legislation on the cutting and exportation of wood. In this respect, the superintendent indicated that the navy's need for lumber could be met "by reserving for its use and benefit the forests considered sufficient." In this sense the commissioned study of state-owned land on the island would be extremely useful because instead of their trade in wood being impeded, "the owners of woods [should be] left in complete freedom to dispose of their property, as occurs with any other article of speculation."[108] Despite this optimism, the investigation into state-owned property was not very helpful, since the only jurisdictions it found to possess lumber were those of Manzanillo, Baracoa, Bayamo, Guantánamo, and Mantua.

The proceedings in the case of Naumann's request for a permit entailed the reiteration of the agreement not to allow export of wood through unauthorized ports. On February 23, 1859, it was announced that the 1845 measures remained in effect, that permits became invalid, and that "in the future no petitions will be accepted or studied that request such concessions, nor will anything contrary to the present measures."[109] Three years later permission was denied an English company to remove wood purchased in Puerto Príncipe and held in the port of Mayanabo, which was closed without warning.[110]

The war of 1868–78 contributed to a reduction in the wood trade, since it took place in the center east of the island, where most of the forests were located. This does not mean that the commerce disappeared entirely: for example, the liquidation of duties for pieces of wood shows an increase from 32,550 pieces in 1875–76 to 39,369 in 1876–77.[111] The wood trade often combined export with supply of the domestic market. In the 1850s, for example, different companies were created that had both objectives, such La Explotadora, S.A., founded in 1857. It proposed, among other goals, (1) to exploit the greatest area of forests possible, providing as much lumber as possible for industry and for families; (2) to raze forests for its own benefit and that of others, harvesting the wood when the clearings were for agriculture; (3) to establish logging operations at as many locations as was judged appropriate; (4) to supply docks, wharves, mills, and the like or provide the wood needed for these purposes; (5) to export and import lumber of as many types as were needed for buildings and other purposes; (6) to supply crossties for railroads and firewood to fuel machines and for all applications in this sector; (7) to facilitate the construction of boats, launches, coastal vessels, and ships of greater draft, as well as the repairs they require; and (8) to provide lumber of all dimensions and qualities for piles, telegraph lines, carts, mills, and other objects. It also proposed to establish sawmills in towns and in the countryside, to buy ones already in service, and to purchase woodlands, lands, and estates for forest exploitation.[112] This list of goals gives an idea of some of the applications for which wood was used on the island, not taking into account the many other products of Cuba's forests.

Despite this and in keeping with the vanishing of forests as the plantations advanced, Cuba became a major importer of wood from the United States.[113] The origins of this commerce, as we have seen, went back to 1772, the goal being to replace the cedar used in sugar crates with cypress from Louisiana. The trade was maintained unproblematically until the sugar boom and the warfare of the 1790s.[114] The lack of wood from New Orleans for crates was first experienced in 1796, as a result of floods that had affected sawmills along the Mississippi the summer before. This and other factors, such as the absence of buyers in Havana and a lack of ships and warehouses for the cargo, led the price to increase to 14 reales per crate. It was believed at the time that wood for crates would not be lacking by the following harvest, since the shortage was thought to result from short-term circumstances, and that prices would return to their ordinary level.[115] Three years later, however, the shortage of containers was much worse.

In September 1799 twelve *ingenio* owners petitioned the Royal Consulate of Agriculture, Industry, and Commerce expressing their fear of an "absolute lack of cypress to build crates in which to pack their produce."[116] The situation was worsened by the imminence of the harvest and by the urgent need for at least a third of the containers. The war brought a great shortage and high prices of wood for crates, which cost up to 20 reales in 1798 and 26 reales in 1799. In the latter year many growers had to use crates made of jobo, pine boards from the United States, casks, vats, and even vases and flour barrels. Fears increased because the 1799–1800 harvest produced 170,000 crates' worth of sugar, to which had to be added the sugar on estates along the coast and that which remained unloaded in the market. In the estate owners' opinion, the only solution was to authorize the United States and neutral nations to ship wood from New Orleans to Havana.

The solution to the container problem subsequently centered on obtaining permanent authorization for U.S. traders to import wood into Cuba in exchange for molasses from the *ingenios*, which according to advocates did not interfere with trade with Spain. In January 1802 Francisco de Arango y Parreño, syndic of the Royal Consulate, told the panel that the island needed to supply itself with articles that could not be obtained through domestic commerce, beginning with all types of wood from the United States.[117] He pointed out that it was so cheap that many estate owners hauled it up 10 or 12 leagues to their mills and that without this trade the consumption of Cuba's wood and the destruction of its forests would have been greater. In April of the same year a new petition was sent to Spain, which began by mentioning the shortage and high price of wood in the Havana jurisdiction owing to restrictions imposed to benefit the navy. About two hundred thousand crates were needed, in addition to the great consumption of boards, rafters, and other pieces "for the innumerable quantity of houses, machines, pieces of furniture, and other public and private buildings that have been built in recent years with wood from the North." For the New Orleans merchants, there was no reason to fear competition, since the abundance of cypress and the ease of transport along the river allowed them to sell wood for crates more cheaply.[118]

The container shortage worsened with the imminent onset of the harvest. In October 1802 the Royal Consulate requested permission for the North Americans to import 150,000 containers, failing which the "sugar might be entirely lost."[119] The uncertainty was all the greater because New Orleans was unable to provide about a third of the wood needed until the end of the harvest and because of Spain's cession of Louisiana to France, "which was already considered certain." In addition the Tobacco Agency (Factoría de Tabacos) needed a supply of 300,000 board feet, and more would be needed for the general use of the population, which was "calculated by informed people at a third of what is used for sugar." The consulate did not share the royal treasury's opinion that wood for containers should be obtained on the island, "when the fact remains that jobo, in addition to being quite distant and remote, requires preparation time that we no longer have." In conclusion the consulate members recalled "the repeated negative responses" of the navy for the use of cedar, and yet they conceded that the wood could not be used owing to the lack of time and the high cost for containers, which entailed a significant surcharge, "since we cannot do any better for them in European markets,"[120] where nothing was paid for containers.

The importation of wood from the United States did not occur without controversy, especially after wood was declared free from tariffs. This motivated José de Arango to write his essay on jobo, in which he declared it a disgrace that Cubans paid U.S. companies a tribute of more than 600,000 pesos for their boards. As a remedy he proposed making sugar containers from jobo, a wood that had fallen in disrepute as a result of the difficult circumstances of its use when wood for crates was in short supply, "without attending to the waning or waxing of the moon and with no subsequent benefit than to saw them, making them into crates, and fill them with sugar." This led the sugar to become moist "with the sap of green boards," which led to "our striving to recommend what comes from elsewhere and to discredit our own resources."[121]

To show the advantages of jobo Arango cited experiences such as that of the Marquis del Arcos, who always packed his sugar in this wood, selling more than forty thousand crates of all grades. The marquis sought to convince others that jobo, when appropriately prepared, made better containers than pine or even cedar, among other reasons because, unlike those woods, it gave off no odor. Its only disadvantage was that it was difficult to saw, but even so jobo crates were 40 percent cheaper than cedar ones, "which are being used today [for this purpose] to the detriment of more notable applications." Arango recommended that authorities focus on increasing the number of sawmills and noted that, since not all types of wood introduced were used in sugar crates, royal tariffs should be applied to all of them equally, to stimulate the national industry.[122]

A November 1817 petition signed by twenty Cuban wood merchants stressed the same arguments, complaining of grave losses "due to the excessive introduction of American boards absolutely duty free, while our woods, whether uncut or sawn, pay 6 percent." After citing Arango's essay on jobo, they denounced the use of two-thirds of the imported boards for other purposes: "Generally they are employed as can be seen in the enormous pieces in bullfighting rings, horse pens, the building and repair of vessels, as well as the construction of houses and the fences of large gates, gardens, and country homes." Domestic businessmen could not compete on such an uneven playing field. The petitioners cited the steam-powered sawmill established in Havana by Enrique Disdier "when the Americans, at war with the British, did not bring boards" and dismantled when these imports resumed. To make matters worse, the Americans clandestinely took "from our own forests the wood that they then sell us manufactured."

The object of the petition was to have foreign wood taxed "so long as the need for pine finds no more support than a steady worry"; meanwhile they agreed with "the just relief of freeing from tax our woods destined for domestic consumption."[123]

The administrator of royal income, Diego J. Sedano, replied to the petition that imported wood's freedom from duties had been repealed. As for the difference between its use for containers and its use for other civilian purposes, he did not see this as prejudicial, since "so long as the country's wood sector is not sufficient to replace it, we must not lose" the option of importing foreign wood. Other reasons to deny the petition included the rapid increase in the population and in the receipts of the royal treasury. What is clear is that while the plantation lands were experiencing intense deforestation, the importation of U.S. wood increased. So, as the Cuban wood merchants made their complaint, estate owners and businessmen in Matanzas were requesting the exemption from the tax on barrels for U.S. ships arriving with wood and leaving with molasses.[124]

The importation of wood continued to meet protest because of the contradiction entailed by the island's still extensive forests. During the 1847 harvest, faced with a shortage and high price of containers, some planters again argued that they should be made from jobo and cedar, "where abundance permits." This would open "a new path for local industry considerably prejudiced by its foreign counterparts." These farmers correspondingly requested that the tare per container be reduced from 50 to 40 pounds, in accordance with the lesser weight of these two woods.[125] And yet this type of request was more than ever a product of its circumstances. The import of U.S. wood increased almost as fast as the export of Cuban sugar. According to an 1818 report by Sedano, 7,466,098.5 feet of boards per year arrived in Havana in 1815 and 1816, an average that increased to about 18 million feet a year from 1860 to 1864.[126] Another source indicates that between 1866 and 1875 the port of Havana received an annual average of 18,670,000 feet of boards, 470,376 box pieces, and 32,354 cask pieces.[127] Most used during this period were crates with a capacity of 16 to 22 arrobas for refined sugar and casks with a capacity of 40 to 60 arrobas for unrefined sugar. The import of pieces gave rise to a container-assembly industry on the island, which became "an industry worth millions of pesos per harvest."[128]

It is possible to find sources that contradict an increasing importation of wood. The 1845 balance of trade, which analyzes the previous five years, recorded an increasing export of precious woods and a nearly 50 percent decline in the import of foreign wood, with an especially marked reduction in pine boards. Nonetheless, these reductions were short term.[129] Over the course of the nineteenth century, the main ports in plantation areas became, like Havana, entry points for large amounts of U.S. wood, used for containers and diverse urban and rural purposes. We could conclude that this slowed somewhat the rapid disappearance of Cuba's forests but also limited the development of a system of forest exploitation aimed at the domestic market and based on the conservation and regeneration of the harvested resource.

Steps to Organize the Exploitation of Forests and Reticence in the Colony

In 1812, a long and conflict-ridden process began in Spain known as the *desamortización* (disentailment), through which vast tracts of land passed into private ownership. According to Erich Bauer, the coronation of Fernando VII and the consequent repeal of the Cádiz laws on woodlands and small fields (*plantíos*) led to a certain moderation, with measures such as those of 1818, which organized the sale of communal woodlands, whether owned privately or by the state, but without negative impact on the woodlands indispensable for each town's supply of firewood, lumber, and acorns. Nevertheless, in Bauer's opinion, political changes in 1833 led to the progressive annulment of these "prudent restrictions."[130]

General Woodlands Ordinances were enacted that year that again declared privately owned woodlands "absolutely free." A few critics argued that the effects of these laws were negligible given their theoretical nature, inspired by the French forest code of 1827 without a sufficient adaptation to conditions in Spain and undermined by unpropitious circumstances linked to the Carlist War of 1833–40. Other observers saw them as evidence of growing awareness of the need to counter the increasing degradation of woodlands, as noted by scientists linked to the Madrid Botanical Garden and the Economic Societies. Vicente Casals Costa underlined their importance "to the extent that they were the matrix that inspired, with more or less substantial variations, all of the forest legislation of the nineteenth century."[131] In particular, the creation of the General Directorate of Woodlands to administer state-owned property and that under public trusteeship showed the need for employees trained in forest science, a discipline that was being developed to increasing sophistication in countries like Germany. In Spain, creation of the Special School of Woodlands Engineers was ordered in 1835, although its definitive inauguration was delayed for various reasons until January 1848.

This teaching center and the later constitution, by its graduates, of the Woodlands Engineers Corps, following the royal decree of October 18, 1853, played an important role in solidifying a modern forest administration and modern forest policies in Spain.[132] It was a complicated relationship, since at the same time measures favoring the individualization of agrarian property reached their apex. Josefina Gómez Mendoza argues that "because of the disentailments (1821–23, 1833–49, and after 1855) Spain's true forested area declined during the nineteenth century from a quarter to a tenth of its territory."[133] Given this situation, forest engineers advocated the state's retaining control of the high woodlands (forests) richest in lumber because of their social and physical importance, since individual interest did not lead to their conservation. The engineers' judgment of the importance of forests was often included in disentailment measures and in forest laws.[134]

The wave of disentailments in Spain and the debate about their consequences had limited impact in Cuba. This was largely due to the old polemic over the ownership of woodlands. When the king granted absolute freedom to clear forests, he decreed that "although on this Island it seems that there are no woodlands intended for the common use of towns, there may be some that belong to my royal crown because they have not been distributed, sold, or composed; with respect to these the general rules dictated on this point will be observed." The survey of state-owned property remained neglected for several years, so that when another attempt was made to investigate state woodlands, their size was not known. In 1853 the Superintendence of the Treasury, which was charged with the study, claimed not to know "whether [woodlands] actually exist that are designated or known as such, unless they are the mangrove swamps that line the island's coasts and those points where the Royal Navy has its lumber logging sites." The situation was further complicated by the fact that as soon as state-owned land was discovered, "it is immediately alienated for the purposes of agriculture or whatever benefit one seeks."[135]

That the metropole and the colony were out of phase on forest matters was well known. While the former stepped back from the Cádiz measures on woodlands and small fields in 1814, the latter reaffirmed its postulates barely a year later. From then on, private interests jealously defended the privilege they had obtained to freely dispose of forests, opposing any attempt at limitation by the central administration. This occurred when the metropole began to show interest in what had happened since 1815, through the royal order of December 10, 1844, issued by the Ministry of the Navy, Commerce, and Overseas Government, which inquired about the effects of free clearing on the island. The reply of the Development Committee was categorical: the reforms "having been so fortunate and satisfactory, as can be measured by the present state of agriculture, without presenting the least drawback, or giving rise to the slightest complaint, the Committee whose creation was ordered has had no reason to meet, limiting itself to being installed in May 1816."[136]

But not everyone in the colony felt this way. In August 1845 Primo de Rivera, the commander of the navy, sent to the court his reflections on the need for measures that would cut out at the root "the abuse that is done in the extraction of wood." Among other examples he included a letter from the commander of the register of Remedios reporting on the considerable removal from his coasts of all kinds of wood for foreign shipbuilding, bound especially for England.[137] In another letter to his superiors Primo de Rivera urged that a committee be established to protect the woodlands.[138] From the metropole the Overseas Committee for the Revising of Laws of the Indies agreed that measures were needed to develop and conserve forests "in favor of shipbuilding, whether military or commercial," according to a report by the War and Navy Commission. It criticized the effects of the 1812 measures but considered that it was still possible "to remedy what has been done" if landowners were roused from their apathy and supported "to achieve the conservation of such an important sector."[139] In short, a special solution should be found "through a Law that, while respecting property, cuts short the abuses that . . . owners believe they can commit," a law based partly on the principle "that woods cannot be thinned, burned, or subjected to any other risky operation without previous permission from the civil authority." A navy expert would mark trees so they would be preserved until they attained sufficient size to be cut down or sold, preferably to the navy and the state. In the case of royally or communally owned woodlands, "if there still are any on the island," the Overseas Committee proposed that they be sold in order to avoid expense and that they enter "in the general measure, being balanced with those of private citizens."

The War and Navy Commission found that the royal edict of August 30, 1815, was "the foundation on which the organization of such an important sector should be based." The panel pointed in particular to the edict's

Article 5, which stipulated the creation of a committee to treat "with the proper care all that is considered useful and appropriate to the development of woodlands." As for the prerequisites, the committee members suggested various topics for debate: "This Committee must consider and act on the issue of property, which must be respected to the fullest degree; the Navy's interest in conserving lumber and its preference as a buyer for it; the correction of abuse in the cultivation and logging of trees to prevent forests from being razed out of pure caprice, with no use being made of the wood; and the measures of economy and vigilance that must be taken."[140] These were contradictory guidelines, a defense of private property rights combined with restrictions on logging by landowners. One result of this report was the royal edict of March 23, 1846, which ordered the creation of a woodlands protection commission, charged with drafting a woodlands ordinance. Until it took effect, clearing and thinning required permission of the Civil Superior Government, "which in order to grant it, may make optional visits to mark trees that are to be preserved."[141]

The first meeting of the Woodlands Protection Commission for the Island of Cuba took place on July 26, 1846. The commission was presided over by Captain General Leopoldo O'Donnell, and its members included, among others, the Count de Villanueva, superintendent of the treasury, and Primo de Rivera. Its first decision was to suspend the second point in the March 23 edict. To offset this, the commission determined that in addition to the 1845 ban on the export of wood from unauthorized ports, it would require certain dimensions for wood whose export was allowed. Both measures should have an indirect and discrete influence, "without attacking directly the right of ownership of woodlands."[142] Three days later, in a lengthy letter to the court, Count de Villanueva detailed the commission's reasoning, fearing that the act communicating the agreement did not express this clearly enough.[143] His arguments recall those made by Havana estate owners at the end of the eighteenth century.

The first part of the letter summarizes the situation prior to the royal edict of August 30, 1815, when there existed a "manifest violation of the right of property." In contrast, after this decree and that of July 16, 1819, which guaranteed "the property of estates in a stable and formal manner," together with free trade, "all the sources of public prosperity" grew surprisingly quickly. The application of Article 2 of the edict of March 23, 1846, in Villanueva's opinion, would entail falling back into disadvantages and abuses "that made revocation of the former prohibitions necessary."[144]

Villanueva acknowledged that after the 1815 and 1819 decrees part of the island's forests had been "cleared" (*descuajado*), but he noted that "at least two-thirds of its extensive length" remained wooded. In his judgment, the occasional need to move *ingenios* to virgin terrain, the growth of other agricultural sectors, and the export of lumber contributed to the reduction of woodlands, but never "with the gratuitously exaggerated celerity." Without a doubt, his concern was the need to extend the plantations at the expense of forests. After mentioning "the construction of many *ingenios* that has begun in wooded terrains," he summarized his true fears: "The dismantlement or division of the great woodland estates, so recommended by various royal resolutions and so necessary for the development of the white population, would be entirely blocked; and it would become impossible to move *ingenios* to virgin terrains, slowly diminishing their production until the exhaustion of the soil and the cost of maintaining it would require demolishing them, something that happens today with almost all where there have been more than forty harvests."[145]

His proposed remedy was to plant artificial forests to replace the destroyed natural ones. He invoked the *Informe sobre la ley agraria* (Report on the Agrarian Law; 1795) by Gaspar Melchor de Jovellanos, according to whom, as Villanueva paraphrased, woodlands could be increased only through the free dismantlement of estates and through the absolute freedom to clear woodlands. As an example, he observed that in some areas trees of construction timber had been planted in soils exhausted by agriculture. He concluded by insisting that the fear of wood shortages was exaggerated, since the colony's thick forests could provide all kinds of trees for the navy "for many scores of years." The consequences of the "antieconomic" order of March 23 could not be offset by "the possession of a few new warships"; nor could the lost income for the royal treasury be compensated by the wood trade. But the worst, most inevitable outcome would be "the progressive decline of the sugar industry."[146]

The superintendent's letter had the desired effect: that December 10 another royal edict approved the agreement reached by the Woodlands Protection Commission in its first meeting, although only provisionally until the woodlands ordinances that the panel had been charged with drafting were complete.[147] Nevertheless, once this objective was reached, the colony's lack of interest in regulating forest exploitation again became clear. Three years later nothing had been done, and in an apparent delaying tactic the Woodlands Protection Commission asked the Secretariat of State and of the

Government of the Kingdom for documents relative to discussions of the woodlands sector in Spain's current logging operations and regulations.[148]

From then on the insistence on the need to adopt measures for the exploitation and conservation of Cuban forests was led by state forest administrators in Spain. At the end of 1852 the director of the Special School of Woodlands Engineers proposed sending three brigades of woodlands engineers to perform a scientific survey and propose plans to develop the forests of the Philippines, Puerto Rico, and Cuba, with the aim of containing logging that could severely prejudice agriculture and the navy. Referring specifically to Cuba, he wrote:

> The Cuban woodlands, bountiful as they are little known in the island's interior, are experiencing on the coast and plains the effects of destructive logging by the sugar industry, which is so developed there and its *ingenios* so dependent on plentiful and inexpensive fuel. This threatening evil can already be witnessed on the west coast, not only in the high price of this resource but, even more grave and prejudicial, in alterations of climate and in long and [previously] unknown droughts.[149]

Thus began a slow process of implanting a modern forest administration in Cuba, as we will see in the next chapter. Part of these efforts was the early work, amid vicissitudes and difficulties, of the first graduates of the Special School of Woodlands Engineers. The outbreak of war in 1868 provided another reason for delaying this work, since the areas where the insurrection was strongest were also the ones with the most forest, and especially the most public woodlands.

In 1876 the Woodlands Ordinances for Cuba and Puerto Rico were finally promulgated. By coincidence, this was also the year when Rodríguez Ferrer's *Naturaleza y civilización de la grandiosa Isla de Cuba* was published in Madrid. Offering his conclusions on what had occurred since 1815, the naturalist observed that his contemporaries had paid far less heed to the subject of woodlands "than the legislative attention that our ancestors dedicated to this sector." How to use the forests had been left to the caprice of passing need or made into an object "of permanent profit and vandalic speculation," in private as well as public woodlands. "In Cuba, which in terms of cane and the sugar industry has attained the ultimate progress of practice and science[,] . . . nothing relative to woodlands, their conservation and yield, has led to a single forward step." This was due, above all, to the fact that "above the interest in conserving woodlands is . . . the more immediate interest of sugar, beside whose fabulous product all the woodlands are little, in its development and fuel." In an observation that conformed with the opinions of Spain's Woodlands Corps and of scientists and other observers aware of the grave consequences of Cuba's accelerated deforestation, Rodríguez Ferrer expressed the basic logic of the change that would be attempted beginning in 1876: "All the more so if private citizens operate without looking further than their individual interest, it is the duty of governments to defend and protect at all costs the collective interest; and the first thing needed in Cuba is to catalog the state's woodlands, which requires a preliminary survey, determining ownership, studying species and their distribution, and calculating their size and stock."[150]

5

Centralization
of the Sugar Industry
and the Forests,
1876–1898

The Transition from Ingenio
to Central and the Forests

In the last third of the nineteenth century Cuba experienced a technical and organizational transformation known as the concentration and centralization of the sugar industry. It was not entirely unprecedented, and the process did not end with the beginning of the twentieth century, but this first phase was decisive.[1] During this time there began to take shape some of the main reformist aspirations to leave behind the slavery-based system of production by separating the agricultural and manufacturing sectors of agroindustry. Increasingly, the tendency was to process the greatest quantity of cane possible in mills equipped with the era's most advanced industrial technology. Thus emerged the *central*, amid vast cane plantations that, unlike in previous periods, did not need to belong to the same owner (see figure 5.1).

FIGURE 5.1. Landscape of the Caridad *ingenio central* in Rancho Veloz, area of Sagua la Grande.

(*Informe sobre el censo de Cuba, 1899* [Washington, DC: Government Printing Office, 1900])

Different factors contributed to the centralization of sugar production and decentralization of sugar supply. On the one hand, the circumstances of the international sugar market, with competition from European beet sugar and other cane producers such as Java and Hawaii, combined with low price levels. On the other hand, there was increasing mechanization and the successful experiments of other producing areas in the separation of cultivation from refining and in new work regimes. The process of the abolition of slavery, finally accomplished in 1886, accelerated the transition.[2] The principal solution to the related problems was the *colonato*, a system composed of producers with different backgrounds, former slaves, who supplied the *central* with its raw material.[3] The Ten Years' War (1868–78) had a direct impact, destroying many sugar farms on the eastern half of the island and forcing a pause in eastward expansion.

The appearance of the mechanized *ingenio* in the middle of the century largely marked the end of the sugar industry's itinerant character. Production growth based on farms that exploited the same terrain for thirty or forty years, then moved on to other virgin areas, was not very compatible with the great investments required by mills that were increasingly expensive, large, and technologically complex. The framework of the *ingenio* as a unit of production that encompassed the agricultural and refining sectors entailed more rapid exhaustion of forest reserves and high cane yields, which were in great part responsible for the plantations' profitability. Both issues commanded the attention of people who wrote about the sugar industry from the mid-1800s.

The Count de Pozos Dulces, his brother José Jacinto de Frías y Jacott, Alvaro Reynoso, Ramón de La Sagra, and other contemporaries expressed serious reservations about the viability of large-scale production combined with large-scale cultivation on the same farm. La Sagra's reflections on his trip to Cuba in 1859–60 are typical. After visiting a mechanized *ingenio*, with *al vacío* boilers and centrifuges, a "beautiful farm" on which "all is grandiose," he asked, "Is all this useful? Is all this necessary?" The matter required fuller examination, and any conclusion could be premature, but he was at least disconcerted by "this complex assemblage of highly costly apparatuses, compared with the simplicity and wealth of the juice they refine." After noting the method of a French scientist for obtaining sugar by sunlight and after clarifying that he was not suggesting that all this modern production apparatus be replaced, he wrote, "What I am trying to do is call attention to the simple methods used by the great resources of nature, preferable to the complicated systems that seem, on the contrary, to flee nature, seeking in industry costly auxiliaries."[4]

Despite reservations of this type, technology triumphed, although its implantation was slow. For Manuel Moreno Fraginals, the mechanized *ingenio* launched the Cuban industrial revolution: it doubled industrial yields, improved quality, and separated the agricultural from the refining sectors. It was "the germ of the great *central*."[5] In 1860, 4.86 percent of sugar farms qualified as mechanized *ingenios*, but they produced 14.8 percent of the country's sugar. After the early experiments, they most commonly were constructed as a new type of mill. Between 1876 and 1898 new machines were set up as well as large *trapiches* to crush cane, triple-effect evaporators and centrifuges for the separation of molasses and sugar became widespread, as did implements such as shakers, choppers, and clearing pans (*defecadoras*). According to Fe Iglesias García, during these years Cuba began to import the most important technology for large-scale sugar production.[6] Chemistry laboratories were established to aid in refining, green-pulp burners became common, bringing greater energy efficiency, and important efforts were made to improve the agricultural sector (see figure 5.2).

The industrial modernization of Cuban sugar production was accompanied by a greater concentration of exports toward the U.S. market. The

FIGURE 5.2. Interior of the Caracas *central*, area of Cienfuegos, province of Santa Clara.

(*Informe sobre el censo de Cuba, 1899* [Washington, DC: Government Printing Office, 1900])

increasing development of the refining industry in the United States led to the creation of the so-called Sugar Trust, with seventeen businesses and twenty mills grouped in 1891 into the America Sugar Refining Company, and Cuban producers were required to specialize in the production of raw sugar of 96 degrees polarization, which could be achieved only through the standardization permitted by the use of centrifuges. Simultaneously sugar began to be shipped in bags, which kept the product fresh longer. In 1890 the U.S. Congress approved a protectionist duty known as the McKinley Tariff, which favored the importation of raw sugar and made the introduction of refined sugar more expensive. Under these circumstances Cuba and the United States signed a commercial reciprocity treaty that stayed in effect from 1891 and 1894 and was decisive in the growth of the Cuban sugar industry.[7] Thanks to this stimulus the threshold of 1 million tons of sugar for a single harvest was passed in 1892, and 1894 saw the greatest harvest of the century: 1,110,991 metric tons.

Unlike the increases of earlier periods, the increase in sugar production from 1878 to 1894 was caused not by a greater number of producing units but by the greater production capacity of the new *centrales* and the disappearance of farms that were less technologically advanced. In 1877, 1,200 *ingenios* were recorded on the whole island, with 958 of them on the western half. The record crop of 1894, in contrast, was processed by about 400 mills. The 1899 census reported about 600 sugar farms destroyed by the war of 1895–98, of which 217 were judged likely to be able to restart production in the more or less short term.[8]

If the average area of an *ingenio* in 1860 was a little more than 40 caballerías, or 100 caballerías including the largest ones, with in both cases half the land in cane, at the beginning of the 1890s the average *central* required about 100 caballerías of cane fields. As Oscar Zanetti indicates, this entailed, under the old production scheme, pushing the investment potential "to prohibitive limits."[9] In this sense the generalization of the *colonato* resulted both from changes in the work regime and from the set of transformations that eventually required the separation of cane refining from its cultivation. The success of the two phases' interconnection depended on costly investments in private railways to transport the cane to the *central*, to workshops, or to warehouses, as well as on obtaining privileges allowing the grower to use certain local resources, such as private ports to load and ship the product.

The process that culminated in large-scale industrial sugar production produced a new offensive on Cuban forests. In this case one can differentiate what happened on the western half of the island from what occurred on the eastern half. On the former, much land already had been occupied by sugar, so the pattern was the creation of large *centrales* from already existing parcels. For example, at the end of the 1870s, the province of Matanzas had 517 *ingenios*; in 1899 it had 271 (120 of which had been dismantled) and 354 cane *colonias* (farms supplying *ingenios centrales*). In 1899, the total amount of land dominated by sugar in the province was 21,108 caballerías, about 5,000 more than had been recorded in 1860 as belonging to the 442 *ingenios* in the jurisdictions of Matanzas, Cárdenas, and Colón. Nevertheless, the total cultivated area fell from 14,355 caballerías in 1862 to 11,087 in 1895. During the same time, forests declined from 19.3 percent (7,384 caballerías) to 8.4 percent (3,909) of the surface area. By contrast, the total share of territory in livestock farms and arid land, which in 1862 was 41 percent of the jurisdiction of Matanzas, Cárdenas, and Colón, increased by 1899 to 81.7 percent in the categories of livestock farms (*potreros y haciendas de crianza*) and "unproductive" terrain.[10]

The occupation of the province's forested areas may have been more significant during the Ten Years' War, but this does not mean that it ceased afterward. The colonization process did not entail a radical break with ancestral practices of cutting, burning, and planting. On the contrary, in many cases it helped extend them to unexpected distances, again with the help of railroads, now also used to transport cane. In this sense public railroad companies played an important role, and private ones proliferated. Both were important agents in the transformation of space, promoting expansion to the most remote regions and linking the cane fields of old properties with the new mills. In short, "the railroad would become a decisive element in the process of centralizing agrarian property, one that would make the large latifundist plantation the typical economic unit of the sugar sector" (see figure 5.3).[11]

Partly responsible for the end of the sugar industry's itinerant nature, the emergence of the *central* also promoted the formation of ever larger cane plantations. The technological modernization that allowed planters to forgo firewood and convert many former *ingenios* into cane colonies made the forests that had survived previous eras appealing terrain for new cane fields. The *central* and the use of railroads for cane transport led to a new colonization of territories long occupied by sugar. The *Revista de agricultura* noted in 1890 that "the railroads extended their iron tentacles in search of new, fertile colonies, and one day two *ingenios* that a few years before had been separated by thick forest found themselves at the end of the rail lines, fighting over some area of recognized value for cultivation."[12]

A slightly different case from the same Colón Plain was the expansion of the rail networks of Matanzas and of Cárdenas and Júcaro toward the south in the 1870s and 1880s. The goal was to exploit one of the few parts of the province that sugar had not yet reached, at a time when the older sugar regions were beginning to show signs of exhaustion. For example, in 1888 the *Diario de la Marina* said of the lands around the town of Colón: "The yield here has become nothing, completely losing the reputation of being . . . the main sugar center."[13] In contrast, the new territories traversed by the public railroads of Matanzas, heading south toward Jagüey Grande and southeast toward Yaguaramas, were more promising. In 1882 *La nueva era* wrote of the transformation of the Santa Isabel *ingenio* into a modern *central*, located in Calimete and owned by Carlos de La Rosa: "He plans to link the San Pablo *ingenio* to the aforementioned farm and extend a rail line to Jagüey Grande, passing through virgin terrain, on which, given the good prices now offered, cane surely will soon be planted."[14]

But the real offensive on the forests in sugar's process of concentration and centralization came from the outside the old plantation regions. The

FIGURE 5.3. Railroad for transporting sugarcane, late nineteenth century.
(*Informe sobre el censo de Cuba, 1899* [Washington, DC: Government Printing Office, 1900])

forests again largely became the hope for overcoming the crisis in the sector. If the dominant tendency at first was to establish a *central* in an area where several *ingenios* already existed, the end of the war in 1878 was one of several incentives to renew sugar's eastward movement.

The new big *centrales* and the *colonato* were the prevailing solution to the crisis caused in the industry by the drop in prices; they were also the main motor of socioeconomic reconstruction after the war. On the western half of the island this led to lower production costs and on the eastern half to a more effective means of economic reactivation of territories affected by the conflict.[15] In both cases a source of income was created for an impoverished population, which in supplying the *centrales* with cane found its best option for subsistence. Centralization thus reinforced dependency on sugar, with the destruction of the forests once again as backdrop. In 1882 *La nueva era* described both factors in this way:

> It is probable that with the great development of the sugar trade, we will see an annual increase in the clearing of woodlands so that cane can be planted in open lands, with the prolongation of some railways and the building of others. It is also probable, in the state of misery in which the country finds itself, that many formerly in other lines of work will take

up farming, from which they formerly were excluded, as the only means that today offers a good future and the hope of well-being.[16]

The appearance of *centrales* in areas where *ingenios* already had been present was generally accompanied by an emphasis on improving cultivation. Nonetheless, the same backers of *centrales* were also quick to point out the advantages of setting up modern sugar industrial installations in new areas. One of the most cited of these promoters was the estate owner Francisco Feliciano Ibáñez. His advocacy came in the context of great uncertainty about sugar production on the island as a result of competition from other producing countries, low prices, and the imminent abolition of slavery, with the consequent impact on the labor market. In his opinion the only remedy that could save agriculture and the sugar industry, "the life of the country," would be creating large *ingenios centrales* through the association of various neighboring *ingenios*, with the goal of increasing production and reducing costs. He was well aware, however, of the possibility of this new type of agroindustrial organization of sugar in virgin land; he therefore proposed that the government create fifty *centrales* staffed entirely by free workers. The 1881 project consisted of developing these *centrales* on an average area of 300 caballerías of virgin land, with the aim of attaining quickly and economically a production of more than 1 million tons of sugar a year. Ibáñez based this goal on the estimate that 1 caballería of virgin land "that had just been cleared" could produce more than 100,000 arrobas of cane, although in his calculations he preferred to use an average yield of just 70,000 arrobas. In the initial phase, between 600 and 800 men worked on the clearing, planting, and cultivation of the first 200 caballerías, then moving on to the remaining 100. In selling the fifty *centrales*, the government would obtain 250 million pesos, in addition to annual tax revenues.[17]

Another well-known project was José Curbelo's 1882 effort to develop six 120-caballería *centrales* able to produce 1 million arrobas of sugar each year. These would also be established in wooded areas, and with families from the Canary Islands. Curbelo offered more details about the advantages of trees. He estimated that a caballería of virgin woodland contained a minimum of two hundred large trees, and that in four months 180 men could clear of smaller trees and brush the 120 caballerías necessary for the first *ingenio*. To fell the large trees, he estimated an expense of 20,000 pesos for nine steam-powered saws, plus a similar amount to pay laborers to cut and process the wood and take it to the port. The investment to buy land, seeds, and houses, as well as to pay for clearing, planting, and maintenance, came to 180,000 pesos for the first *central*. For the five remaining ones, the cost was cut in half, since the railroad was now nearer and there were now fewer expenses for transport to the docks and warehouses of ports, as well as for the steam-powered saws and pottery and smelting works. All these expenses, Curbelo said, could be covered with the sale of lumber. The 120 caballerías yielded a minimum of twenty-four thousand lengths of hardwood, whose price according to the Havana workshops never went below 10 pesos each. Therefore 240,000 pesos could be made from their sale, which would pay off part of the investment, specifically the 8 percent of shareholders' outlay to be distributed among them.[18]

We can see, therefore, why the dominant tendency was to start new *centrales* in wooded areas. Sale of precious wood and lumber offset part of the investment, and the trees could also be used on the plantation itself to make ties for private railroads and other needs. For instance, during these years there was much demand for construction of private docks and warehouses, which always entailed significant amounts of Cuban wood for such uses as pilings. In some cases, forest exploitation was the specific object of petitions.[19] Moreover, there was the well-known guarantee of high cane yields, given the persistent custom of planting in cleared land, despite the agricultural advances furthered by the extension of the *colonato* system. Finally, one could add other comparative advantages, such as the ease, for the owners of and stockholders in new *centrales*, of imposing their conditions on farmers kept under control by tenant contracts or other forms of subjection to and dependency on the industrial sector.

Sugar centralization and concentration can thus be seen as impacting Cuban forests in two contrasting ways. Although it helped end the industry's portability, the existence of abundant woodlands on the eastern half of the island allowed planters to keep establishing sugar plantations on virgin land, now with a much greater impact per unit. The fact that during this period sugar's occupation of the east of the country was just beginning meant that deforestation generally declined relative to the 1815–76 period. Eliseo Matos estimated that between 1878 and 1900 527,409 hectares (39,358 caballerías) disappeared, 12 percent of the woodlands that existed in 1878 and 5 percent of the island's original forested area.[20] Between 1828 and 1877 the number of caballerías felled annually declined from 3,763 to 1,956.

Centralization heightened many of the old social and environmental problems entailed in sugar expansion. The switch to cane cultivation by many small landowners, tenant farmers, and former slaves worsened the traditional shortage of subsistence crops and reduced the possibility for agricultural diversification. In 1888 the agronomist Nicomedes P. de Adan wrote: "Stop this work of destruction. . . . Continue at the appropriate time, if it is desired, in our central and eastern provinces, where magnificent *centrales* are being developed that in a few years will be the only ones able to compete with foreigners. . . . But not another banana tree, palm tree, or coffee bush must be felled by the very hands that should be protecting them!"[21]

Sugar plantations were the island's main representation of this opposition between a wild rural nature and one transformed and domesticated by humans. Nevertheless, from the same civilizing perspective, the increasing scale of production relative to agroecosystems also was a reason for concern, as the high price of lumber continued to be. In 1881 *El repertorio* noted that in Cuba 1,000 feet of lumber cost as much as 1,000 pounds of sugar. For the same amount of the latter, planters in Louisiana could buy 4,500 feet of lumber.[22] Partly as a result of deforestation during this period, the Zapata Swamp grew, a phenomenon that the engineer Juan A. Cosculluela studied and described in the 1910s. The planting of sugarcane that began in the first decades of the twentieth century in the regions of Alacranes and Macuriges, in the southeast of the Artemisa Plain and the south of the Colón Plain, increased as a result of the renewed expansion of sugar in the last third of the nineteenth century. Forests of the northern edge of the swamp were cleared for the planting of cane, and estate owners soon began to feel the results of their carelessness. Rainfall became increasingly irregular, and "floods swept away the land, drowned livestock, and caused infinite evils" in an area that had been fertile and productive before it was deprived of its plant cover. "Little by little," Cosculluela wrote, "cane has been disappearing from land where erosion has been the most intense, and one sees vast expanses of barren, rocky, and arid terrain, with no crop whatsoever, and which are entirely useless, especially where the slope most favors erosion, as occurs on land bordering the swamp, which is slowly dominating this land as it expands its sphere of action."[23]

Agricultural Improvements and the Green-Pulp Burners

During the final third of the nineteenth century, Cuba's forests were affected by significant changes in the cultivation methods and fuel used by the sugar agroindustry. In the older sugar regions, planters had to adopt an intensive cultivation system in order to revive soil that had been worked for several decades, although generally speaking more projects and expectations were created than working farms.[24] And in the late 1880s the so-called green-pulp burners were introduced and put into general use, an innovation that allowed for important savings in the labor that had been spent drying cane pulp in the sun and that helped reduce the need for firewood.

As sugar mills modernized, the need to find a less itinerant method for exploiting the soil became more urgent. In the introduction to Alvaro Reynoso's *Ensayo sobre el cultivo de la caña de azúcar* (Essay on the Cultivation of Sugarcane), the Count de Pozos Dulces had noted that "fortunately" the mood was becoming more favorable toward the improvements proposed by Alvaro Reynoso. Some of the largest farms of the period pioneered the application of such innovations as the use of plows and fertilizers, the drainage of soil, and even the introduction of the *colonato*. Moreover, the Ten Years' War, which made it impossible to continue expanding sugar cultivation to the east, affirmed the belief of many that refining improvements had to be accompanied by agricultural ones.

In general farmers became increasingly receptive to the application of scientific knowledge in agriculture, and cane farming in particular. Newspapers and magazines played an important role, continuously calling for reform of the island's dominant cultivation system. Between the late 1870s and the mid-1890s a number of agricultural periodicals appeared, including the *Revista de agricultura* (first published by the Estate Owners' Circle [Círculo de Hacendados] in 1879), *El ingenio* (1878–79), and *La nueva era* (1881–84). *La nueva era* is a particularly noteworthy because it was published in El Roque, a small town in the heart of the Colón Plain, an area that was reaching the end of its sugar hegemony.[25] In Havana and other towns, the press informed readers of the main advances in industry and agriculture, created a forum for debate of sugar-production concerns, and frequently referred to the issue of forests.

The greater interest in agricultural reform found expression in the creation of the School of Agriculture, a private initiative sponsored by the Estate Owners' Circle. Also prominent was the work of a group of professional agronomists trained in Europe and the United States who propagated modern agricultural ideas on the island. The *colonato* in particular was seen as a way to improve cultivation, based on the general notion that "careful attention to the countryside is profitable, and a small well-cultivated area will always be more productive than a large abandoned one."[26] This view was shared by major agricultural scientists of the period, including Francisco de Zayas y Jiménez, Francisco Javier de Balmaceda, Juan Bautista Jiménez, and Gabriel de Castro Palomino.[27]

In their writings these authors warned about the dangers of the transformations brought about by Cuba's agricultural boom. A good example is Bautista Jiménez's *El ingenio: Segunda parte de la adventuras de un mayoral* (The *Ingenio*: Part Two of the Adventures of a Farm Manager; 1883). Through a three-part dialogue, it shows the differences between lands recently cleared and those that have been farmed for several years. One of the characters, a count, speaks of a farm where cleared land is planted and where "the fields remain quite lovely, without suffering from excess water." A character named Picabia (the author) replies that this is because these fields have natural drainage thanks to the root systems that remain in the earth and that form "true underground conduits through which excess water goes to lower levels of the subsoil." These soils were made moister by the abundant humus, which allowed them to absorb more water, but the roots later rotted and the conduits thickened, dragged by heavy rains and trampled by livestock, carts, and farmworkers. After six to ten years the cane fields suffered from excess water, and drainage works had to be undertaken.

Another subject of the conversation was whether it rained as much as or less than before. Picabia found rainfall to be more irregular: "Sometimes it rains too much, two or two and a half weeks without stopping, and at other times there is remarkable drought." In his opinion the cause was the vanishing of the forests, whose humidity attracted clouds and regularized rainfall, while their moister soils absorbed more water. Arroyos thus formed in the lowlands. Dry most of the year, they channeled water that could not be absorbed by the soil. A third interlocutor exclaimed, "Listen, my Lord Count, Señor Picabia is quite right! When I was a boy the arroyos were so small I could jump them with my feet locked together; while today, during the rainy season, they become true rivers. When they swell up, they flood vast areas."[28]

Despite the changes, we cannot say that there was a radical and general turning point in the agricultural sector of the Cuban sugar industry. The author of an 1881 manual on sugar refining noted that, "with the exception of well-known and honorable exceptions, Cuban sugar agronomy consists of simply felling, planting, and clearing; much is said about fertilizers, but they are almost never used, and irrigation is entirely unknown." For this writer it was not surprising with such a system that production would decline and farms have to be dismantled when there was no more land to clear. He thus argued for the use of pulp as fertilizer, since in his opinion soil improvement was "the prime necessity of an *ingenio*."[29] At the same time *La nueva era* affirmed that fertile terrain was "one of the most sinister elements" for the progress of agriculture, "since false ideas and principles flourish there." Cuban farmers therefore should not be so eager to abandon tired land for virgin terrain.[30]

True, both of these sources are from the early years of the transition from the *ingenio* to the *central*, but at the end of the period cane farming had not changed substantially. At least this was the opinion of the sugar chemist Gastón Alonso Cuadrado when he argued, in 1901, for the founding on the island of a school for sugar engineers, where experiments could be carried out in cultivation and refining, since "the individual efforts of estate owners are lost in the ether."[31] Another issue was the increasing number of areas where the clearing, burning, and planting method was becoming impossible, and in these cases sooner or later there would be no alternative but to seek higher yields from worn-out soils.

The introduction and generalized use of green-pulp burners had a greater impact on the relationship between sugar and the forests. The importation of coal helped to resolve in part the crisis that the sugar industry had been experiencing since the mid-1900s as a result of the shortage and high price of fuel, as did the increased use of pulp despite the difficulties of its use. Nevertheless, firewood continued to be the caloric source par excellence in many cases. The type of fuel used on each farm varied according to whether it included forests or wood reserves and depending on the farm's distance from ports authorized to engage in foreign trade. The predominant practice was the use of different fuels in proportions dictated by the circumstances of each *ingenio*. For example, during his tour of the island in the late 1850s, Ramón de La Sagra wrote of his visit to a semimechanized *ingenio*: "The use of fuel is enormous, as it is in all *ingenios* set up by this method. The furnaces consume all the pulp, more than two thousand cartloads of firewood, and 150 to 200 tons of coal, the last of which is resorted to when rain makes the use of pulp impossible." He reached a similar conclusion about a mechanized *ingenio*, with two large steam engines for two powerful mills and two complete triple-effect Derosne trains, of which he wrote: "The problem of fuel has not been resolved there, as is desired and was promised a priori, because far from cane pulp's being sufficient, each year two or three thousand cartloads of firewood are required."[32]

Fuel remained a subject of concern for sugar planters until the late 1800s. Coal was expensive for many, and cane pulp continued to present the same disadvantages. In 1882 a writer in *La nueva era* suggested that the oldest *ingenios* press cane as much as possible and dry it on a series of plots, with the goal of reducing the labor required to stretch out the pulp and gather it up after it had dried in the sun. Among other advantages, the author noted that if it rained, only the wet part needed to be removed, and that it was easier to carry the pulp to the furnaces. In sum, the article concluded, economy of labor was preferable to that of fuel, since the former could be imported from overseas.[33] That same year a writer in the same journal praised the solution found by an *ingenio* for the use of coal, whose use had only recently become generalized. The remedy consisted of combining undried pulp with coal in finely broken pieces, which were then dampened and spread over the pulp, "obtaining an almost perfect combustion." The proof was that "although this farm has woodlands where it can harvest firewood, the owner chooses to buy coal."[34]

Another recurring topic was the disjunction between using pulp as fuel and using it as fertilizer. In 1867 Reynoso argued that "pulp is clearly an expensive fuel, because of the workers needed to handle it and considering the lost benefits for the fields given the organic matter that pulp would introduce." His view was that any system of refining that economized its use would be beneficial for both reasons but that the tariffs and difficulties entailed in transport limited the use of other fuels.[35] E. Pimienta's *Manual práctico de la fabricación de azúcar de cañas* (Practical Manual for the Making of Sugarcane; 1881) argued that estate owners failed to understand how much pulp cost them, since they did not take into account the labor invested in its preparation. In his opinion coal was cheaper, no matter how high producers might find its cost, and its use would require "intensive farming and refining reforms, with the result that our current production would increase by half." If coal was generalized, railroads would have return loads for *ingenios* and would reduce their rates, while "the successive increase in harvests due to the use of fertilizer would profit everyone."[36]

Several of sugar farms' fuel problems were solved with cane pulp burners, which allowed the direct use of cane's woody residue without the need for drying. The burners originated in Louisiana in the mid-nineteenth century, according to the sugar engineer Gastón Descamps, one of their most fervent promoters. In Cuba, the first efforts to use them were made in the early 1870s, but these met little success, hampered by routine, ignorance, and above all "lack of necessity."[37] During the same decade various types of green-pulp burning ovens began to be used in other sugar-producing areas of the world, such as Java and Egypt.

In 1880 efforts in Cuba began again, using the so-called Jarvis oven. The first ovens were set up in *ingenios* on the Colón Plain, in the town of Bolondrón. Descamps put one in the Armonía *ingenio* in 1881, together with two new boilers. In that year and the following ones some two hundred boilers with the Jarvis oven were installed in different *ingenios* around the island. In 1882 *La nueva era* wrote that this system was beneficial because it saved fuel, labor, and fertilizer.[38] Rillieux ovens enjoyed similar success, although their placing of grates under the floor was problematic, since many *ingenios*, including those on the Colón Plain, had underground water currents close to the surface. Other green-pulp burning ovens were patented on the island in the 1880s, some shipped from abroad and others built on the farms.[39]

But the true generalization of this new technology came after the final abolition of slavery in 1886. The significant savings in labor was an additional incentive to accelerate the burners' implantation, the doubts about models that had been used thus far on the island notwithstanding.[40] An 1890 promotional brochure for Fiske green-pulp burners also stressed these advantages. It included a letter from the owner of the Soledad *ingenio*, Edwin Atkins, who claimed that with the Fiske oven he could dispense with the work of 60 to 70 men needed in his previous system, as well as 30 pairs of oxen. If we estimate that the 1,000 *ingenios* on the island needed an average of 40 workers for the different tasks involved in drying pulp (and some used 80 or 100), we find that green-pulp burners saved the work of 20,000 men "who, employing their strength and activity in other work, can powerfully impel our agricultural development."[41]

The Fiske green-pulp burner was first used in Louisiana in 1885 and came to Cuba three years later. Among its most noteworthy qualities was its possible use with any type of boiler, although the brochure also announced that Fiske was developing a system of multitubular steel boilers that would increase the burners' advantages. Samuel Fiske made several trips to Cuba's main sugar-growing regions to promote his inventions.[42] Among their virtues, the brochure noted, was the assurance that harvests would not be interrupted by rain or fire. Moreover, no other fuel would be needed; some pulp would even be left over for other applications.[43]

Another important sugar manual of the period cited fuel as one of the most pressing concerns at harvest time. Nevertheless, the uncertainty did not seem to be as great as in previous decades. The manual's author argued that earlier estate owners had not believed that the island's immense forests could be completely exhausted and that the day would come when "in order to continue making sugar they would need pulp, not as fuel but rather in order to fertilize their cane fields, made poorer by continual production." By then most sugar plantations had used up their woodlands and had to buy firewood or coal. Some used these fuels exclusively, reserving pulp for fertilizer. But on many farms the use of green-pulp burners resolved the fuel issue "in such a favorable manner that today the refiner can grind his cane without fear of fire, obtaining this fuel, which had cost him so dearly, with great savings in labor, livestock, and time."[44] In 1900 Gastón Alonso Cuadrado expressed a similar opinion, arguing in his assessment of how much sugar production had been improved by the new industrial methods that the latter had saved some estate owners from "an almost certain ruin."[45]

Finally, it is important to note that the possibility of the sugar industry's using petroleum instead of coal was already being evaluated. In April 1888 the *Diario de la Marina* reprinted a Cárdenas newspaper's report on the establishment there of a refinery to process the "mineral liquid" extracted from the nearby mines of Delicias and Perseverancia. If large-scale extraction could be achieved, as was hoped, a new source of wealth for the country would emerge, "not only because of the use this product currently has among us, but also because with it we will resolve one of the main problems related to our sugar industry, the need for inexpensive fuel."[46]

Postwar Reconstruction and Ingenios Centrales in the Eastern Half of the Country

Reconstruction in the eastern half of the island after the Ten Years' War was supported by the region's still abundant forests. The end of hostilities allowed resumption of the export trade in precious woods, as well as the commerce in various forest products with cities in western Cuba. The lands of the former sugar plantations were a good point of departure for the new *ingenios centrales*, thanks to the destruction of the mills and their owners' inability to resume sugar production. Many of these properties still included large forests, a guarantee of high cane yields.

The export of wood did not entirely disappear during the war, but it immediately resurged in 1878. Foreign ships devoted to this trade became a common sight in ports in the eastern half of Cuba. The traditional wood centers of Santa Cruz and Manzanillo, which maintained their importance, were joined by others such as Gibara and Nipe on the northern coast. Santiago de Cuba and Guantánamo remained loading ports for wood from their areas, as did Cienfuegos and Trinidad, although these were less important than they had been in previous eras. Cuban wood was sent to such destinations as London, Liverpool, Bremen, Rotterdam, Le Havre, and New York. In addition to precious woods such as cedar and mahogany, other forest products exported included fustic for ink and yarey.[47] Statistics on some of the principal exports passing through Cuban customs, with exception of Havana, for 1884–85 and 1888–89 show the continuing importance of wood relative to other products (see table 5.1).

The harvesting of wood in the provinces of Camagüey and Oriente awakened the interest of investors who came to the island in those years. For example, in early 1885 a Santiago de Cuba newspaper announced that several North Americans would be arriving in the city to develop mining and other industries. Their plans included establishing "on a large scale and with mechanical elements a logging operation for local wood that should provide work for many men."[48] Many economic development projects on the eastern half of the island included exploiting the region's forest wealth.

One of these development projects was promoted by the Agricultural and Industrial Society of Nipe Sites (Sociedad Agrícola e Industrial de los Terrenos de Nipe), formed in the early 1880s to develop 5,600 caballerías (75,000 hectares) of sites adjoining the bay, an important arrival point for European immigrants. Its plans included harvesting forests with modern systems in order to provide the market with all types of lumber and dyewoods found on the sites, which had "immense forests and the richest woods." Once the woodlands had been cleared, the land would be devoted to cane cultivation to supply several large *centrales* in the area, "outfitted with the most complete equipment" and accessible by extensive railways.[49] The society, constituted in Matanzas in 1881 and based in Madrid, had to suspend its work in 1884, leaving the initiative to French investors in 1886. In 1888 a French vice-consul described the area as still including "forests with abundant ebony, cedar, mahogany, and other fine woods. The harvesting of forests in Nipe according to the same method followed in Santa Cruz and Manzanillo . . . would yield satisfactory results."[50]

TABLE 5.1. Main Products Exported through Cuban Customs,
except in Havana, 1884–1885 and 1888–1889

| | | 1884–85 | | 1888–89 | |
Product	Unit of Measure	Amount	Value (Pesos)	Amount	Value (Pesos)
Aguardiente (liquor)	Barrel	16,237	416,720	2,633	78,990
Aguardiente	Liter	1,200,773	327,643	405,880	60,222
Yellow wax	Kilogram	164,606	55,049	189,113	85,100
Wood	Foot	17,910,222	564,687	18,403,618	451,958
Honey	Gallon	271,698	103,345	141,700	45,449
Cocoa	Kilogram	728,327	263,578	1,131,756	452,702
Copper	Kilogram	30,777	2,754	44,277	3,143
Iron	Kilogram	71,315,014	108,540	283,641,000	425,461

Source: "Estado comparativo de los principales artículos exportados por las Aduanas de esta
Isla, excepción hecha de La Habana, con los valores que han alcanzado en los años de 1884
a 1885 y 1888 a 1889," Boletín de la Cámara Oficial de Comercio, Industria y Navegación de La
Habana, May 31, 1890.
Note: In 1888, 13,928,815 ft. of wood were exported, with a value of 33,749 pesos.

Among the society's proposals for developing the Nipe sites was the
large-scale cultivation of banana and coconut trees, as was already done
in Baracoa for export to New York and Boston (the same was done with
coffee). Nonetheless, the group's true future was in sugar and tobacco. To
this end it planned to establish a large *ingenio central* named Santa Isabel
de Nipe, with the goal of attracting many colonists to the area. The project's
promoters were no doubt aware of the successful sugar *centrales* developed
in the provinces of Santa Clara, Puerto Príncipe, and Santiago de Cuba.

This new expansion focused on the border of the older sugar plantation
area, beginning in Cienfuegos and Sagua la Grande. This was the case of
the eastern half of the Plain of Corralillo-Yaguajay and of the Heights of
the Northern Range and the Plain of Santa Clara–Sancti Spíritus. Also in
the physico-geographic province of Eastern Cuba, the natural regions of
Manzanillo Plain and Guantánamo Plain were two pioneering zones in
the founding of *ingenios centrales*. Other regions in the eastern half of the
island were settings for new sugar mills, but these were isolated and not
very representative, as on the extensive plains and heights of the subdistrict

of Camagüey-Maniabón. In general, sugar's occupation of these areas was conditioned by the proximity of loading ports — thus the enthusiasm for the Ferrocarril Central's projected extension into the east, which at first did not materialize.[51]

Sources on sugar's new eastward expansion nearly always mention the destruction of forests to make way for cane fields. Describing this process in Manzanillo, for instance, an 1883 article in *La nueva era* said that a person traveling through the 84 kilometers between Manzanillo and the town of Belic, to the south, could see smoke from the stacks of a number of *ingenios centrales* and that crossing the vast areas formerly wooded and now cleared for cane he would be convinced that "this district is progressing rapidly." That same year more than 30 caballerías of San Ramón had been cleared for cane, and large-scale clearings were being undertaken around Niquero for the next processing season. This town, which had grown rapidly since the logging had begun, promised to be important for the *ingenio central* of the same name, "as will its spacious and sheltered port and the fertile soil that surrounds it."[52] At the time the port of Manzanillo had an active trade in the coastal shipping of forest products.[53]

The sugar boom on the Manzanillo Plain was partly the result of the reconstruction of *ingenios* destroyed during the war and the conversion of others into *colonias*. A similar situation could be found in the old sugar areas of Puerto Príncipe and Nuevitas, as reflected by the 1880 project of Reed, Ruiz, and Company to establish the Redención *ingenio central* in the Tínima area, along the railroad between the two cities and 18 kilometers from the former. The developers could see the excellent condition of this area for returning to sugar production, favored by the fact that "in many areas, ten years' abandonment has increased the fertility of the soil and moisture of the subsoil, thanks to luxuriant vegetation." They noted the preference for growing cane because it could be planted without great expense and because not everyone could plant vegetables, whose abundance lowered prices. Small-scale activities such as the production and collection of honey, wax, yucca starch, and guano could be undertaken so long as the competition was not ruinous, while the wood trade was not within everyone's means.[54]

The owners of the old *ingenios* around Tínima, some of whom had returned to sugar growing, were enthusiastic about the idea. Twenty-one of them committed to ship the required cane on the narrow railway being built, at a price of 2.25 gold pesos per 100 arrobas. Among the favorable

circumstances mentioned were the fertility of the soil, which would produce several harvests; the low lease rates due to low land values; the reduced salaries that would be accepted by laborers who could not otherwise
find work; and a five-year exemption from taxes. The society would focus
on harvesting and selling lumber as longer as this was practical, and if it
could not get good prices in Cuba, it would sell the wood internationally.
The draft project included an appendix with data on thirty-three farms in
the area in 1868, including twenty-eight *ingenios* with abundant woodlands
and firewood.[55] In 1883 *La nueva era* announced that the Redención *ingenio*
would process 83 caballerías that year but that in 1884 this number would
increase to 120, and in 1885 it would rise to 150.[56] Another sugar project
proposal, offered by a group of Havana businessmen and landowners, described the farm Las Mercedes de Santa Cruz, located a short distance from
Minas, as "one of the best in Camagüey, in terms of its complete health and
its flat and very fertile terrain, mostly woodland, which abounds in all kinds
of fine wood."[57]

The creation of *centrales* in the province of Puerto Príncipe resulted in
a production increase from 107,880 arrobas in 1880 to 750,200 arrobas in
1889. In addition to Redención, other noteworthy *centrales* included Congreso and Senado, joined in 1891 by Lugareño. And yet Puerto Príncipe's
sugar production remained insignificant until the end of the nineteenth
century. In 1894 it made up 0.84 percent of Cuba's total output. The province of Santiago de Cuba increased its share from 2.46 percent in 1878 to
9.56 percent in 1894. The true resurgence of expansion occurred in hitherto
unoccupied areas in the natural regions of the island's center. While the
Havana-Matanzas region saw its share of national sugar production drop
during this period from 76.96 percent to 57.5 percent, what was then the
province of Santa Clara increased its percentage from 20.59 to 32.1. This rise
was impelled by the process of concentration in areas that had been occupied before 1868 but also by the building of new *centrales* in virgin territory
near the old sugar frontier. This was the case of the area of Yaguajay, on the
eastern half of the northern Las Villas Plain.

Transformation of Northern Las Villas: Part Two

The sugar boom that took place in the 1840s in the jurisdiction of Sagua
la Grande, in the eastern part of the northern Las Villas Plain and of the
Heights of the Northern Range, reached its peak during the Ten Years' War.

In 1883 it was cited as an example of the crisis experienced by growers unable to make the technological leap or to be sure of exceptional fertility in their soil. Their plight was explained partly by their inability to replace the old Jamaican trains with modern double- or triple-effect machines, which also required more cane fields "in proportion with their increased value and the quantity of their product."[58] In following years the concentration process took hold in the area, promoted by new branches of the railroad from Sagua to Caguaguas, heading west toward the area of Quemado de Güines, and east from Encrucijada to Camajuaní, where it joined the Caibarién railway.

In the 1860s there was a notable difference in the development of sugar plantations in the western and eastern halves of northern Las Villas. The Sagua la Chica River could serve as a dividing line, with the two administrative centers in the towns of Sagua la Grande and San Juan de los Remedios. Carlos Rebello's statistics show the different degrees of occupation by sugar. In the jurisdiction of Sagua la Grande he recorded 119 *ingenios*, 89 using steam power and 30 using oxen. The average area per farm was 44.4 caballerías, 13.4 of them in cane. The jurisdiction of Remedios had 44 *ingenios*, 27 using steam power, with an average area of 53.9 caballerías, 8.4 of them in cane. The differences between the two regions' cane yields in 1860 were great: the former produced 72,533 crates and 58,262 casks, while the latter produced 2,696 crates and 22,583 casks.[59]

Despite being the scenes of significant forest exploitation since the early days of colonization, both jurisdictions were among the most abundant in forests, according to the 1862 census. But Remedios, which until then had been less impacted by commercial agriculture, was the most so, with 77.9 percent of its 28,750 caballerías in woodlands. Large and small livestock continued to be responsible for the bulk of the region's economy, together with forest products, fishing, and other agricultural items such as tobacco and cocoa.[60] At the same time, sugar was reinforcing its position, with 71 *ingenios* and *trapiches* according to the 1862 census.[61] Unlike in Sagua, the direct impact of the war on some of its area led to a reduction in the number of sugar plantations. When we look at the 1877 figures, we see that the largest survived. That year the municipal jurisdiction had 38 *ingenios*, 15 of them in the *partido* of Camajuaní, and 9 in that of Yaguajay, on the northeastern coast. In the former the average area increased by 20 caballerías compared with 1860, and that in cane tripled; in the latter the average area increased by 30 caballerías, and that in cane nearly doubled.

The jurisdiction of Remedios was one of the principal backdrops for sugar concentration and centralization between 1878 and 1898, as is shown by studies of the region's sugar production during this period.[62] The number of sugar plantations dropped from 38 in 1877 to 31 in 1888 and 23 in 1899. Total production, in contrast, rose from 3,231,606.8 arrobas in 1887 to 4,045,042.8 in 1890. Other signs of change included the increase in centrifugal refining and shipping in bags.

These changes led to an intense transformation of the landscape. Comparison of 1862 and 1899 data reveals tendencies similar to those in regions previously invaded by sugar, but they were now more pronounced. The figures on which the statistics are based are different, but the percentage variations are clear enough to show the strong impact of sugar's arrival in its new industrial phase. Table 5.2 indicates that the proportion of forests fell by more than 65 percentage points, more than double the decline in Sagua la Grande during the same period (just over 25 percent, though both jurisdictions are given a smaller area in these figures). Hernán Venegas notes that the new sugar colossuses were located in two basic areas of Remedios, one in the west and southwest, along the axis Placetas-Camajuaní-Vueltas-Remedios-Caibarién, and the other in the east, around Yaguajay and Mayajigua.[63] In both sugar's expansion depended on the clearing of woodlands to ensure high yields and to enlarge cane fields. But the impact was greatest in the latter as a result of its smaller population and geographic conditions better suited to cane: a long coastline, which reduced transport costs, and a flat topography, which facilitated construction of portable and private railways.

The territories of Yaguajay and Mayajigua are located to the east of the axis between the towns of Remedios and Caibarién and are bordered by the Jatibonico del Norte River. Like the rest of the Plain of Corralillo-Yaguajay, they are very active hydrologically, with a slight elevation above sea level, have plentiful rainfall throughout the region, and possess generally fertile soil, though it is prone to swamping. These conditions created drainage problems for sugar farming that had to be attenuated over time with new canals.

Of the nine *ingenios* in Yaguajay when the war ended in 1878, those with the most cane fields relative to their total area were Santa Catalina, with 26 caballerías in cane out of 44.5 total, and Océano, with 32 of 46, respectively. In other cases the cultivated area was significantly less: Soberano, 15 caballerías out of 55; Urbanza, 7.5 of 79; Encarnación, 10 of 80; Aurora,

TABLE 5.2. Changes in Land Use in Remedios, 1862–1899

Year	Area[a]	Cultivated	%	Pasture[b]	%	Forest	%	Arid	%
1862	28,750	814	2.8	3,498	12.2	22,382	77.9	2,054	7.1
1899	11,665	1,831	14.7	6,684	57.3	1,425.6	12.2	1,843	15.8

Source: Noticias estadísticas de la Isla de Cuba en 1862, in Memoria del año fiscal de 1899 a 1900: Estados (Havana: Secretaría de Agricultura, Comercio e Industria, 1900).
[a] In caballerías. For 1899, data was collected for the municipalities of Caibarién, Camajuaní, Placetas, Vueltas, Remedios, and Yaguajay.
[b] "Pasture" includes land that in 1862 was categorized as artificial and natural pastures and in 1899 was categorized as potreros and livestock farms.

9 of 78.5; and Luciana, 9 of 144. There are no figures for the two remaining ingenios: Belencita and Noriega. We thus see a remarkable difference relative to the sugar areas around the cities of Matanzas, Cárdenas, Colón, Cienfuegos, and Sagua, where the old ingenios did not have access to as much land in which to increase their cane fields and ensure high yields. Yaguajay became one of the most attractive areas for relaunching sugar's eastward expansion.

At the beginning of the 1881–82 harvest, La nueva era announced increased yields for the Océano, Santa Catalina, Belencita, and Urbanzas ingenios, while on the Noriega ingenio much land had been cleared, but the fruits of this labor would not be seen until future harvests. At the same time, the newspaper referred to Ibáñez's idea of establishing a central in the area, about which he had written to the owners of Urbanza and Luciana. It defended the proposal, pointing out that the land of the district was in excellent condition, especially for cane, "whose plants withstand ten or twelve cuttings without damage to the stalk." Both farms were near the coast, "with enough depth for a good wharf," and had "vast virgin terrain, which could be devoted to cane cultivation."[64]

In the proposal cited above for founding the Redención central in Puerto Príncipe, the promoters mentioned Yaguajay as an example to follow. Specifically, they praised Bernal, Hermano, and Company for bringing together "a good number of temperate, honorable, and intelligent colonists, some of whom have brought their families and their own resources in order to establish themselves in the area." The seven-year contract granted the colonists a certain area of terrain, "of thick woodland," to plant cane and other essentials. Estate owners committed to pay 2 to 2.5 gold pesos for each

100 arrobas of cane. The proposal noted the results of the first attempts at growing cane there, which had produced, in fields of ⅛ and ¼ caballería, yields that amounted to 125,600 and 146,032 arrobas per caballería, respectively. The other cane fields already established had yields that fell between these extremes, despite having been planted in some haste.[65] With such high production, the fruit of the traditional system of clearing, burning, and planting, we should not be surprised by Venegas's 1890 affirmation that progress in Yaguajay was "perhaps more pronounced than in other towns in the province [of Santa Clara or Las Villas], and even on the island as a whole."[66]

In the 1880s intense lumbering took place in the area, in general associated with the clearing of woodlands for expansion of sugar plantations (see figure 5.4). In January 1888 the *Diario de la Marina* echoed an article in *El avisador comercial* announcing the details of what it termed a "new industry." Manuel Carrera, the owner of the Meneses farm in Yaguajay, had installed a large steam-powered sawmill that cut between 5,000 and 6,000 feet of lumber a day. It employed between 150 and 200 men and was served by a railway 11 kilometers long, which took the wood to the coast for shipping. The farm was located on land abundant in large cedar trees, the timber most worked there. New techniques also allowed it to work wood such as jobo and ceiba, previously considered to be unusable.[67] Three years later, in 1891, Carrera sold land on his Alicante farm, also in Yaguajay and said to be virgin terrain fertile for sugar and tobacco, to one hundred families.[68]

This increasing deforestation was reflected in the arrival in Havana of ever more forest products from Yaguajay, which became, at least between 1886 and 1891, one of the main originating ports for coastal traffic in these goods. This sawed wood was generally cedar and in smaller proportion majagua[69] and other Cuban hardwoods. Unsawed lengths of these trees were also marketed, as were articles such as cedar planks, packs of small boards (*tablilla*), broom handles, packs of majagua, bags of charcoal, firewood, and railroad ties made of júcaro. A number of schooners were used for this traffic, including the *Trafalgar, Joven Blanca, Natividad, Joven Magdalena, Joven Gertrudis, Joven Balear, Cuba,* and *Sofia,* some sporadically and others making regular monthly trips. Table 5.3 shows how many feet of wood these schooners took from Yaguajay to Havana during six-month periods between 1886 and 1891, based on daily entries in the *Diario de la Marina.*[70]

The export of wood to Havana seems to have reached its apex between

FIGURE 5.4. Length of mahogany hauled by oxen.

(Robert P. Porter, *Industrial Cuba* [New York: G. P. Putnam's Sons, 1899])

TABLE 5.3. Coastal Shipping of Wood from Yaguajay to Havana, 1886–1891

	First Six Months			Second Six Months		
Year	Entries	Schooners[a]	Feet of Wood	Entries	Schooners[a]	Feet of Wood
1886	7	2	142,415	9	4	600,401
1887	9	6	444,833	—	—	—
1888	4	3	160,424	1	1	48,006
1889	3	2	99,809	—	—	—
1890	—	—	—	19	8	164,050
1891	5	4	2,668	—	—	—

Source: Diario de la Marina, 1885–91. Records for the six-month periods that do not appear in this table could not be found.

[a]Indicates the number for schooners coming from Yaguajay. A schooner may have made more than one entry.

1886 and the first half of 1888, one of sugar's periods of most rapid development in this region. The subsequent drop could indicate that the trade began to weaken as a result of the intense deforestation and the lack of interest in regenerating forest wealth and establishing a durable system of harvesting. The wood industry had already begun to turn a hungry eye east of Yaguajay. A newspaper in Sagua la Grande wrote in 1891 that "on the vast plateau that includes Mayajigua and borders the coast are immense forests rich in excellent wood that vegetates there eternally due to the difficulty of hauling it. Three leagues from the town is the cove of Punta de Judas, deep enough for schooners, and the railroad passes within four or five leagues of the hamlet. . . . It is indeed a pity that this large and rich area is not developed."[71]

In 1900 the municipality of Yaguajay had seven *ingenios centrales* and two *colonias*. Its lands included 160 cultivated caballerías (or 7.5% of the total area), 363.5 caballerías of woodland (16.4%), 1,092 caballerías of livestock farms (48.8%), and 620 caballerías classified as "unproductive" (27.7%). The war of 1895–98 did not cause significant damage to the sugar farms in the Remedios area, allowing sugar production and deforestation to resume their acceleration as soon as the conflict was over.[72] Robert Porter, a special envoy of U.S. president William McKinley charged with evaluating the situation on the island, reported that interest in sugar had caused "the numerous sugar properties in the area to burn forests in order to plant in . . . virgin soil, leading to the disappearance of the large forests" (see figures 5.5 and 5.6).[73]

In 1913 only two *centrales* remained in Yaguajay: Vitoria and Narcisa. The two together controlled 1,442 caballerías. Vitoria had 842 caballerías, with 419 in cane farmed by *colonos* and 130 in woodlands. It had an average yield of 57,000 arrobas per caballería. Narcisa's 600 caballerías included 420 in cane and 80 in woodlands. Its average yield was just 42,000 arrobas per caballería.[74] Three decades after Yaguajay's sugar boom, the proverbial fertility of its land was already history. In their study of Cuba's soils Hugh Bennett and Robert Allison said of "Yaguajay Clay" that excess humidity often harmed cane and that the main problem was to eliminate surface water through lateral canals and drains. They also noted that because of the lack of soil aeration, weeds thrived. In these conditions, they concluded, this soil was not favorable "to the growing of cane or of any other crop." They recommended control of weeds and excess water and moderate use of shallow plowing to improve crops in these types of terrain.[75]

FIGURE 5.5. *Batey* of the Narcisa *central* in Yaguajay.

("Informe del Secretario de Obras Públicas por el semester que terminó en 31 de diciembre de 1900," in Leonard Word, *Civil Report of Brigadier General Leonard Word, Military Governor of Cuba, from the Period from December 20, 1899 to December 31, 1900,* vol. 10 [Washington, DC, 1900])

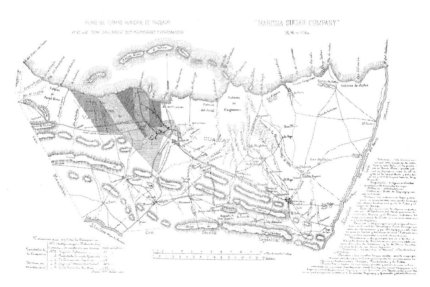

FIGURE 5.6. Municipality of Yaguajay in 1898, lands and railroads of the Narcisa *central.*

(*Memoria sobre el central Narcisa* [Havana: Rambla y Bouza, 1898])

The Establishment of a
Modern Forest Administration

In April 1876, after several years of attempts, the Woodlands Ordinances for Cuba and Puerto Rico were enacted, marking the formal beginning of modern forest administration in the two Spanish possessions.[76] This fact is little known in the case of Cuba, perhaps because the new laws did little to restrain the vanishing of the island's forests. But this does not mean we should be ignorant of the changes that were made in this direction, especially after several decades of nearly total lack of interest by the government.

Early on, the desire of the Ministry of Overseas Territories to bring order to forest management in Cuba encountered various difficulties, including open opposition from private property owners. The first mission sent, in 1853, to take charge of the effort was hindered by the death of two commissioners from yellow fever the following year. In 1858 one of two commissioners sent to resume this work met the same fate. The other commissioner, however, was the only Cuban who studied at Spain's School of Woodlands Engineers: Francisco de Paula Portuondo y Bravo, son of the Marquis de Las Delicias de Tempú, of Santiago de Cuba.[77]

As the story is told in the family, young Portuondo was recommended to Miguel Rodríguez Ferrer to travel to Spain and study for a career in weapons manufacturing, but the naturalist convinced the family that it would be better for the young man to undertake studies more appropriate to his future as an estate owner on the island, and so Portuondo enrolled in the School of Woodlands Engineers, recently established in Villaviciosa de Odón, a town 20 kilometers from Madrid. Once he had earned his degree, vacancies in Cuba's civil service created an excellent opportunity to apply his new knowledge in his native country. By a royal order of December 28, 1858, he was named to a post on Cuba's Woodlands Reconnaissance Commission, and beginning in 1859 he was a member of the Woodlands Engineers Corps.

Portuondo returned to Santiago de Cuba and lived there briefly before moving to Havana. In 1860, at his urging, Captain General Francisco Serrano promulgated four provisional measures to serve until the woodlands ordinance and the regulations for the sector could be finalized. Portuondo explained then that it was indispensable to begin with a reconnaissance of the woodlands, since the reports supplied by the Quartermaster Corps did not give the slightest idea of their limits, for instance, or of what species were suitable for firewood. He noted that these woodlands remained in the same virgin state as in primitive times, in terrain difficult to access, far from the coast and from the centers of consumption, and were not lands considered suitable for agriculture. These, after all, "make up most of the State's forest property on this island, and we should apply to them first and foremost the fecund principles of dasonomy."[78]

Portuondo argued that if the state woodlands were numerous and if their prudent exploitation was a guarantee that climatological conditions would not change and the navy not lack for lumber, "the use and benefit from forest property on the rest of the island [could be left] absolutely free." In the opposite case, however, it might become necessary to impose "some restrictions on the use of private property in the name of that superior right based on the conditions of existence of these provinces' inhabitants and on the requirements of the entire nation." The measures he proposed were approved at court, with the recommendation that the demands of the navy, which had prompted consideration of the question, play a direct role in the drafting of the ordinances.[79]

In 1868 Miguel Bosh y Juliá, a Spanish naturalist and professor at the School of Woodlands Engineers, claimed that the sad state of Cuba's woodlands resulted "from ignorance of their value, from the ineluctable and constant tendency of individuals to extend cultivation beyond natural limits, from the absolute freedom with which logging has always been carried out." Commenting on the proposed woodlands ordinance sent from the island in March 1866 in the hope it would put a stop to these abuses and that woodlands harvesting would be submitted to a rational plan, he wrote: "According to our forest adversaries, agriculture in Cuba has been represented and led by a wealthy and intelligent class, able to neutralize with its management the bad effects of prolix and invasive rules established in the Ordinances, so there is no reason to discuss applying the latter in the Antilles. This appraisal contains the most atrocious, most bloodthirsty attack on the fundaments of our social organization."[80]

Bosh y Juliá was delighted that the project would be undertaken on the island with the participation of the engineers and that it met the approval of higher authorities and of "men interested in the prosperity of the country."[81] One of these men was the naturalist Rodríguez Ferrer, who donated collections of Cuban plants to the School of Woodlands Engineers. In his work on the island he reiterated the criteria that Portuondo outlined in his annual *memorias* on public woodlands, such as those of 1869, in which he complained of being unable to present them as he wished because the woodlands were administered by the Quartermaster Corps. Compounding this problem was the lack of organization of forest property, of a sufficiently large and competent "warden staff," of forest legislation, and of "a single administration of national woodlands, with the participation of the engineers."[82]

In 1875 the colony's Superior Government enacted new regulations for the harvesting of public woodlands, while in Spain a new model was approved for the personnel and material involved in woodlands inspection on the island.[83] At stake was not only conserving forests for their physical importance but also exploiting their commercial value through auctions, as a source of revenue for the treasury. Finally, on April 21, 1876, the long-awaited Woodlands Ordinances for Cuba and Puerto Rico were promulgated in Madrid.[84] They included eight titles with 118 articles and regulated such aspects as the demarcation and harvesting of public woodlands, their policing, and the forest administration's penal code and personnel. Article 1, Title 1, classified as woodlands all terrain intended for the production of lumber and firewood, as well uncultivated pasture land. Woodlands were divided into the public and the private. The first include those of the state, of towns, and of corporations linked to the state; the second were those that, by just title, belonged to the private domain.

The dispositions of the ordinance fundamentally concerned woodlands of the state, since individuals would not be subjected to more restrictions than those set out in the general policing rules. Only private woodlands that adjoined public ones would be subject to the ordinances, and owners were warned in these cases to put them under the custody of state woodlands personnel and contribute to common expenses. The fact that private woodlands were left out of the ordinance regulations limited the effectiveness of forest administration on the island. Nevertheless, the ordinances were a step forward and provided an adequate framework for the action of an administration dedicated specifically to the planning, exploitation, and conservation of state and municipal woodlands. They also emerged at a moment when, despite difficulties, the work of woodlands engineers was beginning to bear fruit, particularly thanks to the efforts of Portuondo. In 1875 the latter expressed concern in one of his *memorias* that the number of woodlands, "whether private or of the state and towns, included in the area of the island of Cuba is impossible to indicate due to the lack of forestry statistics." Despite this, he was confident that the number could not be very large and that the amount of private woodlands, "diminishing each day due to the constant growth of agriculture, true wealth of this country, may disappear entirely in the not too distant future."[85]

Reports such as this one were key to the decisions made by the Ministry of Overseas Territories about Cuban forests. The increase in number of personnel was one example. When they arrived on the island, woodland engineers expressed alarmed at the state of forest husbandry there. In an 1876 *memoria* Ernesto Ruiz Melo, who worked in eastern Cuba, blamed "the ancient and constant struggle of the ignorant and avaricious man against nature" and people who, "guided by ambition and selfishness, shielded perhaps by impunity," destroy everything within reach. After more than a year on the island, he wrote:

> Personal interest, or rather, the selfishness and avarice of individuals, sometimes without understanding their own interest, and indifferent to the general interest, some in the erroneous belief that their wealth increases just by increasing the area of their property, and others in order to make their fortune quickly and cheaply, cutting down everything within reach, as well as the majority's ignorance of the effective influence of and many general needs satisfied by woodlands, this spirit so developed here of enriching oneself without concern for the means, has no doubt been the cause of the complete disappearance of vast lumberable woodlands in the central and western Departments. It appears that in the eastern Department . . . they have been saved from the fury of the axe, although the pernicious practice of disordered harvesting remains, with all its negative consequences, making these elements of destruction instead of the means of conservation and development that they should be.[86]

During these years the structure of forest administration was organized as a dependency of the General Government. The name changed several times, but the function did not. It was known variously as the General Inspection of Woodlands, the Central Section of Woodlands, or the Department (Negociado) of Woodlands. In 1878 three forest districts were created. The first included the provinces of Pinar del Río, Havana, and Matanzas; the second, Santa Clara and Puerto Príncipe; and the third, Santiago de Cuba. This subdivision was the most stable, although on occasion the first two districts were merged into one. Each district was led by a woodlands engineer with a team of woodlands assistants and office personnel.

Through the periodic *memorias* sent to his superiors in Madrid by Portuondo, who was chief engineer during almost this entire period, we can follow the process by which a modern forest administration was implanted in Cuba. In an 1879 report, for instance, Portuondo characterized each of the forest districts. About the first he indicated that thanks to the employees under his direction various state terrains had been recovered in which fraudulent logging was occurring; these operations immediately established a growing production because of the shortage of private woodlands, "and due to the need they have of wood products for the consumption of their sugar plantations." Also influential were the advantageous conditions for supplying the capital "with the fuel indispensable for everyday needs and for industrial speculation." Of the second and third districts he observed that, having been a "theater of the separatist war," many properties needed resources for their subsistence, which led many landowners to obtain them by harvesting their woodlands, as could be seen from the sending of guides to lead the transport of forest products.

Portuondo also argued for several measures that he said were essential if the island was to profit better from lumbering, such as the elimination of tariffs on exported wood. He reasoned that the cost of laborers and the difficulty of harvesting and hauling the wood to port limited large-scale exploitation of woodlands and thus prejudiced the interests of the state and of private landowners. For the latter the loss was even greater, since the expense and difficulty of selling their wood led many to focus exclusively on agricultural exploitation of their land: "Discounting the wood's possible usefulness, they reduce the woodlands to ashes, losing many large trunks and different species that are highly valued and which, harvested and transported to the sites of consumption, could have been sold advantageously."[87]

Portuondo added that the Woodlands Inspection was destined to play a great role in legitimizing property ownership, offering owners of rural farms the chance to possess a title that would allow them to use their land freely. Among his service's achievements he listed its revitalization of and putting into production large public woodlands, its contribution to an increase in agricultural wealth through land distribution, and generally speaking the present and future advantages of establishing the woodlands sector in Cuba.

A major concern was determining precisely how much land could be considered public or state woodlands. Figures are different and contradictory for different years. Prior to 1876 area estimates were offered such as 223,300 or 300,000 hectares.[88] Portuondo's 1879 *memoria* gives a much larger area and specifies a figure for each forest district: 200,000 hectares for the first, 350,000 for the second, and 480,000 for the third, a total of 1,030,000 hectares, or about 10 percent of Cuba's territory. But estimates in subsequent years reduce the area of public woodlands by half. Although all these estimates are tentative figures not based on a demarcation of property, they could be influenced by factors such as the auctioning of public woodlands or the 1879 figure's inclusion of "seized property." Another *memoria* for 1892 and 1893 calculated the area of state woodlands at 500,000 hectares, with keys and maritime areas, and admitted that an unknown amount might remain.[89] According to 1899 statistics, the area of public woodlands was at least 496,540 hectares (37,000 caballerías).[90]

This last estimated area represented 5 percent of Cuban territory, indicating from the outset that the work of forest administrators could not lead to great woodlands conservation. In 1893 Portuondo pointed out that it would be difficult to develop harvesting in public woodlands owing to competition from privately owned forests, which found themselves in an advantageous situation thanks to the sale of lumber and secondary products. Nevertheless, he foresaw possible change if the greed of private landowners led in the near future to the disappearance of their woodlands. In that case, he predicted, "the misfortune in which state woodlands find themselves today due to their low production would become an inappreciable asset, because having been conserved, even if this was because of the impossibility of harvesting them, . . . they will serve to satisfy the urgent needs of agriculture and industry."[91]

Two years later, the chief engineer calculated that a third of the consumption of forest products could be supplied by public woodlands.[92] He sought to demonstrate the importance of a centralized woodlands administration by a professional corps of engineers and to counter the possibility that budget reforms could limit this administration to a local service. He cited the example of more progressive towns, which could even be said to "overindulge" forest production as an important source of wealth through assiduous vigilance and "respecting the property of the state to such an extent that they consider it more sacred than their own, because it satisfies general needs, and thus everyone benefits from conserving it." He also stressed the unity of forest management in Spain itself, where the Woodlands Engineers Corps had been created "with the goal of applying with a broader perspective the technical principles of dasonomic science."[93]

Portuondo and other forest administrators in Cuba shared the viewpoints predominant among their colleagues in Spain, such as the idea that the state was the natural owner and administrator of high, lumberable woodlands, "since it is the only one who can conserve what is needed by wood consumers and the requirements of public interest, in conformity with the income corresponding to [the woodlands'] conservation." Nothing in this sense could be expected of private landowners, however, since they were "only attentive to the greatest and most rapid use, forgetting the advantages of the conservation . . . of lumberable woodlands that might redound to future generations."[94] Portuondo was taking into account not simply the influence of woodlands on public health, their regularization of river levels, their defense of smaller terrains devoted to agriculture, and other such benefits. He began with the principle that, among state property, forested area was "the social capital of the most public and general nature," something "recognized by all legislators and economists." In favor of this precept he cited the same law opposed by the Woodlands Inspection, which granted local administrative counsels the income from forest harvesting, but only in usufruct, "the state's reserving, in its high mission of inspection and trusteeship, the ownership of the funds, in order to avoid a reduction of this social capital due to a lesser interpretation of the nature of the capital, which, belonging in all its integrity to future generations, as well as to the present one, does not allow us either now or later to use more than its product or interest, represented by the growth of the total arboreal mass."[95]

Many forest products, such as lumber, railroad ties, dyes, charcoal, and firewood, vivified the coastal shipping industry and created jobs, although these were sometimes in difficult conditions and poorly paid. Forests also supplied other articles for the domestic market, including skids, telegraph poles, lumber packs, lathes, small boards, júcaro stakes, frames for drying tobacco (*cujes*), bark of peralejo, yarey, thatch palm, and various products made from majagua (such as cords and threads). Despite their decreasing size, the island's forests still supplied important resources that sustained its inhabitants.

This domestic demand created additional pressure on Cuban forests, such as in the clearing of mangrove swamps and coastal areas for firewood and charcoal. In 1886 the botanist Sebastián Alfredo de Morales, writing about the coastal hicaco,[96] gave the example of the damage caused by firewood and charcoal merchants, both of whom practiced an excessive type of clearing, removing trees indiscriminately by the roots. To prevent this, Morales called for laws and regulations such as those that existed for hunting, measures that would reduce "such clearing that tends to strip us of these advance sentinels of our flora." He warned that if this situation continued many plant species would disappear that would then have to be obtained overseas. He thus urged that authorities limit the species that could be used for each purpose, "since we should not allow the use for fuel of precious woods needed in rural, urban, and naval construction, as well as cabinet making, which would be an attack on the laws of economy."[97]

One of Morales's goals was to make clear the wealth of Cuba's flora that could be harvested but at the same time "to defend this same wealth from the uprooting hand of ambitious speculators."[98] More than sixty years earlier, the abundance and diversity of these forests had led La Sagra to claim that "it can be said that there is no country wealthier than ours in this domain, and we can be just as certain that in none are known more than ten or twelve of those [trees] we possess."[99] This view was still predominant at the end of the nineteenth century. An administrative geographer of the era affirmed that no country in the world possessed, relative to its land area, "a greater quantity of beautiful trees and of wood for construction, cabinet making, and dyes."[100]

The variety of trees and plants that covered the island was a resource of great value for many applications, as is demonstrated by catalogs that appeared throughout the nineteenth century. One of the first was published in 1868 by José María Fernández y Jiménez.[101] His prologue is an eloquent testimony to the fears of what might result from the accelerated disappearance of forests. In his opinion, if there was an evil worthy of all types of remedies, it was "the nakedness of our woodlands, the depopulation of fields, the ominous neglect in reviving them, and the general effort to make sterile the terrain of this fertile island." This was largely due to the fact that Cuba's estate owners, "without a care for the future and without taking into account the tremendous harm that this clearing brings to the country in general, have ruined most of the woodlands of this fertile island for the selfishness of their personal gain."[102] Like other of his contemporaries, Fernández y Jiménez grounded his concerns in broader considerations of the function of forests in nature and society: "The conservation, multiplication, and regularization of woodlands is not a simple matter of individual, economic, and present interest; its nature is higher and its reach broader; it is a matter of public interest, a matter of natural interest, a matter of universal interest, a matter of health and life, a rigorous matter of existence for the current generation as well as future ones."[103]

The subject of the disappearance of the forests and its consequences appeared frequently in the press and in the scientific publications of the era. Examples include the references by the German scientist Johannes Gundlach, who lived in Cuba for several decades, to the reduced bird populations in different locations due to agriculture and clearing of woodlands, together with what he called "the unnecessary war against birds." In the mid-1860s, he asked, "What older Cuban does not recall having seen, when he was young, an abundance of certain birds that today have disappeared?"[104] He specifically noted the cases of the royal woodpecker and the caraira, as later, in his *Ornitología cubana* (1893), he would lament the disappearance of the Cuban macaw, which shortly afterward was considered extinct.

Attracting greater attention during this period were artificial forests, whose origins could be traced to the founding of the Royal Botanical Garden of Havana or to the appearance of urban parks.[105] The concern in this regard increased as Cuban deforestation worsened and as similar experiences overseas were noted. As José Francisco Arnao observed in *La nueva era* in 1882, artificial forests were more quickly available and more profitable than those that grew naturally. According to Arnao, they were best developed by people of greater means, although "the formation of artificial forests on a regular scale does not require great expense." Their full usefulness took time, but value was guaranteed from the beginning, since "the cost of fuel in the towns and countryside of this department increases daily."[106]

In this case the discussion was of artificial forests composed of native trees, such as cedar, mahogany, majagua, pine, dágame, guásima, baría, and ateje. But more often authors wrote of acclimating exotic species. Francisco Javier de Balmaceda, for example, mentioned among others eucalyptus, rubber, coconut, cinchona, white mulberry, and ivory palm trees. "It is necessary," he wrote, "that inhabitants . . . think of creating artificial forests, principally in the western region, in order to live in a pure and healthy atmosphere." This was of primordial interest given transformations in the environment and the ills caused by "sterility and meteorological disorder." He noted the drying up of many springs in sites of large-scale clearing, as well as the reduced flow of rivers, the rapid alternation of drought and flood, the appearance of plant epidemics, and even the effects of yellow fever, which slowed European emigration. He was also worried that agriculture would become "extremely laborious and its fruits puny," such that, with increasing human population, "how difficult it will become to provide food for those with the misfortune to live in a country where the gifts of nature overflowed and were scorned and annihilated!"[107]

In rural areas farmers were advised to plant useful trees along the edges of property, as a way to "improve greatly the climate in parts of the island where scarcely a single tree now exists." Recommended trees in such cases included species such as corojo, date, pomo rosa, guava, guásima, caimitillo, mango, and palm.[108] The greatest hopes, however, were for eucalyptus, in cities as well as in the countryside. Efforts were made to imitate successful experiments in different parts of the world, including neighboring Latin American countries. During the entire 1876–98 period there were constant allusions to the necessity of planting more eucalyptus on the island, particularly *Eucalyptus globulus*, because of its healthful and pharmaceutical properties, as well as for reasons of industry, agriculture, and forestry.[109] In 1882 *La nueva era* wrote: "The more this tree is tried and studied, the more the suitability of its propagation becomes clear. In many parts of Cuba it has become a necessity that one cannot consider with indifference, since for them it is health and even more, life."[110]

We cannot end this chapter without noting that the new war of 1895–98 again increased the clearing of forests for military fortifications. Describing her journey with three colleagues along the road from Júcaro to Morón, the journalist Eva Canel wrote in 1897, "Before and behind us, after we have crossed the wide clearing also made by the engineers: the brushland, silent, dark, mysterious, immense curtain of leaves and plains that cloaks the landscape, hiding from view what hides behind it. There, perhaps, is the enemy, fleeing the Spanish colonies that pursue him, hidden in the shadows of the thicket."[111]

North American
Capital and Sugar's Final
Assault on the Forest,
1898–1926

*Dependence on the United States
and Giant Sugar Corporations*

In 1898 the end of the Cubans' war of independence against Spanish colonial domination opened a new phase in sugar's impact on the forests. The Republic of Cuba was formally established on May 20, 1902, but
its sovereignty was limited by the Platt Amendment, approved by the U.S.
Congress the year before and incorporated as an appendix into the Cuban
constitution. It gave the U.S. government the right to intervene for "the
maintenance of a government adequate for the protection of life, property,
and individual liberty." This regulation of future political relations between
the two countries was complemented in 1903 by a reciprocal trade accord
that reduced tariffs on Cuban sugar and other products entering the U.S.
market by 20 percent; in compensation the United States enjoyed special
tariffs (between 25% and 40%) for various of its products.[1]

During the first U.S. intervention legislation was adopted to promote privately used railroads, and steps were taken to facilitate the buying and selling of land in eastern half of the country, as in Military Order 62, which concerned the demarcation of communal estates. Another important factor in sugar's development was the elimination of yellow fever, thanks to the discovery of the transmitting agent by the Cuban physician Carlos J. Finlay and to the eradication program administered by the provisional military authorities. But perhaps the most important change after 1898 was the arrival of massive investment by U.S. capitalists, who in a few years became the producers of most of the island's sugar, under the protection of Cuba's singular politico-economic status. Ramiro Guerra y Sánchez argued that the extraordinary measures to promote the inflow of foreign capital opened the country to the unfettered action of capitalist enterprise, "free of the restrictions it encountered even in the United States."[2] At no other time in Cuban history did the country experience a greater increase in its "productive potential," just as at no time were deforestation and general environmental change more intense, as consequences of what Richard P. Tucker has called the first flowering of American ecological imperialism.[3]

Sugar production began to recover shortly after the war ended, and its growth continued almost uninterrupted for a quarter of a century. Nevertheless, two phases can be distinguished, marked by the outbreak of World War I and its impact on U.S. investment. The war also led to a drop in the production of beet sugar, from 8.6 million metric tons in 1913 to 3.6 million metric tons in 1919, which sparked a great sugar fever in Cuba. The country's harvest rose from 2,244,500 metric tons in 1914 to 4,104,100 metric tons in 1919 and 5,200,800 metric tons in 1925. Cuba's percentage of world sugar production increased from 14 percent in 1914 to 26 percent in 1919. The period from mid-1918 to mid-1920 has become known in Cuban history as "the dance of the millions" and "the fat cows." According to Leland H. Jenks, the worldwide orgy of speculation in the two postwar years was particularly intense on the island, whose fortunes paralleled those of the sugar market.[4] Thirty-four *centrales* were founded in Cuba between 1915 and 1919 and another sixteen between 1920 and 1926, for a total of fifty, double the number built between 1900 and 1915. This led William Showalter to proclaim in a 1920 *National Geographic* article that Cuba was "El Dorado" and cane its king, producing more than enough sugar in 1920 to build two pyramids of Cheops.[5]

The high prices during the war and the need to increase production rapidly attracted the attention of U.S. capital as never before. Oscar Pino Santos estimates the total U.S. investment in sugar until 1915 at about $50 million, a figure that rose by 1,200 percent in just six years.[6] César Ayala observes that in 1924 the Caribbean, and Cuba in particular, was the site of the greatest U.S. investment in the world, relative to land area and population, representing 63 percent of the total U.S. investment in agricultural enterprises.[7] This great influx of capital was used to build ever more powerful new mills and to expand the capacity of existing ones. It also helped purchase vast territories and multiply private railroads for transporting sugar.[8]

Until the mid-nineteenth century sugar expansion had developed through the subdivision of former *hatos* (cattle ranches) and *corrales* (hog farms), alongside diversified economic exploitation of land. In the last third of the 1800s, at the beginning of the process of concentration and centralization, livestock estates were dismantled and subdivided, with a much greater area of cane fields. In contrast, the *centrales* built after 1898 could control by themselves the area of one or several of these former estates. Lands that before had been composed of forests, grassy savannas, and crops, or subdivided into *ingenios*, *potreros*, estancias, and other types of farms, were now devoted exclusively to cane fields and pastures for oxen. The constant increase in the productive capacity of the *centrales* led to an unprecedented simplification of agroecosystems: from an average 7,949 metric tons on the 186 *centrales* existing in 1907, capacity rose to 14,249 metric tons on 176 in 1913 and 19,455 metric tons on 192 in 1919. The area in cane per *central* increased from 131 caballerías in 1907 to 267 caballerías in 1913, to 346.7 caballerías in 1919.[9]

The impact of sugar expansion on the landscape during these years becomes even easier to understand when we consider the differences between the growth that took place in the provinces of Pinar del Río, Havana, Matanzas, and Santa Clara with that which occurred in Camagüey and Oriente. In table 6.1 we see that the latter went from 20 percent of total national sugar production in 1904 to 35 percent at the outset of World War I, to 60 percent in 1929. Never in the nineteenth century had there been so rapid an occupation of natural regions by sugar, expansion that would have been impossible with the technology of the era.

This acceleration of sugar was due largely to the emergence of the "colossal *ingenios*,"[10] thus known for the enormous quantity of sugar that they could produce in a single day and a single harvest. A study from the 1940s included 27 *centrales* in this category, all built during the first quarter of the

TABLE 6.1. Sugar Production by Province, 1904, 1914, and 1929

	1904		1914		1929	
Province	Metric Tons (Thousands)	%	Metric Tons (Thousands)	%	Metric Tons (Thousands)	%
Pinar del Río	21	2.0	51.5	1.9	192.7	3.7
Havana	132	12.8	322	12.4	355	6.9
Matanzas	318	30.7	565.5	21.8	524.6	10.2
Santa Clara	358	34.6	760	29.4	1,001.7	19.4
Camagüey	28	2.7	273	10.5	1,564	30.4
Oriente	178	17.2	620.5	24	1,517	29.4

Source: L. V de Abad, *Azúcar y caña de azúcar: Ensayo de orientación cubana* (Havana: Mercantil Cubana, 1945).

century in Camagüey (15) and Oriente (12). To satisfy the milling capacity of these *centrales* gigantic latifundios took shape, with private railroad networks that allowed cane to arrive in the time required (see table 6.2). In both provinces the length of the private railroad lines was greater than that of the railroads that had existed on the entire island before 1898, while the production of more than 1 million metric tons of sugar on just 12 or 15 *centrales* equaled the late nineteenth-century yield produced by some 400 *centrales*.

These gigantic sugar mills, dominating thousands of caballerías of land, represent the triumph of industrialization over people who had expressed reservations in the mid-nineteenth century. Modern technologies had tripled yields in sugar refining and notably reduced the costs of production. In economic terms we could speak of greater efficiency, especially in the industrial sector. This would not have been possible without the political and economic factors that I indicated earlier, which created, in the words of Allan Dye and Antonio Santamaría, an adequate "institutional framework" to attract great investments of U.S. capital to the sugar industry and release its maximum productive potential.[11] The fact that the investment flow was directed primarily to the provinces of Camagüey and Oriente is explained by the region's economic incentives, which made it easier to own large swaths of land, establish private railroad networks, and exercise greater control over farmers. In 1904, 1 caballería of land in Camagüey and Oriente sold for 100 to 800 pesos, but if one bought large lots, the price fell

TABLE 6.2. "Colossal *Centrales*" in Camagüey and Oriente, 1920s and 1930s

Province	Number of Colossal *Centrales*	Greatest Production (Metric Tons)	Total Area of Privately Owned or Controlled Land (Caballerías)	Average Area of Privately Owned or Controlled Land (Caballerías)	Total Length of Private Railways (km)	Average Length of Railway (km)
Camagüey	15	1,231,233	43,573	2,904	2,358	157.2
Oriente	12	1,070,937	45,160	3,763	2,467	205.6

Source: L. V de Abad, *Azúcar y caña de azúcar: Ensayo de orientación cubana* (Havana: Mercantil Cubana, 1945).
Note: Greatest production is for harvests between 1922 and 1929.

to less than 100 pesos, while in other provinces it was never less than 300 to 400 pesos.[12]

In truth these sugar colossi could not be called a great economic success, although their more negative repercussions were felt in the social, political, and environmental spheres. In increasing the scale of production, sugar planters aggravated in similar proportion many of the old problems generated by the advance of sugar. For example, Luis V. de Abad concluded of the milling time: "The result is that these huge plants and this network of railroads that cross an area larger, taken together, than the island of Puerto Rico only can be in service one Sixth of the year!"[13] Along with the "dead time" there was the increasing scarcity of subsistence foods, parallel to the destruction of small- and medium-sized property or, rather, its exclusive devotion to sugar farming. In the words of Guerra y Sánchez *latifundismo* reduced Cuba to an "immense field to produce sugar at a low price." The grand scale of sugar monoculture and the production for export and not for domestic consumption made the community "into a mere dependency, a simple satellite, a workshop, in the service of an outside economic metropole."[14]

It has not been stressed enough, however, that sugar's expansion in the first quarter of the twentieth century toward Camagüey and Oriente largely continued the logic of the old slaveholding plantations in the western half of the country. The high yields of planting in cleared land and the availability of low-cost lumber, railroad ties, and firewood as supplementary fuel again played a central role in the conquest of the east for sugar production. Forests also offered initial profits through the wood trade (see figures 6.1 and 6.2).

The great forest masses in the provinces of Puerto Príncipe and Santiago de Cuba were seen at the end of the nineteenth century as one of the most attractive resources. In the pages of *Cuba y América*, a weekly published in New York by Cuban independence activists, Ramiro Cabrera wrote in 1897 about the perspectives for American capital. No opportunity "in the agricultural circle," he wrote, was "more attractive than the exploitation of the magnificent lumber of which the ancient forests of the island are full."[15] Although he exaggerated the quantity in claiming that there were 13 million uncultivated hectares, and that 10 million of these were virgin forest, he was still correct about the agricultural possibilities. As far as the true wooded area at the end of the nineteenth century, estimates vary. Eliseo Matos gave a figure for 1900 of 4,547,857 hectares (339,392 caballerías), or 41 percent of Cuba's area.[16] Statistics for the 1899 census indicate far fewer, but they counted only land on farms.[17]

What is certain is that the forests of the eastern half of the country were an obligatory topic in the books and articles that publicized Cuba's natural resources to the U.S. public, and investors in particular. Books published between 1898 and 1902, by authors such as Albert J. Norton, Robert T. Hill, William J. Clark, and Robert B. Porter, always included estimates of the forested area and discussed the possibilities offered by their exploitation, together with data on wood exports from Cuba to the United States.[18] In general they supposed the existence of 13 to 15 million acres (5.3 to 6.1 million hectares) of forest.[19] Before the war began in 1895, the greatest amount of wood, particularly mahogany and cedar, bound for the U.S. market left from Tunas de Zaza, Santa Cruz del Sur, Manzanillo, and Gibara. With the new transportation infrastructure, the growth potential of this trade was thought to be enormous.[20]

The export of wood and other forest products from the island increased sharply in the first decade of the twentieth century. According to the 1907 census, the value of exported wood that year was 2,375,733 pesos, significantly more than the 966,999 pesos in 1899 or the 1,428,574 in 1902. Exports of fibers, dyes, and tanning agents set records in 1902 and 1903. From 1907 to 1913 the wood trade grew slightly, then declined precipitously during World War I. In 1914, 10,458,050 cubic feet of cedar and 10,254,902 cubic feet of mahogany were exported, figures that fell to 561,000 and 161,000,

FIGURE 6.1. Logging of ties for the Central Railroad.

(Antonio Duque, "Ferrocarril Central de Cuba: Compañía de Cuba y construcción del ferrocarril," *Cuba y América* [April 1903]: 313)

FIGURE 6.2. Sawmill in the vicinity of the Central Railroad.

(*Cuba Review and Bulletin,* June 1907)

respectively, by 1919. During this period wood harvesting was reduced by half and supplied mostly the domestic market. Production of other items such as railroad ties and telegraph poles remained stable or increased. One category that grew significantly was that of "other woods," whose annual averages of 1 million to 2 million feet rose to 10,921,000 feet by 1918.[21]

In the opposite direction, the census figures from 1907 and 1919 show the increasing dependency on imports of wood and other plant materials, mostly coming from the United States. The abrupt drop in the export of forest products due to World War I occurred in the midst of the greatest destruction of Cuban forests in the shortest time ever.[22] Thousands of caballerías were converted to cane fields to satisfy the demands of the sugar market and of U.S. refineries where the final product was processed, often without leaving margins where wood or other forest products could be cultivated. Thus in under two decades the landscapes of Camagüey and Oriente underwent a radical transformation whose magnitude depended both on *centrales* with the most advanced technology and on the ample network of public and private railroad networks that allowed them to access the most remote regions. Other technology, such as the first tractors, chemical fertilizers, and increasingly used petroleum helped make Cuba one of the earliest settings for industrial agriculture in the tropics (see figures 6.3, 6.4, and 6.5). It would be an exaggeration, however, to say that the sugar boom of those years resulted from a substantial improvement in agricultural technology, in the use of irrigation, or in the use of fertilizers. Apart from the great production capacity of the new mills and their high industrial yields, the new and definitive expansion of sugar was rooted for some time in the proverbial fertility of cleared land (see figure 6.6).

Studies of Cuban agriculture and soils published between 1900 and 1930 noted the persistence of a cultivation system whose success depended on occupying wooded areas. In 1905 the director of the Agronomic Station in Santiago de las Vegas, Franklin S. Earle of the United States, wrote: "The planting of cane in cleared land is a matter perfectly known in Cuba, and it always gives satisfactory results. Such land, when it is properly planted and cared for, continues giving productive harvests for ten or even twenty years, depending on its richness and nature."[23] Years later another director of the same institution, Josiah T. Crawley, also of the United States, described the method of cultivation that had been followed on the island since the seventeenth century, then claimed: "For those unfamiliar with such matters this will seem a quite crude method for planting and yet, if the land is rich, the

FIGURE 6.3. España *central* in the province of Matanzas.

(República de Cuba, *El libro de Cuba* [Havana, 1925])

FIGURE 6.4. Canal for irrigating land of the Gómez Mena *central* in the province of Havana.

(Josiah T. Crawley, "El cultivo de la caña de azúcar en Cuba," *Boletín de la Estación Experimental Agronómica*, no. 35 [February 1917]: 77)

FIGURE 6.5. Studies on the use of chemical fertilizers.

(Franklin S. Earle, *El cultivo de la caña de azúcar en las Antillas*
[Havana: Germán Kali Works, Imprenta La Prueba, n.d.], 59)

Despite her extraordinary present wealth and development she still is only well started on the road to improving her potentialities. Sugar cane on virgin land may be cut for thirty years without replanting.

FIGURE 6.6. Reference in a tourism book to the fertility of Cuban soils
after clearing.

(Rotary Club of Havana and Asociación Nacional de Fomento del Turismo, *Cuba*
[Havana: Artes Gráficas de La Habana, 1920])

harvest's first cutting will yield from eighty thousand to one hundred thousand arrobas of cane per caballería . . . and, with very little cost for weed removal, it will produce good harvests for ten to twenty years."[24]

Crawley also commented on the difference between the east and west of the island: "The virgin soil of Camagüey and Oriente can produce sugar cane for fifteen years or more, without plowing, without replanting, and without fertilizer, but the soil of Santa Clara, Matanzas, or Havana in general only produces five harvests, more or less, afterward requiring replanting." Works such as those of Earle and Crawley called attention to the problems that this system caused in the long term, and they sought to improve cultivation methods in relation to the different types of soils. Also at the beginning of the twentieth century a new system was proposed by Francisco Zayas, with the same goal as that behind Alvaro Reynoso's method developed decades before: the improvement of cane cultivation without needing to resort to virgin soils.[25] As Earle put it in his article from 1905, "Almost all the old *ingenios* on this island are surrounded by thousands of acres of this kind of terrain, which remain useless so long as the cane has to be taken each day to very distant points."[26]

Warnings about the long-term consequences of the system of clearing and burning had limited impact so long as there were forests to clear and exploit for their natural fertility, notwithstanding the visible adverse effects of this system on much of the island's geography. In the middle of the post-1898 sugar boom, and particularly during World War I, Cuba had a clear advantage owing to its high cane yields and the possibility of obtaining harvests for several years without needing to replant. Authors such as A. D. Hall, in his book *Cuba: Its Past, Present, and Future* (1906), described soils unrivaled in other parts of the world that gave an enormous advantage over competitors.[27] Some time later, in 1920, William Showalter's *National Geographic* article claimed that Cuba's advantage over any other country in producing cheaply was due to the fact that the others had to plant every two years and some each year, while in Cuba the average was once every seven to twelve years.[28]

The temptation of rapid profits during the exceptional circumstances of the war momentarily kept at bay any large-scale attempt to improve cultivation on the new lands of Camagüey and Oriente. Tranquilino Frasquieri described the result as "a superdestruction favorable only to the sugar latifundio and the greed of those who seek to buy land temporarily fertilized with the ashes of centuries-old forests."[29] The new sugar boom, like the booms of previous eras, depended largely on the destruction of forests. A comparison of the forested area of the late nineteenth century with that existing less than thirty years later shows this quite eloquently. According to Matos, this area shrank from 4,547,857 hectares in 1900 to 2,242,166 hectares in 1927, or from 41.3 percent to 20.4 percent of the national territory. According to sources from the period, the difference could be even greater. In 1923 the director of woodlands and mines of the Secretariat of Agriculture, Commerce, and Labor, José Isaac del Corral Alemán, claimed that the forested area was 135,848 caballerías, divided into 92,363 caballerías of high woodlands (forests), 30,415 of low woodlands (brushland, pasture, and savanna), and 13,070 of mangrove and other swamps.[30] The total represented 16.5 percent of Cuban territory. Compared with the estimates from the beginning of the century, which put the forests at about 50 percent of Cuba's land area, this would indicate the disappearance of forests from more than 30 percent of the country in just two decades.[31]

This great escalation in the transformation of forests into cane fields bore ephemeral fruit compared with the damage to the ecosystems. In mid-1920 the price of sugar on the world market began to fall abruptly, and thus "fat cows" gave way to the "thin" ones. One result was the consolidation of U.S. companies' domination of Cuban sugar production. Jenks notes that in 1913 they produced about 35 percent of the total, but by the 1926–27 harvest their share had increased to 62.5 percent, to which one should add the 8 percent owned by "cubano yanquis" and the 4 percent that belonged to Canadians. This dominance was possible thanks to their owning or leasing no fewer than 2,540,000 hectares (189,552 caballerías), about 22 percent of the country, as well as 6,400 kilometers of railroad serving these *centrales*. These properties were concentrated in Camagüey and Oriente, where the North Americans generally controlled the best land.

After the transitory wartime prosperity, the historical problems entailed by sugar's advance accentuated. The dependence on a single product and a single market was greater than ever. Unlike in previous eras, when most plantations belonged to criollos or foreigners settled on the island, the country had become "a huge latifundio governed and administered by absentee landlords." Large investments in sugar transformed life in vast regions, to which were brought such symbols of modernity as railroads and electric lights, and in many cases these helped improve living conditions in urban centers and in the countryside, although ephemerally for many. Nevertheless, they also further reduced economic independence and increased vulnerability to the ups and downs of the market. As Jenks concluded, "Cuba's problem concretely symbolizes the modern struggle of the individual, of local idiosyncrasy, of self-confidence, against the process of global uniformity." He further wondered, "What role will remain for democracy in a completely industrialized society? If Cuban liberty proves in the end illusory, where will freedom be safe?"[32]

By the time the perverse effects of sugar's vertiginous growth on the economic, political, and social order were obvious, the damage to the environment was already irreversible. The desire to profit from the economic circumstances and obtain quick profits swept away most of the forest wealth that still existed, which had been a resource for the local economy and one of the bases of sugar's splendor. In November 1920 an editorial in the *Revista de agricultura, comercio y trabajo* (the organ of the Secretariat of Agriculture) offered this judgment of the intense deforestation of those years:

> Our forest reserves suffered enormous loss with the considerable increase in fields devoted to the growing of sugarcane. In less than four years, the demolishing ax has felled thousands and thousands of the best forests in Cuba, among the scant forests that are left to us, and soon the country will find itself without the shade of a tree, to make room for ephemeral cane. . . . One has no right to destroy this fundamental and eternal wealth to enrich those whom circumstance makes owners of the land. And we now see, too late, the fatal result of our carelessness and our fever to make all of Cuba into a vast cane field. We have not even been able to obtain the present good at the expense of the future.[33]

Faced with this situation, lawmakers began trying to contain the clearing of forests in Camagüey and Oriente. A crucial moment was the approval of Decree 495, signed by President Gerardo Machado on April 13, 1926, which ordered the "absolute prohibition to clear in high woodlands belonging to the state or to private landowners." This banned the clearing of high woodlands in order to plant cane and was extended each year until the 1930s, when the decree became a law. It clearly represented an important change in attitude, but it came lamentably late to avoid the enormous clearings for cane fields that sometimes failed. Some years later the report *Problemas de la nueva Cuba* detailed the effects of the period of growth that followed World War I: "Millions of pesos were lost in the useless extension of cane fields. . . . Examples are known where a large *central* was built only to discover later that the local soil was not suited for cane."[34] This razing of centuries-old forests in order to pursue a goal doomed at the outset to failure was sadly symbolic.

The Offensive against the Natural Regions of Camagüey and Oriente

The 1898–1926 period saw the culmination of the conquest, on an unprecedented scale, of Cuba's natural regions most suited to the production of sugar. Until the end of the nineteenth century the industry took several decades to exploit the fertility of cleared land in each of the regions involved. It set up in an area and in successive moves within it occupied the surrounding terrain so long as it could find virgin land for the expansion of cane fields or to relocate entire farms. Between 1900 and 1926 the transformation of entire natural regions took much less time and occurred simultaneously in many of the regions of eastern Cuba.

Until the end of the nineteenth century the bulk of sugar production took place in the physico-natural regions of Havana-Matanzas and the Center. Two stages can be differentiated: the first, from the seventeenth century to 1815, encompassed natural regions with an approximate area of 5,863 square kilometers; the second, from 1815 to 1900, completed the expansion of sugar through the Colón Plain and the regions of the Center, a total of 19,235 square kilometers. Sugar production took place outside this zone, but without achieving an absolute dominance over other economic activity and without transforming the ecosystems so radically as had been done from the Havana area to the center of the island. Exceptions to this general pattern, to a certain point, were the natural regions of the plains of Santiago de Cuba (279 km²), Palma–San Luis (765 km²), and Songo–La Maya (525 km²), as well as the development of sugar in the second half of the nineteenth century around the regions Manzanillo Plain (2,025 km²) and Guantánamo Plain (1,350 km²).

At the beginning of the twentieth century, these regions of Camagüey and Oriente still retained much of their forest wealth. In a study comparing them with the west of the island, Juan Pérez de La Riva called them "Cuba B," untransformed by sugar and the slave plantation. The contrast with "Cuba A" was significant in all senses. For instance, in 1860 Cuba A's share of foreign trade was 89.9 percent and Cuba B's only 10.1 percent. In the latter, a self-sufficient livestock economy predominated, while in the plantation area some indexes of progress, such as the extension of rail lines, could be compared with those of Europe's advanced industrial countries.[35] The sugar development of Cuba B was based on small *ingenios* and *trapiches*. At the end of the Ten Years' War (1868–78), a few *ingenios centrales* set up in parts of the region, but with more local impact.

As the nineteenth century drew to an end, the 1899 census shows, the provinces of Puerto Príncipe and Santiago de Cuba together had 70.5 percent of the high woodlands and 64.3 percent of the low woodlands on Cuban farms. For an impression of the forest wealth of the two provinces one can consult the census of 1919.[36] In Camagüey the average number of trees in 1 caballería of high woodlands near the coast was 300 mahogany, 50 cedar, 50 yaba, 100 ocuje, 100 baría, 200 júcaro, 50 sabicú, 100 jiquí, and 50 of other species. This totaled 1,000 trees of useful wood, with 200 feet of boards. For woodlands of the interior, the average number of trees was as follows: 300 cedar, 50 mahogany, 100 yaba, 100 baría, 100 ocuje, 50 sabicú, 50 jiquí, and 50 of other species, for a total of 900 useful trees. The average amount of firewood available per caballería was estimated at 1,000 cords of 128 cubic feet each. Thus, according to these figures, the forests of Camagüey produced per caballería about 200,000 to 500,000 feet of boards along the coast and between 180,000 and 480,000 feet in the interior.

For the province of Oriente the estimated average was up to 20,000 feet of cedar or mahogany per caballería and up to 50,000 feet of other hardwoods such as jiquí, almiquí, and yaba, although the average production was reckoned at 25,000 feet. As for firewood, 2,000 to 2,500 metric tons could be produced, depending on how abundant the woodland was in soft- and heartwoods. A valuable resource in assessing the area of hardwood forest in the two forests at the onset of the twentieth century is the military map made between 1906 and 1908, which Leo Waibel used in his study of Cuba's original vegetation (see map 6.1).[37]

In the first three decades of the twentieth century these forests were the principal suppliers of forest products and wood for export. Despite having been weakened by uncontrolled clearing for cane fields and pastures, Camagüey in 1933 still was the leading site for extraction of various such products, followed by Oriente.[38] Nonetheless, there were notable differences with forest statistics from before World War I. Extraction of cedar and mahogany was 10 percent that of 1914. Other woods declined considerably or disappeared from the records entirely — for example sabicú, which yielded 2,653,350 poles in 1918 and just 20 in 1933, or yaba and ácana, which

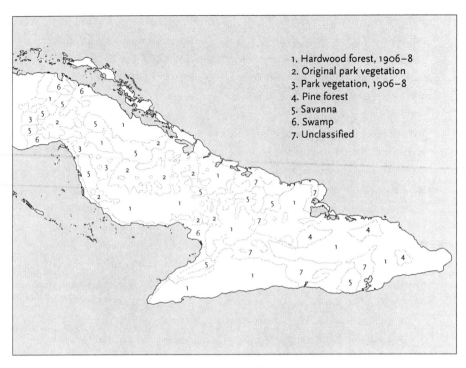

1. Hardwood forest, 1906–8
2. Original park vegetation
3. Park vegetation, 1906–8
4. Pine forest
5. Savanna
6. Swamp
7. Unclassified

MAP 6.1. Hardwood Forests in the Provinces of Camagüey and Oriente,
Early Twentieth Century

Source: Leo Waibel, map based on *Mapa militar de Cuba, 1906–1908*
(Washington, DC: U.S. War Department, 1908).

in several years between 1914 and 1919 surpassed 200,000 feet but do not
appear in the statistics for 1933.

But the interest in the vast forests of eastern Cuba after 1898 had much
more to do with the new possibilities for sugar's expansion. Very early,
buyers began to purchase the thousands of caballerías of wooded land in
order to build large *centrales*, exploiting natural, political, economic, and
commercial advantages that Cuba offered in comparison with other sugar-
growing countries and according to the demand from U.S. refineries. In
1899 Manuel Rionda, a U.S. Hispanic and owner of the Tuinicú *central* since
1893, joined with other U.S. interests to acquire 2,000 caballerías in the area
of Santa Cruz del Sur (Puerto Príncipe Province). The goal was to develop
the Francisco *central*, founded in 1901 in the wood trade's most important
zone. In 1913 it was recorded that this *central*, with 399 caballerías of cane

and another 100 of pasture, had 500 caballerías of woodland and 539 of unspecified use.[39]

During the years of the first U.S. intervention lands were also bought for large *centrales* around the main bays of the northeastern coast, which were surrounded by abundant forests and had excellent conditions for rapid commercialization. A turn-of-the-century case was the acquisition of 6,000 caballerías in the Nipe Plain region (1,200 km²) for the derisory price of 31 pesos per caballería. Here the Boston (1901) and Preston (1904) *centrales* were established. Around another northeastern bay, Puerto Padre, were founded the *centrales* of Chaparra (1901) and Delicias (1911) (see figure 6.7). One year after that the Manatí *central* was created near the port of the same name. In 1913 records, each of these sugar plantations is credited with having 1,000 or more caballerías of woodland.[40] Chaparra, with a total of 2,663 caballerías, that year had 947 in cane, 500 in pasture, and 1,216 of woodland. The maximum yield was 115,000 arrobas per caballería and the minimum 40,000. Manatí, just one year old, had 180 caballerías in cane and 100 in pasture, as well as 1,320 of woodland and savanna. Mark J. Smith's study of Manatí's latifundio clearly shows the abundance of forests in the area, described in the documents as a solid jungle in which the sun did not reach the ground and with valuable hardwoods such as mahogany and cedar. Smith also notes the forests' important role in providing the soil with organic material, in contrast with the nutrient deficits characteristic of savannas.[41] Manatí's cane yields reached the stunning levels of 70,000 (minimum) and 180,000 (maximum) arrobas per caballería (see map 6.2).

All these mills near various of Oriente's northern ports, where sugar could be loaded, formed one of the most important nuclei of the industry's expansion before World War I. This area covered much of the east of the Camagüey-Maniabón district (in the east of the regions Plain of Northern Camagüey-Maniabón [4,937 km²], Plains and Heights of Maniabón [900 km²], and Plains and Heights of Banes-Cacocum [1,133 km²]).

The forests continued to be a very useful resource during the early years of an investment. Their importance as suppliers of lumber and firewood may have been less, but this may have been offset by their value for other products such as railroad ties needed for sugar's transportation infrastructure. Some wood may also have remained for export overseas or to other provinces. All these were characteristics shared by a second group of *centrales* established in the interior of the two provinces, along the Central Railroad (Ferrocarril Central). During the period that began in 1898 the

FIGURE 6.7. Delicias and Chaparra *centrales* in the north of Oriente Province.
(República de Cuba, *El libro de Cuba* [Havana, 1925])

idea of building this line to link western and eastern Cuba was quickly taken up again. The man charged with making this railroad a reality was the famous builder of the Canadian Pacific, Sir William Van Horne, who in 1900 founded the Cuba Company to link the cities of Santa Clara and Santiago de Cuba. Two years later, on December 1, 1902, the long-awaited

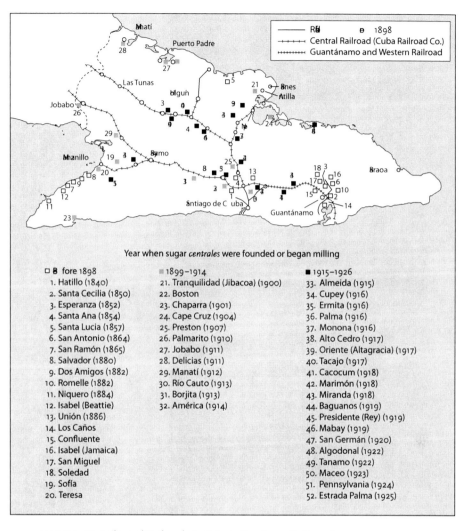

Year when sugar *centrales* were founded or began milling

□ B fore 1898	▨ 1899–1914	■ 1915–1926
1. Hatillo (1840)	21. Tranquilidad (Jibacoa) (1900)	33. Almeida (1915)
2. Santa Cecilia (1850)	22. Boston	34. Cupey (1916)
3. Esperanza (1852)	23. Chaparra (1901)	35. Ermita (1916)
4. Santa Ana (1854)	24. Cape Cruz (1904)	36. Palma (1916)
5. Santa Lucia (1857)	25. Preston (1907)	37. Monona (1916)
6. San Antonio (1864)	26. Palmarito (1910)	38. Alto Cedro (1917)
7. San Ramón (1865)	27. Jobabo (1911)	39. Oriente (Altagracia) (1917)
8. Salvador (1880)	28. Delicias (1911)	40. Tacajo (1917)
9. Dos Amigos (1882)	29. Manatí (1912)	41. Cacocum (1918)
10. Romelle (1882)	30. Río Cauto (1913)	42. Marimón (1918)
11. Niquero (1884)	31. Borjita (1913)	43. Miranda (1918)
12. Isabel (Beattie)	32. América (1914)	44. Baguanos (1919)
13. Unión (1886)		45. Presidente (Rey) (1919)
14. Los Caños		46. Mabay (1919)
15. Confluente		47. San Germán (1920)
16. Isabel (Jamaica)		48. Algodonal (1922)
17. San Miguel		49. Tanamo (1922)
18. Soledad		50. Maceo (1923)
19. Sofía		51. Pennsylvania (1924)
20. Teresa		52. Estrada Palma (1925)

MAP 6.2. *Centrales* and Railroads in Oriente Province, 1898–1926

Central Railroad began operation. During the first decade of the century the company expanded its network in both provinces under the name of the Cuban Railroad Company, with 935.6 kilometers designed to remove vast territories from their isolation though exploitation of their valuable natural resources.[42]

These public railroads and the private ones established by the sugar *centrales* networked together, extending like tentacles to the remotest places

Construida para el Central Jaronú

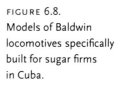

FIGURE 6.8.
Models of Baldwin
locomotives specifically
built for sugar firms
in Cuba.

(República de Cuba,
El libro de Cuba [Havana,
1925])

Construida para United Railways of Havana

Construida para el F. C. Norte de Cuba

Construida para United Fruit Co.

Construida para el Central Siboney

Construida para el Central N. S. del Carmen

to supply cane to industrial colossi that appeared like transatlantic steamers in a sea of cane fields (see figures 6.8 and 6.9). As usual, one of their first services was transporting wood and other forest products. Among the Cuban Railroad Company's first investments were lumbering sites and saw mills.[43]

FIGURE 6.9.
Advertisement for tools
for transporting cane, as
well as products and by-
products of sugar refining.
(*Cuba Review*, published in
several issues in 1923)

After several years of meager profits, the company's lines began to make it indispensable to the new sugar boom. The company developed two large *centrales* along its tracks, Jatibonico and Jobabo, which began their first harvests in 1906 and 1911. The first was located at Camagüey's border with Santa Clara and the second in the west of Oriente, near the border with Camagüey. Independent of the time of operation, location seems to have determined the difference in the amount of forest in 1913. While no woodlands were mentioned for Jatibonico (for which 526 caballerías of cane and 100 of pasture are recorded), Jobabo was credited with 107 caballerías in cane, 200 in pasture, and 2,500 of woodland. During this time a visitor, the journalist Carlos Martí, described the distribution of parcels as "extensive fields of virgin land," part of Jobabo, for the planting of cane and predicted: "It is some distance from Manatí to Jobabo, but with time the cane plantations will join through the woodland." He saw a similar future for other areas of Oriente. It was 1915, and World War I had broken out, which led the poet to reflect on the landscape around the Bay of Nipe: "From Antilla . . . one overlooks the wide Bay of Nipe and a broad green plain that is nothing but cane plantations in production. The smokestacks of the Preston Central are like gallant dominators of the cane fields. The bay will be enclosed by cane plantations, the woodlands harassed by cane plantations, the towns besieged by cane plantations. Oh, famous year! God grant that the calculations of wealth in no way err! But what will we eat?"[44]

Before the war began there were few *centrales* along the Central Railroad. The Río Cauto *central* was established along the line from Bayamo to Manzanillo and had its first harvest in 1913. Its 1,000 caballerías of land included 30 in cane, 470 in pastures, and 500 of woodland. Two other *centrales* were founded in the province of Camagüey, where the former line from Júcaro to Morón impelled an area of development linked to the Central Railroad near Ciego de Avila. The rise in prices caused by the war led to sugar's definitive conquest of the virgin lands of Camagüey and Oriente. The province of Las Villas increased its production during the conflict and maintained its dominance until 1920, when it was quickly overtaken.

The most spectacular growth occurred in Camagüey, as we will see in the next section, but that in Oriente was nearly as astonishing. This was due both to modifications that increased the capacity of existing mills and to the building of new ones. Many were constructed along the lines of the Cuban Railroad Company, with exceptions such as the Tánamo *central* in the region Plain of Sagua de Tánamo (900 km^2), near the bay of the same name. We can say that this was the stage of sugar's irruption in the natural region Cauto Plain (5,650 km^2) and in other areas of the Plains and Heights of Cauto subdistrict (Heights of Báguanos, 648 km^2; and parts of the Nipe Plain, 1,200 km^2, and the Manzanillo Plain, 2,025 km^2). Writing about the repercussions of the war on the provinces of Oriente and Camagüey, Jenks observed: "Few forests escaped clearing. For several months, whole gangs of firewood merchants set to their destructive work. Then the trees that remained caught fire, producing a simultaneous conflagration in several thousand hectares." He went on to note that agriculture proved so lucrative that "contracts were drawn up with clauses much more favorable to the *central* than was customary in more stable regions of Cuba."[45]

While much terrain in western Cuba was considered exhausted and unproductive, that on the eastern half of the island became the great hope for a new sugar boom. The eastern soils were praised as most fertile and best suited for cane; few observers understood that this land could decline similarly. Josiah Crawley was an exception: in a February 1909 session of the Havana Academy of Sciences he warned: "A vicious cycle of cultivation is responsible for the poverty of soils in the long-colonized districts, and one need not be a prophet or a wise man to see that the provinces of the east will become barren and sterile in the same way."[46] He believed that Cuba's wealth was in its land and that the prosperity, power, and endurance of the nation depended on solving the soil problems energetically and intelligently. He explored this topic in greater depth in a 1917 article on cane farming in Cuba. He noted planters' preference for "black soil," the most abundant kind from Santa Clara to Oriente. Nonetheless, he called attention to the difficulty of working it due owing insufficient drainage and the rapid invasion of weeds. In areas where this type of soil predominated, arroyos were common in red earth, but these areas did not have equal access to underground water. In the east, therefore, *ingenios centrales* were often located near rivers.

The impact of the sugar boom of those years on the forests of Camagüey and Oriente caused growing concern, at least among the scientists, journalists, and politicians who put their thoughts in writing. In 1918 the botanist Juan Tomás Roig warned after two working trips: "Someone who visited these provinces ten years ago and returns to them now can only be alarmed by the rapid disappearance of those magnificent forests that before could be contemplated in all directions and that today have been replaced by cane fields and pastures." He maintained that if the clearing continued at the same intensity in ten years no forests would remain, except in "places that are inaccessible or that, like Baracoa, lack railroads and have not yet been reached by sugar's fury." Roig was not against clearing forests for fields of cane and other crops, since he saw this as indicating "progress and well-being for the country." But if clearing was indispensable, it would be highly unwise "to destroy with one blow all forest wealth in the entire country."[47]

In order for the necessary conservation of forests to be achieved, Roig asked that not only the need for fuel and lumber be taken into account but also the influence on the climate, the regularity of rainfall, and the protection of fields against erosion. What could not be seen by farm owners "alert only to their own private and immediate interest" had to be attended to by foresighted governments, "which are obligated to look out for the future of national agriculture." Among other remedies, Roig pointed to the need for a forest reserve or national forest in each province, imitating the United States and Puerto Rico's Sierra del Luquillo. These forests should be "sacred places for everyone" and could be formed by preventing wood extraction on state lands and by the propagation of the principal lumberable species by provincial woodlands and mines authorities. He also proposed the issuing of a decree compelling landowners in regions whose wood was being harvested to reserve the "equivalent of at least 10 percent of the total area currently covered by forest." Similarly, he recommended a ban on the felling and harvesting of rare and valuable or nearly extinct species.[48]

Proposals such as Roig's stumbled on the obstacle of the greatly reduced area under the state's direct jurisdiction. In this respect the situation had worsened during the first two decades of the twentieth century. In November 1920 the *Revista de agricultura, comercio y trabajo* published an editorial on the heavy deforestation of those years, noting that "in Cuba we lack modern laws to protect forest wealth. Each farm owner considers himself the absolute and eternal owner of his property, as if he had acquired it for all time at the Creation, and he simply does what he pleases with his trees, so that the case often arises where highly valuable fruit trees are destroyed to be converted into charcoal, or to make way for immediately exploitable crops."[49]

The editorial therefore called on the Congress of the Republic to establish "intangible laws that defend the forest and the tree against ignorance, disdain, or greed."[50] Shortly thereafter, measures began to appear promoting the conservation of still-existing forests and the multiplication of efforts to restore the lost wealth. There were frequent allusions in this sense to the vast tracts of land that had been cleared during the sugar expansion and that later proved inapt for cane. In 1929 Alberto Fors, then director of the forest nursery of Pinar del Río, wrote: "We now find ourselves with the important problem of repopulating forests in regions whose woodlands were cleared for the planting of cane and whose land proved unsuitable for this crop."[51] The same thing happened in Camagüey and Oriente, but especially in the former, where in fewer years the most forest had been destroyed in the history of Cuba.

Sugar on the Plains of Camagüey

The scale of this period's sugar expansion surpassed that of the previous era, so in this case we will take as our example not a specific natural region but what was then the province of Camagüey.[52] This includes most of the five regions of the Camagüey-Maniabón district. In its far west is the Plain of Júcaro-Morón region (5,050 km²), bordered to the east, in four parallel horizontal strips from north to south, by Plain of Northern Camagüey-Maniabón (4,937 km²), Plain of North-Central Camagüey (5,800 km²), Plain of South-Central Camagüey (7,150 km²), and Plain of Southern Camagüey (4,500 km²).

These territories include the greatest area of plains in Cuba, interrupted by the small natural region of Heights of the Sierra de Cubitas (392 km²). Its central band (the subdistrict of Plains and Heights of Central Camagüey-Maniabón) has an average elevation of 100 to 200 meters above sea level, while the three remaining natural regions rarely exceed 50 meters. One particularity of Plain of Júcaro-Morón compared with the others is the low density of its river network, with 0.25 to 0.5 kilometer of waterway per square kilometer, with fundamentally underground drainage. In contrast, the other four regions are traversed by numerous rivers and arroyos, which spring from the watershed in the central plain (Plain of South-Central Camagüey, for instance, has fluvial density of 1 to 1.5 km per km²). The soils of the northern and southern plains are considered fertile but with some drainage problems, while those in the center are largely classified as of average fertility, as well as being sandy and prone to erosion. The highest quality soils are in the center of Plain of Júcaro-Morón, where they are considered to be fertile and deep.

The extensive plains of Camagüey are today emblematic of Cuban savannas, but they clearly were covered with forest when the European colonizers arrived. Much of the savannas of Puerto Príncipe, famous in the nineteenth century, were artificial and often the result of livestock farming. For example, the 1862 census ranked Puerto Príncipe as the jurisdiction having the most natural pasture, with 37,960 caballerías (46.6% of its designated area). The fact that the administrative area that year was much less than that of the future province prevents us from taking this percentage as representative, but it does illustrate the impact of traditional clearing and burning for pastures. Since the eighteenth century, bans had been issued against this practice on livestock farms, but they were outweighed by the impossibility of verifying adherence to the regulations and later by landowners' absolute freedom to clear forests on their farms.[53]

Also influencing the modification of the Camagüey landscape before the twentieth century was the trade in wood and forest products, domestic and industrial necessities, and agriculture. After the 1815 edict granting freedom to clear forests, individuals and companies devoted to the trade set up shop. The nuclei of the wood trade were Nuevitas and Santa Cruz del Sur, although wood was also shipped from the coves of Júcaro and Vertientes on the southern coast. The best trees of precious wood and lumber were felled, taking advantage of river crests during the rainy season for transport to the coast. Among the destinations of this wood were the ports of London, New York, Bremen, Rotterdam, Philadelphia, and Boston. Apparently the extraction of wood through Santa Cruz was more directed toward export, while Nuevitas was more involved in coastal shipping to Havana.[54]

The area of Nuevitas and the territory around the city of Puerto Príncipe were in fact the principal scenes of the reduced sugar production in the future province. In 1860 these areas had 102 *ingenios*, 36 of which used steam engines. This represented 35 percent of farms, while for the *ingenios* of the Western Department the proportion was 78.2 percent. While in the west 43 percent of all land occupied by *ingenios* was in cane, in this jurisdiction the figure was only 10 percent.[55] Much of the land not devoted to cane was covered with forest, as Father Escolapio Antonio Perpiñá described in the 1860s. Writing about his visit in 1860 to the Oriente *ingenio*, one of the most modern in the region,[56] he recalled what one of his hosts had told him: "Do you see all those vast cane fields, Father? Well, they are the smallest part of the terrain owned by the large farm. If they were instead sown with cane many thousand blacks would be needed to farm the land. In contrast, you will note in these woods and green pastures a multitude of cattle and horses running in all directions."[57]

The completion in 1851 of a 72-kilometer railroad line between Puerto Príncipe and Nuevitas contributed to sugar's limited impact on this area. The project is to be credited more to the persistence of its promoter, Gaspar Betancourt Cisneros, than to objective economic conditions. As in other regions, rail facilitated the transport of forest products and became a consumer of firewood, charcoal, and railroad ties.[58]

During the Ten Years' War the region's agricultural and livestock wealth was largely destroyed, this area being one of the conflict's main battlegrounds. After the signing of the Zanjón Accord (Convenio de Zanjón) reconstruction began, with sugar one of its pillars. But instead of farms like those of 1860, when the largest area in cane was 16 caballerías, Puerto Príncipe saw the creation of its first *ingenios centrales*: Redención, Congreso, Senado, and later Lugareño. The outbreak of another war in 1895 again led to the region's economic ruin, and like the previous war it transformed its landscape, with the digging of trenches and other military actions.

The 1899 census provides data that can help us understand how Camagüey would evolve. Although it had the smallest number of farms, these occupied a much larger area, an average 25.8 caballerías, far ahead of its closest competitor in this category, Matanzas, with 7.5 caballerías per farm. These properties were composed of 41.2 percent high woodland and 19.6 percent low woodland, a total of 60.8 percent of the 61,365 caballerías in the province's farms and 34.5 percent of high woodlands on farms on the entire island.[59] The fact that according to the 1899 census farms formed only 29.2 percent of the province does not mean that the rest was without owner or belonged to the state. The contrary is closer to the truth, since among provinces Puerto Príncipe also had the second smallest amount of land in public woodlands.[60] Whatever the form of land ownership, what interests us here is the large amount of forest that the province had in 1900. While forests were about 60 percent of the area on working farms, on other lands they were often a larger proportion. The 1899 census specifies that "columns relative to forests only include forest on working farms and do not include the vast and limitless prairies located outside working farms."[61]

The end of war gave a new push to the harvesting of lumber and precious wood in Camagüey's forests. In the category of transport permits (guías) issued by the Department of Woodlands for the extraction of forest products during the 1899–1900 fiscal year, Puerto Príncipe ranks far ahead of the other provinces, with 181 for private woodlands and 14 for communal estates, followed by Santiago de Cuba, with 69 and 37, respectively. Puerto Príncipe was the leader in lumber-transport permits, with 179, followed by Santiago de Cuba, with 95, and Santa Clara, with 21.[62]

During the first quarter of the twentieth century the province of Camagüey maintained its leadership in the wood trade. Its topography offered excellent conditions for large-scale clearing. Wood transport was done through the traditional system of hauling by oxen (up to eight pairs) to rivers with sufficient flow, so that during the rainy season logs could be led on rafts to the sea and the ships that awaited them. The arrival of the Central Railroad facilitated the transport of wood to areas along its lines. The wood's destinations were principally the United States, Germany, and Great Britain, although during the 1920s Germany and Belgium were primarily mentioned.[63]

In a 1910 book recounting his travels to Cuba, the French geographer Charles Berchon describes Camagüey as the region of forests and livestock: "Its countryside is three-quarters full of trees, interrupted by natural prairies, offering numerous winding rivers and scattered savannas." He also mentions the many deposits of wood he observed on different branches of the Central Railroad between the province's main towns.[64]

Santa Cruz del Sur still stood out in the active wood trade. The author of a 1913 work of local history, Rafael Pera y Peralta, ranked it as the most important wood-trading town on the island. During the dry season, he said, there were always boats in its port waiting to load wood, at least three sailing ships of regular tonnage, without counting the boats that loaded from nearby docks. According to figures he offered, the municipal district's forests included 9,302 of its 18,111 caballerías. They produced woods of all kinds, for cabinetmaking and construction, with markets in Europe and the United States. Of its 238 farms, 60 were devoted to wood harvesting, and the local industries included sawmills that were "well put together." One of these, Pera y Peralta recounted, had opened with an 8-horsepower motor for a steam-powered saw and been converted to a magnificent saw mill, with 150 horsepower and a 60-bulb dynamo, that provided work for many people.[65]

Before World War I the center of sugar expansion in Camagüey was the old military line from Júcaro to Morón. South of the city of Ciego de Avila were founded the *centrales* of Jagüeyal (1904) and Stewart (1906), which in 1914 had 1,200 and 1,100 caballerías, respectively. On the former, 355 were in cane, 445 in pastures, and 400 in woodlands, with an average yield of 74,884 arrobas per caballería and a maximum of 150,000. The second had 746 caballerías in cane, 40 in pastures, and 314 of woodlands. Two other *centrales* were located in the same region between 1912 and 1914: that of Ciego de Avila, near the city of the same name, and that of Morón, with 213 caballerías of land at first, 132 in cane, 9 in pastures, and 72 of woodlands.

In the remaining natural regions, sugar had barely appeared, with the exception of the late nineteenth-century *ingenios centrales* in Nuevitas and the Francisco *central* near Santa Cruz del Sur. On the plains crossed by the Central Railroad the only *central* at the time was that of Camagüey, also founded around 1914, with 325 new caballerías (80 in cane, 5 in pastures, and 240 of woodlands). According to the data in the 1912–14 sugar portfolio, the cane fields of the province offered an average yield of 67,330 arrobas per caballería. The next most productive province was Oriente, with 57,314 arrobas per caballería; the other provinces all had averages below 50,000 arrobas. Similarly, the use of firewood as a supplementary fuel distinguished the new sugar regions. According to the same source, the eight *centrales* of Camagüey consumed an annual average of 8,648.4 metric tons of firewood, followed by Oriente, with 3,397 metric tons, and Matanzas, with 1,972 metric tons. During the 1913 harvest, Francisco used 18,065 metric tons, Stewart 18,750 metric tons, and Jagüeyal 13,400 metric tons. The data from the 1919 census on amount of firewood per caballería in the woodlands of Camagüey indicate a wooded area of about 10 caballerías.[66]

Until 1914 sugar's penetration into Camagüey was relatively slow. At 2.6 percent of Cuba's total sugar production in 1902, it had increased to 10 percent by 1915. True, sugar farms had increased more than tenfold the total amount of cultivated land around 1899, but this expansion, which included equally cane fields, pastures, and woodlands, represented 7.3 percent (10,932 caballerías) of land in the province. Camagüey continued to be a region of livestock and forests, although with the important contribution of the Central Railroad and gradual penetration by the sugar industry. Graphic depictions of the province during this era show this trilogy of wood, livestock, and sugar, which soon would come to an end.

Sugar's definitive conquest of Camagüey was rooted in the outbreak of World War I in Europe. At the beginning of 1914 the province had 9 *centrales*. From 1914 to 1920–21 another 14 were established, and 6 more were founded between 1921 and 1926. In 1915 Camagüey's sugar production was 263,300 metric tons, ranking it fifth among Cuba's provinces. A few years later the situation was different. In 1923 Camagüey was the leading producer among the provinces, with 1,111,100 metric tons, 30.9 percent of the island's total production. This amount continued to rise until it hit a record 1,564,000 metric tons in the 1928–29 harvest (see map 6.3).[67]

This notable increase in production was brought about by the foundation of new *centrales* and the augmented capacity of those already existing. In 1913–14 the province's 9 mills had an average capacity of 2,167 metric tons a day, a figure that during the war rose to 4,987 metric tons a day. The most remarkable case was that of Morón, which went from 1,496 to 8,631 metric tons. The *centrales* developed during and after the war had great productive potential. The 14 created from 1915 to 1921 could attain an average 3,691 metric tons a day, with highs like that of Cunagua, with 6,905 metric tons, and that of Baraguá, with 5,754 metric tons. Among the 6 founded between 1921 and 1926, Vertientes increased from 1,841 metric tons a day in 1921 to 8,631 in 1925. The largest sugar mill in the world, Jaronú, went from 7,480 to 11,507 metric tons (see figure 6.10).

Camagüey became the province with the greatest installed capacity per

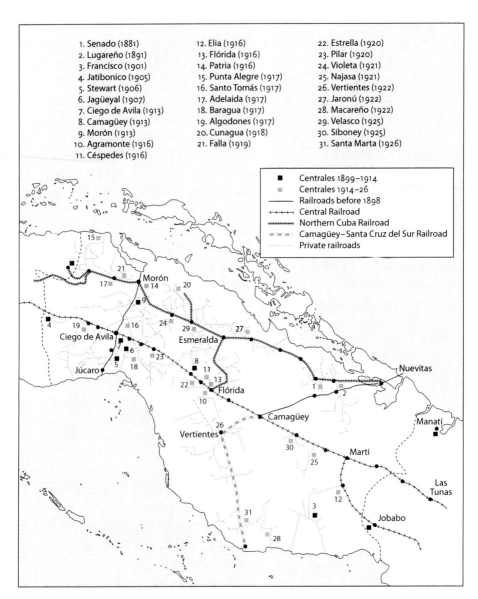

1. Senado (1881)
2. Lugareño (1891)
3. Francisco (1901)
4. Jatibonico (1905)
5. Stewart (1906)
6. Jagüeyal (1907)
7. Ciego de Avila (1913)
8. Camagüey (1913)
9. Morón (1913)
10. Agramonte (1916)
11. Céspedes (1916)

12. Elia (1916)
13. Flórida (1916)
14. Patria (1916)
15. Punta Alegre (1917)
16. Santo Tomás (1917)
17. Adelaida (1917)
18. Baragua (1917)
19. Algodones (1917)
20. Cunagua (1918)
21. Falla (1919)

22. Estrella (1920)
23. Pilar (1920)
24. Violeta (1921)
25. Najasa (1921)
26. Vertientes (1922)
27. Jaronú (1922)
28. Macareño (1922)
29. Velasco (1925)
30. Siboney (1925)
31. Santa Marta (1926)

■ Centrales 1899–1914
▨ Centrales 1914–26
—— Railroads before 1898
+++++ Central Railroad
╫╫╫╫ Northern Cuba Railroad
▨▨▨▨ Camagüey–Santa Cruz del Sur Railroad
······· Private railroads

MAP 6.3. *Centrales* and Railroads in Camagüey Province, 1898–1926

FIGURE 6.10. Vertientes *central*, province of Camagüey.
(*Cuba Review*, May 1925)

unit, with an average in 1928 of 4,472 metric tons a day, followed by Oriente, with 2,955 metric tons.[68] This augmentation of industrial scale was accompanied by the reinforcement of sugar interests' tendency to impose their control over vast areas of land. Both the old farms and the ones established since the war participated in this process. Morón, created in 1914 with 213 caballerías, had 4,795 in 1928. Stewart, which had 1,100 caballerías in its first harvest of 1906, swelled to control 3,055 in 1928. The increase in production and in controlled land translated, of course, into an unprecedented area of cane fields. Francisco, for example, went from 399 caballerías in cane in 1914 to 1,322 in 1928.

Similarly, the *centrales* founded between 1914 and 1916 based their productive structure on the creation of large latifundios. Cunagua and Jaronú, developed by the same company, together covered more than 10,000 caballerías. Vertientes came to dominate 7,521 caballerías, the most land under any single *central*. For the entire province the area occupied by sugar reached about 11,000 caballerías in 1914 and more than 60,000 in the three subsequent decades. The correlation between the maximum amount of land controlled by the *centrales* according to the 1936 sugar census and the area of the province's judicial districts (*partidos judiciales*) in 1928 is telling (see table 6.3).

TABLE 6.3. Territory Controlled by *Centrales* in Camagüey according to the 1936 Sugar Census and Area of 1928 Judicial Districts

Judicial District	Area (km²)	*Centrales*	Area (km²)	% of Judicial District
Camagüey	4,000	4	1,547	38.7
Florida	1,500	5	1,016	67.7
Guaimaro	1,152	1	377	32.7
Santa Cruz	2,270	3	997	43.9
Nuevitas	4,000	2	807	20.2
Ciego de Avila	1,757	6	1,590	90.5
Morón	4,244	7	3,709	87.4
Jatibonico	1,200	1	356	29.7
Total for province	20,122	29	10,399	51.7

Sources: Carlos de La Torre and A. M. Aguayo, *Geografía de Cuba* (Havana: Cultural, 1928); *Censo azucarero de la República de Cuba, 1936* (Havana: Cuba Importadora e Industrial, 1936). *Note:* The proportions are not exact because the lands of some *centrales* could appear as part of different judicial districts or even different provinces. Of the total in *centrales*, 61 percent was owned by *centrales* and 39 percent was leased or controlled.

Camagüey's case was the most representative of the massive arrival of U.S. capital, inspired by high prices and increased demand for sugar during World War I, as well as the remodeling of enterprises in the sector as incorporated companies. Leland Jenks has noted that in 1926 twenty-one of Camagüey's *centrales* could be considered as having U.S. ownership, and two others were owned by Cuban Americans.[69] The dimensions of the sugar latifundio become clearer when we notice that most of these were administered by a much smaller number of companies.[70]

The latifundio's expansion was primarily impelled by the networks of public and private railroads. During the war the plan to build a line traversing the north of the province took shape. It was promoted by José Miguel Tarafa, founder of the Northern Cuba Railroad (Ferrocarril del Norte de Cuba). Between 1917 and 1921 it connected lands from the Chambas River to Nuevitas, where the island's largest sugar port, christened Puerto Tarafa, was built.[71] This line served several *centrales* established since 1914, including Cunagua, Velasco, Violeta, and Jaronú, as well as the older Morón, Lugareño, and Senado. A new branch linked Esmeralda, halfway point between Morón and Nuevitas, where it met the Central Railroad. During the 1920s a line also opened between Camagüey and Santa Cruz del Sur, accessible to *centrales* like Santa Marta and Vertientes.

The rapid expansion of cane fields to supply the demands of the market triggered the most intense deforestation in the history of the province. The new *centrales* of 1915–26 generally located in areas with abundant forests. The 1907 census reported that "the north and south of the province remain almost entirely uninhabited, with large areas of excellent arable land that has been abandoned due to the lack of means of transporting the innumerable products that could be grown there."[72] None of the natural regions was spared by sugar's violent invasion during those years. Plain of Júcaro-Morón, which had the most *centrales* before 1914, saw the arrival of new colossi like Punta Alegre, near the bay of the same name on the northern coast, as well as others with vast cane fields between Punta Alegre and the western side of the four natural regions to the east, including the *centrales* of Baraguá, Violeta, Patria, and Velasco. Along the Central Railroad, on the central plains, were built the *centrales* Céspedes, Florida, Estrella, and Agramonte, which with the Camagüey *central* encircled the city of Florida. Farther to the east Siboney and Najasa were built.

But perhaps the greatest impact of sugar between 1914 and 1925 was experienced on the northern and southern plains. With the Cunagua and Jaronú *centrales*, and with the lands controlled by Velasco and Violeta, the occupation of the Plain of Northern Camagüey-Maniabón was completed, aided by the Northern Cuba Railroad. The occupation of this plain by *ingenios centrales* began in the late nineteenth century with the founding of Senado and Lugareño and continued in the first fifteen years of the twentieth century with the construction of the eastern colossi Chaparra, Delicias, and Manatí. To get an idea of sugar's impact on this region (4,937 km²), we can note that from the 1920s to the 1940s the Senado, Lugareño, Cunagua, Jaronú, Manatí, Delicias, and Chaparra *centrales* came to control 4,476 square kilometers. Although for some of them part of their territory lay in neighboring regions, this figure is still eloquent testimony to sugar's presence in these areas. Something similar occurred on the Plain of Southern Camagüey. Before 1914 it included only the Francisco *central*, joined in the following decade by Santa Marta, Elia, Macareño, and part of Vertientes. The municipality of Santa Cruz del Sur, whose farms in 1900 were 82.9 percent forest, saw this proportion reduced to only 9.1 percent in 1945.[73] Despite the fact that farm area doubled that of the beginning of the century, the forested area fell between these years from 7,298 to 1,151 caballerías, so that Santa Cruz ceased to be "a town of fishermen and wood traffickers," as it is categorized in the 1907 census.

Aside from the advantages of occupying virgin territory from the point of view of controlling the supply of cane, clearly the felling of thousands of caballerías of forest during and after the war was related to the ancient tradition of planting in cleared land. Nevertheless, after the market highs many of the cleared areas in Camagüey proved poorly suited to the planting of cane, or at least they did not produce the high yields to which people were accustomed. In 1928 the province still had Cuba's highest cane yields, with an average 53,751 arrobas per caballería, but this was well below the 67,330 arrobas per caballería obtained in 1913.

In the part of Hugh Bennett and Robert Allison's *Los suelos de Cuba* (The Soils of Cuba) dedicated to Camagüey, there are constant references to land recently cleared so it could be devoted to cane fields. For example, writing about the red plain of Ciego de Avila and Cubitas, they note that most of the "rather dense" forest vegetation that characterized this area had been eliminated. They point out that on the interior plain of southern Camagüey the planting was generally good in virgin land. Among the types of soils that they classify are "Camagüey Clay," originally covered with hardwood and royal palms, and "Florida Clay." In both soils they observed yields in clearings of 135,000 arrobas per caballería.[74] In contrast, the province's northern and southern coastal plains did not give the best results because of salinity, poor drainage of the soils, and invasions of weeds, great obstacles to agricultural success.

To get an idea of the great transformation of Camagüey's landscapes in such a short period we can consult the national agricultural census of 1946. That year 161,558 caballerías (21,686 km^2) were reported to be part of the province's farms, or more than three times the amount recorded in 1899 and 82.5 percent of the total area estimated for the province that year: 196,612 caballerías (26,391 km^2). Compared with the distribution of lands in 1899, the proportion covered with forest declined from more than 60 percent to 11 percent. It is true that Camagüey had 18.8 percent of the nation's woodlands on farms, second to Oriente, which had 34.2 percent, but we must not lose sight of the fact that Camagüey was also second in total land area and in farm area. Other indicators show that it ranked first in pasture land (48%) and "other areas" (21.2%), and second in cultivated land (16.4%) and in land dominated by marabú (3.2%).[75] The change relative to the beginning of the twentieth century was significant. Camagüey was no longer the region of forests.

The inclusion of marabú in the 1946 statistics is a sign of the transformations that were taking place parallel to the disappearance of forests. Marabú is the most invasive plant in twentieth-century Cuba, and the vast plains of Camagüey are one of the areas most afflicted. Uncontrolled clearing and burning for the development of cane fields and their subsequent abandonment when sugar prices fell or when land proved infertile left wide areas more vulnerable than ever to invasion by weeds. Thus marabú thickets, a subject of concern as early as 1910, became one of the main enemies of Cuban agriculture and livestock farming, in Camagüey in particular.[76]

The size of the sugar latifundios and of area grazed by livestock is largely responsible for the marked deterioration of soils in the region, considered today as one of its most serious environmental problems. Today, 75 percent of Camagüey's soils are considered to be affected by erosion, 35 percent by poor drainage, and 18 percent by salinity. Thirty-nine percent are classified as shallow.[77] Agricultural yields would never return to the levels of the golden years of the "fat cows," despite the constant use of chemical fertilizers, pesticides, and agricultural machinery. Among the effects of the large *centrales* on Camagüey meriting further study is the contamination of rivers and other more debatable consequences such as the reduced rainfall in the region or, rather, their benefits, insofar as there is a greater or lesser proportion of forest in given locations. As early as in the 1940s Luis de Abad noted, among the causes of Cuba's reduced cane yields, which had fallen below those of almost all other sugar-producing countries, the reduced rainfall that had resulted from the clearing of woodlands during the first two decades of the twentieth century, especially in Camagüey and Oriente. Of course, none of these environmental consequences of the sugar latifundio can be considered separately from other economic and social implications studied by numerous authors.

The Republic's Forest Administration until 1926 and Other Efforts in Favor of the Forests

In his first *memoria* on the state of the forests after the end of Spanish rule, Francisco Portuondo reported on the uncontrolled harvesting of private and public woodlands. The Woodlands Inspection set as its priority the functioning of the woodlands service as determined by the ordinances and other regulations, through measures such as indicating to the Customs Administration that all ports must require the presentation of transport permits and the elimination of unauthorized harvesting. The inspections chief expressed satisfaction with the results of these measures for the working of the service and predicted their quick normalization.[78]

Portuondo believed that the state's forest property would increase considerably when private landowners demarcated their farms; the demarcation of public woodlands could also be rectified and inscribed in the property register. In other *memorias* from this period, he insisted on the need for surveys to ascertain the area of state woodlands, an operation not yet undertaken because it would be "long and costly," but that was essential to any application "benefiting the island's general interests." Important for this goal was the military government's Civil Order 60, issued on February 10, 1900. Proposed by the Secretariat of Agriculture, Commerce, and Industry, it created six woodlands commissioner and clerical assistant posts for each province. This staff would report to the chief engineers and the Woodlands Inspection and aid the engineers in their operations as well as perform all nonprofessional work.[79]

These measures opened a new era in Cuba's forest administration. Portuondo remained its director until the creation, by the Organic Law of Executive Power on January 12, 1909, of the Direction (or Department) of Woodlands and Mines in the Secretariat of Agriculture, Industry, and Commerce, charged with the surveillance, demarcation, and conservation of woodlands, as well as with recording statistics and issuing transport permits for forest products. The scientist José Isaac del Corral Alemán was named director of the department, while Portuondo became section chief, a position he held until his death in 1912. That same year the Department of Woodlands reported that in under three years it had attended to more than thirty-two hundred proceedings (*expedientes*); it presented a plan for policing and punishing violators of woodlands regulations, focusing on damage due to illegal harvesting.[80] From then until the early 1920s there were few innovations in the forest service.

The rapid disappearance of forests resulting from World War I led to renewed efforts at regulation. Although the Woodlands Ordinance of 1876 would remain the fundamental law for many years, successive decrees and complementary laws sought to modernize it and to respond to the serious problems brought about by the intensive deforestation that had occurred since the founding of the republic. On the initiative of the director of woodlands and mines and with the signature of Cuban president Alfredo Zayas, and Pedro E. Betancourt, secretary of agriculture, commerce, and labor, several decrees were promulgated between 1922 and 1924 to regulate forest harvesting and to promote the protection of wooded areas.[81]

In the preamble to the first, Decree 1831 of December 16, 1922, which laid out the foundation to which forest projects in state woodlands should be subject, Isaac del Corral Alemán reviewed the situation of forests since the beginning of the republic, when the Cuban state took possession of many rural farms, especially in the east, which often had rich forests. For two decades, however, the state was unable to attend to these properties or to investigate whether others might belong to it, with the result that much of this terrain was absorbed by neighboring private landowners. Efforts to prevent this property from passing into private hands were in vain. Isaac del Corral Alemán gave the example of the directors of woodlands and mines in Oriente, who for fifteen years had been fighting in vain to defend the property of the state, "since the winners are always the neighboring landowners, the Administration being unable to produce irrefutable documents to demonstrate the disputed ownership."[82]

Faced with this reality, the Direction of Woodlands proposed "opening the doors to private initiative" to improve public woodlands. Private landowners were therefore allowed to present to the Secretariat of Agriculture ten-year projects to exploit the land scientifically. This would promote forest conservation, as well as provide income for the state and, indirectly, surveillance of the woodlands at no expense whatsoever. The nearly thirty introductory articles (*por cuanto*) took up these and other considerations showing the need for order in the harvesting of the state's high woodlands. Low woodlands, most in littoral areas and on adjoining cays, were also regulated during these years.

Other measures focused on protecting and repopulating the damaged forests. In March 1923 President Zayas signed the first decrees of this type. Number 295 required that in areas where forests were harvested loggers have corresponding permits and that they carry a registry of the extracted products and the locations where they were stored. Number 318 regulated the harvesting of yana, a tree that, in addition to its use for lumber, was the preferred species for making charcoal. The fact that not only the trunks but also the large roots were used prevented the tree from reproducing, making charcoal increasingly expensive and many yana forests "useless savannas."[83]

Decree 753, issued on May 24, 1923, was very important because it established the "Regulation for the System of Protective Woodlands and Forest Reserves." Among its essential justifications, the decree mentioned once again the beneficial influence of forests and the imperative need, "demanded by the conscientious elements of the community," to reduce the grave harm being done to them. The edict was grounded in a belief that the government was obligated to dictate technical rules to prevent the destruction of forests in which the public had an interest and that it must take adequate measures to increase the proportion of the national territory covered with forest. Official protection was needed not only for the "fiscal forests of the Nation" but also for those belonging to municipalities and to private citizens. It should be provided through the creation of regional nurseries, which would distribute trees in accordance with local soil conditions.

Landowners, as well as those overseeing or leasing farms devoted to pasture or any kind of cultivation and having an area of 5 caballerías or more, were required to set aside at least 5 to 15 percent of their total area for a permanent forest reserve, an obligation that also applied to estates still covered with forest. In each case the required area would be determined according to local conditions and could be reduced by half if the land was devoted to fruit trees. Nevertheless, two types of farms were exempted from having to maintain such a reserve: those with irrigation and those devoted entirely to cultivation. This clarification was no doubt related to sugar plantations.

Other articles of the decree concerned repopulation of forests, requiring owners and leasers of land traversed by rivers, streams, brooks, and springs in whose valleys forests had been destroyed to plant trees that grew rapidly and plentifully in a 50-meter band along the edges of the property. If zones established as protective woodlands and forest reserves had already been cleared, owners and leasers were required to plant trees in at least half the area foreseen. Owners had a similar obligation to plant rows of poplar trees along property boundaries, highways (*caminos reales*), and public roads. The Secretariat of Agriculture would contribute to reforesting with regional nurseries, technical assistance, seeds and seedlings, and prizes for trees successfully planted and well maintained.

Decree 772, also enacted on May 24, 1923, banned the felling of royal palms and fruit trees. Palms provided great benefits, including feed for pigs, oil, lumber for rural dwellings, and cisterns, aside from the beauty they brought to the Cuban countryside. But in many areas they were being weakened and killed by pollarding. Fruit trees, often "the object of felling for trivial ends," were suffering a similar fate. Cutting down both types of trees was therefore declared a fraudulent use; clearing them was allowed only if the trees were sick or to make way for public works projects (buildings, roads, highways, railroads, bridges, dams, aqueducts, and so on) and provided the appropriate permits had been issued. No exception was made for clearing for cultivation or to thin dense palm groves.

Other decrees sought to prevent the disappearance of valuable species of timber. A July 1923 edict banned the felling and clearing of two categories of species from land under any type of ownership. The first category included trees such as guayacán and fustete, which could not be harvested if their trunks were 12 inches or smaller in diameter; larger trees of this type could be felled, but the cut had to be 1.3 centimeters from the ground, and three trees had to be planted for each one that was cut. Felling trees in the second category, which included sabina, ebony, walnut, and cork, was banned in all circumstances except if the tree was sick, of poor quality, or clearly near the end of its life.[84] Other measures from September 1923 and February 1924 protected the red mangrove (mangle colorado) and prohibited the felling of guaimaro and guana.

These decrees fulfilled the aspirations of Isaac del Corral Alemán, expressed in his 1923 article "El problema forestal en Cuba," published in *Cuba contemporánea*. The first thing to note is his contention that all "civilized nations" had placed limits on landowners' right to clear and raze woodlands; that is, "Official intervention in privately owned farms enclosed in the woodlands zone has become a principle of public law." After reviewing the situation of forests in various countries, Isaac del Corral Alemán argued that to ensure biological and economic equilibrium every nation had to maintain a forested area equivalent to a third of its territory. In Cuba the proportion was only 16.5 percent, making it urgent to reforest areas unsuited for cultivation, since the island's prosperity depended "on the increased wealth of crops characteristic of each zone." The woodlands director noted that the continued existence of forests could be guaranteed only for those belonging to the state, privately owned woodlands being constantly threatened by the temptation to profit from their wealth, "worrying very little about the well-being of those who will follow."[85]

Cuba was among those nations needing "special protection for its woodlands." But the forests of the state were not sufficient to guarantee the necessary proportion of forest area so that trees could play their important role in regulating climate, hydrology, and the wealth of the soil: "Many of the forests on private property or on land of a similar category appropriate to silviculture are in all respects indispensable for the maintenance of the country's forested area, which makes it necessary to submit these forests or wooded terrain to an adequate forest regime that guarantees the conservation of trees, as well as their restoration."[86]

Isaac del Corral Alemán found that in general the state of Cuban forest conservation was lamentable. In his opinion, nothing had been done to prevent the forests' merciless clearing, "made considerably powerful from 1915 to 1920." It declined somewhat in 1921 and 1922 but resurged with hikes in sugar prices, "which stimulated the conversion of the vast and bountiful forests of the eastern provinces into cane fields." The damage caused by the "immense burning" was palpable and obvious, and it could get worse if the government did not impose restrictions to prevent the complete destruction of forest wealth. He therefore criticized the absolute powers that the Woodlands Ordinances of 1876 granted to landowners, without any rule "that would prevent razing of centuries-old forests." The 1909 Law of the Executive Power of the Republic, inspired by the principle that no forest harvesting could be undertaken without a permit, concluded with this "scientific monstrosity [enormidad]," but regulations were needed to fix the limits imposed on private citizens.[87]

The early 1920s decrees on the forest question meant that after a century of free clearing limits were being put on private property ownership. Although none took on sugarcane as the principal historical cause of the island's deforestation, the edicts showed that the ancestral practice of extending cane fields at the forests' expense was about to end. President Gerardo Machado's signing of Decree 495 on April 13, 1926, placed an absolute ban on the "a hecho" clearing of high woodlands, whether these belonged to the state or to private citizens. By "a hecho" the decree meant clearing carried out on one or more hectares, with the result that the land was completely stripped of vegetation. The first provision stated that "clearing on vast areas of Cuban territory" had created a state of opinion favorable to the defense of forests and to reforestation, both because of the beneficial influence on the country's health and because increased forestation would help Cuba stop being "dependent on foreigners" for wood that the island could provide. The second provision cited the doctrine that each nation should maintain a forested area equal to one-third of its territory: "Currently Cuba's woodlands do not cover even 10 percent of its territory; since the period of high sugar prices and the planting of cane that has resulted from 1922 to the present threaten to finish off the rare woodlands that are left to us, the

FIGURE 6.11. Virgin land, planted with cane.

(Josiah T. Crawley, "El cultivo de la caña de azúcar en Cuba," *Boletín de la Estación Experimental Agronómica*, no. 35 [February 1917]: 25)

state must intervene in privately owned forested estates, imposing on them justified limitations, in the public interest" (see figure 6.11).[88]

Another reason for this measure was that "in forests that are cleared . . . only some hardwood for railroad ties and a few thick trunks for boards are harvested." All the forests' wealth was thus lost "due to the sinister custom of burning thousands of caballerías of woodlands without benefit for their owners and with great harm to the nation. This double error of destroying an existing wealth to develop crops leads to economic difficulties if no limit is placed on this clearing." The decree warned that existing measures had not resolved the matter definitively, although they had restrained the greed "excited by the high prices that forest products attained during the European war." It also admitted that it was not easy "to transform abruptly the habits of a country, passing from complete freedom to rigorous restriction."[89]

The Direction of Woodlands and Mines would cease to issue permits for clearing in virgin woodlands unless it could be demonstrated that a location's topographical conditions, the nature of its soil, or the lack of transportation infrastructure made clearing necessary for the cultivation of smaller crops, pasture, henequen, coffee, tobacco, and rubber. In privately owned high woodlands thinning permits would be granted to cut down timber of the established dimensions so long as this did not endanger the forest. By coincidence, on May 3, 1926, less than a month after the signing of Decree 495, the so-called Verdeja Law was passed, with provisions to limit production and prevent the development of new *centrales* as a means to counter falling prices.[90] Independent of the fact that discussion of this legislation could have influenced the decree banning clearing in high woodlands, we cannot ignore the fact that, for a government that aspired to "regenerate" the country, the forest issue could be a good theme for political propaganda.

One sign of the change in attitude toward woodlands was that just a few days after clearing in privately owned high woodlands was banned, several decrees from previous years for the protection of forest wealth were made law. On the first anniversary of the ban on clearing high woodlands for cane, it was renewed for another year. The Ministry of Agriculture declared, "It is the aspiration of this Government to repopulate forests in barren lands unsuited for cultivation, undertaking in this way a patriotic effort that will tend to increase the country's wealth and free it from its current dependency on a single crop." In following years the renewals were repeated, until 1930, when this measure became law, in response to general public acclaim and the persistence of the scientific and economic problems that had inspired the decree. A contemporary pamphlet in favor of the measure warned that "the prohibition on complete clearing of woodlands should remain in effect for a long time, because such clearing has ruined our legendary forests, without the rich woods that these forests contain being used."[91]

The ban certainly came late, when few forests remained to save in flat and gently rolling regions, but it still was an important step in the defense of those forests that survived. This does not mean that forests stopped disappearing or that sugar stopped being one of the causes, as it was with the post-1926 clearings that responded to favorable market conditions or government policy. Nonetheless, we can say that in general terms cane yields ceased to depend on planting in land that had been cleared.

In his 1933 article, Frasquieri argued that the forest issue was not simply technical, administrative, economic, and financial; it was above all social and educational. Buttressed by the success of similar institutions in other fields, he called for the creation of a forestry school to train rural wardens and personnel to adapt scientific teachings to the island's conditions and products, the only way to end dependency on other countries and "to develop the great wood resources of our soil." The state should be responsible for artificial forest repopulation—even in the case of cedar and majagua, which had high value and grew rapidly — since this was a public work that should not be left "to private initiative, which is generally ephemeral."[92]

At the end of this period the first general study of Cuban soils was carried out by the U.S. experts Hugh Bennett and Robert Allison, as the basis for a more detailed classification of the land and its relationship to agriculture and other uses. One of the causes of low cane yields, Bennett and Allison found, was "excessively inferior" soil with inadequate drainage, uncontrolled weeds, and insufficient fertilization. They concluded: "There is probably no other place in the world where the soil's influence is more important than on the sugar plantations of Cuba." Their description testifies well to the landscapes generated by sugar's expansion: "Traveling through the provinces east of Havana it seems that the island is an immense cane field. In many places these fields seem completely uninterrupted, extending across the plain to the horizon. One might see some tobacco or fields of corn, bananas, beans, yucca, sweet potatoes, *malangas*, or other fruits and vegetables, and small groves of avocados and mangos, but these are generally erased from the mental frame by the enormous and ubiquitous cane fields."[93]

The second phase of Bennett and Allison's study was not carried out because of the drop in sugar prices, according to the report *Problemas de la nueva Cuba* (1935), which claimed that a detailed study of the terrain and its uses would show that much of the land devoted to cane or to "submarginal sites" should be made back into forest.[94] In addition to exhausting the soil and the supply of wood, deforestation had other effects on living conditions in Cuba arising from the loss of natural resources and biodiversity.

In a solemn session marking the anniversary of the Havana Academy of Sciences on May 19, 1928, Isaac del Corral Alemán, a member of the academy, gave his address "Forest Devastation and the Harm It Causes." In the presence of the Cuban president, the director of woodlands and mines stated that immense negative effects could be felt in the entire country as a result of the almost complete destruction of its forests, impacting the nation's hydrology, its weather, the increasingly impoverished soil, and its ability to produce, not to mention "the rarity and complete disappearance of animals and birds who are born and live in the woodlands." Already in Cuba one noted the greatly reduced number or the extinction of many woodland birds "who gave charm and utility to our countryside." Among the birds whose numbers had dropped sharply in many locations were the yaguaza, torcaza salvaje, torcaz morada, sevilla, Cuban crane, royal woodpecker, partridge, parakeet, huyuyo, and flamingo, while the Cuban macaw was largely considered to be extinct.[95]

Isaac del Corral Alemán recalled that the war in Europe had considerably worsened the forest situation, since the high price of sugar had promoted "the clearing and burning of the millennial forests of Camagüey and Oriente." In his opinion, if foresighted laws had existed such as the ones since enacted, "such catastrophic destruction" could have been avoided. To top it off, "the clearing was so excessive that today there are vast expanses of terrain of such bad quality that they are now abandoned and have become useless brushland." In addition to heart- and firewood, forests could produce many chemical products such as acetic acid, methylic alcohol, creosote, acetone, and other derivatives of high market value. "All this wealth has evaporated without benefit to anyone, so that today we find ourselves impoverished, in addition to having lost woodlands that were the pride of the Cuban nation." He concluded by proposing, among other measures, the creation in each province of a forest park, which would be a reserve for the country's principal trees, a refuge for forest animals, and a site of learning for future generations.[96]

Scientific institutions and administrative agencies acknowledged these subjects in different ways. The Experimental Agronomic Station of Santiago de las Vegas and the Secretariat of Agriculture, Commerce, and Labor, for example, published articles in their journals that stressed the economic, physical, and social importance of forests. In 1909, the Experimental Agronomic Station's *Circular* published an essay by Antonio Ponce de León on trees along roadways that noted a phenomenon parallel to deforestation — the replacement of native trees with foreign ones: "On the one hand, we cut down júcaros, mahogany and cedar trees, etc.; on the other, we increase the number of laurels and poplars. Soon Cuban flora will be unknown. The majagua, varía, jiquí, and sabicú will be history. We will speak of the scented oak [*roble de olor*] the way we speak today of the Siboney."[97]

The *Revista de agricultura, comercio y trabajo* published studies very critical of the destruction of forests. In 1919 the interim chief of the Department of Botany of the Secretariat of Agriculture, Commerce, and Labor, Marcelino Cremata, recalled José María Fernández y Jiménez's prediction half a century earlier, in *Arboricultura cubana*, of what would happened as a result of the systematic exploitation of forests to harvest their wood and of the enormous increase in the cultivation of sugarcane, "which when it expands or when it needs new, unexhausted soil, causes precisely those places where forests now exist to be chosen." Not only had short-sightedness created a need to import great quantities of wood and led to the vanishing of Cuban timber, but it also meant that much of the island was taking on "the aspect of a great desert."[98] A 1923 article by Roberto Luaces cited Alvaro Reynoso's warnings and his call to restore the country's climate by establishing a proper proportion between cultivated land and forests. He quoted the famous Cuban agronomist's affirmation that "we are experiencing the effects of clearing and the lack of formation of new forests, if not to the extent that our descendants will, at least to a degree very prejudicial to our interests." A half century later Luaces remarked, "These descendants are us, and yet we continue the thoughtless destruction unperturbed."[99]

The attention of the republic's government to forest matters was heightened, and in response it hired more scientific and administrative personnel. Although the measures came late, there was increasing awareness of the state's role in forest protection. Beginning with Gerardo Machado's first government, reforestation took on a more prominent role in the country's political life. An example of this was the "Festival of Cuban Reforestation," celebrated in September 1929 at the Experimental Agronomic Station in Santiago de las Vegas. In the presence of the Cuban president and the secretary of agriculture, Eugenio Molinet, local public school students planted about two hundred lumberable trees in a field "full of Cuban flags, which gave joy and beauty to the scene." The station's librarian read a speech praising Molinet for his program of reforestation with Cuban trees, "proclaiming cedar and mahogany as preferred, the scale of harvestable woods continuing with majagua, júcaro, sabicú, yaba, ocuje, guaimaro, and paraíso and ayua, which grow quickly."[100]

In the mid-1920s the reforestation campaign intensified. Free publications detailed the existing forest-protection laws and their multiple benefits, in addition to calling attention to the commercial potential of forests. One fruit of these efforts was the brochure *Cuban Forestry Primer: For the Use of Authorities and Citizens*, which had three editions in 1927. Other pamphlets bore titles such as *Desirability of Undertaking Reforestation in Terrain Unsuited for Agriculture*, *Usefulness of Trees*, and *Reforestation Is a Business*.[101]

Finally we should note that the campaign against the accelerated disappearance of forests and its economic, environmental, and social effects was not led only by the government and its agencies. Worth mentioning are the efforts of associations and initiatives that emerged out of civil society, such as the Felipe Poey Cuban Society for Natural History (founded in 1913) and the Geographic Society of Cuba (1914). Among the earliest initiatives was the celebration of Arbor Day, a tradition in various countries that was promoted beginning in 1904 by the Association of Owners and Neighbors of Private Preserves (Asociación de Propietarios y Vecinos del Vedado).[102] Some years later, in 1912, Ramón García Osés, then director of the Agronomic Station, reiterated in a *Circular* the need to imitate more advanced countries and establish by law an Arbor Day. In his judgment this holiday should be indicated on public school calendars in order to instill in the people affection for trees and the habit of planting and caring for them. Forests, he argued, were "natural resources of common wealth that we receive from our ancestors, with the responsibility to use and care for them, bearing in mind that they belong less to this generation than to future ones."[103]

Up to that time, however, the exact opposite had happened, the result, García Osés said, of cultivation that was "without rules or economic considerations of any kind, without consideration of the future, and without calculation of its fatal consequences." In another article that appeared in the same *Circular*, he wrote of the important role that forests had played in the island's economic growth: "Our industries have developed more rapidly, we must acknowledge, because we have had inexpensive fuel, because we have had abundant lumber and firewood that is easy to obtain in any location."[104]

The director of the Agronomic Station advocated regulation of forest harvesting by the state, which was charged with caring for the people's interests and with developing the property of future generations. He noted also that as a result of improving communications technology, "the depopulation of our countryside is greater every day."[105] Despite such warnings, the republic's government reacted too late to prevent a new wave of sugar fever from finishing off the forests that remained in the island's flat and undulating regions. Thus, while Cubans were given more and more information about the role of trees, and while tree planting was promoted in cities through civic campaigns in the schools or through actions with a mentality close to the so-called environmentalism of the rich, the natural forests of Camagüey and Oriente were vanishing at an unprecedented pace. Obviously this great change in land use disordered the living conditions of these regions' inhabitants, areas now reached by symbols of modern life but at the same time deprived of an important local resource and made more vulnerable to the circumstances of the world sugar market.[106]

Conclusion

From Forests to Sugar
An Insignificant Change?

In the mid-nineteenth century Ramón de La Sagra asked whether Cuba's forests could be destroyed without compromising the island's admirable fertility, characterized by lush perennial and woodland vegetation. Although it was still far from generalized, since the history of Cuban agriculture "was very recent," the naturalist observed that there were daily examples of such destruction on the scale of each new district opened to cultivation: "Forests are cleared or burned; fields are planted not in relation with the needs of the country but according to commercial demand; production is continued so long as it is productive, then exhausted fields are abandoned and others sought, opened by the ax and by fire, destroyers of forest vegetation." Considering this situation, "To what point can clearing Cuba's forests be insignificant, and from what point does it cease to be so?" The basis for a wise and foresighted system of agriculture, he said, should be maintaining a proper proportion between arboreal and herbaceous vegetation, so that the healthy, fertile, and fecund conditions of the island's climate and terrain would not decline or be altered.[1]

These were not new warnings. During the dispute with Havana land-owners over the exploitation of forests, navy officials called attention to the dangers entailed by the surge in cultivation of sugarcane, which required large parcels of treeless land. Other contemporaries such as the German scientist Alexander von Humboldt, who visited the island in 1800 and 1804, immediately understood the growing imbalance between commercial crops, especially sugar, and the scarcity of subsistence ones. His belief that the imprudent activities of Europeans had transformed the order of nature, here as in other intertropical regions, synthesizes a socioeconomic reality marked from the beginning by foreign trade of a few products of high commercial value for manufactured goods or basic articles of consumption. Humboldt was confident that Cuba could change this relationship "as its inhabitants, having learned more about their true interests, and having become discouraged by the low price of colonial articles," varied their crops and gave free reign "to all branches of the rural economy."[2] But things did not turn out this way; on the contrary, Cuban sugar production increased in subsequent decades at a rate that the most foresighted person could not have imagined.

In 1935, less than a century after La Sagra's warnings, the so-called Cuban Studies Commission, made up of U.S. scientists and humanists, listed agricultural diversification, small-scale property ownership, and a forestry program as elements that would be essential to Cuba's rehabilitation. Developing these would not be an easy task, however: "There are currently no absolute rules for land use, for the basic reason that this use is necessarily affected by the circumstances and conditions of the market."[3] By then the impacts were not simply the local ones La Sagra had observed: practically the entire island would at one time or another be home to sugar plantations. What had been the conjecture of a few scientists or civil servants interested in preserving forest wealth for shipbuilding or to produce revenue for the treasury was now a reality affecting the whole country. Forests had disappeared to make way for sugarcane, and for other crops to a lesser degree, as well as for livestock pastures. Cuba's proverbial fertility was thus seriously endangered. The question was no longer how long these changes could remain insignificant; the need to revive the land had become urgent for the country's future.

Cuba had come to the same point as neighboring Caribbean sugar islands, whose land had begun to show signs of exhaustion after losing its forests and sustaining years of monoculture, and in Cuba this had occurred faster, especially relative to its larger land area. The fundamental reason for this difference was the scale on which space for sugar was conquered. Cuba offers one of the most representative cases of early industrial agriculture in the Americas. It would be difficult to situate the island's plantation system in the model of sedentary agriculture, where continuing cultivation depends on returning to the earth the nutrients extracted from it. In such a system what predominates is a circular flow of energy and nutrients typical of traditional organic agriculture or of a more or less rational exploitation of the resources on which agriculture depends. This could come about on other Caribbean islands to the extent that they produced sugar on smaller tracts of land, or in more difficult topographical conditions, and because their sugar production reached its height before the industrial era. In Cuba, in contrast, sugar production took off at the dawn of the industrial age and functioned like strip mines, the metaphor used by the Count de Pozos Dulces in the mid-nineteenth century.

The arrival of the steam engine made possible a noteworthy increase in production, but it also required new clearings to increase the size of cane fields and the amount of firewood available. The railroad was a key facilitator of the occupation of more distant wooded areas, and later it provided a way to send raw material to the *central*. The transition from animal-powered *ingenios* to semimechanized and mechanized ones, and from these to the *ingenio central*, subordinated ever vaster regions to the requirements of industrial technology. Just one indicator of the huge boom is the size of the engines used in sugar production: the first ones used on the island's *ingenios* in the 1820s had 6 to 12 horsepower; a century later, the largest sugar mill in the world, Jaronú, had engines with a combined 14,124 horsepower.

If we note the growing impact of the mechanized sugar industry on the environment and the degree of the former's dependence on the latter in the early days, we cannot be surprised by the fears of more and more scientists and estate owners about the ecological difficulties created by sugar's growth. Part of the solution was to import coal. Nevertheless, the use of organic fuels, specifically firewood, for machinery was common on *ingenios* as well as for locomotives and steamships into the early twentieth century, during which time the use of fossil fuels increased.

Agriculture was dominated until this time by the traditional system of clearing and burning woodlands to obtain high yields without needing to apply animal or plant fertilizers, inorganic fertilizers, or agricultural techniques such as plowing, leaving land fallow, crop rotation, or irrigation.

The advantages of this system—reduced production costs and savings in labor—were too tempting for the rapacious slave system to change. To the degree that complex technology put an end to the industry's portability, new efforts were made to improve cane cultivation through agronomic science. Even thus, wooded areas remained an irresistible temptation for the sugar business.

The rapid growth in sugar production enabled by industrialization accelerated the conquest of Cuba's natural regions because of the need for fuel and for land that had been fertilized for centuries by forests. This process essentially ended by the mid-1920s, after the final offensive impelled by World War I and by large North American investment, which led to the building in eastern Cuba of the world's most modern and powerful sugar mills. This does not mean that no more land was cleared for cane fields, but after this time growth in yields depended on other factors, such as agricultural mechanization, chemical fertilizers, and other components of the so-called green revolution.

If we compare the area in cane during one period with that several decades later, we see that the difference in total area is not great. This phenomenon, largely the result of increased industrial yields, can deceive us as to sugar's true impact on the environment. Considering the surface area in cane in different periods leaves out of the equation a large amount of land that was abandoned in the intervening years. In 1860 the area of cane fields was 2,786 square kilometers and that of sugar farms 7,979 square kilometers, or 2.5 percent and 7.2 percent of the island's total area, respectively. This proportion seems very small for the radical transformation of space in just over a century, even if we take into account only flat or rolling land (75%) or total agriculture area (62.7%). Even with the date from the early twentieth century, it could seem that sugar production did not occupy enough land to finish off the forests. In 1919, cane fields represented 8 percent of the island's total area, although that occupied by latifundios was three times greater.

Powerful plantation interests could buy vast tracts of virgin land located in traditional livestock estates in order to convert them to agriculture. Since these were abundant, it was more "profitable" to leave behind an equal amount of "tired" land, which was converted to pastures or used for smaller crops, whose rate of land occupation was insignificant compared with that of commercial crops. Sugar was, directly and indirectly, the most potent factor in the savannization of Cuban territory.

The eagerness of *ingenio* owners to invade wooded areas was restrained so long as the Havana shipyard was given a predominant role by the strategic and military interests of the Spanish Empire. Beginning in the seventeenth century the Crown reserved for itself control of the Havana regions' forests in order to privilege shipbuilding, one of the principal causes of deforestation until the end of the eighteenth century. Sugar's arrival in the *hatos* and *corrales* spelled the forests' doom, sooner or later, since the planting of cane and the need for firewood left woodlands unable to regenerate themselves in the short or medium term. For this reason restrictions on forest harvesting were tightened beginning in 1772, especially those concerning the use of wood on sugar *ingenios*.

The confrontation between shipbuilding and commercial agriculture is an example of the changes produced on the island between the last third of the eighteenth century and the beginning of the nineteenth. Until then, neither livestock farming, forest harvesting, nor agriculture clearly predominated over the others. Estates of small and large livestock had abundant forests, partly because their need for pasture was not great and partly owing to the island's climate and the importance of forests to the animals' diet. For its part, shipbuilding was not a model for rational forest exploitation, since its goal was to have the best lumber. But despite the destruction it left in its path, shipbuilding was unlikely to compromise the regeneration of the forest masses. In contrast, commercial agriculture, specifically that of sugar, required an ever larger, treeless area.

Until the 1772 *ingenios* often were built on land abandoned by the Cortes del Rey, the royal bureaucracy charged with logging for shipbuilding; from that time on it became more and more difficult to contain them within these limits. For this reason the navy attempted to control the dismantlement of traditional estates, which increased sharply as landowners sought to make room for agriculture and more intensive forms of livestock farming. But the Haitian Revolution, the rise of economic liberalism, and the decline of Havana shipbuilding imperiled the navy's age-old privileges over Havana forests. *Ingenios* entered the zones of the Cortes del Rey definitively, provoking what could be considered an "ecological revolution."[4]

These changes were accompanied by a long debate over the best way to exploit forest resources, in the sense not only of obtaining the greatest economic benefit but also of how best to conserve them. The royal navy argued for more forceful measures to ensure control of the forests for shipbuilding and to a certain degree in order to guarantee the necessary public supply of lumber and fuel. The owners of *ingenios* and estates, in contrast, maintained that securing individual property was the best guarantee of beneficial exploitation, both for the economy and for forest conservation.

Until 1791 backers of the former position prevailed, fundamentally because of strategic considerations, but the Haitian Revolution turned the order on its head. Final attempts to preserve the navy's forest-harvesting privileges offered economic, juridical, and environmental arguments against turning the forests over to the exclusive will of private landowners. But the sugar boom's great benefits for criollo oligarchy and for the Spanish Crown eclipsed reasoning that opposed the "sacred" rights of property. Echoing arguments in vogue in Spain, such as those of the Agrarian Law of Gaspar Melchor de Jovellanos, the Havana estate owners proclaimed the dangers of any intervention into or limitation of the rights of individuals to exploit the resources of their property. Logically, we must bear in mind the period of this polemic and admit that an argument that then appeared incontrovertible was not unreasonable: that the island's forests were inexhaustible and could last hundreds of years.

The navy was concerned less that the forests might disappear than about the increasing distance from the forests to the shipyard as the former receded, which made hauling the wood more costly. But it is true that navy officials were much more foresighted about the negative consequences of sugar's uncontrolled deforestation for the environment and the economy. The question is much more complicated because the navy's privileges gave it a kind of monopoly increasingly rejected even in Spain, making it one of the most characteristic symbols of the old regime.

The conflicts between the Havana *ingenio* owners and the Spanish royal navy were the point of departure for a great economic, ideological, and environmental transformation. Two different conceptions of colonial exploitation, and two ways of conceiving of the use of natural resources generally, confronted each other. The viewpoint of the navy was more favorable to a subsistence economy, to a balance among different products and to a certain degree to the communal use of property that in the final instance belonged to the Crown. That of the estate owners focused on the production of merchandise for export and on the individualization of the use of resources. The royal decree of August 30, 1815, was the final triumph of the most exaggerated form of liberalism in the exploitation of forests. The colony's sugar boom allowed the concession of land to go further than it had in Spain, perhaps induced not only by the benefits one could obtain but also by the belief that the island's forests really were unending.

The importance of the freedom to clear forests is underscored when we take into account land distribution in the colony, with an almost absolute dominance of the private citizen. In Cuba, unlike in Spain, communal, municipal, and other territorial forms of property ownership had limited significance. We could say that while in the metropole the individualization of agrarian property ownership evolved in several waves during the disentailment process of the nineteenth century, in Cuba this occurred all at once, through the delivering over of the forests to individual will and through the recognition in 1819 of full property rights over land conceded by the town councils.

Private property owners in the colony jealously defended the rights over the forests granted to them in 1815. All efforts to slow the uncontrolled deforestation of the island met the determined opposition of sugar producers, who understood that the success of their business largely depended on their freedom to dispose of the forests. The owners generally ignored other considerations — be they scientific, social, or even economic — which no doubt accentuated their predatory attitude toward the environment, which in itself was characteristic of colonial life and favored by the abundance of resources. This mentality guided the relationship of sugar to the environment until the forests of the island's flat and rolling regions were almost entirely eliminated. Following John McNeill, we could say that economic growth, or in this case the growth of sugar, became a seductive religion that put itself above all social or ecological precautions.[5]

Finally, in 1876, the Woodlands Ordinance was passed, after more than thirty years of Cuba's inquiring, for the first time, into the effects of free clearing of forests. The island could not remain completely alien to the modernization of forestry in Spain, where a school and a scientific body were formed with the specific mission of administering state and communal forests. The ordinance represented a significant change of attitude by the metropole with respect to Cuban forests. Nevertheless, its significance was very limited. Since it did not encompass privately owned woodlands, the area it governed was just 5 to 10 percent of Cuba's territory. The rest remained subject to the free will of landowners, who, as forest engineers in the colony were quick to warn, could not be counted on because they were interested only in immediate profit.

We must acknowledge that an effort was made to demarcate state property after years of almost total abandonment and to put some order to the exploitation of forests through harvesting concessions and permits to transport forest products. During the first two decades of the twentieth century there were few changes in the administration of state woodlands, and none in that of privately owned woodlands, despite the limitations foreseen when the Direction of Woodlands and Mines was created in the Ministry of Agriculture in 1909. It was not until the last great offensive against Cuban forests, impelled by World War I, that the need to impose restrictions on the exploitation of privately owned forests was understood to be urgent. The presidential decree of April 13, 1926, which banned the clearing of high woodlands even to plant sugarcane, was the first direct intervention since 1815 against the right of private property over trees.

Between these two dates Cuban sugar production increased 120-fold. Forested area, for its part, shrank from nearly 80 percent of the island at the end of the eighteenth century to 15 or at the most 20 percent by 1926. By itself private property ownership of woodlands could not have brought about such a transformation of the Cuban landscape in so short a time, but it was a fundamental factor in the reinforcement of industrial agriculture and its growing power to simplify ecosystems. Without the mechanization of the industry, with the railroads and other modern means of communication and of broadening the market (among other factors characteristic of the Industrial Revolution), the complete freedom to clear privately owned woodlands could not have had such a devastating impact on the forests. It was the combination of these two factors that brought about a radical change in most of Cuba's natural regions between 1815 and 1926.

The sugar boom sparked by World War I was the culmination of this process. There still being no restrictions on the freedom to cut down privately owned forests, thousands of caballerías of land were cleared and converted to cane fields in the midst of exceptional market circumstances. Some of the wood was used in the sugar industry itself or in railroads, but much of it succumbed for no other purpose than giving organic matter to the fields. How much biodiversity was consumed or extinguished so that Cuba could be for a few years the world's "El Dorado"? The great irony, as occurred so many times after sugar became the god of colonial economic interests, was that the wealth that wooded areas destroyed by sugar fever had sheltered did not produce the great economic benefits expected. At the beginning of the 1940s the agricultural representative of the U.S. embassy in Cuba noted that in some regions the lack of forests was so severe that campesinos could not find wood for fuel or other farm needs and that more than 40 percent of wood required for industrial use had to be imported.[6]

The principal negative economic effects of deforestation—the scarcity and high cost of wood and fuel—may have helped contain clearing given the urgent need to find alternatives and save the sugar industry from ruin. But another factor, less visible in the short term, had a powerful impact on sugar's fate: the "exhaustion of the land." The dominance of a rapacious agriculture was partly due to the short supply of labor, which made any attempt to improve the system of cultivation expensive, but this was essentially an economic calculation. Yields in cleared woodland were the highest and in the end more "economical" than those that could be obtained through more agricultural techniques, such as the ones practiced in Europe on land that had been farmed for hundreds of years. Only the most foresighted estate owners made changes. Sometimes the owners of the largest mills were pioneers in this regard, since the wearing out of more land and especially the cost of machinery required in the short term that the ancestral routine of itinerant farming be abandoned. Both questions were associated in the beginning with centralization and the *colonato*. Not only was this work system a solution to the scarcity of labor in the aftermath of slavery, but it also was reason for hope that Cuban agricultural practices could be reformed.

The appearance of the *ingenio central*, however, did not entail the end of clearing forests in order to plant cane. If the tendency to group farms together predominated on the western half of the island, in the east, after the Ten Years' War, new *ingenios centrales* began to be built with great production capacities and generally in areas with plentiful forest. Again the railroads helped increase the scale of space occupied, now especially through the extensive private networks for the transport of cane to the mill. This procedure was maintained until the end of sugar's expansion through the natural regions of Camagüey and Oriente. Political and economic dependence on the United States promoted the definitive triumph of industrialized agriculture in the sugar sector on a scale unprecedented in Cuba and without parallel in the world's other sugar-producing regions. This enormous industrial sugar production, together with its adverse economic, political, and social consequences, accentuated as never before the historical problems in the relationship with the environment.

During the different stages there was no lack of warning: many contemporaries sounded the alarm about the possible implications of uncontrolled deforestation. We could even say that there was no shortage of means and alternatives for a different kind of cane cultivation, one that, in today's terminology, could have been undertaken in a more sustainable manner. But economic interests ignored the forecasts of scientists, as they did with the so-called Reynoso system, which was based on local conditions and sought to replace the traditional system of clearing and burning to plant sugarcane. With reason, Alvaro Reynoso lamented that the attitude of producers was one of "after me the deluge."

Largely as a result, the soils' fertility was exhausted. When sugar's occupation of the natural regions was complete, evidence confirmed in spades La Sagra's fears of the consequences of large-scale clearings to make room for commercial agriculture. To begin with, this process was not limited to the soils most suited to cultivation, since often the simple existence of trees was considered a sign the land was fertile. Nor can we ignore the fact that at various times this may have been a deliberate practice to expand cane fields, since after all one could obtain favorable yields at least as long as good market conditions lasted. There was certain empirical experience with the handling of different types of soil, and producers had to adapt to local conditions, but even so the trend was to abandon land when it was considered "tired." Sugar thus left in its wake vast expanses of land converted back into livestock farms or dismissed as "unproductive." When there were no more forests to clear for cultivation, increasing yield would require the use of great quantities of external additives, chemical fertilizers, herbicides, agricultural mechanization, and so on.[7] Even so, the former yields of more than 100,000 or 150,000 arrobas of cane per caballería after clearing, and cane fields that lasted twenty, thirty, or forty years, today are a distant memory of Cuba's sugar splendor.

The problem of deteriorating soil that Cuba confronts today is largely rooted in the characteristics of sugar expansion, which, as it advanced, invaded vast areas that never should have been cleared for cane. It is estimated now that only 5.4 percent of arable land can be considered very productive and 17.8 percent as productive, while 30.8 percent is rated as poorly producing and 46.8 percent as very poorly producing. Other, more significant types of degradation that affect soils today are expressed by the following percentages of agricultural area: medium and heavy erosion, 43.3 percent; poor drainage, 40.3 percent; salinity and sodicity, 14.9 percent; extensive compaction (natural or caused by human activity), 23.9 percent. Perhaps the statistics that best show the difference from the former fields of cleared woodland are those of very low organic material content and of low fertility, 69.6 percent and 44.8 percent, respectively.[8]

Other environmental consequences of forests' disappearance were cause for alarm from early on. Changes in the hydrographic system and in rainfall were matters of growing concern for contemporaries. Whether deforestation directly caused the decrease in rainfall is debatable, but there is no doubt that it helped reduce rainfall's benefits and accentuate its harmful effects. References to droughts and floods, and to reduced flows of some rivers during the rainy season, were frequent during the nineteenth century. The greatest concern, apparently, was prolonged drought. Reynoso's work is significant in this regard for its effort to promote a cultivation system with irrigation as a central component.

Deforestation had much more direct impact on the disappearance of numerous plant and animal species from habitats characterized by high endemism. Naturalists have compared the Cuban archipelago to a long and narrow florist's shop, one that has the greatest floral diversity in the Caribbean, with 51.4 percent endemism, surpassed worldwide only by the Cape region in South Africa, Hawaii, and some areas of Australia. Of the more than 6,700 species of vascular plants in Cuba, no fewer than 500 have some economic, alimentary, medicinal, or textile value.[9] Nevertheless, only a few dozen native plants have been used for such purposes, as forest products, medicines, or fodder. This potential has been considerably reduced and in some cases lost forever, as can be seen in a preliminary study for the preparation of a Red Book of the country's flora.[10]

The archipelago's fauna also has suffered the effects of deforestation. Its species originally had a broader distribution, and some have disappeared forever. At the beginning of the twentieth century some species of avifauna already were considered extinct, such as the Cuban macaw (guacamayo cubano), the most visually impressive of native birds. Just a few decades before, Esteban Pichardo Tapia had written in his dictionary of Cuban terms: "In the island's interior there are many Guacamayas (as both sexes are referred to there) and so friendly that they let themselves be shot point-blank: it is a strange and wondrous sight [cosa peregrina] to see the many branches of a tree speckled with so many beautiful colors continuously in movement, covered with innumerable and raucous Guacamayas."[11]

During the first half of the twentieth century other birds were considered extinct or extremely rare, such as the royal woodpecker and the traveling dove (paloma viajera). The former was rediscovered in densely wooded parts of the eastern mountains in the 1980s, but then its trail was lost again.[12] Other birds that once lived in several regions now are found in very restricted habitats, such as the gallinuela de Santo Tomás, now limited to the Zapata Swamp. The different species of hutia, which were important to the diet of Cuba's indigenous people, are similarly threatened. Other mammals, such as the almiquí, a giant among insectivores that in pre-Columbian times lived in all parts of Cuba, are now found only in very small numbers in densely wooded mountain locations. Of course, the disappearance of fauna is not solely attributable to the deforestation provoked by sugar. Uncontrolled hunting is just one other factor that played a role. But no other crop or economic activity, including livestock, could rival with cane fields in their simplification of ecosystems. It is no accident that Cuba ranks fourth among New World countries most affected by the transformation of nature due to human activity.[13]

While some species of plants and animals became rare or ceased to exist, other native and especially exotic ones became dreaded plagues for the development of agriculture and livestock farming. In the nineteenth century there was the famous case of so-called Don Carlos grass, very difficult to extirpate from cultivated fields, and paraná grass was mentioned as a similar pest, despite its being one of the best artificial pastures for livestock. But no case is so revealing as what happened in the twentieth century with marabú and other plants that are known by this popular name. Introduced in the late nineteenth century as an ornamental plant or through the importation of livestock, this bush has invaded an ever vaster area, particularly in lands abandoned by agriculture and now devoted to livestock. Its growth in compact masses has made its eradication very difficult, none of methods tried thus far having offered definitive results.[14]

The story of the direct and indirect environmental consequences of deforestation could be even more detailed. I do not pretend to have enumerated them all here; nor is it possible to go into depth about all their aspects, which can be done in future studies. In this book I have sought, rather, to show the great transformation of the island's landscapes from the point when sugar production began to take shape in the last third of the eighteenth century until the cane plantations completed their occupation of most of the flat and gently rolling natural regions in the 1920s. Commercial crops and especially sugar, together with other factors to a lesser extent, brought about a radical change in Cuba's landscape through the intense conversion to agriculture of vast territories until then often covered by thick forests.

The enormous amount of material and nutrients stored for centuries in these forests was an essential resource for the full flowering of the Cuban sugar industry. Of course, it was not the only one; we need mention only the Africans torn from their continent to work as slaves on the plantations. But Cuba's sugar boom might not have been possible without the lumber, abundant firewood, and fantastic yields. Someday it will have to be calculated how much of the island's rich biodiversity was consumed to supply the food needs of the nascent European and U.S. industrial centers. Certainly it would be very revealing to compare the value of resources that ended up in boilers and steam engines, or simply rotted on the ground to fertilize cane fields, with how much was obtained in sugar, mostly to enrich the powerful group of planters on the island and foreign investors in the enormous latifundios.

The comparison should be grounded in a specific historical context, but it will make sense if it takes into account other, not necessarily economic, indicators that called attention in those years to the dangers of putting all efforts into commercial agriculture: scarcity of subsistence crops, ever greater dependence on foreign countries for basic and essential products, accentuation of social inequality, and environmental degradation. This type of argument is generally inseparable from the denunciation of the rapacious mentality of the slave system toward human beings and the environment. If one was free to trade in black slaves, why not be free to exploit the forests? In this sense there is no doubt that the decree of August 30, 1815, strengthened the proposition that the landowner could dispose, without limitation, of resources that had taken years to form. From then on the owner could use them according to his or her interests and personal benefit, without having to consider their importance as a common good or their influence on local living conditions.

The disproportion between the rate of resource formation and that of their consumption was increasing, and it was clear that this was not due to overpopulation. In the 1950s the geographer Gerardo Canet expressed it in this way: "We have developed ... [,] to an almost fantastic degree, the propagation of a few plants and animals that offered us the means to satisfy an immediate need, often transforming the original garden only for the sake of ephemeral benefit, discounting the best offerings of nature."[15]

But all was not in vain, and one could make a long list of what today's Cuba — in its economy, its society, and its culture — owes to the legacy of sugar. There also were few choices owing to Cuba's status as a colony, peripheral to industrial centers and centers of consumption. But none of this could justify an indulgent evaluation of the way some of our ancestors acted with respect to nature. The elements advanced in this study and others still to be written about the coevolution of human beings and the environment allow us to note that La Sagra and his contemporaries were correct to warn that the great changes caused by the sugar fever would have significance for living and production conditions on the island.

The long-term economic results were also less than one might have predicted, if one bases one's considerations on the peak moments of the primary export model. As David Watts observes, the benefits of commercial crops for the West Indies, including Cuba, have been doubtful or at least have had an enormous cost from social and environmental points of view.[16] As Cuban and Caribbean environmental history is constructed, the voices that denounced from the beginning a mode of exploiting nature with profound long-term implications for the social and environmental order will become more audible. Together with the traditional national heroes — politicians, soldiers, and champions of progress and of the growth of sugar — there should always appear those who dedicated themselves to the more anonymous and patient work of better understanding the earth and promoting a more sustainable means of interacting with it. Many of the authors cited here, independent of political tendency or nationality, deserve a special place. This was the case of José Martí, who, considering other contexts, expressed similar concerns.[17] All these works repeat the idea that future generations will demand an accounting of people who thoughtlessly destroyed the forests. Of course, it is impossible to do this with those directly responsible, since they have long ceased to exist. But we can look around us and ask ourselves to what point Cuba and the world of today and tomorrow have been or could be unchanged by a relationship between society and nature such as that of sugar and the Cuban forests from 1815 to 1926, which was dazzling but unsustainable.

Appendix 1

Scientific Names of Plants and Animals

I would like to thank Ramona Oviedo, a specialist in ecology and systematics, for her valuable assistance with this appendix.

Flora

Abey, *Abarema glauca* Urb. Barneby & J. W. Grimes and *Jacaranda arborea* Urb.
  or its sister, *Jacaranda coerulea* Griseb.
Acana, *Manilkara albescens* Griseb.; *Manilkara wrightiana* Pierre; *Manilkara*
  valenzuela (A. Rich.) Penn.
Aceitunillo, *Capparis cynophallophora* L.; *Beilschmieda pendula* (Sw.) Benth & Hook
Aguacatillo, *Alchornea latifolia* Sw.; *Nectandra antillana* Meisn.
Almácigo, *Bursera simaruba* L.
Ateje, *Cordia colococc* L.
Ateje de costa, *Cordia nitida* Vahl; *Bourreria suculenta* Jacq.
Avocado, *Persea americana* Mill.
Baría (or varía), *Cordia gerascanthus* L.
Bayúa, *Zanthoxylum elephanthiasis* Macfad.
Boniato, *Ipomoea batatas* L.
Cane palm, *Sabal palmetto* (Walt.) Lodd. ex J. A. et J. H. Schult.
Cayman oak, *Ekmanianthe actinophylla* (Griseb.) Urb.
Cedar, *Cedrela cubensis* Bisse.
Cedar, *Cedrela mexicana, Cedrela odorata* (L.) Roem.
Ceiba, *Ceiba pentandra* L., Gaertn. var. *Caribaea* (DC) Bakh.
Chicharrón (dark), *Terminalia eriostachya* Rich.
Cocoa, *Theobroma cacao* L.
Cuajaní, *Laurocerasus occidentalis* (Sw.) Roem., *Prunus occidentalis* Sw.

Cuban or Caribbean mahogany, *Swietenia mahogani* L.

Dágame, *Calycophyllum candissiumum* (Vahl) DC.

Don Carlos grass, *Sorghum halepense* Pers.

Eucalyptus, *Eucalyptus globulus* Labill.; *Eucalyptus resinifera* Smith.;
  Eucalyptus saligna Sw.

False acacia, *Robinia pseudo-acacia* L.

Fustete, *Chorophora tinctoria* (L.) Gaud.

Granadillo, *Brya ebenus* (L.) DC; *Brya microphylla* Bisse.

Guaimaro, *Brosimum alicastrun* Sw.

Guara (female), *Cupania americana* L.

Guara (white), *Cupania macrophyla* A. Rich.

Guásima, *Guazuma ulmifolia* Lam.

Guayabo, *Psidium guajaba* L.

Guayacán, *Guaiacum officinale* L.

Guinea grass, *Panicum maximum* Jacq.; *Urochloa maxima* (Jacq.) R. D. Webster

Hicaco (coastal), *Chysobalanus icaco* L.

Holm oak, *Quercus cubana* A. Rich.; *Quercus oleoides* Schlecht. and Cham.,
  ssp. *Sagraeana* (Nutt.) Borhidi

Indian laurel, *Ficus retusa* Thunb.

Ingenio torchwood, *Hypelate trifoliata* Sw.

Jagüey, large native species of the genus *Ficus* and the family *Moraceas*;
  Ficus benjamina L.

Jaimiqui, *Manilkara jaimiqui* (C. Wright ex Griseb.) Dubard

Jobo, *Spondias mombin* L.

Jocuma, *Syderoxylon foetidissimum* Jacq.

Júcaro (black), *Bucida buceras* L.

Jurabaina, *Hebestigma cubense* Urb.

Laurel, *Laurus nobilis* L.

Levisa, *Licaria jamaicensis* Ness.

Majagua, *Hibiscus tiliaceus* L.; *Hibiscus elatus* Sw.

Majagua (common), *Hibiscus elatus* L.

Mango, *Mangifera indica* L.

Mangrove (red), *Rhizophora mangle* L.

Marabú, *Dichrostachys cinera* (L.) Wright & Arn.

Oak, *Tabebuia angustata* Britt

Ocuje, *Calophyllum antillarum* Britt; *Calophyllum inophyllum* L.

Palo de caja, *Allophylus cominia* (L.) Sw.

Paraná (grass), *Panicum purpurascens* Raddi.

Patabán, *Laguncularia racemosa* L.

Pine (female and white), *Pinus tropicalis* Morelet.

Pine (male), *Pinus caribea* Morelet.

Poplar, *Ficus religiosa* L.

Quiebrahacha (caguairán), *Pseudocopaiva hymenifolia* (Moric.) Britt. & Wils.

Ramón, most common is known as *Ramón de caballos*, *Trophis racemosa* (L.) Urb.

Royal ebony, *Diospyros grisebachii* (Hiern.) Standl.

Royal oak, *Ekmanianthe longiflora* (Griseb.) Urb.

Royal palm, *Roystonea regia* (HBK) O. F. Cook

Sabicú (or jigüe), *Lysiloma sabicu* L.; *Lysiloma sabicu* Benth.

Sabina, *Juniperus lucayana* Britt.

Scented oak, *Macrocatalpa puntacta* Griseb.

Sugarcane, *Saccharum officinarum* L.

Vigueta (name for various trees), *Chione cubensis* A. Rich.

Walnut (native) (Nogal del país), *Juglans jamaicensis* DC

White oak, *Tabebuia leptoneura* Britt.

Wild avocado (aguacate cimarrón), *Dendrocereus nudiflorus* (Eng.) Britt Et Rose

Yaba, *Geofrea inermis* Sw.

Yagruma, *Cecropia schreberiana* Miq.

Yaití, *Gymnathes lucida* Sw.

Yamao (or yamagua), *Guarea guidonia* (L.) Sleumer.

Yamaquey (various), *Belairia ternata* Wright.

Yarey, various of the genus *Copernicia*

Yaya, *Oxandra lanceolada* Benth.

Yucca, *Manioth esculenta* Crantz.

Sources: J. Bisse, *Arboles de Cuba* (Havana: Científico-Técnica, 1988); Instituto de Ecología y Sistemática, *Arboles de Cuba* (Madrid: Academia, Lunwerg, 1999); Juan Tomás Roig, *Diccionario botánico de nombres vulgares cubanos*, 3rd. ed. (Havana: Editorial del Consejo Nacional de Universidades, 1965).

Fauna

Almiquí, *Sonelodon cubanus*

Cuban crane, *Grus Canadensis nesiotes*, *Grus mexicana nesiotes*

Cuban macaw, *Ara tricolor*

Flamingo, *Phoenicopterus rubber*

Gallinuela de Santo Tomás, *Cyanolimnas cerveral*

Huyuyo, *Aix sponsa*

Parakeet, *Aratinga eups*

Partridge, *Starnoenas ganocephala*

Royal woodpecker, *Campephilus principalis*

Sevilla, *Ajaia ajaja*

Torcaza salvaje or Torcaza morada, *Columba squamosa* and *C. inornata*

Yaguasa, *Dendrocyma arborea*

Source: Félix Guerra, *Los funerales del Rey: Ecología y fauna* (Santiago de Cuba: Oriente, 1999).

Appendix 2

Temperature and Precipitation in the Natural Regions of Cuba

Natural Region	Temperature (°C)	Annual Rainfall (Meters)
Plains and Heights of the North of Havana and Matanzas	24–26	1,200–1,400
Plains of Ariguanabo–Almendares–San Juan	22–24	1,600–1,800 and 1,400–1,600 east
Heights of Bejucal-Madruga-Coliseo	22–24	1,400–1,800
Artemisa Plain	24–26 and 26–28 littoral	1,400–1,600 and 800–1,000 littoral
Colón Plain	22–24 and 24–26 littoral	1,400–1,600 and 1,000–1,400 littoral
Plain of Corralillo-Yaguajay	24–26	1,000–1,200 and 1,400–1,600 east
Heights of the Northern Range	22–24	1,200–1,400 west, 1,400–1,600 center east, and 1,600–1,800 east
Plain of Los Arabos–Real Compañía	22–24	1,200–1,400 and 1,400–1,600 Damují River basin
Plain of Manacas-Cienfuegos	22–24	1,200–1,400
Plain of Santa Clara–Sancti Spíritus	22–24	1,200–1,400

Natural Region	Temperature (°C)	Annual Rainfall (Meters)
Plain of Trinidad-Banao	24–26 coast and 22–24 north	800–1,000 coast and 1,000–1,200
Plain of Júcaro-Morón	24–26	1,200–1,400 and 1,000–1,200 littoral
Plain of Northern Camagüey-Maniabón	25–26	1,200–1,400 west, 1,000–1,200 center, and 800–1,000 east
Plain of Southern Camagüey	25–26	1,200–1,400 and 1,000–1,200 littoral
Plain of North-Central Camagüey	24–26	1,200–1,400
Plain of South-Central Camagüey	24–26	1,600–1,800
Plains and Heights of Maniabón	25–26	1,200–1,400 and 1,000–1,200 littoral
Plains and Heights of Banes-Cacocum	24–26	400–500 littoral and sublittoral and 1,200 from east to west
Cauto Plains	24–25 littoral and 25–26 interior	800–1,000 and 1,000–1,200 coast and elevations
Manzanillo Plain	24–25 littoral and 25–26 interior	800–1,000 and 1,000–1,200 coast and elevations
Nipe Plain	24–25 littoral and 25–26 interior	800–1,000 and 1,000–1,200 coast and elevations
Plain of Palma–San Luis	24–26	800–1,000
Plain of Songo–La Maya	24–26	1,000–1,200
Guantánamo Plain	24–26	600–1,000 south and 2,400 north
Plain of Santiago de Cuba	+26	800–1,000 south and 600–800 north

Source: Roberto Gutiérrez and Manuel Rivero, *Regiones naturales de la isla de Cuba* (Havana: Científico Técnica, 1999).

Appendix 3

Units of Measure, with Equivalents

Measures of Length or Longitude

Cuban vara	0.848 meter
Meter	1.179 Cuban varas
Cuban flat league	4.24 km (4,240 km)
Spanish league	5.55 km (5,572 m)
U.S. league	4.83 km (4,828)
Kilometer	0.236 Cuban leagues

Surface Area

Cuban vara	0.719 square meter
	7.74 ft.²
Caballería	13.4 hectares
	33.55 acres
Square kilometer	7.45 caballerías
	100 hectares
	247 acres
Square Cuban league	133.96 caballerías
	1,798 hectares
	4,494 acres
Corralera league	0.78 Cuban leagues
	105.3 caballerías
	1,413 hectares
	3,533 acres

Volume

Cubic meter	35.314 ft.^{3}

Weight

Arroba	11.5 kg
	25 lbs.
Quintal	46 kg
	100 lbs.
Metric ton	1,000 kg
	86.9 arrobas
	2,200 lbs.
Spanish ton	920 kg
	80 arrobas
	2,024 lbs.

Notes

Abbreviations

AACH	*Anales de la Academia de Ciencias de La Habana*
AGI	Archivo General de Indias, Seville
AHC	Academia de la Historia de Cuba
AHN	Archivo Histórico Nacional, Madrid
AJF	*Anales de la Junta de Fomento* (former name of *MSEH*)
AMN	Archivo del Museo Nacional, Madrid
ANC	Archivo Nacional de Cuba, Havana
DM	*Diario de la Marina*
GG	Gobierno General
GSC	Gobierno Superior Civil
IG	Indiferente General
IH	Intendencia de Hacienda
ME	Miscelánea de Expedientes
ML	Miscelánea de Libros
MSCHN	*Memorias de la Sociedad Cubana de Historia Nacional*
MSEH	*Memorias de la Sociedad Económica de La Habana*
RACT	*Revista de Agricultura, Comercio y Trabajo*
RCJF	Real Consulado and Junta de Fomento
RCO	Reales Cédulas and Ordenes
SD	Santo Domingo

Introduction

1. Ramiro Guerra y Sánchez, *Azúcar y población en las Antillas* (1927; Havana: Ciencias Sociales, 1971), 5–6.

2. Cuba has the greatest land area of the Caribbean islands, followed by Hispaniola (the Dominican Republic and Haiti), 76,484 km²; Jamaica, 11,424 km²; and Puerto Rico, 8,897 km², which, together with the Cayman Islands, 241 km², form the Greater Antilles, which constitute 88% of the Caribbean's land area. The Bahamas, 11,826 km², have 5%, while the Lesser Antilles (of which Guadeloupe, 1,702 km², and Martinique, 1,090 km², are the largest) form 3%. The islands of Trinidad and Tobago (4,828 km² and 300 km², respectively) have 2% of the area, while the islands off the Venezuelan coast have 1%.

3. Here I follow the classification system offered in R. Guha and M. Gadgil, "Los hábitats en la historia de la humanidad," *Historia y ecología: Ayer*, no. 11, ed. Manuel González de Molina and Joan Martínez Alier (1993): 45–110.

4. Manuel González de Molina and Joan Martínez Alier, eds., *Naturaleza transformada: Estudios sobre historia ambiental en España* (Barcelona: Icaria, 2001).

5. Fernando Tudela, coord., *Desarrollo y medio ambiente en América Latina y el Caribe: Una visión evolutiva* (Madrid: MOPU, 1990); Guillermo Castro Herrera, *Los trabajos de ajuste y combate: Naturaleza y sociedad en la historia de América Latina* (Havana: Casa de las Américas-Colcultura, 1994); Allen Wells, ed., *The Second Conquest of Latin America: Coffee, Henequen and Oil during the Export Boom, 1850–1930* (Austin: University of Texas Press, 1998).

6. E. A. Wrigley, *Cambio, continuidad y azar: Carácter de la revolución industrial inglesa* (1988; Barcelona: Crítica, 1993).

7. Juan A. Cosculluela, *Cuatro años en la ciénaga de Zapata: Memorias de un ingeniero* (1918; Havana: Comisión Nacional Cubana de la UNESCO, 1965), 211.

8. Hernán Venegas, *La región en Cuba* (Santiago de Cuba: Oriente, 2001); Eduardo Torres Cuevas, "El azúcar y la formación de los complejos económico-sociales regionales," in *Le sucre dans l'espace Caraïbe hispanophone aux XIXe et XXe siècles: Stratégies et représentations*, ed. Michèle Guicharnaud-Tollis (Paris: L'Harmattan, 1998), 51–70. These two authors, and other historians, usually employ the concept of historical regions. Although I will not ignore such regionalizations, I have given preference to the geographer's concept of physico-natural regions in an effort to combine these broader spaces with the successive politico-administrative delimitations within each region.

Chapter One

1. Juan Pérez de Tudela, ed., *Colección documental del descubrimiento (1470–1506)*, vol. 1 (Madrid: Real Academia de la Historia, CSIC, Fundación MAPFRE América, 1994), 136–64.

2. Bartolomé de Las Casas, *Historia de las Indias . . .* , vol. 4 (Madrid: Miguel Ginésta, 1875–76), 73.

3. Alejandro de Humboldt, *Ensayo político sobre la isla de Cuba*, ed. Miguel Angel Puig-Samper, Consuelo Naranjo, and Armando García (Madrid: Doce Calles, 1998),

144. The first French edition was published in 1826 and the first Spanish one in 1827, both in Paris.

4. Ramón de La Sagra, *Historia física, política y natural de la isla de Cuba* (Paris, 1861), 50–51.

5. The cultural thesis argues that the savannas are the result of human action in certain zones prior to the Europeans' arrival. Studies that find that natural factors were more important can be divided into two groups: those that point to a climactic origin and those that find it had an edaphic basis. Leví Marrero, *Cuba: Economía y sociedad*, 15 vols. (Madrid: Playor, 1971–86), 1:29–33.

6. Lourdes Domínguez, Jorge Febles, and Alexis Rives, "Las comunidades aborígenes de Cuba," in Instituto de Historia de Cuba, *Historia de Cuba: La colonia*, vol. 1 (Havana: Política, 1994), 5–57. Neolithic communities applied different agricultural systems according to the ecological circumstances and learned to choose the type of soil best suited to specific crops; Ramón Dacal and Manuel Rivero, *Arqueología aborigen de Cuba* (Havana: Gente Nueva, 1984).

7. Pérez de Tudela, *Colección documental*, 159.

8. Domínguez, Febles, and Rives, "Comunidades aborígenes de Cuba," 43.

9. David Watts, *Las Indias occidentales: Modalidades de desarrollo, cultura y cambio medio ambiental desde 1492* (Madrid: Alianza, 1992), 75.

10. Hugh H. Bennett and Robert V. Allison, *Los suelos de Cuba* (1928; Havana: Comisión Cubana de la UNESCO, 1962).

11. República de Cuba, *Censo de 1943* (Havana: P. Fernández y Cía, 1945), 166.

12. Leo Waibel, "Places Names as an Aid in the Reconstruction of the Original Vegetation of Cuba," *Geographical Review* 33.33 (1943): 376–96.

13. The actual size of the island is smaller than the figure given by Waibel (114,500 km^2). In 1925, the Army Staff calculated Cuba's area at 111,111 km^2. In 1965, the Cuban Academy of Sciences offered the figure I use in this book: 110,920 km^2; Antonio Núñez Jiménez, *El archipiélago cubano* (Havana: Letras Cubanas, 2000), 91.

14. Leo Waibel and Ricardo Herrera, *La toponimia en el paisaje cubano*, edited with a prologue by Ernesto Chávez (Havana: Ciencias Sociales, 1984).

15. Herrera used the map of *hatos* and *corrales* in Ricardo Rousset, *Historial de Cuba*, 3 vols. (Havana: Librería Cervantes, 1918). See also Laird W. Bergad, *Cuban Rural Society in the Nineteenth Century: The Social and Economic History of Monoculture in Matanzas* (Princeton, NJ: Princeton University Press, 1990). *Hatos* and *corrales* were the names given to estates destined for raising livestock conceded in usufruct by the island's town councils from the mid-seventeenth century to about 1729. Their size and the type of livestock raised there varied over time. The original dimension for a *hato* (cattle and horses) was a radius of 2 Cuban leagues, and for a *corral* (hogs) a radius of 1 Cuban league.

16. Earl E. Smith, *The Forests of Cuba* (Cambridge, MA: Maria Moors Cabot Foundation, 1953).

17. Eliseo Matos, "Breve historia de los montes de Cuba" (Instituto Nacional de Desarrollo y Aprovechamiento Forestal, Havana). This unpublished manuscript appeared in the early 1970s and can be found at the Institute of Geography in Havana. It estimates that in 1492 5.5% of the island may have been cleared for agriculture.

18. Academia de Ciencias de Cuba (ACC), *Nuevo atlas nacional de Cuba* (Havana: Instituto de Geografía [ACC] and Instituto Geográfico Nacional [Spain], 1989).

19. This estimate concurs with studies of potential vegetation in A. Borhidi and O. Muñiz, *Mapa de la vegetación potencial de Cuba* (Havana: JUCEPLAN, 1984).

20. Enrique del Risco Rodríguez, *Los bosques de Cuba: Su historia y características* (Havana: Científico Técnica, 1995).

21. Ibid., 14.

22. I borrow here the explanation in the legend of the *Nuevo atlas* as well as in del Risco's book, which doesn't use the same terms.

23. This concept does not exclude socioeconomic elements. I take the concept of physico-natural regionalization from the *Nuevo atlas* and from Roberto Gutiérrez Domenech and Manuel Rivero Glean, *Regiones naturales de la isla de Cuba* (Havana: Científico Técnica, 1999).

24. I will refer little to the Pinar del Río district, since it was not one of the principal areas into which sugar expanded.

25. Matos, "Breve historia," 7. Matos estimates that between 1492 and 1774 786,609 hectares of forest were felled. This represented 7.87% of what the wooded area had been in 1492.

26. Arturo Sorhegui and Alejandro de La Fuente, "El surgimiento de la sociedad criolla de Cuba (1553–1608)," in Instituto de Historia de Cuba, *Historia de Cuba*. The authors indicate that beginning in 1553 "economic prosperity began to be considered based on the amount of land that an individual owned" (124).

27. Francisco Carrera y Justiz, *Introducción a la historia de las instituciones locales de Cuba* (Havana: Moderna Poesía, 1905), 58–78.

28. Marrero (*Cuba*, 2:58–78) cites the case of New Spain, where the emperor rescinded the right of town councils to concede lands.

29. With time few livestock estates maintained these ideal dimensions. To measure their area the legua corralera was created, equal to 105 caballerías, or 1,407 hectares. A *hato* thus measured 16 leguas corraleras and a *corral* 4 leguas corraleras.

30. This Spanish term refers both to the mill and to the estate of which it is the center. — Trans.

31. Julio Le Riverend, *Historia económica de Cuba* (Havana: Instituto Cubano del Libro, 1971), 3. A relative shortage, of course.

32. Marrero (*Cuba*, 2:245) argues that "the concept of communal lands did not predominate in Cuba, due to the abundance of land relative to the scant population during the colony's first two centuries."

33. "Carta del obispo Fray Diego Sarmiento al Emperador dando cuenta de su visita a villas e iglesias de Cuba, julio 25 de 1544," in Luis Torres de Mendoza, *Colección de documentos inéditos relativos al descubrimiento, conquista y organización de las antiguas posesiones españolas de Ultramar*, vol. 6 (Madrid: Sucesores de Rivadaneyra, 1891). Cited in Alejandro García Alvarez and Luis Miguel García Mora, comps., *Textos clásicos de la historia de Cuba*, Clásicos Tavera, ser. 1, vol. 9 (Havana: Fundación Histórica Tavera, 1999).

34. Nicolás Joseph de Ribera, *Descripción de la isla de Cuba, 1755–1756: Compilación*

e *introducción de Olga Portuondo Zúñiga* (Havana: Ciencias Sociales, 1986), 138–56; Ribera, "Discurso sobre el comercio y navegación de España con las Indias Occidentales," in ibid., 178–91.

35. Marrero, *Cuba*, 2:121–24.

36. Manuel Moreno Fraginals, *El ingenio: Complejo económico social cubano del azúcar*, 3 vols. (Havana: Ciencias Sociales, 1978), 1:157.

37. Sorhegui and La Fuente, "Surgimiento de la sociedad criolla," 124.

38. Havana's jurisdiction came to include quite vast territories, but for the purposes of this study it will comprise essentially the natural regions of the Havana-Matanzas district.

39. Marrero, *Cuba*, 2:119–20.

40. Ibid., 120–21.

41. Ovidio Ortega Pereyra, *El Real Arsenal de La Habana: La construcción naval en La Habana bajo la dominación colonial española* (Havana: Letras Cubanas, 1998), 30; Marrero, *Cuba*, 2:200.

42. Marrero, *Cuba*, 2:200. Marrero cites Pierre Chaunu, who claims that Havana became a second Biscay or the Biscay of the Indies.

43. Francisco Pérez de La Riva, *Origen y régimen de la propiedad territorial en Cuba* (Havana: Siglo XX, 1946), 93–94.

44. *Recopilación de las leyes de los reinos de las Indias*, vol. 2 (Madrid: Boix, 1841), 132. Law 13: "Que en La Habana no se corten caobas, cedros ni robles sino para el servicio real o fábrica de navíos" (In Havana mahogany, cedar, and oak are not to be cut save in the service of the King or the building of ships), Felipe IV, June 9, 1622; Law 15: "Que no se corte madera en la chorrera de La Habana, y si se cortare, no se traiga por el río hasta media legua antes de la presa" (Wood is not to be cut in the Havana channel, and if any is cut, it can not be taken to the river for a distance of half a league before the dam) and that "en diez leguas a Barlovento, y diez a Sotavento de la ciudad, no se corten maderas ningunas sin licencia del Gobernador" (within ten leagues Windward and Leeward of the city, no wood is to be cut without permission of the Governor), Felipe IV, August 6, 1624.

45. Pérez de Oporto had the support of Governor Francisco de Venegas, who warned that for 20 leagues around the port "there has been such haste in the felling of cedar, mahogany, and oak that scarcely a stick can be found of this wood that is so important in the building of ships"; ANC, AHC, box 87/419, "Carta a SM acerca de los desmontes y otros particulares" (Letter to His Majesty about clearing and other particulars), August 12, 1622.

46. Ortega Pereyra, *Real Arsenal*, 36, 39.

47. Douglas G. Inglis, "The Spanish Naval Shipyard at Havana in the Eighteenth Century," in *New Aspects of Naval History: Selected Papers Presented at the Fourth Naval History Symposium, United States Naval Academy, 25–26 October 1979* (Baltimore: Nautical and Aviation Publishing Co. of America, 1985), 47–58; Marrero, *Cuba*, 8:1–23, 12:174–85.

48. Gaspar de Aranda y Antón, "Las maderas de Indias," *Asclepio* (CSIC, Madrid), no. 45 (1993): 217–48; Aranda y Antón, *Los bosques flotantes: Historia de un roble del*

siglo XVIII (Madrid: Ministerio de Agricultura, Pesca y Alimentación, 1990); Erich Bauer, *Los montes de España en la historia* (Madrid: Ministerio de Agricultura, 1980), 173–79.

49. Aranda y Antón, *Bosques flotantes*, 21–22. Aranda y Antón estimates the area to be approximately half. Emilio de La Cruz Aguilar, in *La destrucción de los montes: Claves histórico-jurídicas* (Madrid: Facultad de Derecho, Universidad Complutense de Madrid, 1994), observes that the navy came to administer two-thirds of Spain's woodlands.

50. The ordinances were part of plans by the Marquis de La Ensenada (Zenón de Somodevilla; 1702–1781) to restore Spain's naval power. The marquis was the architect of administrative reforms during the reigns of Felipe V and Fernando VI. Judgments of these reforms have been divided. La Cruz Aguilar, in *Destrucción de los montes* (84–137), notes that they "put in place a true monster of natural, jurisdictional, mercantile, and technical complexity." Bauer and Aranda y Antón acknowledge that the reforms had flaws such as their impoverishment of the forests' quality through selective cutting, but they defend the role of the navy. An intermediate position is that of Luis Urteaga, *La tierra esquilmada: Las ideas sobre la conservación de la naturaleza en la cultura española del siglo XVIII* (Barcelona: SERBAL-CSIC, 1987).

51. Marrero, *Cuba*, 8:21–22.

52. AGI, Cuba 1694, royal order of October 8, 1748. These distances in Cuban leagues correspond to a length of about 170 km to either side of the port and a depth of 25.6 km inland along the northern coast and a total of 170 km along the southern coast.

53. Ibid. Cowherds driving draft animals could lop off the branches of orange and other trees "to maintain their oxen" but "without cutting them at the root because of the ruin that this would bring in the future." It was stipulated that no lumber could be conveyed along the Zanja Real aquaduct.

54. "Corte de Maderas, Artículo 5 . . . ," *AJF* 4 (*MSEH* 42) (1851): 27–37, "Respuesta de la Comandancia de Marina de Cuba a la pregunta de si existía orden del Rey en esa dependencia por la que SM declarase reservarse los montes de esta Isla o si se observaba por la Ordenanza de montes de 1748," August 27, 1796.

55. Inglis, "Spanish Naval Shipyard," 54–55.

56. J. H. Galloway, *The Sugar Cane Industry: An Historical Geography from Its Origins to 1914* (Cambridge: Cambridge University Press, 1989).

57. Alberto Vieira, *Canavais, açúcar e aguardiente na Madeira, séculos XV a XX* (Funchal, Madeira: Centro de Estudos de História do Atlántico, 2004).

58. Fernando Agete, *La caña de azúcar en Cuba* (Havana: Estación Experimental de la Caña de Azúcar, 1947); Rafael Suárez and Rafael B. Morín, "Caña de azúcar y sostenibilidad: Enfoques y experiencias cubanas," in *Transformando el campo cubano: Avances en la agricultura sostenible*, ed. Fernando Funes A. et al. (Havana: ACTAF, 2000), 127–44.

59. Ramiro Guerra y Sánchez, *Azúcar y población en las Antillas* (1927; Havana: Ciencias Sociales, 1971), 190.

60. In his August 12, 1598, letter to the king in support of the request, Governor Juan Maldonado observed that when he arrived in Cuba in 1593 there had been only small cane fields that did not produce sugar, which was shipped from Santo Domingo. But by 1595 inhabitants had begun to make sugar with mills and boilers. By 1598, the island

shipped 3,000 arrobas' worth to Castile, Cartagena, and Campeche; Marrero, *Cuba*, 2:315–20.

61. Reinaldo Funes, "Del trapiche al ingenio, 1600–1827" (tesis de licenciatura, Universidad de La Habana, 1991), 4–13. Tables with the number of requests for land concessions in the seventeenth century appear in Arturo Sorhegui and Alejandro de La Fuente, "La organización de la sociedad criolla (1608–1699)," in Instituto de Historia de Cuba, *Historia de Cuba*, 139–79.

62. From the registry of the ANC's *Anotaduría de Hipotecas* (starting in 1632); Heinrich Friedlaender, in his *Historia económica de Cuba*, vol. 1 (Havana: Ciencias Sociales, 1978), 20, gives a total of eighty for the entire century.

63. ANC, AHC, box 91/669, "Carta del gobernador Severino de Manzaneda y el Cabildo de La Habana a SM acerca del tabaco y el azúcar como únicas fuentes de riqueza de la Isla. 14–7–1690." The crisis was attributed to the entry in Spain of sugar and tobacco from foreign colonies.

64. Marrero, *Cuba*, 4:30.

65. Ibid., 2–9. In 1728 a letter from the governor to the royal offices in the colony mentioned the dismantling in recent years of several of the most substantial mills for reasons including the high cost of slaves, their high mortality, costly freight, and high taxes.

66. Ibid., 7:14–16.

67. Bernardo de Urrutia y Matos, "Resumen de los intereses y posibles aumentos de la isla de Cuba en cuanto comerciable . . . ," in Leví Marrero, *Bernardo de Urrutia y Matos: Cuba — Fomento de la isla, 1749* (Capiro, Puerto Rico: Capiro, 1993).

68. Marrero, *Cuba*, 7:13.

69. ANC, ML, 2646, "Libro de cargo y data de las proporciones de azúcar con que contribuyen los dueños de ingenio para el 5% correspondiente a SM, 1759–1765."

70. Nicolás Joseph de Ribera, *Descripción de la isla de Cuba*, ed. Olga Portuondo Zúñiga (Havana: Ciencias Sociales, 1971), 144, 157–58, 161–63.

71. Moreno Fraginals, *Ingenio*, 1:20–21, 35–36.

72. Allan James Kuethe, "El Marqués de Esquilache, Alejandro O'Reilly y la reforma económica de Carlos III en Cuba," in *Memoria del IV Congreso venezolano de Historia*, vol. 2 (Caracas: Academia de la Historia, 1983), 119–33.

73. David Watts (*Indias occidentales*, 424) mentions different writings on the industries of other Caribbean islands, from the mid-seventeenth century through the eighteenth. Nothing similar exists for Cuba for this period.

74. Funes, "Trapiche al ingenio," 38–43.

75. Fe Iglesias García, "La estructura agraria de La Habana, 1700–1775," *Arbor* (Madrid), no. 547–48 (1991): 103; Mercedes García Rodríguez, "Ingenios habaneros del siglo XVIII," *Arbor*, no. 547–48 (1991): 118. See also Pablo Tornero, *Crecimiento económico y transformaciones sociales: Esclavos, hacendados y comerciantes en la Cuba colonial, 1760–1840* (Madrid: Ministerio de Trabajo y Seguridad Social, 1996), 203–4.

76. Moreno Fraginals, *Ingenio*, 53.

77. Watts, *Indias occidentales*, 427–29.

78. Marrero, *Cuba*, 4. The figure for Barbados comes from Noel Deer, *The History of Sugar*, vol. 2 (London: Chapman and Hall, 1949), 332–33.

79. Mercedes García, *Misticismo y capitales: La Compañía de Jesús en la economía habanera del siglo XVIII* (Havana: Ciencias Sociales, 2000), 105–9.

80. Moreno Fraginals, *Ingenio*, 52.

81. The group of boilers used for this purpose.

82. The Spanish term refers to the harvest as well, since the sugar is made as the cane is harvested. — Trans.

83. Julio Le Riverend, *Problemas de la formación agraria de Cuba, siglos XVI–XVII* (Havana: Ciencias Sociales, 1992), 202.

84. Ibid., 202–3. On December 17, 1648, it was noted that the mills required 4,000 to 6,000 caballos of wood per harvest (*zafra*) and that "in a few years these woodlands will be ruined."

85. Marrero, *Cuba*, 4:18–19.

86. Both Spanish terms also refer to the plantations of which the mills were the center. — Trans.

87. The "dismantling" or *demolición* of an estate was the subdividing of it into smaller parcels, which were then assigned another use.

88. ANC, AHC, box 86/373, Letters of Governor Francisco Rodríguez Ledesma: "Of the *monte vedado* and clear-cutting, and the resolution to preserve the *monte*" (September 1, 1670); "Of the *monte vedado*, clear-cutting, the mills, and other particulars" (September 29, 1670).

89. The Ordinances of Cáceres only limited the establishment of cattle ranches and livestock farms in this area. Ordinance number 70 stipulated that "no one may be licensed to establish cattle or livestock farms within eight leagues of this city, because estates [*estancias*] may be authorized at any location within these limits that is not in the common lands next to this city."

90. Pedro Agustín Morell de Santa Cruz, *La visita eclesiástica*, selection and introduction by Cesar García del Pino (Havana: Ciencias Sociales, 1985). Outside the Havana jurisdiction were the *ingenios* in Santa Clara (26); Sancti Spíritus (25); Trinidad (25), and Puerto Príncipe (56). The 63 mills in Bayamo and the 6 in Santiago del Prado (El Cobre) were classified as *trapiches*.

91. Pedro M. Pruna, *Los jesuitas en Cuba hasta 1767* (Havana: Ciencias Sociales, 1991), 43. Quotation from AGI, Cuba section/1098.

92. Elpidio de La Guardia, *Guanabacoa, 1511–1927: Apuntes históricos* (Guanabacoa: I. F. Mora, 1927); Gerardo Castellanos García, *Relicario histórico: Frutos coloniales y de la vieja Guanabacoa* (Havana: Librería Selecta, 1948).

93. The *Anotaduría de Hipotecas* lists 18 *ingenios* in this region in the seventeenth century. In the first half of the following century, 11 were dismantled in the area around Guanabacoa and 5 in Cojimar; Iglesias García, "Estructura agraria."

94. Marrero, *Cuba*, 7:11–18.

95. Juan Pérez de La Riva, "Presentación de un censo ignorado: El padrón general de 1778," *Revista de la Biblioteca Nacional José Martí*, September–December (1977): 5–17.

96. La Guardia, *Guanabacoa*, 52–53. The royal decree was drafted in response to a letter from Havana's governor; Manuel Hernández González, "La pugna por la jurisdic-

ción de Guanabacoa entre su cabildo y el de La Habana en el siglo XVIII," *Tiempos de América*, no. 7 (2000): 3–9.

97. Marrero, *Cuba*, 4:22–23. Marrero gives 1653 as the date around which the dissolution of the livestock farms began.

98. Le Riverend, *Problemas de la formación agraria*, 210.

99. According to the Spanish Royal Academy's *Diccionario de la lengua española*, 21st ed., vol. 2 (Madrid: Espasa Calpe, 1992), this word (which ordinarily is translated in English as "field" or "pasture") is also used in the Americas to mean a "rustic farm, enclosed by a fence and with trees, intended principally for raising and maintaining all species of livestock." — Trans.

100. Marrero, *Cuba*, 3:244–45. Marrero cites the city council's ordinance of June 17, 1622, as evidence of the deterioration of the Almendares River basin and a dam that fed into the Zanja Real. Any Spaniard, mulatto, or black found to be cutting wood in these woodlands would receive a penalty "of 200 lashes and 4 years in the Castillo del Morro, so that he may labor in the service of His Majesty." Marrero notes that "in the penalty indicated for those who cut down woodlands, members of different ethnic groups were equal, counter to penal tradition in the Indies."

101. ANC, AHC, box 90/652, "Carta del Gobernador Diego A. Viana de Hinojosa a SM, acerca del teniente General Francisco Manuel de Roa, el Monte Vedado, su ingenio azucarero y otros particulares," Havana, April 18, 1689.

102. ANC, AHC, box 91/677, "Carta del Gobernador Severino de Manzaneda a SM, acerca del Monte Vedado, las fortificaciones y otros particulares," Havana, August 11, 1691.

Chapter Two

1. Manuel Moreno Fraginals, *El ingenio: Complejo económico social cubano del azúcar*, 3 vols. (Havana: Ciencias Sociales, 1978), 1:34.

2. Francisco de Arango y Parreño, "Discurso sobre la agricultura en La Habana y medios de fomentarla," in *Obras*, 2 vols. (1792; Havana: Imagen Contemporánea, 2005), 1:144–73.

3. "Sugar gave a notable agility to the Austrians' paralyzed monopoly system, to a point that the latter found irresistible, giving way in 1765 to an extensive experiment in free trade"; Jaime Vicens Vives, *Historia económica de España* (Barcelona: Vicens Vives, 1967), 517, 526.

4. Moreno Fraginals, *Ingenio*, 1:44–46. Commercial relations did not disappear with prohibition. In May 1785, seventeen of twenty-four ships anchored in Havana harbor were from the United States, loaded with flour, slaves, and tools for mills.

5. Ramiro Guerra y Sánchez, *Azúcar y población en las Antillas* (1927; Havana: Ciencias Sociales, 1971), 195.

6. Antonio de La Paz, "Discurso sobre el principio, progreso y decadencia del comercio y fomento de La Habana, sus causas y remedios," *MSEH* 38 (1849): 115–73.

7. Moreno Fraginals, *Ingenio*, 1:47.

8. Arango y Parreño, "Discurso," 158.

9. ANC, ME, file 2033/BO, "Expediente para que los dueños de ingenio den relación jurada de los azucares que producen," 1771; Juan Pérez de La Riva, "Presentación de un censo ignorado: El padrón general de 1778," *Revista de la Biblioteca Nacional José Martí*, September–December (1977): 5–17; "Padrón General por orden de D. Luis de Las Casas," *MSEH* 32 (1846): 197.

10. There were *cajas* of different sizes, but the most common volume was 16 to 17 arrobas.

11. ANC, RCJF, file 92/3933, "Estado que manifiesta el número de cajas de azúcar blanca y terciada embarcadas en el puerto de La Habana en los años que indican 1786–1797."

12. ANC, ME, file 945/P, "Renta decimal del ramo de ingenios de Guanabacoa, 1801."

13. ANC, IH, file 502/11, "Renta decimal del ramo de ingenios de Guabanacoa (1784)," and file 1020/10, "Renta decimal de ingenios de Guanabacoa, 1789."

14. For the year 1792 see the census of Las Casas and ANC, IH, file 7/14, "Expediente instruido a virtud de informe del Contador de glose de las cuentas prestadas por la Administración General correspondiente al año de 1792."

15. Pérez de La Riva, "Presentación de un censo ignorado"; 1796, ANC, IH, file 7/14.

16. Moreno Fraginals, *Ingenio*, 1:40.

17. ANC, RCJF, file 184/8325, "Expediente sobre la formación de un mapa topográfico del terreno demolido en la jurisdicción de esta ciudad. La Habana," January 21, 1801. Formally dismantled, since beyond this limit many *ingenios* still existed.

18. José R. O'Farrill, "Exposición . . . a la sociedad del método observado en la isla de Cuba en el cultivo de la caña dulce y elaboración de su jugo," *MSEH* 1 (1793): 119–45.

19. Antonio del Valle Hernández, *Sucinta noticia de la situación presente de esta colonia, 1800*, ed. Juan Pérez de La Riva (Havana: Ciencias Sociales, 1977), 71–112.

20. Alejandro de Humboldt, *Ensayo político sobre la isla de Cuba*, ed. Miguel Angel Puig-Samper, Consuelo Naranjo, and Armando García (Madrid: Doce Calles, 1998), 225.

21. Juan José Díaz de Espada, "Diezmos reservados," in *Obispo Espada: Ilustración, reforma y antiesclavismo*, ed. Eduardo Torres Cuevas (Havana: Ciencias Sociales, 1990), 242.

22. ANC, IH, file 901/13, "Remate de la renta decimal de ingenios de Güines, 1800."

23. Moreno Fraginals, *Ingenio*, 1:171. Moreno Fraginals considers that around 1792 an average of one hundred slaves and an annual production of 115 metric tons were the optimal figures.

24. Ramón de La Sagra, *Historia económica-política y estadística de la isla de Cuba, o sea de sus progresos en la población, la agricultura, el comercio y las rentas* (Havana: Viudas de Arazoza y Soler, 1831).

25. See Arango y Parreño's notes in Humboldt, *Ensayo político*, 226–27.

26. Valle Hernández, *Sucinta noticia*, 11–12.

27. O'Farrill, "Exposición," 121–22.

28. Valle Hernández, *Sucinta noticia*, 177.

29. "Although black soil is generally preferred for growing sugarcane, because it keeps moisture better, and vermillion soil is more esteemed for growing coffee, nevertheless, much sugar cane has been grown in vermillion soil"; Humboldt, *Ensayo político*, 144.

30. Antonio de Morejón y Gato, *Discurso sobre las buenas propiedades de la tierra bermeja para la cultura de la caña de azúcar y sobre su excelencia respecto a la negra en determinadas circunstancias* (Havana: Imprenta de la Capitanía General, 1797).

31. Humboldt, *Ensayo político*, 144.

32. O'Farrill, "Exposición," 122.

33. Ibid., 123–24. O'Farrill avoids a definitive judgment of the value of harvesting corn before planting cane. In his *Ensayo político*, Humboldt notes that diminishing productivity after years of growing cane, and a drop in sugar prices, led many farms to switch to rice (227).

34. Humboldt, *Ensayo político*, 239.

35. ANC, RCJF, file 92/3933, "Ingenios de nueva planta: Representación en que se da cuenta de las novedades introducidas en el ramo de ingenios, a beneficio de los esfuerzos de esta Junta de Agricultura y de los vecinos más ilustrados," August 8, 1798.

36. ANC, RCJF, file 92/3939, "Expediente sobre introducción de la caña de Otahití"; Moreno Fraginals, *Ingenio*, 178. There were two varieties of Otahití cane, white and yellow. Only the first was planted in nineteenth-century Cuba.

37. O'Farrill, "Exposición," 128.

38. So-called black or dark soils retain moisture better, thus promoting the cane's growth, but they also are more susceptible to weeds. Red or vermillion soils are looser, allowing weeds to be more easily controlled, but cane shoots are more vulnerable in them during the dry season. Hugh H. Bennett and Robert V. Allison, during their travels through the red plain of Matanzas, described as predominant the "Matanzas" soils, where they noted good production in fields that had been farmed for a hundred years without fertilizers or irrigation; Bennett and Allison, *Los suelos de Cuba* (1928; Havana: Comisión Cubana de la UNESCO, 1962), 116–23.

39. O'Farrill, "Exposición," 140–45.

40. In Cuban Spanish, a *canoa* can be either a canoe (small boat made from a tree trunk) or a wooden conduit, closed on both ends, and also made from the trunk of a single tree. — Trans.

41. AGI, SD, 1599 A., "Representación de dueños de ingenios," February 20, 1784.

42. AGI, IG, 1663, "Método que debe esperarse para la conservación de los montes: Francisco de Borja," September 5, 1783; "Juan B. Bonet, sobre consumo de cedro en los ingenios."

43. Ibid.

44. AGI, Ultramar 9, no. 7–39, "Representación de Comandante de Marina," February 24, 1784.

45. AGI, IG, 1663, "Método que debe esperarse para la conservación de los montes."

46. AGI, Ultramar 9, "Reglamento para el corte de maderas: Bando del 17 de abril de 1784," Luis de Unzaga y Amezaga.

47. Domingo Cabello de Robles, "Disposición sobre corte y uso de maderas," Havana, March 8, 1790. According to O'Farrill ("Exposición," 141): "[The *trapiches*] are three

pounders or cylinders of solid wood, . . . ten years old here in nearly all the *ingenios* with cast iron drums, of various dimensions."

48. AGI, Cuba 1694, Junta de Maderas, "Comisión sobre la demarcación de terrenos que sirvan para socorrer todas las necesidades de maderas, tanto para los agricultores, como para los ciudadanos," Andrés de Jáuregui and Miguel de la Puente, August 26, 1802.

49. AGI, SD, 1599 A., "Papel en que pone a la vista de VM Dn. Nicolás de Villa los motivos que atrasan claramente la fábrica de navíos en La Habana; que destruyen los montes con daño del público, y atrasos del Real Erario," 1784.

50. On the remaining 416 caballerías he estimated that no fewer than sixteen coffee plantations and sixteen small farms and livestock farms could be founded, with a consumption of more than fifty lengths of wood each, depending on their size.

51. Francisco de Arango y Parreño, "Corte de Maderas . . . Voto del Sr. D . . . , Síndico del Consulado," *AJF* 3 (*MSEH* 41) (1850): 303–5.

52. Mercedes García Rodríguez, "Ingenios habaneros del siglo XVIII," *Arbor*, no. 547–48 (1991): 121.

53. ANC, RCJF, file 92/3933, "Ingenios de nueva planta."

54. Marqués de la Torre, *Noticias de la isla de Cuba con que se acompañó el padrón del año de 1775*, ser. 1, vol. 9 of *Textos clásicos de la historia de Cuba*, comp. Alejandro García Alvarez and Luis Miguel García Mora (Madrid: Fundación Histórica Tavera, 1999).

55. Arango y Parreño, "Discurso," 152–53.

56. O'Farrill, "Exposición," 138–39.

57. ANC, RCJF, file 92/3933, "Ingenios de nueva planta."

58. Ibid.

59. "In many [*ingenios*], finally, reverberatory furnaces are being made in different ways, with the goal of saving and reducing as a result the share of woodlands needed by the mills" (Valle Hernández, *Sucinta noticia*, 79–80).

60. Moreno Fraginals, *Ingenio*, 1:88–90.

61. José Ricardo O'Farrill, *Sobre la conservación de montes . . . presentado a la Sociedad Económica de La Habana el 22 de octubre de 1796*. Printed book distributed with the *Papel periódico de La Havana* of February 9, 1797. In it O'Farrill indicated that 673 livestock farms and 4,359 small farms (*sitios y estancias*) existed in Havana's jurisdiction.

62. Moreno Fraginals, *Ingenio*, 1:157–58. Moreno Fraginals notes that in 1819 1,000 caballerías of forest were raised for sugar, although he does not specify how the wood was used. For the end of the eighteenth century he divides this use into 500 for firewood and 500 for cane fields.

63. The tarea, the most common measure of firewood, was a bin with a capacity of 3.6 or 4.3 cubic meters.

64. Humboldt, *Ensayo político*, 240–41.

65. Ibid.

66. Moreno Fraginals, *Ingenio*, 199; Alvaro Reynoso, *Ensayo sobre el cultivo de la caña de azúcar* (1862; Havana: Ministerio de Industrias, 1963).

67. Moreno Fraginals, *Ingenio*, 199–200. Moreno Fraginals claims that large *ingenios* of the 1820s cleared 2 or more caballerías for firewood during each harvest.

68. Humboldt, *Ensayo político*, 240; Reynoso, *Ensayo sobre el cultivo de la caña de azúcar*, 4.

69. ANC, RCJF, file 38/1664, "Expediente formado para contratar leña necesaria al consumo de las máquinas del camino de hierro." The second point said: "I place here all kinds of useful wood, excluding jagüey, almácigo, jobo, yagruma, and others of this poor category, the thickness of each tree or cut being upward of three inches."

70. Ovidio Ortega Pereyra, *El Real Arsenal de La Habana: La construcción naval en La Habana bajo la dominación colonial española* (Havana: Letras Cubanas, 1998), 57.

71. José P. Merino, *La Armada española en el siglo XVIII* (Madrid: Fundación Universitaria Española, 1981). From the reign of Carlos III, Merino singles out the creation of the Navy Engineers Corps in 1770 and the Arsenals Ordinance of 1776.

72. José Manuel de Villena, *Instrucción para los Cortes del Rey, acordada con el Excmo. Sr. Comandante General de Marina, por el Capitán de Navío, Don José Manuel de Villena, Encargado de la Dirección de ellos* (Havana: Imprenta de Don Estevan Boloña, Impresor de la Real Marina, 1790); copy in AGI, IG, 1663, "Prohibición de cortas de madera en Cartagena de Indias." José Manuel de Villena, born in Havana in 1744, was a sailor like his father, who bore the same name and was first marquis of the royal treasury, a title the younger Villena inherited in 1790.

73. From Jaruco to Matanzas were located the *cortes* of contractors paid by the king to supply ácana wood that was transported by sea from El Rincón.

74. AGI, SD, 1599 A, "Motivos que atrasan la fábrica de navíos, Nicolás de Villa, 1784."

75. AGI, Cuba 1158, "Informe de Félix Estrada, sobre reconocimiento de los montes de la Isla, a Juan B. Bonet. Daños de los Ingenios, Colmenas y cercados y quemas, 1775."

76. Consuelo Naranjo, "Los reconocimientos madereros en Cuba (1780–1810)," in *El bosque ilustrado: Estudios sobre la política forestal española en América*, ed. Manuel Lucena (Madrid: ICONA, Instituto de la Ingeniería de España, 1991), 107–23; Miguel Angel Puig-Samper, "La exploración científica de Cuba en el siglo XVIII," *Arbor: Monográfico — Las raíces del pueblo cubano* 1.547–48 (1991): 55–82; *Cuba ilustrada: La Real Comisión de Guantánamo*, 2 vols. (1796–1802; Barcelona: Lunwerg, 1991).

77. María Dolores González-Ripoll, "Una aproximación a la expedición 'secreta' de Ventura Barcáiztegui (1790–1793) y los reconocimientos de la parte oriental de Cuba," *Asclepio* (Madrid: CSIC) 43.2:165–80.

78. AGI, Cuba 1158, "Informe de Félix Estrada, 1775."

79. An edict by Antonio María de Bucarely on October 3, 1767, designated woodlands (estates) where individuals could cut cedar trees, so that "only for these are licenses granted, and it is determined that wood of this type may not be taken from any other location for use in sugar crates."

80. AGI, Cuba 1201, "Documentos y papeles concernientes a la contrata celebrada entre los cosecheros de azúcar de La Habana y un vecino de Nueva Orleans para la provisión de las cajas acomodadas al envase de este fruto."

81. AGI, Cuba 1201, "Términos de la contrata, La Habana," November 26, 1772.

82. AGI, Cuba 1157, "Del conde Macuriges al marqués de la Torre," September 19, 1772.

83. There was more rigor in the granting of licenses, but it had been agreed that the captain general would give them with the approval of the navy commander.

84. It did not escape Bonet that the two men intended to set up various *ingenios* and estates on their lands after the royal order of March 23, 1774, which deprived them of their tobacco mills.

85. AGI, Ultramar 9, "Representación de Juan B. Bonet en respuesta a otra del marqués de la Torre sobre embargo de maderas al marqués de Jústiz y al conde de Jibacoa," March 12, 1775.

86. AGI, Ultramar 9, "Real Orden del 29 de febrero de 1776."

87. AGI, Cuba 1158, "Bando del 7 de marzo de 1777, por el marqués de la Torre."

88. AGI, Cuba 1148, Havana, July 1, 1776. It is interesting to note that crossed out beneath the word *vecino* in the document is the term *hacendados* (estate owners).

89. AGI, Ultramar 9, "Gobernador de La Habana a Gálvez. Informa de conflicto por el tema de los bosques," July 8, 1776.

90. Ibid.

91. Ibid.

92. AGI, Ultramar 9, "Gálvez al Gobernador de La Habana," September 18, 1776. It previously had been determined that Bonet would take over the one thousand lengths of wood confiscated in Matanzas, paying the owners their cost, in order to ship the lumber to the arsenals of the metropole; AGI, Cuba, 1148, "Del marqués de la Torre a Bonet," September 14, 1776.

93. In his missive to Gálvez the Marquis de La Torre said he had come to consider these conflicts as the matter that made his "the most tiresome work in any branch of the Government."

94. AGI, Ultramar 9, "Juntas de Maderas, 1777–1779."

95. The goal was to increase the number of trees on estates, such as those operated by the Royal Company and Ponce de León's own Las Ciegas, where, although "trees had been cut in the past for shipbuilding, [trees] are today abundant." If the increase in population required more land, this could be requested of the navy, "with the assurance that the King will cede that of his whose Wood has been most harvested."

96. AGI, Ultramar 9, no. 7–13, "Informe de Diego Miguel de Moya Colón sobre Consulta de Junta de Maderas," February 23, 1779. The navy defended "the absolute dominion of His Majesty in the woodlands," following the royalist arguments in vogue in the metropole, especially during the reign of Carlos III, defending the preeminent right of the Crown. He cited the June 3, 1751, judgment of Cagigal y de La Vega's government ensuring "the total reservation that His Majesty has taken in his supreme authority to concede lands and to revalidate their sale," thus "prohibit[ing] the dismantlement of said estates and the variance of their initial concession without prior approval of His Majesty."

97. Ibid, February 23, 1779.

98. AGI, Ultramar 9, no. 7–12, February 19, 1779. To the second category of people, the law gave such absolute dominion "that once the requirements are met for which it provides as regards the sale, composition, division of the land, states *that they are granted the power to sell it and do with it as they desire, freely, as their own thing*" (underlined in the original).

99. He mentions the estates of Jaruco, Magdalena, Aguacate, Bainoa, Nombre de Dios, Quivicán, Santo Cristo de la Salud, Aguas Verdes, Ariguanabo, Guanajay, "Vane," and Mosquitos.

100. AGI, Ultramar 9, "Representación Diego J. Navarro a José de Gálvez," October 6, 1779.

101. AGI, Ultramar 9, no. 7–32, "Junta de Maderas del 3 de septiembre de 1783." The committee was charged with "agreeing separately on the way to reconcile this need with that of estate owners and farmers for their buildings and uses."

102. AGI, IG, 1663, "Método que me parece debe ponerse en práctica para la conservación de los montes, de donde han de sacar las maderas de construcción para este Arsenal, y los de España, sin que este preferente objeto prive al público las que necesite para sus fábricas y agricultura," Francisco de Borja, September 5, 1783.

103. Ibid. With respect to mahogany, he asked that harvesting it be strictly prohibited, since the king needed it "for the Artillery works in La Cavada, whose urgent need can not be concealed."

104. AGI, Ultramar 9, no. 7–39. "Representación Comandante de Marina," February 24, 1784.

105. Ibid.

106. AGI, SD, 1599 A, "Representación de dueños de ingenio," February 20, 1784. The *ingenio* owners were responding to an earlier report by Borja, of September 5, 1783, and to his pretensions generally.

107. Ibid.

108. Ibid.

109. AGI, SD, 1599 A, "Carta a Gálvez: Escrita a nombre del Ayuntamiento de La Habana por Baltasar de Sotolongo y Pedro Julián de Morales," July 15, 1784.

110. AGI, Ultramar 9, "Real Orden," October 4, 1784.

111. Ibid.

112. AGI, SD, 1599 A, "Informe sobre reglas para cortes de maderas y Nuevas reglas para el fomento de montes, por José Manuel de Villena," Havana, July 3 and 8, 1787.

113. In Villena's view the way to achieve adequate oversight was to give this responsibility to the district magistrates (*capitanes de partido*) and their lieutenants, with the additional incentive of half the sum of fines.

114. AGI, SD, 1599 A, "Sobre excesivo número de maderas que se conceden a particulares en los montes de la Marina," August 13, 1788. The inspector general of the arsenals believed that "Villena's reflections on the economics and governance of wood, its cutting, working, and transport, could not be produced by a person who did not have the understanding of agriculture and the authority of the Navy that this official brings together in himself."

115. AGI, Ultramar 9, "Real Orden del 15 de febrero de 1789."

116. Domingo Cabello de Robles, *Disposición sobre uso y corte de maderas* (Havana: Imprenta del Gobierno y Capitanía General, 1790).

117. AGI, IG, 1663, "Incidencias relativas al corte de maderas en La Habana, 1790–1791."

118. AGI, IG, 1663, "Expedientes acerca de la dimisión de Villena." It was noted that it

would be "very disagreeable to His Majesty if controversies and disputes arise over the felling, storage, shipping, and uses of wood, and much more [unpleasant] if . . . these overshadow the people, since His Majesty is confident in the merits of all those who make up the Committee, and most especially in this area the knowledge and impartiality of Villena."

119. AGI, IG, 1663, "Proyectos para garantizar el abasto del Astillero de La Habana y los envíos a los de España, por José Manuel de Villena."

Chapter Three

1. Manuel Moreno Fraginals, *El ingenio: Complejo económico social cubano del azúcar*, 3 vols. (Havana: Ciencias Sociales, 1978), 2:120–25; Nadia Fernández de Pinedo, *Las balanzas de comercio exterior de La Habana, 1803–1807* (Bilbao: Universidad País Vasco, Servicio Editorial, 2000). For a broader context, see John R. Fisher, *El comercio entre España e Hispanoamérica (1797–1820)* (Madrid: Banco de España, 1993).

2. María Dolores González-Ripoll Navarro, *Cuba, la isla de los ensayos: Cultura y sociedad (1790–1815)* (Madrid: CSIC, 2000), 155–94; Izaskun Alvarez Cuartero, *Memorias de la Ilustración: Las sociedades económicas de Amigos del País en Cuba (1783–1832)* (Madrid: Real Sociedad Basconganda de Amigos del País, Delegación en Corte, 2000).

3. AGI, Cuba, 1694, "Comisión . . . Andrés de Jáuregui y Miguel de la Puente," August 5, 1802.

4. ANC, GSC, file 864/29229, "Resumen de la riqueza civil e industrial de la provincia de La Habana dividida en partidos," 1820.

5. ANC, RCJF, file 92/3933, "Estado que manifiesta el número de cajas de azúcar blanca y terciada embarcadas en el puerto de La Habana en los años que indican," 1786–97.

6. Rafael A. Cowley, *Los tres primeros historiadores de Cuba*, vol. 1 (Havana: Andrés Pego, 1876–77), 169.

7. Diego José Sedano, *Dos preguntas que el Capitán General de la isla de Cuba . . . Sobre decadencia del ramo del azúcar en la misma Isla* (London: C. Wood, 1812).

8. Ibid.

9. Juan José Díaz de Espada, "Diezmos reservados," in *Obispo Espada: Ilustración, reforma y antiesclavismo*, ed. Eduardo Torres Cuevas (Havana: Ciencias Sociales, 1990).

10. Alejandro de Humboldt, *Ensayo político sobre la isla de Cuba*, ed. Miguel Angel Puig-Samper, Consuelo Naranjo, and Armando García (Madrid: Doce Calles, 1998), 267. The opinions he gives in his diary are in the same vein. Sandra Rebok, "Alejandro de Humboldt en Cuba: Reflexiones historiográficas," in *El Caribe hispano: Sujeto y objeto en política internacional*, ed. Josef Opatrny (Prague: Universidad Carolina de Praga, 2001).

11. The prices are in Humboldt, *Ensayo político*, 224.

12. For 1771, ANC, ME, file 2033/BO, "Expediente para que los dueños de ingenio den relación jurada de los azucares que producen"; for 1778, Juan Pérez de La Riva, "Presentación de un censo ignorado: El padrón general de 1778," *Revista de la Biblioteca Nacional José Martí*, September–December (1977): 5–17; for 1792, "Padrón General por orden de D. Luis de Las Casas," *MSEH* 32 (1846): 197; for 1796, Antonio del Valle Hernández,

Sucinta noticia de la situación presente de esta colonia, 1800, ed. Juan Pérez de La Riva (Havana: Ciencias Sociales, 1977); and for 1820, ANC, GSC, file 864/29229, "Resumen de la riqueza civil e industrial de la provincia de La Habana dividida en partidos."

13. Laird W. Bergad, *Cuban Rural Society in the Nineteenth Century: The Social and Economic History of Monoculture in Matanzas* (Princeton, NJ: Princeton University Press, 1990), 2–45.

14. Juan Pérez de La Riva, "El país de La Habana en los albores del siglo XIX, según Antonio del Valle Hernández," in Valle Hernández, *Sucinta noticia,* 50–54.

15. ANC, ME, file 3772/Añ, "Resumen general de partidos, números de esclavos de la dotación de ingenios nuevos y viejos que molieron antes del año 1804 y de los cafetales que se hallan en el obispado de La Habana, 1804–1835." Among the *ingenios* that appear in other sources, including in the jurisdiction of Güines, are those in the jurisdiction of Macuriges, to the east. In Guanajay and Güines, respectively, 8 and 5 new *ingenios* (and 65 and 25 old ones) are recorded.

16. Valentín Cuesta, *Evolución de la villa Real de San Julián de los Güines* (Guanabacoa: n.p., 1953).

17. ANC, IH, file 901/13, "Remate de la renta decimal de ingenios de Güines, 1800."

18. Moreno Fraginals, *Ingenio,* 60. Calvo was charged by Las Casas with continuing the project of founding San Julián de los Güines as a town. It was given this title in May 1815.

19. Closer to the navy's position was the reduction of tariffs on iron pounders and crushers from Biscay, in December 1789, as well as the royal order of January 11, 1790, freeing Spaniards to take to the peninsula timber cut with the permission of the Woodlands Committee and requiring that foreigners introducing slaves into the colony be treated like Spaniards, "lumber being included among the products that according to said article can be used to pay them"; José A. Escudero, *Los orígenes del Consejo de Ministros en España: La Junta Suprema de Estado,* vol. 2 (Madrid: Nacional, 1979), 471, 477–80.

20. Acevedo recommended granting the dismantlement requests of Santo Domingo del Rosario, Cayajavos, and San Andrés. He recommended rejecting the petitions of San Felipe de Pipián, Cayajavo, Gabriel, and San José de Arroyo Barbudo.

21. AGI, Cuba 1694, "Informe de Pedro Acevedo al Presidente y demás señores de la Junta de Maderas," Havana, November 22, 1794.

22. AGI, Cuba 1694, "En conformidad con lo prevenido por SM en RO de 15 de febrero de 1789 en caso de no acordarse los vocales de la Junta de Maderas . . . ," Havana, May 23, 1795.

23. Ibid. One reason for this was that the landowners themselves did not do the clearing but rather hired this out to "mercenary men in their pay who indiscriminately cut down everything they see."

24. AGI, Cuba 1694, "Voto de Josef de Coca en Junta de Maderas," May 23, 1795.

25. AGI, Cuba 1694, "Voto de Miguel García Barreras en Junta de Maderas," Havana, June 15, 1795. If it was not convenient to leave the trees standing, the landowners could be ordered "to fell and mark them, leaving them in the field at the disposition of the Inspector."

26. AGI, SD, 1599 A, Juan de Araoz, "Representación a la vía reservada de Marina," September 8, 1796. Araoz acknowledged the need to allow the woodlands of the metropole to rest for one hundred years, "enjoying meanwhile, with method and economy, the abundance of this Island of Cuba." This despite the "excessive consumption of fine lumber that is used in the mills of the more than four hundred sugar-making *ingenios* now found in the Jurisdiction of Havana."

27. José Ricardo O'Farrill, *Sobre la conservación de montes . . . presentado a la Sociedad Económica de La Habana el 22 de octubre de 1796.* Printed book distributed with the *Papel periódico de La Havana* of February 9, 1797. The society, "wishing to show the author its appreciation of his report, and desiring that the public take all the benefit that will come from reading it, agrees among other things to its printing."

28. In the jurisdiction of Havana, O'Farrill counted 217 *ingenios*, 61 *ingenios* in development, 673 *potreros*, and 4,359 *sitios* and estancias.

29. This claim had already been made to the Economic Society. See "Informe de la Diputación de los medios que puede ser fomentada la parte oriental de esta Isla," *MSEH* 2 (1794): 53–61.

30. AGI, Ultramar 9 (no. 7–77i), "Informe del Director de Cortas," February 28, 1797.

31. Tomás Romay, "Sobre los obstáculos que han impedido progresen las colmenas en la isla de Cuba, y los medios de fomentarlas," in *Obras completas*, vol. 1, *Trabajos científicos*, comp. José López Sánchez (1796; Havana: Academia de Ciencias de Cuba, 1965): 357–73.

32. ANC, RCJF, file 92/3932, Tomás de Piña, "Sobre escasez y carestía de maderas," February 1797.

33. Ibid., "Testimonio de Francisco Peñalver," November 3, 1797. Peñalver claims that Acevedo went "to the extreme of seizing me by the shirt and ordering me to leave."

34. During one logging operation, he said, a day did not go by without a navy official "coming to the saw mill until it became necessary to give him a couple of half lengths . . . because even the ácana we were cutting looked to him like cedar."

35. The council argued that dismantlement of *corrales* had not led to a perceptible drop in livestock, thanks to "new breeds from abroad, of which each one is worth three of those from the island," which had propagated widely and which guaranteed public supply even during the dry season.

36. AGI, Ultramar 9/7, 2, "Expediente del Real Consulado sobre que se reforme el reglamento de maderas . . . en aquella Isla por los perjuicios que dice ocasiona a la agricultura y al comercio," Havana, May 22, 1798. Also in *AJF* 3 (*MSEH* 41) (1850): 73–93.

37. Ibid. One may wonder if Arango y Parreño included these documents to show the bias behind the woodlands director's veto. If this is the case, he attained his objective. As the report notes, it was learned "extrajudicially" that the subinspector testified against the claims of the twenty-two witnesses.

38. The consulate members claimed that the Wood Committee was "flabbergasted" by its new member and "even more so by the interim presidency that a man of great age and little rank (Colonel Domingo Cabello) unfortunately exercised in favor of everything he proposed."

39. AGI, Ultramar 9/7, 2, "El Prior y Cónsules de la Habana remiten una información sobre los precios a que han corrido las maderas desde el año de 1780," Havana, May 31, 1798.

40. The navy could choose forests for its exclusive use in anchorages and ports, "whose surroundings are virgin woodland for several leagues from the water."

41. In AGI, Cuba 1694, and AGI, Santo Domingo 1599 A.

42. AGI, SD, 1599 A, "Representación a la vía reservada de Marina," July 2, 1800. Araoz recommended that "the appropriate reports [be requested] of Ship Captain don José Manuel de Villena, today Marquis of the Royal Treasury . . . and that all the many documents about these Woodlands in the secretariat of the Supreme Council of the Indies be consulted."

43. La Puente's replacement of Bouyón posed an immediate problem, since the former acknowledged not having thoroughly studied the documents provided by his predecessor.

44. AGI, Ultramar 9, "Dictamen de Juan de Araoz," December 31, 1801.

45. Corte de Maderas, Article 3, *AJF* 3 (*MSEH* 41) (1850): 261–64. The restrictions were an impediment "to giving land the ventilation it needs" and on livestock reproduction, as well as a hindrance because landowners had to have on their lands wardens "who exercise rigorism."

46. AGI, Cuba 1694, "Junta de Maderas," June 3, 1802. Someruelos recommended that two locations be chosen for the building and careening of commercial ships, that logging for the royal treasury be suspended, and that rules be established for the interior of the island.

47. He denied that Law 1, Title 12, Book 4, gave full property rights to individuals, and he cited Laws 13 and 14, Title 17, Book 4; the municipal ordinances 63, 68, 70, 71, 72, 73 and 75 on the concession of lands; the report of Diego de Moya; the royal order of April 6, 1791, confirming the fining of Lázaro Chávez; and resolutions on and regulations of woodlands.

48. The total included 16,872 cedars, 4,589 mahogany trees, 2,053 sabicúes, 1,760 chicharrones, 2,394 oaks, and 50 guaiacums. As for the requirement to bring to the shipyard two futtocks for each length of lumber cut, more than half of these were returned, and the rest were paid for at their just price. Hauling them was not burdensome because in practice they were carried on top of the lengths.

49. AGI, Cuba 1694, Andrés de Jáuregui and Miguel de La Puente, "Junta de Maderas . . . para la lectura de Comisión sobre demarcación de terrenos que sirvan para socorrer todas las necesidades de maderas," August 26, 1802.

50. Matanzas, Jaruco, Güines, Santa María del Rosario, Guanabacoa, Santiago, Bejucal, and San Antonio. Havana also included Jesús del Monte, El Cerro, and Regla, with eighty thousand inhabitants.

51. Of the other towns Jáuregui and La Puente said: "Some of their inhabitants, although only a few, can be given the title of property owner. Most of the others have enough to live on; all would like to become more comfortable as their means increase. This is why one finds furniture never before seen . . . in said Towns . . . [and] an increasing number and quality of buildings."

52. Francisco de Arango y Parreño, "Corte de Maderas, Art. 4° . . . ," *AJF* 3 (*MSEH* 41) (1850).

53. He cited the San Pedro *potrero*, which the navy had bought from his family for 400 pesos and which could be sold for 1,600: "It is well known that those who build and plant always profit when they sell, so much so that our country folk regularly seek their fortune by buying wooded lands . . . later selling them at a higher value" (298).

54. Miguel Fernández de La Puente, "Corte de maderas, Art. 3° . . . ," *AJF* 3 (*MSEH* 41) (1850): 264–73.

55. He argued that "the Navy should by rights be the unique depositary of the woodlands Jurisdiction, and this jurisdiction should have its rules, its statutes, its guarantees."

56. He lamented that although Cuban tobacco was of higher quality, "the pestilential [tobacco] of Virginia is smoked instead." This "scandalous decline" was due to the "unequal care and disproportionate aid . . . given to some sectors over others."

57. AGI, Cuba 1694, "Dictamen de Someruelos" (n.d.). In his opinion "such loyal vassals" would not oppose the regulations if they benefited royal service.

58. AGI, Ultramar 9 (no. 7–80), Juan de Araoz, "Cuenta final de las juntas celebradas a consecuencia de la Real Cédula de 14 de febrero de 1800," January 31, 1804.

59. This was the "first time that a leader has been denied common documents on which wisdom is sought, and in which the State and the public has an interest."

60. AGI, Cuba 1694, "Juntas de Maderas, 1803–1806."

61. AGI, Cuba 1694, "El Teniente Gobernador de Trinidad da cuenta . . . de las voluntarias e indebidas demoliciones de las haciendas y pide resolución," December 18, 1804. Complaints were received from Trinidad *ingenio* owners about the shortage of lumber in the estate destined for the public (1795). They also requested permission to ship sugar in cedar crates for the duration of the shortage caused by the war (1798).

62. AGI, Cuba 1694, "Testimonio de lo acordado por este Ayuntamiento sobre elección de montes para la saca de maderas de fábricas y demás usos comunes," Santiago de Cuba, November 30, 1803.

63. Joaquín de Ozés y Alzúa, "Representación hecha al Consejo de Indias sobre el remedio que necesita el nuevo obispado de Cuba para su fomento dirigida por su obispo en 30 de noviembre de 1794," in Ana Irisarri Aguirre, *El Oriente cubano durante el gobierno del obispo Joaquín de Osés y Alzúa (1790–1823)* (Pamplona, Spain: EUNSA, Ediciones de la Universidad de Navarra, 2003), 329–59. Ozés y Alzúa based his description on his journey from Havana to Santiago de Cuba in 1789.

64. AGI, SD, 1599 A, Juan de Araoz, "Perjuicios del comercio extranjero de maderas," July 22, 1804. Up to January 1804, 110,019 pieces of lumber had been harvested under license. The grantees "fell and work the lengths without respecting the prescribed quota . . . and eat the livestock of the estates without obtaining the owners' permission or paying the animals' value."

65. Ibid. José del Río confirmed the shortcomings of this trade during a visit to Trinidad, Sancti Spíritus, and Manzanillo, where the English bought lumber "for whatever they wanted and however they wanted."

66. AMN, Ms. 438, Villavicencio, "Informe del Comandante General de Marina de La Habana sobre fuerzas navales para los Apostaderos de América, sobre maderas de construcción y sus montes en la isla de Cuba . . . ," June 20, 1809.

67. Emilio de La Cruz Aguilar, *La destrucción de los montes: Claves histórico-jurídicas* (Madrid: Facultad de Derecho, Universidad Complutense de Madrid, 1994), 126–35. La Cruz Aguilar notes that during a December 21, 1811, meeting a deputy listed the navy's woodlands, smuggling, and freedom to publish as the topics that had concerned the *cortes* since its investiture.

68. Luis Urteaga, *La tierra esquilmada: Las ideas sobre la conservación de la naturaleza en la cultura española del siglo XVIII* (Barcelona: SERBAL-CSIC, 1987), 142. Urteaga points out that "Enlightenment thought slips progressively toward a full assumption of private initiative."

69. ANC, RCJF, file 94/3955, "Expediente instruido con los antecedentes del recurso dirigido a las cortes generales y extraordinarias sobre las reservas hechas en la Junta de Maderas de 22 de junio de 1812 por el ingeniero D. Diego de la Parra contra el decreto que restituye a los particulares el dominio de los arbolados."

70. José A. Piqueras Arenas, "Azúcar y comercio: Los confines del liberalismo cubano (1808–1814)," *Revista mexicana del Caribe* 8 (1999): 128–56. The Regency's interpretation was that land concessions "have the condition that dominion over woodlands and trees is reserved for the King."

71. AGI, SD, 1599. In this file appear the motions of the Cuban deputies, together with the responses of the navy and the captain general.

72. "Corte de Maderas, Artículo 6°," *AJF* 4 (*MSEH* 42) (1851): 161–244.

73. AGI, Ultramar 9, Pedro Aparici, "Informe de la Contaduría General," August 31, 1805. The General Accounting Office reduced the area that the Royal Forest Reserves should abandon from 40 leagues around the port of Havana to 30. It also supported suggestions such as establishing wood committees in other towns on the island.

74. "Corte de Maderas, Artículo 6°," *AJF* 4 (*MSEH* 42) (1851): 167.

75. Ibid., 170.

76. Urteaga, *Tierra esquilmada*, 153–57.

77. AGI, SD, 1599 A.

78. The decree sought "to protect the sacred right of property, to perpetuate the woodlands of this island, and to ensure, through the increasing supply and low price of lumber, the most rapid progress in shipbuilding and civil construction, and at the same time to protect the population, agriculture, and commerce."

79. AGI, Ultramar, 26/13, signed by Juan Ruiz de Apodaca, Havana, May 11, 1816.

80. AGI, Ultramar 27/8, "El Consulado de La Habana al Fiscal, pide imprimir y distribuir ejemplares de la Real Cédula de 30 de agosto de 1815."

81. Arango y Parreño believed this to be one of his most important achievements. In "Resumen de méritos y servicios," one reads: "No. 1 . . . It would not be excessive to recall now that . . . he has written different Essays that have resulted in great advantage to the Treasury and the country, such as those relative to freedom of our overseas commerce, the abolition of weighing of livestock, the slavery in which the Navy held our

woodlands, the destruction of the infernal Factoría [the institution through which the Crown controlled the cultivation and sale of tobacco], and the wrongheaded design of promoting the political independence of this Island"; Francisco de Arango y Parreño, *Obras*, 2 vols. (1792; Havana: Imagen Contemporánea, 2005), 2:445.

Chapter Four

1. The relationship between slavery, the environment, and agricultural underdevelopment is taken up in Manuel Moreno Fraginals, *El ingenio: Complejo económico social cubano del azúcar*, 3 vols. (Havana: Ciencias Sociales, 1978), which views the slaveholding system as hindering agricultural improvements. The smaller size of other Caribbean colonies required them to adopt agricultural and manufacturing innovations earlier. David Watts, *Las Indias occidentales: Modalidades de desarrollo, cultura y cambio medio ambiental desde 1492* (Madrid: Alianza, 1992); Richard H. Grove, *Green Imperialism: Colonial Expansion, Tropical Island Edens and the Origins of Environmentalism, 1600–1860* (Cambridge: Cambridge University Press, 1996); José Augusto Pádua, *Um sopro de destruição: Pensamento político e crítica ambiental no Brasil escravista (1786–1888)* (Río de Janeiro: Jorge Zahar, 2002).

2. Heinrich Friedlaender argues that few countries were as enthusiastic as Cuba in their reception of Adam Smith's ideas on the international division of labor and those of Gaspar Melchor de Jovellanos on the perniciousness of state intervention; Friedlaender, *Historia económica de Cuba*, vol. 1 (Havana: Ciencias Sociales, 1978), 342.

3. Vicent Sanz Rozalén, "De la concesión de mercedes a los usos privativos: Propiedad y conflictividad agraria en Cuba (1816–1819)," in *Las Antillas en la era de las Luces y la revolución*, ed. José A. Piqueras (Madrid: Siglo XXI, 2005), 247–73.

4. The only possible impediment to the sugar boom was the 1817 treaty between England and Spain decreeing an end to the slave trade north of the equator beginning on May 20, 1820, but Cuba's greatest arrivals of slaves in fact came after that date.

5. Moreno Fraginals, *Ingenio*, vol. 3. For statistics on Cuban and world production of cane and beet sugar, see 35–40; on Cuban sugar exports and destination countries, see 67–76. Some years Cuba produced more than 40% of the world's cane sugar.

6. Ibid., 1:203–14. Moreno Fraginals calculates that large-scale sugar mills with a capacity of 350 to 450 metric tons saved fifty to eighty pairs of oxen to move the *trapiches*, as well as about thirty slaves.

7. In Trinidad the ratio was 10 steam-powered *ingenios* out of a total of 43. The new areas of Jagua (Cienfuegos) and Sagua la Grande had ratios of 8:71 and 12:59, respectively.

8. Carlos Rebello, *Estados de la producción azucarera de la isla de Cuba* (Havana: Intendencia del Ejército y Hacienda, 1860).

9. José Luis Casaseca, "De la necesidad de mejorar la elaboración del azúcar en la isla de Cuba y de las mejoras de que es susceptible esta fabricación," *MSEH* 27 (1843): 325–53.

10. Justo Germán Cantero, *Los ingenios: Colección de vistas de los principales ingenios de azúcar de la isla de Cuba* (Havana: Litográfica Luis Marquier, 1857). La Ponina had a

60-horsepower machine moving its *trapiche* and a 370-horsepower Rillieux sugar kettle battery, and Flor de Cuba with 53-horsepower machine to run the mill (and an effective power of 100 horsepower) as well as a 400-horsepower Derosne y Cail boiler train.

11. Dale Tomich, "Material Process and Industrial Architecture: Innovation on the Cuban Sugar Frontier, 1818–1857," *Nature, Raw Materials and Political Economy: Research in Rural Sociology and Development* 10 (2005): 289–309.

12. *Cuadro estadístico de la Siempre Fiel isla de Cuba, correspondiente al año 1846* and *Noticias estadísticas de la isla de Cuba en 1862* (Havana: Imp. del Gobierno, Capitanía General y Real Hacienda, 1864). The recorded area in 1846 was 731,770 caballerías and in 1862 626,886 caballerías. Neither reflected the true area (826,342 caballerías).

13. Ramón de La Sagra, *Historia económica-política y estadística de la isla de Cuba, o sea de sus progresos en la población, la agricultura, el comercio y las rentas* (Havana: Viudas de Arazoza y Soler, 1831).

14. Miguel Rodríguez Ferrer, *Naturaleza y civilización de la grandiosa isla de Cuba*, 2 vols. (Madrid: J. Noguera, 1876), 1:690.

15. Jacobo de La Pezuela, *Diccionario geográfico, estadístico, histórico de la isla de Cuba*, 4 vols. (Madrid: Imp. del Establecimiento de Mellado, 1863), 1:39. He notes that these statistics are full of imprecision — for instance, the figure he gives for the island's surface area: 978,788 caballerías (131,380 km^2).

16. Eliseo Matos, "Breve historia de los montes de Cuba" (Instituto Nacional de Desarrollo y Aprovechamiento Forestal, Havana).

17. J. Emilio Santos, "Costumbres Cubanas," *Revista forestal, económica y agrícola* 4 (1871): 522–36, 581–97, 645–54; 746–56. The figure is on 646.

18. ANC, RCJF, file 115/4844, "Expediente instruido en excitación del Sr. Síndico Don Francisco de Arango y Parreño con el fin de que se efectúe el antiguo proyecto del Sr. Conde de Macuriges, de abrir un canal que reuniese los ríos de los Güines y de la Prensa," 1795.

19. Moreno Fraginals, *Ingenio*, 1:151.

20. Cuba was second in the Americas after the United States and seventh in the world: Oscar Zanetti and Alejandro García, *Caminos para el azúcar* (Havana: Ciencias Sociales, 1987); Eduardo L. Moyano, *La nueva frontera del azúcar: El ferrocarril y la economía cubana del siglo XIX* (Madrid: Consejo Superior de Investigaciones Científicas, 1991).

21. Laird W. Bergad, *Cuban Rural Society in the Nineteenth Century: The Social and Economic History of Monoculture in Matanzas* (Princeton, NJ: Princeton University Press, 1990), 107–15.

22. Moyano, *Nueva frontera*, 151–53. On the Cárdenas railroad the amount of lumber carried decreased from a high of 3,758,502 feet in 1845 to 205,256 feet in 1851.

23. ANC, RCJF, file 38/1664, "Expediente formado para contratar la leña necesaria al consumo de las máquinas del camino de hierro," April–May 1839.

24. ANC, RCJF, file 105/4510, "Expediente relativo a la solicitud del Administrador de la Cía de Caminos de Hierro de esta ciudad para que la introducción de leña extranjera sea comprendida en las gracias concedidas a la del carbón de piedra," 1853.

25. Esteban Pichardo Tapia, *Diccionario provincial casi-razonado de vozes y frases cubanas* (1836; Havana: Ciencias Sociales, 1985), 65–66.

26. Rodríguez Ferrer (*Naturaleza y civilización*, 1:701–2) gives the example of the United States, where railroads were estimated to be the main cause of deforestation. There 160 million crossties were used, equal to 50,000 acres of forest. These pieces were no shorter than 8 to 10 inches and had to be replaced every seven years.

27. Known as Santa Clara Province until 1940, Las Villas included the current provinces of Cienfuegos, Villa Clara, most of the current province of Sancti Spíritus, and part of Matanzas. In 1976, Cuba reorganized from six provinces to fourteen provinces and one special municipality (what is now Isla de la Juventud).

28. Antonio M. Alcover y Beltrán, *Historia de la villa de Sagua la Grande y su jurisdicción* (Sagua la Grande: Imp. Unidas *La historia* y *El comercio español*, 1905), 21.

29. Tomás Romay, "Memoria en que se manifiestan las ventajas que conseguirán los colonos que pretenden establecerse en esta Isla, prefiriendo su parte oriental; y las leyes que deben observar para mantenerse sanos," *MSEH* 6 (1819): 343–51, 346–47.

30. Idelfonso Vivanco, "Sagua la Grande," *La siempreviva* 3 (1839): 45.

31. "Sagua la Grande," *MSEH* 21 (1840): 462–66, 464; Alcover y Beltrán, *Historia de la villa de Sagua la Grande*, 83–87.

32. Ramón de La Sagra, *Historia física, económica-política, intelectual y moral de la isla de Cuba: Relación del último viaje del autor* (Paris: L. Hachette y Cia., 1861), 214.

33. A rodent 30–50 cm long with a 15–30 cm hairy tail that lives in Cuba's dense forests.

34. J. M. J., "Apuntaciones históricas y geográficas del partido de Sagua la Grande en 1844," *MSEH* 33 (1846): 286.

35. ANC, GSC, file 1279/50103, "Sobre la habilitación del puerto de Granadillo o estero Caunao: Su agregación al territorio de Villa Clara," 1847–48.

36. ANC, GG, file 334/16062, "Expediente de subdivisión interior del distrito de Sagua la Grande," 1849–52.

37. "Ferrocarril," *Hoja económica del puerto de Sagua la Grande*, no. 81, October 8, 1858.

38. La Pezuela, *Diccionario*, 4:374–76.

39. The 1877 averages are for ninety-eight *ingenios: Noticia de los ingenios o fincas azucareras que en estado de producción existen actualmente en toda la Isla* (Havana: Dirección General de Hacienda de la Isla de Cuba, 1877). For number of *ingenios* in 1871, Alcover y Beltrán, *Historia de la villa de Sagua la Grande*, 266.

40. "Maderas," *DM*, October 10, 1845.

41. "Riqueza rústica del término municipal de Sagua," *DM*, July 25, 1888.

42. "Ingenios de Sagua," *La nueva era* (Roque), May 15, 1883, 149.

43. Hugh H. Bennett and Robert V. Allison, *Los suelos de Cuba* (1928; Havana: Comisión Cubana de la UNESCO, 1962), 137–45, 157–81.

44. ANC, GG, file 72/3043, "Expediente relativo a la descomposición del río Sagua."

45. Antonio M. Alcover y Beltrán, *La villa de Sagua la Grande (República de Cuba): Bosquejo crítico descriptivo* (Havana: Cuba y América, 1909), 24.

46. Josef Opatrny, "Los cambios socio-económicos y el medio ambiente: Cuba, primera mitad del siglo XIX," *Revista de Indias* 56.207 (1996): 367–86, and Vicente Casals Costa, "Las ideas sobre la protección del bosque en Cuba y Filipinas durante el siglo

XIX," in *Estudios sobre la ciencia: Ciencia, vida y espacio en Ibero América*, ed. José Luis Pesset, vol. 3 (Madrid: CSIC, 1989), 357–88.

47. Watts, *Indias occidentales*; Grove, *Green Imperialism*; John Perlin, *Historia de los bosques: El significado de la madera en el desarrollo de la civilización* (Madrid: GAIA, 1999), 255–69.

48. Jamaica's highest point is 2,257 meters, while Cuba's is 1,972 meters. In the Havana-Matanzas district, the highest elevation, the Pan de Matanzas, is just 381 meters.

49. Warren Dean, *With Broadax and Firebrand: The Destruction of the Brazilian Atlantic Forest* (Berkeley: University of California Press, 1995); Stanley Stein, *Vassouras: A Brazilian Coffee County, 1850–1890* (New York: Atheneum, 1970); Pádua, *Sopro de destruição*.

50. Ramón de Arozarena and D. Pedro Bauduy, *Informe presentado a la Junta de Gobierno del Real Consulado . . . sobre el estado de la agricultura, y elaboración y beneficio de los frutos coloniales en la de Jamaica . . .* (Havana: Fraternal de los Díaz de Castro, 1828), 23.

51. Alejandro Oliván, *Informe a la Junta de Gobierno del Real Consulado de Agricultura y Comercio . . . de un viaje de investigación a Jamaica, Inglaterra y Francia para mejorar la elaboración de azúcar, y obtener noticias sobre varios puntos interesantes al fomento de este país* (Havana: Fraternal, 1831).

52. José Antonio Saco, *Colección de papeles científicos, históricos, políticos y de otros ramos sobre la isla de Cuba . . .* (Paris: D'Aubusson et Kugelmann, 1858), 1:43–49; "Montes o bosques en la isla de Cuba," *Mensajero semanal*, August 25, 1828, 43.

53. Conde de Mopox y de Jaruco, "Ruina de nuestros preciosos montes: Necesidad de reponerlos," *MSEH* 27 (1843): 233–34.

54. Ibid., 235, 236.

55. José Pizarro y Gardín, "Reposición de los bosques que se consumen anualmente en el combustible de los ingenios," *MSEH* 33 (1846): 373.

56. The *penca de guano* is the leaf and the *palmiche* the fruit of the palm tree. The *yagua* is the fiber that surrounds the upper part of its trunk.

57. Alejandro Dumont, *Guía de ingenios que trata de la caña de azúcar desde su origen, de su cultivo y de la manera de elaborar sus jugos* (Matanzas: Imp. del Gobierno de CAMPE, 1832), 94–95.

58. Andrés de Zayas, "Observaciones sobre los ingenios de esta Isla," *MSEH* 12 (1835–36): 255–56.

59. José Montalvo y Castillo, *Tratado general de Escuela Teórico Práctica para el gobierno de los ingenios de la isla de Cuba en todos sus ramos . . .* (Matanzas: La Aurora, 1856), 24–32. "Can we save firewood and the expense of fossil fuels? We respond to these questions with a resolute 'no,' and yet we must put ourselves in a position to answer with a complete 'yes'" (24).

60. *Cartilla práctica del manejo de ingenios o fincas destinadas a producir azúcar, escrita por Un Montuno, y dedicada al Excmo. Sr. Duque de Alba* (Irún, Spain: Elegancia, 1862), 17.

61. AHN, Ultramar, file 23/4, "Instancia a la Junta de Fomento de Francisco Diago solicitando la libre importación del carbón de piedra," 1847–48, n.p.

62. Ibid., n.p.

63. J. A. Cosculluela, *El regadío en el valle de Güines* (Havana: Ruiz, 1914), 203–6.

64. *Viajes de Don Jacinto de Salas y Quiroga* (1840; Havana: Consejo Nacional de Cultura, 1964), 146–47.

65. Roland T. Ely, *Cuando reinaba Su Majestad el azúcar: Estudio histórico sociológico de una tragedia latinoamericana — El monocultivo en Cuba, Origen y evolución del proceso* (1963; Havana: Imagen Contemporánea, 2001), 569–81; Hernán Venegas, "Apuntes sobre la decadencia trinitaria en el siglo XIX," *Islas*, no. 46 (1973): 159–251.

66. Francisco de Frías y Jacott (Count de Pozos Dulces), *Colección de escritos . . .* (Paris: Jorge Kugelmann, 1860), 21, 144.

67. Bergad, *Cuban Rural Society*, 116–40.

68. José J. Frías y Jacott, "Ingenios de fabricar azúcar: Beneficios productivos que deja el capital invertido en estas fincas — Ventajas y desventajas de los ingenios monstruos," *MSEH* 42 (1851): 60–61.

69. "Utilidades comprobadas del uso del arado en los ingenios," *MSEH* 32 (1846): 342–43; José María Dau, *Memoria sobre adaptar en la isla de Cuba el sistema de abonos verdes para mantener en perpetua fertilidad los terrenos sembrados de cañas de azúcar . . .* (Havana: Imp. del Gobierno, 1849); "Trabajos agrícolas y fabriles puestos en planta en los ingenios Tinguaro y Santa Elena, por el Sr. Francisco Diago," *MSEH* 54 (1863): 130–43.

70. Alvaro Reynoso, *Ensayo sobre el cultivo de la caña de azúcar* (1862; Havana: Artes Gráficas, 1963), 5. Reynoso (1829–1888) graduated from the University of Paris with a PhD in science and became internationally famous as an agricultural chemist. He was a disciple of and collaborator with the German chemist Justus von Liebig (1803–73), a pioneer in recommending adding nutrients to the soil.

71. Ibid., 7.

72. In Cuba, paths that separate cane fields.

73. Alvaro Reynoso, *Apuntes acerca de varios cultivos cubanos* (Madrid: M. Rivadeneyra, 1867), 370; see also Reynoso, *Consideraciones respecto de los abonos, dirigidas a los agricultores cubanos* (Madrid: M. Rivadeneyra, 1867).

74. He believed that this intervention should be limited to establishing a rural code and employing forest wardens to prevent the theft of wood, "as if the property of trees were not as sacred as that of any other object"; Mopox y de Jaruco, "Ruina de nuestros preciosos montes," 237.

75. La Sagra, *Historia económica-política*, 84–85.

76. La Sagra, *Historia física*, 39.

77. Ramón de La Sagra, *Cuba, 1860: Selección de artículos sobre agricultura cubana* (Havana: Comisión Nacional Cubana de la UNESCO, 1963), 27.

78. Ibid., 28–30.

79. Rodríguez Ferrer, *Naturaleza y civilización*, 1:685–732, 733–69.

80. "This liberty, which would better be called a scandalous license, dates back to 1812. It allows one to dispose as one likes, according to the whims of one's caprice, with trees that belong not to the current owners of the land but rather to future generations"; ibid., 694.

81. Ibid., 695.

82. Ibid., 702–3.

83. Arthur Morelet, "Observaciones sobre la conservación de arbolados: Carta remitida por Arturo Moselet [*sic*] en su viaje por la isla en el año 1847," *MSEH* 37 (1848): 93.

84. "Memoria sobre los trabajos en que se ha ocupado la Sección de Agricultura y Estadística en el año próximo pasado, leída por Lucas Ugarte," *MSEH* 32 (1846): 139–40. The Agriculture Section also noted that "we must either adopt a coercive measure to contain this ruin and reestablish the woodlands and cedars already in short supply or eventually see their total absence."

85. "Corte de maderas: Artículo 7º," *AJF* 4 (*MSEH* 42) (1851): 343.

86. Ibid., 345.

87. AMN, Ms. 437, Honorato Bouyón, "Informe sobre la construcción de buques de guerra en la isla de Cuba . . . , consecuente con la Real Orden de 5 de noviembre de 1817," January 18, 1818.

88. Enrique Edo, *Memoria histórica de Cienfuegos y su jurisdicción* (Havana: Ucar, García y Cía., 1943); Consuelo Naranjo and Miguel A. Puig Samper, "Les Bordelais, colons-fondateurs de Cienfuegos à Cuba, 1819–1842," in *L'émigration aquitaine en Amérique Latine au XIXe siècle*, ed. Bernard Lavalle (Bordeaux: Maison des Pays Ibériques, 1995), 75–96.

89. ANC, RCJF, file 76/2955, "Sobre el tráfico de maderas de caoba y cedro en la colonia de Fernandina de Jagua, 1826–1836."

90. Ibid.

91. Ibid., "Firmado en Fernandina de Jagua el 10 de enero de 1828 por Francisco Guerrero."

92. Ibid., "La instancia firmada por Francisco de La Cruz Gallardo, Gobernador interino," January 13, 1836. The commissioners of the Development Committee replied that any prohibition would amount, for an increased number of families, "to forbidding them to use the very soil they were called to fertilize and make the enterprise begun there into an illusion."

93. AHN, Ultramar, Fomento, file 225/10, "Noticia de la madera de las clases de ligera de cedro y duras de caoba, sabicú y chicharrón, yaba y demás propias para construcciones navales y civiles, que se han exportado del puerto de Jagua para el extranjero . . ."

94. Shortly before, in 1844, officials in Spain had begun to ask for an account of the effects of the royal edict of August 30, 1815. The next section goes further into this question.

95. AHN, Ultramar, Fomento, file 225/10. He noted that "repeatedly" during the construction of the brigantine *Habanero* and the corvette *María Luisa Fernanda* a foreign bidder emerged to "double or triple the market value of this wood."

96. "Balanza general del comercio de la isla de Cuba en 1845," *DM*, August 30, 1845.

97. "Corte de maderas: Artículo 7º," *AJF* 4 (*MSEH* 42) (1851): 341–45.

98. Miguel Rodríguez Ferrer, *DM*, March 24,1849; quoted in Rodríguez Ferrer, *Naturaleza y civilización* 1:732–36. He called for a ban on burning to develop pastures.

99. Ibid., 734–35.

100. Rodríguez Ferrer, *Naturaleza y civilización*, 1:733, 735, 736.

101. Félix Erenchún, *Anales de la isla de Cuba: Diccionario administrativo, económico, estadístico y legislativo, año de 1856* (Madrid: Tejado, 1861), 1707–8.

102. Rodríguez Ferrer, *Naturaleza y civilización*, 1:701.

103. ANC, GSC, file 635/20046, "Expediente que trata acerca de las maderas que se hallan en la playa de Santa Cruz," 1850.

104. ANC, GSC, file 1202-C/47099, "D. José Verdecia y Cª del Comercio de Manzanillo sobre que se les permita embarcar madera por las ensenadas de Júcaro y Vertientes," 1856.

105. ANC, GSC, file 1202-D, "Expediente promovido por D. Federico Naumann solicitando permiso para exportar maderas por el puerto de Zaza," 1857–59.

106. Ibid.

107. Ibid.

108. Ibid.

109. "Sección de oficio," *Revista de jurisprudencia, administración y comercio* 4.1 (March 15, 1859): 255.

110. ANC, IH, file 771/54, "Expediente promovido por A. Leak y Cª para que se le permitiera la exportación de maderas por el puerto de Mayanabo," 1862.

111. *Revista económica* 2.33 (April 25, 1878).

112. ANC, GSC, file 1593/81589, "La Explotadora, S.A.," 1857.

113. Moreno Fraginals, *Ingenio*, 1:162.

114. Ibid., 237–46. Moreno Fraginals notes that U.S. wood was imported for crates because Cuban precious woods transmitted their odor to the sugar. In fact, this was a justification used later, after the time when cedar was banned as material for containers.

115. ANC, RCJF, file 71/2762, "Sobre remediar la escasez de envases para azucares en esta plaza, introduciendo los del Nueva Orleans," 1796.

116. ANC, RCJF, file 72/2785, "Expediente promovido por varios dueños de ingenio sobre la necesidad de importar envases de los Estados Unidos para los azucares de esta Isla," 1799.

117. ANC, RCJF, file 73/2796, "Sobre pedir a SM el comercio recíproco por americanos, de maderas del norte y mieles del país en todo tiempo . . . ," January 27, 1802.

118. AGI, SD, 1599, "Proposición comercio recíproco de maderas con el norte," April 10, 1802.

119. AGI, SD, 1599 A, Oficio del Consulado, October 23, 1802, "Sobre escasez de envases de madera y necesidad de comerciar con el norte." One argument mentioned was Spain's transfer of Louisiana to France in 1800.

120. AGI, SD, 1599 A, "El Capitán General sobre la necesidad de introducir maderas."

121. José de Arango, "Jobo: Discurso dirigido por el Sr. José de Arango al Excmo. Sr. Gobernador y Capitán General . . . ," *MSEH* 4 (1817): 264–65.

122. Ibid., 271, 273. Arango said that cedar lost "none of the qualifications that make it the most notable of plants." He made a comparison full of symbolism: "It can be said that its very hierarchy prohibits its application for certain uses, and that just as a Calabar black is better than a white man for rough labor, jobo is better than cedar for containers" (270).

123. ANC, RCJF, file 103/4386, "Sobre excepción de derechos a las maderas del país a su importación en esta capital, 1817–18," November 26, 1817.

124. ANC, RCJF, file 103/4442, José Pizarro y Gardín, "Sobre la solicitud de los hacendados y comerciantes de Matanzas para que se eximan del derecho de toneladas a los buques angloamericanos que introduzcan maderas y extraigan mieles," October 6, 1828.

125. ANC, RCJF, file 76/2987, "Solicitud de los Sres. Conde de Jaruco y D. José Guerrero para que se fije el abono de 40 libras de tara por cada envase de cedro o jobo para azúcar," April 7, 1847.

126. For 1815–16: ANC, RCJF, file 103/4386, Sedano's report of January 28, 1818. Data for 1860–64 in Leví Marrero, *Cuba: Economía y sociedad*, 15 vols. (Madrid: Playor, 1971–86), 12:171.

127. "Importación por este puerto de los principales artículos de consumo durante los diez años anteriores," *Boletín comercial, agricultura, comercio, industria, navegación, operaciones y anuncios mercantiles en general*, Havana, January 3, 1876. The greatest years for importation of box pieces was 1871, with 884,011, and for cask pieces 1869, with 76,067.

128. Moreno Fraginals, *Ingenio*, 1:238.

129. Rodríguez Ferrer, *Naturaleza y civilización*, 1:701. There was a decline from 2,550,151 pesos in 1841 to 1,258,227 pesos in 1845. The figure rose again to 2,127,846 pesos in 1847.

130. Erich Bauer, *Los montes de España en la historia* (Madrid: Ministerio de Agricultura, 1980), 65–84.

131. Vicente Casals Costa, *Los ingenieros de montes en la España contemporánea, 1848–1936* (Barcelona: Serbal, 1996), 33.

132. Ibid., 34. These were part of the process by which the bases were created in Spain "for the development of teachings and technical bodies in agreement with the new needs posed by industrialization and the full development of capitalist social relationships." See also Bauer, *Montes de España*, 239–73; Josefina Gómez Mendoza, *Ciencia y política de los montes españoles (1848–1936)* (Madrid: ICONA, 1992); and Helen Groome, *Historia de la política forestal en el Estado Español* (Madrid: Agencia de Medioambiente de la Comunidad de Madrid, 90).

133. Gómez Mendoza, *Ciencia y política*, 38.

134. Ibid., chap. 1; see also Xesús Balboa López, "La historia de los montes públicos españoles (1812–1936): Un balance y algunas propuestas," *Historia agraria*, no. 18 (1999): 95–128.

135. ANC, GG, file 388/18518, "Documento referente a la devolución de los únicos antecedentes que en la Secretaría política existen relativos a montes," 1853–54.

136. "Corte de maderas: Artículo 7°," *AJF* 4 (*MSEH* 42) 6(1851): 342.

137. AHN, file 225/10/8, "Trasladando un aviso oficial sobre extracción para el extranjero de maderas de la isla de Cuba . . . ," August 27, 1845.

138. AHN, file 225/10/10, "Carta de José Primo de Rivera al Secretario de Estado y de Marina," October 13, 1845.

139. According to the Overseas Committee, the town governments and local courts should play the central role, with support from the economic societies through prizes, projects, and essays.

140. AHN, Ultramar, Fomento, file 225/10, "Junta de Ultramar Revisora de las Leyes de Indias: Dictamen sobre bosques de Cuba con motivo de cartas del comandante del Apostadero de La Habana," January 24, 1846.

141. AHN, Ultramar, Fomento, file 246/17, no. 39.

142. AHN, Ultramar, Fomento, file 225/10, "Disposición de la Junta de Autoridades Superiores de la Isla," June 21, 1845.

143. Ibid., Conde de Villanueva, "Da cuenta de acuerdo en Junta de Autoridades, proponiendo la reforma del art. 2º de la RO de 23 de marzo último . . . ," July 29, 1846.

144. Ibid. The urgency of planting did not allow for delay in the granting of permits and marking of trees, which "would prevent the total clearing of the burned area, indispensable for the sowing of cane." In addition, trees would be marked "without which [the owner] would find no buyer for the others."

145. Ibid.

146. Ibid.

147. ANC, RCO, file 159/176, "Aprobando la suspensión del Art 2º de la RO de 23 de marzo que trata de los términos en que los propietarios han de hacer la corta de sus montes," December 10, 1846.

148. AGI, Ultramar, 311, "Asuntos de Marina de la isla de Cuba, 1804–1853." The Navy Command continued to demand that action be taken, such as by maintaining watch over uncultivated areas and state lands.

149. AHN, file 246, proceedings 17/2, "Carta del director de la Escuela Especial de Montes al presidente del Consejo de Ministros," November 3, 1852.

150. Rodríguez Ferrer, *Naturaleza y civilización*, 1:754–55. "I respect as much as anyone the sacred right of private property, but I also find that given the state which our societies have reached on this subject, the legislation should require some sacrifice of this right when it is abused and harms associates and future generations" (763).

Chapter Five

1. Fe Iglesias García, *Del ingenio al central* (San Juan: Editorial de la Universidad de Puerto Rico, 1998); José A. Piqueras, comp., *Azúcar y esclavitud en el final del trabajo forzado* (Madrid: Fondo de Cultura Económica, 2002).

2. Rebecca J. Scott, *Slave Emancipation in Cuba: The Transition to Free Labor, 1860–1899* (Princeton, NJ: Princeton University Press, 1985); Imilcy Balboa Navarro, *Los brazos necesarios: Inmigración, colonización y trabajo libre en Cuba, 1878–1898* (Valencia, Spain: Centro Francisco Tomás y Valiente UNED Alzira-Valencia/Fundación Instituto de Historia Social, 2000).

3. Ramiro Guerra y Sánchez, *Azúcar y población en las Antillas* (1927; Havana: Ciencias Sociales, 1971); Consuelo Naranjo, "Trabajo libre e inmigración española en Cuba, 1880–1930," *Revista de Indias* 52.195–96 (1992): 749–94; Naranjo, "Los trabajos y los días:

Colonos gallegos en Cuba en el siglo XIX," *SEMATA: Ciencias sociais e humanidades* 11 (1999): 191–215; Antonio Santamaría and Luis M. García Mora, "Colonos: Agricultores cañeros, ¿Clase media rural en Cuba?, 1880–1898," *Revista de Indias* 8.212 (1998): 131–61.

4. Ramón de La Sagra, *Historia física, económica-política, intelectual y moral de la isla de Cuba: Relación del último viaje del autor* (Paris: L. Hachette y Cia., 1861), 199–205.

5. Manuel Moreno Fraginals, *El ingenio: El complejo económico social cubano del azúcar*, 3 vols. (Havana: Ciencias Sociales, 1978), 1:221.

6. Iglesias García, *Ingenio al central*, 57–70.

7. César J. Ayala, *American Sugar Kingdom: The Plantation Economy of the Spanish Caribbean, 1898–1934* (Chapel Hill: University of North Carolina Press, 1999), 23–47, 48–73.

8. The six hundred farms destroyed included many inactive *ingenios* or ones in the process of dismantlement since before 1895.

9. Oscar Zanetti, "El siglo que se fue: Azúcar y economía en Cuba," *Temas* 24/25 (January–June 2001): 11.

10. Military Government of Cuba, Department of Agriculture, Commerce, and Industry, *Memoria del año fiscal de 1899 a 1900* (Washington, DC, 1900), 238.

11. Oscar Zanetti and Alejandro García, *Caminos para el azúcar* (Havana: Ciencias Sociales, 1987), 149–57. From 1886 to 1894 the railroads built lines for the transport of cane; between 1886 and 1890, two-thirds of the private lines were built. At the end of the century, 93 of 107 private lines belonged to *ingenios*.

12. José de la O. García, "Centrales y colonias," *Revista de agricultura*, no. 7 (February 16, 1890), 77.

13. *DM*, August 26, 1888. The navy newspaper cited the *Unión Constitucional de Colón*, which called on the owners of abandoned *ingenios* around the town to put their farms back in production, which it said could be done "with judicious management" and "without very costly work."

14. "Otro gran central," *La nueva era*, March 15, 1882, 148.

15. Balboa Navarro, *Brazos necesarios*, 49–117.

16. "Datos sobre la maceración," *La nueva era*, no. 11, April 1, 1882, 162.

17. Francisco F. Ibáñez, *Observaciones sobre la utilidad y conveniencia del establecimiento en esta isla de grandes ingenios centrales . . .* (Havana: Obispo, 1880); Ibáñez, *Proyecto para la creación por el Gobierno de la nación, de cincuenta ingenios centrales con empleo exclusivo de trabajadores libres . . .* (Havana: El Sol, 1881).

18. José Curbelo, *Proyecto para fomentar y poner en estado de producción seis ingenios centrales de 1,000,000 de arrobas de azúcar cada uno . . .* (Havana: Propaganda Literaria, 1882). A similar price was paid for lengths of mahogany, júcaro, ácana, ocuje, sabicú, and cedar.

19. AHN, Ultramar, Fomento, file 209/12, "Proyecto de construcción de dos almacenes y una sierra mecánica con sus respectivos muelles en el estero Granadillo, Sagua la Grande."

20. Eliseo Matos, "Breve historia de los montes de Cuba" (Instituto Nacional de Desarrollo y Aprovechamiento Forestal, Havana).

21. Nicomedes P. de Adan, "Cultivos menores," *Revista de agricultura*, September 1883, 242.

22. *El repertorio*, April 1, 1881, 196.

23. Juan A. Cosculluela, *Cuatro años en la ciénaga de Zapata: Memorias de un ingeniero* (1918; Havana: Comisión Nacional Cubana de la UNESCO, 1965), 203–24.

24. For a thorough study of the impact of agricultural science during this period, see Leida Fernández Prieto, *Cuba agrícola: Mito y tradición, 1878–1920* (Madrid: Consejo Superior de Investigaciones Científicas, 2005).

25. El Roque is interesting because of the floods in its region, where 2,000 caballerías could be left under water during the rainy season. A canal was later built to reduce flooding.

26. *Louisiana Planter* 28 (1890): 436; cited in Iglesias García, *Ingenio al central*, 120.

27. Leida Fernández, "Azúcar y ciencia en Cuba: 1878–1898," *Tzintzun: Revista de estudios históricos* (Morelia, Mexico), January–June 2000, 29–54.

28. Juan B. Jiménez, *El ingenio: Segunda parte de las aventuras de un mayoral — Caña de azúcar, su cultivo, su producción, etc.* (Matanzas: Galería Literaria, 1883), 18–19.

29. E. Pimienta, *Los dos primeros libros del Manual práctico de la fabricación de azúcar de cañas* (Havana: Miguel Alorda, 1881), 13, 84, 184.

30. "Ingenios en terrenos feraces," *La nueva era*, June 1, 1882, 230–31.

31. Gastón Alonso Cuadrado, *Necesidades de la industria azucarera cubana* (Havana: La Prueba, 1901), 18–19.

32. La Sagra, *Historia física*, 201.

33. "El manejo del bagazo," *La nueva era*, February 1, 1882, 102–3.

34. "Combustible," *La nueva era*, April 1, 1882, 170.

35. Alvaro Reynoso, *Consideraciones respecto de los abonos, dirigidas a los agricultores cubanos* (Madrid: M. Rivadeneyra, 1867), 53.

36. Pimienta, *Dos primeros libros*, 43–44. He notes the low cost of pulp as a fertilizer: "What other fertilizer has a cost that can compare?" In abandoned purification houses stables could be created to produce manure.

37. Gastón Descamps, *Los hornos de bagazo verde* (Havana: La Lucha, 1892). The first attempt to use them was made by a U.S. citizen named Mitchell.

38. "Hornalla de Jarvis," *La nueva era*, June 15, 1882, 265.

39. Descamps, *Hornos de bagazo verde*, 54. Many farms had "private ovens" that were "conceived and assembled by the estate owners themselves, with the help of the farms' administrators, mechanics, and bricklayers," which gave "excellent results."

40. Juan Tatjer y Risqué, *Fabricación del azúcar de caña tal como se practica con los aparatos más modernos en la isla de Cuba* (Havana: Avisador Comercial, 1887), 195–98. Tatjer y Risqué argued that dry was preferable to wet burning, though he recognized that savings resulted from eliminating the labor of handling pulp.

41. *Hornos de quemar bagazo verde . . . con real privilegio para España y sus posesiones de ultramar de Samuel Fiske . . . .*, Havana, 1890. It includes a letter from Atkins to the inventor dated January 30, 1888.

42. *DM*, March 25, 1891. An article in *El orden* of Caibarién (no date given) announced that Fiske and his lieutenant were visiting several *ingenios*, where they would install his ovens for use in the next harvest.

43. Descamps concluded that green-pulp burners would be successful only when advances such as double milling and improved boiler houses were made.

44. Clodomiro Betancourt, *Método teórico práctico de elaboración de azúcar de caña, por . . (Maestro de azúcar) . . .* , 4th ed. (Havana: Canalejo y Xiqués, 1893), 192–93.

45. Alonso Cuadrado, *Necesidades de la industria azucarera*, 8.

46. *DM*, April 25, 1888.

47. "Estadística de exportación de la Aduana de Santa Cruz durante el año de 1880," *Boletín oficial de hacienda y estadística de la isla de Cuba*, February 28, 1882, 77; "Maderas cubanas en Londres," *Revista de administración*, July 10, 1889, 223. Yarey is a plant of the palm family whose fibers are used to make hats.

48. *DM*, January 30, 1885, quoting *La bandera española* (Santiago de Cuba).

49. *Indicaciones sobre el plan de explotación que llevará a cabo la Sociedad Agrícola e Industrial de los Terrenos de Nipe en sus propiedades* (Matanzas: Aurora del Yumirí, 1883).

50. "Carta a el *Journal du fabricant de sucre*, publicada en su número correspondiente al 11 de enero próximo pasado, dirigida por M. Hautrive, vicecónsul de Francia, en Trinidad y Cienfuegos y Trinidad, fechada el 20 de diciembre último, respecto a la situación agrícola de Cuba," *Revista de agricultura*, February 1888, 3–5.

51. "El Ferrocarril Central," *La nueva era*, February 1, 1882, 108. Landowners agreed to cede, free of charge, 500 meters on either side of the railway in savannas, 200 meters in woodland, and 6 or 8 meters in cultivated fields. They also supplied oxen, ties, and workers.

52. "En Manzanillo," *La nueva era*, June 6, 1883, 173. Notice about the article "Ingenios centrales," *El eco de Manzanillo*, May 17, 1883. See Iglesias García, *Ingenio al central*, 52–55.

53. In coastal shipping with Havana (from 1885 to 1891), Manzanillo was the principal supplier of railroad ties. It also shipped cedar boards and planks, júcaro stakes, and flooring and lathing. The *Diario de la Marina* of April 3, 1888, noted how busy the port was, five or six sailboats continuously loading wood and other regional products.

54. *Memoria sobre un ingenio central en Puerto Príncipe* (Havana: Propaganda Literaria, 1880), 7–8.

55. Ibid., 13, 17.

56. "Ingenios centrales," *La nueva era*, January 1883, 70.

57. "El ingenio central La Santa Cruz," *La nueva era* (La Roque), April 9, 1883, 111.

58. "Ingenios de Sagua," *La nueva era*, May 15, 1883, 149.

59. Carlos Rebello, *Estados de la producción azucarera de la isla de Cuba* (Havana: Intendencia del Ejército y Hacienda, 1860).

60. Hernán Venegas, "Consideraciones en torno a la economía remediana colonial," *Islas*, no. 67 (1980): 11–79. Remedios was the principal producer of charcoal in 1862, with 41,820 bags, followed by Nuevitas with 15,000.

61. Most were in the west of Remedios: fifteen in Camajuaní and eleven in Taguayabón; José M. Gómez, *Camajuaní: La plantación azucarera en el siglo XIX* (Santa Clara: Capiro, 2001).

62. Hernán Venegas, "Acerca del proceso de concentración y centralización de la industria azucarera en la región remediana a fines del siglo XIX," *Islas*, no. 73 (1982): 63–121.

63. Ibid., 77.

64. "Nuestros campos: Noticias de Yaguajay," *La nueva era*, December 15, 1881, 63.

65. *Memoria sobre un ingenio central en Puerto Príncipe*, 12.

66. Venegas, "Acerca del proceso de concentración," 77; citing *Revista de agricultura*, no. 44 (1890): 535–36.

67. "Nueva industria," *El avisador comercial*, December 31, 1887; cited in *DM*, January 3, 1888.

68. *DM*, April 23, 1891.

69. This tree "is very common in lands subject to flooding on the island of Cuba; and its strong and flexible wood is very good for lances and poles, and from the inner bark of its saplings are made cords of long life and use"; Real Academia Española, *Diccionario de la lengua española*, 21st ed., vol. 2 (Madrid: Espasa Calpe, 1992). — Trans.

70. The schooners' cargo included wood in pieces and in poles, as well as other forest products.

71. A Sagua newspaper, quoted in *DM*, March 1, 1891.

72. Manuel Martínez Escobar, *Historia de Remedios* (Havana: Jesús Montero, 1944), 84.

73. Robert Porter, *Appendix to the Report on the Commercial and Industrial Conditions of the Island of Cuba* (Washington, DC: U.S. Government Printing Office, 1899), 186; quoted in Venegas, "Acerca del proceso de concentración," 69. Other contributing factors were the exportation of wood and its use for construction and charcoal (186–89).

74. República de Cuba, Secretaría de Agricultura, Comercio y Trabajo, *Portfolio azucarero: Industria azucarera de Cuba, 1912–1914* (Havana: Moderna Poesía, 1914).

75. Hugh H. Bennett and Robert V. Allison, *Los suelos de Cuba* (1928; Havana: Comisión Cubana de la UNESCO, 1962), 192–93. This does not mean that all of Yaguajay's soils were potentially unsuitable for sugar.

76. Gaspar de Aranda y Antón, *La administración forestal y los montes de Ultramar durante el siglo XIX* (Madrid: ICONA, 1995); Vicente Casals Costa, "Las ideas sobre la protección del bosque en Cuba y Filipinas durante el siglo XIX," in *Estudios sobre la ciencia: Ciencia, vida y espacio en Ibero América*, ed. José Luis Peset, vol. 3 (Madrid: CSIC, 1989), 357–88. For the Puerto Rican case, see Carlos M. Domínguez Cristóbal, *Panorama histórico forestal de Puerto Rico* (San Juan: Universidad de Puerto Rico, 2000).

77. Few biographical details are available about him, despite his importance in the creation of Cuba's modern forest administration. He was born on January 24, 1835, according to Dirección Gral de Agricultura, Industria y Comercio, *Escalafón general del Cuerpo de Ingenieros de Montes rectificado en 1 de enero de 1895* (Madrid: Ricardo Rojas, 1895). He died in 1912.

78. AHN, Ultramar, Fomento, file 247/17, no. 33, Francisco de P. Portuondo, Cuba, June 10, 1862.

79. AHN, Ultramar, Fomento, file 246/17/39, Madrid, November 30, 1863.

80. Miguel Bosh y Juliá, "Rápida ojeada sobre el estado de los montes de Canarias, Puerto Rico, Cuba y Filipinas," *Revista forestal económica y agrícola* (Madrid), March 1868, 39–40. On Bosh y Juliá (1818–79), see Josefina Gómez Mendoza, *Ciencia y política de los montes españoles (1848–1936)* (Madrid: ICONA, 1992), 43–44.

81. The 1866 proposal was drafted following the arrival the previous October of Joaquín María Goróstegui, chief engineer first class. Together with Portuondo, who was absorbed in the reconnaissance of the eastern zone, Goróstegui examined the precedents and agreed on how the work should be done. The proposed ordinances and woodlands regulations were finished in December 1866. Haste may be responsible for their similarity to those in force in Spain, which Bosh y Juliá noted. Goróstegui returned to Spain, and Portuondo went back to leading the island's forest administration.

82. AHN, Ultramar, file 246/16, no. 3, Francisco de P. Portuondo, "Memoria sobre el ramo de montes pedida por el Ministerio de Ultramar," October 2, 1869.

83. *Gaceta de La Habana*, June 20, 1875, "Subastas de aprovechamientos de montes públicos: Con firma del capitán general el 14 de junio — La reorganización del ramo forestal de 1875," in AHN, Ultramar, file 246/18.

84. AHN, Ultramar, file 268/13, no. 4. Also worth consulting is José Isaac del Corral, *Derecho forestal cubano*, vol. 1 (Havana: P. Fernández, 1936), 111–26.

85. AHN, Ultramar, file 246/16, no. 5, Francisco de P. Portuondo, "Memoria sobre los montes públicos de la Isla de Cuba, 1875," Havana, February 26, 1875.

86. AHN, Ultramar, file 246, exp. 16, no. 7, Ernesto Ruiz Melo, "Memoria del servicio y producción de los montes públicos de la Isla de Cuba de 1875–1876," Havana, November 24, 1876.

87. AHN, Ultramar, file 246/16, no. 9, Francisco de P. Portuondo, "Memoria anual general del servicio y producción de los montes públicos de la Isla de Cuba correspondiente al año económico de 1878–79", Havana, December 12, 1879. He noted that export duties were even paid in Cuba for lumber bound for the Canary Islands and metropolitan Spain, "importers of much of this wood."

88. Miguel Rodríguez Ferrer, *Naturaleza y civilización de la grandiosa isla de Cuba*, 2 vols. (Madrid: J. Noguera, 1876), 1:754–55, citing Portuondo's early *memorias*.

89. AHN, Ultramar, file 246/16, no. 30, "Memoria sobre la producción de los montes y estado general del servicio de dicho ramo correspondiente al año económico de 1892–1893," Francisco de P. Portuondo, Havana, November 9, 1893.

90. Francisco de P. Portuondo, "Memoria sobre el servicio del ramo de montes correspondiente al primer semestre del año de 1899," in John R. Brooke, *Civil Report of Major-General John R. Brooke, U.S. Army, Military Governor, Island of Cuba* (Washington, DC, 1899), 79–85. The estimates were Santiago de Cuba, 210,200 hectares; Santa Clara, 124,660; Pinar del Río, 60,000; Matanzas, 46,000; Puerto Príncipe (Camagüey), 35,680; and Havana, 20,000.

91. AHN, Ultramar, file 246/16, no. 26, Francisco de P. Portuondo, Havana, September 28, 1893.

92. AHN, Ultramar, file 246/16, no. 48. Francisco de P. Portuondo, "Anteproyecto del presupuesto general, año económico 1895–1896," Inspección General de Montes, Havana, June 15, 1895.

93. AHN, Ultramar, file 246/16, no. 48, Francisco de P. Portuondo, "Anteproyecto del presupuesto general, año económico 1895–1896," Inspección General de Montes, Havana, June 15, 1895.

94. Portuondo, "Memoria sobre el servicio del ramo de montes . . . 1899," 82.

95. AHN, Ultramar, file 246/16, no. 48.

96. A Caribbean bush 3 or 4 meters high. — Trans.

97. Sebastián Alfredo de Morales, "Flora arborícola de Cuba," *ARACH* (Havana) 23 (1886): 388–90.

98. Ibid., 390.

99. Ramón de La Sagra, "Informe del Director del Jardín Botánico de La Habana," *MSEH* 9 (1828–33): 48–49.

100. Pedro J. Imbernó, *Guía geográfica y administrativa de la isla de Cuba* (Havana: La Lucha, 1891), x. One of the people to whom this book is dedicated is Francisco de Paula Portuondo.

101. José María Fernández y Jiménez, *Tratado de la arboricultura cubana, y lleva agregada la de Isla de Pinos y Puerto Rico* (Havana, 1868).

102. Ibid., 9. He laid part of the blame on overseers, who, "unhappily for us, only know how to plant in virgin fields." The lack of trees caused a decrease in humidity and an increase in the destruction caused by winds, while the soils, deprived of their former fertility, "head rapidly toward sterility and impotence."

103. Ibid., 8.

104. Juan C. Gundlach, "Revista y catálogo de las aves cubanas," *Repertorio físico natural de la Isla de Cuba* (Havana: Imprenta del Gobierno y Capitanía General, 1865–66), 179.

105. Miguel Angel Puig-Samper and Mercedes Valero, *Historia del Jardín Botánico de La Habana* (Aranjuez, Spain: Doce Calles, 1999).

106. José Francisco Arnao, "Bosques artificiales," *La nueva era*, April 15, 1882, 189–90.

107. Francisco Javier de Balmaceda, *Tesoro del agricultor cubano . . .* (Havana: Propaganda Literaria, 1892), 421–38.

108. "El riego y la arboricultura," *La nueva era*, December 15, 1881, 54–55.

109. "Farmacología: El *Eucaliptus globulus*," *ARACH* 13 (1876): 111–12; Arturo del Bosque, "Informe sobre la utilidad de plantaciones de eucaliptos," *ARACH* 36 (1899): 67–68.

110. "El eucaliptos," *La nueva era*, January 1, 1882: "We have in the country much useless terrain that planted with Eucalyptus would become productive property, and in addition would prevent many illnesses from fever." Some believed that *Eucalyptus globulus* was not the most appropriate variety for Cuba and that *Eucalyptus resinífero*, which grew rapidly, should be planted instead.

111. Eva Canel [Eva Infanzón y Canel], *Album de la Trocha: Breve reseña de una excursión feliz desde Cienfuegos a San Fernando, recorrido de la línea militar por cuatro periodistas* (Havana: La Universal, 1897), 30.

Chapter Six

1. Oscar Zanetti, *Los cautivos de la reciprocidad* (Havana: Ministerio de Educación Superior, 1989).

2. Ramiro Guerra y Sánchez, *Azúcar y población en las Antillas* (1927; Havana: Ciencias Sociales, 1971), 87–110. Guerra y Sánchez mentions the Sherman Antitrust Act "and a whole ensemble of measures directed to maintain a prudent equilibrium among the different forces propelling industrial, financial, and commercial development."

3. Richard P. Tucker, *Insatiable Appetite: The United States and the Ecological Degradation of the Tropical World* (Berkeley: University of California Press, 2000), 15–50.

4. Leland H. Jenks, *Nuestra colonia de Cuba* (Havana: Revolucionaria, 1966), 199.

5. William J. Showalter, "Cuba: The Sugar Mills of the Antilles," *National Geographic Magazine*, July 1920, 24.

6. Oscar Pino Santos, *El asalto a Cuba por la oligarquía financiera yanqui* (Havana: Ciencias Sociales, 1977).

7. César J. Ayala, *American Sugar Kingdom: The Plantation Economy of the Spanish Caribbean, 1898–1934* (Chapel Hill: University of North Carolina Press, 1999), 77–78. U.S. investment in 1924 in the Caribbean: $1.1 million; in South America: $1.4 million; in Mexico: $1 million (four times less than in 1897). This was almost double the investment in Asia. Canada was the leading recipient, at US$2.6 million.

8. Allan Dye, *Cuban Sugar in the Age of Mass Production: Technology and the Economics of the Cuban Sugar Central* (Stanford, CA: Stanford University Press, 1998); Antonio Santamaría, *Sin azúcar no hay país: La industria azucarera y la economía cubana (1919–1939)* (Seville: CSIC, EEHA, Universidad de Sevilla, 2001). Both authors indicate that the trilogy of land plus railroad plus labor continued to be key to the sector's growth during the conflict.

9. For 1907: *Censo de la República de Cuba: Bajo la administración provisional de los Estados Unidos, 1907* (Washington, DC: Oficina del Censo de los Estados Unidos, 1908); for 1913: República de Cuba, Secretaría de Agricultura, Comercio y Trabajo, *Portfolio azucarero: Industria azucarera de Cuba, 1912–1914* (Havana: Moderna Poesía, 1914); and for 1919: *Censo de la República de Cuba, año de 1919* (Havana: Maza, Arroyo y Caso, 1919).

10. This term is used in L. V de Abad, *Azúcar y caña de azúcar: Ensayo de orientación cubana* (Havana: Mercantil Cubana, 1945), 391–428.

11. Dye, *Cuban Sugar in the Age of Mass Production*; Santamaría García, *Sin azúcar no hay país*.

12. República de Cuba, *Breve reseña para la Exposición Universal de St. Louis* (Havana: Rambla y Bouza, 1904), 34–37. For Havana the price was between 400 and 2,000 pesos, in Matanzas and Santa Clara between 300 and 800.

13. Abad, *Azúcar y caña de azúcar*, 406. Abad insisted that the colossi were a financial failure generally speaking and that in the past twenty years they rarely had proved themselves useful.

14. Guerra y Sánchez, *Azúcar y población*, 87–92.

15. Ramiro Cabrera, "Los recursos naturales de Cuba y sus perspectivas para el capital americano," *Cuba y América* 1.9 (1897): 2–4.

16. Eliseo Matos, "Breve historia de los montes de Cuba" (Instituto Nacional de Desarrollo y Aprovechamiento Forestal, Havana, n.d. [early 1970s]), 24–26. This unpublished manuscript can be found at the Institute of Geography in Havana.

17. *Informe sobre el censo de Cuba*, 1899. The recorded woodland area totaled 1,478.443 hectares, distributed among the provinces as follows: Pinar del Río, 13%; Havana, 3%; Matanzas, 3%; Santa Clara, 12.5%; Puerto Príncipe, 34%; and Santiago de Cuba, 34.5%.

18. Albert J. Norton, *Norton's Complete Hand Book of Havana and Cuba: Containing Full Information for the Tourist, Settler and Investor* (Chicago: Rand McNally, 1900); Robert T. Hill, *Cuba and Porto Rico, with the Other Islands of the West Indies: Their Topography, Climate, Flora, Products, Industries, Cities, People, Political Condition . . .* (New York: Century, 1898); William Jared Clark, *Commercial Cuba: A Book for Business Men . . .* (New York: C. Scribner's Sons, 1898); Robert P. Porter, *Industrial Cuba* (New York: G. P. Putnam's Sons, 1899).

19. Figures given in Porter, *Industrial Cuba*, "Timber and Fruit Trees," 337–50.

20. Clark, *Commercial Cuba*, 455. Clark cites estimates of the area of virgin forest at more than 18 million acres (190).

21. *Censo de la República de Cuba, año de 1919*, 67–71.

22. Juan T. Roig, *El cedro: Estudio botánico y agrícola*, Circular 79 (Santiago de las Vegas: Estación Agronómica, 1935), 13–14. During the time of greatest inflation, at the end of the war, 1,000 ft. sold for 200 pesos. In 1928 the same quantity of highest-quality wood sold in Havana for 90 to 100 pesos; that amount of third-rate wood sold for 60 pesos. In Oriente 1,000 ft. of unsawed wood sold for 30 pesos; sawed it sold for 40 to 45 pesos. During the first half of 1928 the amount of cedar exported was 415,063 ft.

23. Franklin S. Earle, "La caña de azúcar," *Boletín* (Estación Central Agronómica de Cuba, Havana), July 1905, 7.

24. Josiah T. Crawley, "El cultivo de la caña de azúcar en Cuba," *Boletín* (Estación Experimental Agronómica), February 1917, 24. He noted that in general the island's virgin land was densely forested. If there was valuable wood and if the cleared land was close to a railway, the wood could be sold for fence posts, railroad ties, and other uses.

25. Francisco Zayas, *Política agrícola de la República: Nuevo método de siembras y cultivo de la caña de azúcar . . .* (Havana: La Prueba, 1904).

26. Earle, "Caña de azúcar," 19.

27. A. D. Hall, *Cuba: Its Past, Present, and Future* (New York: Street and Smith, 1906), 154–56.

28. Showalter, "Cuba," 24.

29. Tranquilino Frasquieri, "Nuestra crisis forestal," *RACT*, December 1933, 3–8.

30. Matos, "Breve historia," 29-32. José Isaac del Corral Alemán, "El problema forestal en Cuba," *Cuba contemporánea* 32 (1923): 15.

31. According to Matos's estimates, the annual rate of deforestation during this period was 6,626 caballerías (172,066 caballerías in all). He divided this into two subperiods, 1900–1913, with an annual rate of 7,652 caballerías (102,544 hectares), and 1914–26, with an annual rate of 5,600 caballerías (75,049 ha).

32. Jenks, *Nuestra colonia de Cuba*, 280.

33. "Notas editoriales," *RACT*, November 1920, 1.

34. Comisión de Asuntos Cubanos, *Problemas de la nueva Cuba* (New York: Foreign Policy Association, 1935), 501–19.

35. Juan Pérez de La Riva, "Una isla con dos historias," *El barracón y otros ensayos* (Havana: Ciencias Sociales, 1975), 73–89.

36. *Censo de la República de Cuba: Año de 1919*, 65–71.

37. Leo Waibel, "Places Names as an Aid in the Reconstruction of the Original Vegetation of Cuba," *Geographical Review* 33.3 (1943): 376–96.

38. "Estadística forestal: Año natural de 1933," *Revista de agricultura* 14 (1934): 10–24.

39. República de Cuba, Secretaría de Agricultura, Comercio y Trabajo, *Portfolio azucarero: Industria azucarera de Cuba, 1912–1914* (Havana: Moderna Poesía, 1914).

40. República de Cuba, *Portfolio azucarero: Industria azucarera de Cuba, 1912–1914*.

41. Mark J. Smith, "The Political Economy of Sugar Production and the Environment of Eastern Cuba, 1898–1923," *Environmental History Review* 19.4 (1995): 31–48.

42. Oscar Zanetti and Alejandro García, *Caminos para el azúcar* (Havana: Ciencias Sociales, 1987), 209–27.

43. Ibid., 226.

44. Carlos Martí, *Films Cubanos, Oriente y Occidente: La República será agrícola o no será* (Barcelona: Sociedad General de Publicaciones, 1915), 74–75.

45. Jenks, *Nuestra colonia de Cuba*, 178.

46. Josiah T. Crawley, "Conservación y desarrollo de los recursos naturales de Cuba," *AACH* 45 (1909): 574.

47. Juan Tomás Roig, "Breve reseña sobre una excursión botánica a Oriente," *MSCHN* 3.4–6 (1917–18): 174.

48. Ibid., 174–75.

49. "Notas editoriales," *RACT*, November 1920.

50. Ibid.

51. Alberto Fors, "La restauración de nuestros montes," *RACT*, November 1929, 23.

52. The boundaries here are those of the province created in 1878 (then called Puerto Príncipe), which were little changed until 1975, when the old province was split into the new ones of Camagüey (15,990 km²) and Ciego de Avila (6,253 km²). Since 1975 the western and eastern extremes of the former province have belonged to Sancti Spíritus and Las Tunas.

53. AGI, Cuba, 1171. Responding to the Marquis de La Torre's 1776 proclamation banning unlicensed felling of trees and burning to develop pasture, the town council of Puerto Príncipe argued that the restriction was unneeded in its jurisdiction because the area had "a great abundance of wood, due to the little use made of it and less due to the prohibitions."

54. The importance of Santa Cruz del Sur for wood exports was already notable in the mid-nineteenth century. In 1880s Nuevitas, for example, the schooners *Emilia* and *Dolores* frequently sailed for the capital loaded with railroad ties, mahogany and cedar, firewood, rollers, and other forest products; *DM*, 1885, 1891.

55. Carlos Rebello, *Estados de la producción azucarera de la isla de Cuba* (Havana: Intendencia del Ejército y Hacienda, 1860). The *ingenios* of Puerto Príncipe had an average of 39.3 caballerías, of which 3.5 were cultivated. In Nuevitas the relationship was 58.7 total and 6.3 in cane, most with steam engines (twelve of nineteen *ingenios*).

56. Ibid. The Oriente *ingenio* on the Sibanicú *partido* had a total of 120 caballerías, 10 of them in cane.

57. P. Antonio Perpiña (Escolapio), *El Camagüey: Viajes pintorescos por el interior de Cuba y por sus costas con descripción del país* (Barcelona: J. A. Bastinos y Luis Niubó, 1889), 90–91. He also included his hosts' reflections on the importance of forests: "An *ingenio* needs large forests and vast expanses of terrain to replace in part the old cane fields that are left fallow. . . . An *ingenio* without forests needs lumber and firewood, indispensable for making sugar during the harvest; despite pulp's serving well as a fuel" (90).

58. In 1863 another short railroad, less than 9 km long, united this line with San Miguel y Bagá, near the Bay of Nuevitas.

59. *Informe sobre el censo de Cuba*, 1899. In the report by the Secretariat of Agriculture, Commerce, and Industry for the fiscal year July 1, 1899–June 30, 1900, the area figure given is 52,782 caballerías, with 52.7% in forest, 30.5% in pastures and livestock farms, 16.1% "unproductive," and 0.7% under cultivation.

60. Only the province of Havana had a smaller area of public woodlands, with 20,000 hectares. Those with the greatest area were Santiago de Cuba, with 210,200 hectares, and Santa Clara, with 124,660 hectares. For the whole island the total was 465,540 hectares.

61. *Informe sobre el censo de Cuba*, 1899, 553.

62. Secretaría de Agricultura, Comercio e Industria, *Memoria de los trabajos realizados en el año fiscal que comenzó en 1º de julio de 1899 y terminó en 30 de junio de 1900* (Havana, 1900), 137.

63. República de Cuba, *El libro de Cuba* (Havana, 1925), 510–15.

64. Charles Berchon, *A través de Cuba: Relato geográfico, descriptivo y económico . . .* (Paris: Charaire, 1910), 145–54.

65. Rafael Pera y Peralta, *Ensayo geográfico e histórico del término municipal de Santa Cruz del Sur* (Havana: La Americana, 1913), 6, 12, 116. He offers this image: "The generous saw saves us from the muck! Since it cuts excellent Santa Cruz cedar, it even perfumes the street with its characteristic and pleasing aroma!" (12).

66. República de Cuba, *Portfolio azucarero: Industria azucarera de Cuba, 1912–1914*; *Censo de la República de Cuba, año de 1919* (Havana: Maza, Arroyo y Caso, 1919).

67. Abad, *Azúcar y caña de azúcar*, 397–401.

68. A. B. Gilmore, *Manual de la industria azucarera cubana* (Havana: Metropolitana, 1928). For the other provinces, the figures were Havana, 215,615 arrobas; Matanzas, 190,125; Santa Clara, 173,520; and Pinar del Río, 162,222.

69. Jenks, *Nuestra colonia de Cuba*, 258–59.

70. In 1928, twenty-four Camagüey *centrales* belonged to eight companies: Cuban Cane Sugar Company owned Jagüeyal, Lugareño, Morón, Stewart, Velasco, and Violeta; General Sugar Company owned Agramonte, Camagüey, Estrella, Vertientes, and Pilar; Punta Alegre Sugar Company owned Baraguá, Punta Alegre, and Florida; Sugar Plantation Operating Company owned Algodonales, Ciego de Avila, and Macareño; Intereses

Rionda owned Francisco and Elia; American Sugar Refining Company owned Cunagua and Jaronú; Compañía Azucarera Najasa owned Najasa and Siboney; and Compañía Cubana owned Jatibonico.

71. Zanetti and García, *Caminos para el azúcar*, 259–63. The project was completed around 1930, with the city of Santa Clara as its western extremity.

72. Report of Rogerio Zayas Bazán, inspector for the province of Camagüey, *Censo de 1907*, 691.

73. Farm area in Santa Cruz del Sur in 1900 was 8,815 caballerías; in 1945 it was 16,648 caballerías. The rest of the territory was devoted to cultivation (14.8%), pasture (59.3%), and other uses (9%). Land dominated by marabú (*Dichrostachys cinerea*, an invasive bush or small tree) accounted for 7.6%.

74. Hugh H. Bennett and Robert V. Allison, *Los suelos de Cuba* (1928; Havana: Comisión Cubana de la UNESCO, 1962), 181–224. They remark: "The finest trunks found near a railroad line are separated out to take advantage of the wood, but in general much valuable wood has been destroyed by burning in recent years."

75. Ministerio de Agricultura, *Memoria del censo agrícola nacional, 1946* (Havana: P. Fernández, 1951). The figure given for Cuba's area in this census, 114,524 km², was higher than the true area.

76. The first general historical study was Juan T. Roig, *El marabú o aroma*, Circular no. 50 (Santiago de las Vegas: Estación Experimental Agronómica, 1915). See also Reinaldo Funes, "El fin de los bosques y la plaga del marabú en Cuba: Historia de una venganza ecológica," in Centro de Estudos de História do Atlantico [CEHA], *História e meio-ambiente: O impacto da expansao européia, Actas do seminário internacional* (Funchal, Madeira, Portugal: CEHA, 1999), 369–92.

77. According to the official estimate, barely 17% of Camagüey (including adjoining cays) is forested; Ministerio de Ciencia, Tecnología y Mediomabiente, Delegación Provincial, <www.camagüey.cu/cent_científ/delegacion>.

78. Francisco de P. Portuondo, "Memoria sobre el servicio del ramo de montes correspondiente al primer semestre del año de 1899," in John R. Brooke, *Civil Report of Major-General John R. Brooke, U.S. Army, Military Governor, Island of Cuba* (Washington, DC: U.S. Government Printing Office, 1899), 79–85.

79. *Memoria de los trabajos realizados en el año fiscal que comenzó en 1° de julio de 1899 y terminó en 30 de junio de 1900* (Havana: Gobierno Militar de la Isla de Cuba, Secretaría de Agricultura, Comercio e Industria, 1900), 90–92.

80. Frasquieri, "Nuestra crisis forestal," 4–5. The plan was inspired by the measures promulgated by the U.S. Forest Service regulating use of forest reserves; it adapted some articles from the regulation of May 8, 1884, then in force in Spain.

81. See these decrees in José Isaac del Corral, *Derecho forestal cubano*, vol. 1, *Disposiciones fundamentales* (Havana: Imprenta de Fernández y Cía, 1936).

82. Ibid., 258–59.

83. Another decree of the same date declared two cays south of the Batabanó anchorage to be protective cays, or shipping and bird refuges. On October 2, 1924, logging was banned on four more cays east of the Isla de Pinos, since these served as refuges during the season when the ringdove (paloma torcaz) raised its young.

84. The decree established minimum diameters for trees that could be harvested for use in making different articles. For tobacco-drying frames (*cujes*) these included such species as yaya, mije, guairaje, boniato, and leviza; for posts: arabo, yaití, yamaquey, granadillo, humo or guayabillo, yaicuaje or mulato, and macurije; for rollers and railroad ties: pine, ácana, jaimiqui, jocuma, quiebrahacha or caguairán, moruro, ocuje, sabicú, cocuyo, and júcaro; and for boards: cedar, mahogany, and holm oak. The use of young pine for tobacco frames was banned, except from thick young pine groves where thinning would promote the woodland's development so that its trees could reach the diameter required for railroad ties.

85. Isaac del Corral Alemán, "Problema forestal," 15–16.

86. Ibid., 17.

87. Ibid., 28–29.

88. Quoted in Isaac del Corral, *Derecho forestal cubano*, 173–75.

89. Ibid., 173.

90. It is true that few forested areas remained available and that for this reason, as well as that of harvest restrictions, the sugar industry moved definitively into what different writers have called *intensivismo*.

91. Ministerio de Agricultura, *Conveniencia de efectuar repoblaciones forestales en terrenos inadecuados para la agricultura* (Havana, 1930). The ministry argued against using mahogany for railroad ties, since mahogany forest was being destroyed by this industry, to the point that mahogany was in danger of disappearing entirely in a short time.

92. Frasquieri, "Nuestra crisis forestal," 8.

93. Bennett and Allison, *Suelos de Cuba*, 332. The study was organized by the Tropical Plant Research Foundation and financed by the Cuban Sugar Club (Club Azucarero Cubano), through small contributions from the *centrales* that were members.

94. Comisión de Asuntos Cubanos, *Problemas de la nueva Cuba*, 511–12.

95. José Isaac del Corral Alemán, "La devastación forestal y daños que ocasiona," archive of the Museo Carlos J. Finlay, Fondo Académico, Havana.

96. Ibid.

97. Antonio Ponce de León, "Algo sobre el arbolado de las carreteras," *Circular* (Estación Central Agronómica) 36 (1909): 18. Siboney is a name given to one of Cuba's native groups.

98. Marcelino Cremata, "Algo sobre nuestros bosques," *RACT*, December 1919, 610–11.

99. Roberto Luaces, "Los bosques," *RACT*, no. 6 (1923): 50–52.

100. "Dos grandes acontecimientos agrícolas," *RACT*, October 1929, 6.

101. República de Cuba, *Cartilla forestal cubana: Para el uso de autoridades y ciudadanos* (Havana: Rambla y Bauza, 1927); *Disposiciones vigentes que se han dictado para evitar la destrucción de la riqueza forestal cubana y tendientes a la conservación y repoblación de los montes nacionales* (Havana: Siglo XX, 1923); *Conveniencia de efectuar repoblaciones forestales en terrenos inadecuados para la agricultura, como medio de aumentar la riqueza del país y libertarlo de su actual dependencia económica a un solo cultivo* (Havana: Montalvo y Cárdenas, 1927); José Isaac del Corral Alemán, "La repoblación

forestal es un negocio," in Alberto J. Fors, *Las maderas cubanas* (Havana: Julio y Arroyo, 1929), 99–111.

102. Francisco Carrera y Justiz, *Los árboles y la cultura cívica: Fiesta del Día del Arbol — Su importancia social, sanitaria y estética* (Havana: Moderna Poesía, 1904).

103. Ramón García Osés, "La fiesta del Día del árbol," *Circular* (Estación Central Agronómica), no. 42 (1912): 19–24. In January 1926 Law Decree no. 527 established Arbor Day as October 10.

104. Ibid.; Ramón García Osés, "La influencia de los bosques en la agricultura," *Circular*, no. 42 (1912): 15–18.

105. García Osés, "Influencia de los bosques," 17.

106. It would be worth exploring the extent to which the protests of campesinos and workers against the sugar latifundios during the first half of the twentieth century were a reaction to the loss of access to natural resources; see Joan Martínez Alier, "Justicia ambiental, sustentabilidad y valoración," in *Naturaleza transformada: Estudios sobre historia ambiental en España*, ed. Manuel González de Molina and Joan Martínez Alier (Barcelona: Icaria, 2001), 289–335.

Conclusion

1. Ramón de La Sagra, *Cuba, 1860: Selección de artículos sobre agricultura cubana* (Havana: Comisión Nacional Cubana de la UNESCO, 1963), 22–23.

2. Alejandro de Humboldt, *Ensayo político sobre la isla de Cuba*, ed. Miguel Angel Puig-Samper, Consuelo Naranjo, and Armando García (Madrid: Doce Calles, 1998), 267.

3. Comisión de Asuntos Cubanos, *Problemas de la nueva Cuba* (New York: Foreign Policy Association, 1935), 501.

4. Carolyn Merchant, "The Theoretical Structure of Ecological Revolutions," *Environmental Review* 11.4 (1987): 265–74. Merchant distinguishes in the case of the United States between a colonial ecological revolution, which she situates between 1600 and the War of Independence, and what she calls a capitalist ecological revolution, which she locates from independence to 1860. The first type was generated outside the country by the process of conquest and colonization; the second kind was generated internally.

5. John McNeill, *Something New under the Sun: An Environmental History of the Twentieth Century* (London: Penguin, 2001), 325–35.

6. P. G. Minneman, "The Agriculture of Cuba, by . . . Agricultural Attaché, American Embassy, Havana, Cuba," *Foreign Agriculture Bulletin* (Washington, DC), no. 2 (1942): 10–11. Forests remained on 10–15% of the island, in areas difficult to access and of no value to agriculture.

7. The *Anuario Estadístico de Cuba* for 2000 indicates for state-owned farms a cane yield of 32.2 metric tons per hectare (37,495 arrobas per caballería) and for the nonstate sector a yield of 35.9 metric tons per hectare (41,804 arrobas per caballería). During the nineteenth century, cane fields were generally destroyed when yields dropped below 50,000 arrobas per caballería.

8. Teresita González Novo and Ignacio García Díaz, in *Cuba: Su medio ambiente*

después de medio milenio (Havana: Científico-Técnica), state that 76.8% of the island's soil shows some degree of erosion (73–74).

9. Jorge Ramón Cuevas, "La flora de la Mayor de las Antillas," *Flora y fauna* (Havana), November 1996, 19–21. He notes the high density of species per km².

10. Attila Borhidi and Onaney Muñiz, *Catálogo de plantas cubanas amenazadas o extinguidas* (Havana: Academia, 1983).

11. Esteban Pichardo Tapia, *Diccionario provincial casi-razonado de vozes y frases cubanas* (1836; Havana: Ciencias Sociales, 1985), 287.

12. Félix Guerra, *Los funerales del Rey: Ecología y fauna* (Santiago de Cuba: Oriente, 1999), 11–15.

13. Academia de Ciencias de Cuba (ACC), *Nuevo atlas nacional de Cuba* (Havana: Instituto de Geografía [ACC] and Instituto Geográfico Nacional [Spain], 1989).

14. In 1933 about 30,000 had been invaded by this plague. Between 1975 and 1990 the figure remained more or less stable between 40,000 and 50,000 caballerías, but then it again began to increase, reaching about 85,000 caballerías in the mid-1990s; Juan J. Paretas et al., "Marabú-Aroma II: Obstáculos al rescate ganadero — Programa de control y sus resultados," *Revista ACPA*, no. 1 (1996): 48–49. See Reinaldo Funes, "El fin de los bosques y la plaga del marabú en Cuba: Historia de una venganza ecológica," in Centro de Estudos de História do Atlantico [CEHA], *História e meio-ambiente: O impacto da expansao europeia, Actas do seminário internacional* (Funchal, Madeira, Portugal: CEHA, 1999), 369–92.

15. Gerardo Canet, "Ritmo en la formación de los recursos naturales y la población de Cuba," *Revista bimestre cubana*, January–June 1956, 168.

16. David Watts, *Las Indias occidentales: Modalidades de desarrollo, cultura y cambio medio ambiental desde 1492* (Madrid: Alianza, 1992).

17. On Martí's thought on the relationship between nature and society, see Guillermo Castro Herrera, *Los trabajos de ajuste y combate: Naturaleza y sociedad en la historia de América Latina* (Havana: Casa de las Américas-Colcultura, 1994), 199–206.

Glossary

Barracks (*barracón*)
  Building that housed slaves. Later these structures became lodgings for sugar workers generally.

Batey
  Site of the mill and housing on a sugar plantation. Also, the hamlet around the *central*.

Beam (*bao*)
  Large piece of wood that crossed a vessel at regular intervals from stem to stern to support the sides, to which it was secured at each end. It supported the decks and the full weight of the artillery and other effects. The function of the *bao* was similar to that of beams in houses.

Brigantine (*bergantín*)
  Ship with two masts, the *mayor* and the *trinquete*, with square sails. This type of light ship came into use in the fourteenth century.

Brusca
  Thin plant material used to revive a fire.

Cane field (*cañaveral*)
  Cane fields in general and also the individual plots in which cane is planted.

Cane pulp (*bagazo*)
  Cane residue after the juice is extracted.

Cask (*bocoy*)
  Large barrel used to transport molasses and muscovado. Its use and capacity (between 40 and 60 arrobas) tended to increase with transportation improvements.

Central/Ingenio central
  Around 1880 the term *central* began to replace *ingenio* to refer to the sugar mill and its dependencies.

Centrifuge (*centrífuga*)

Machine that uses centrifugal force to separate molasses from crystallized sugar. Its use became widespread in Cuba in the 1850s.

Clearing (*tumba*)

Deforestation of wooded terrain to plant cane or other crops.

Colonia

Sugarcane farm. This term first came into use to describe towns founded with official support.

Colonist (*colono*)

Workers brought to the island to develop towns or to work on plantations — for example, the Chinese. Beginning in the late nineteenth century, the term came to refer to owners of owners of cane farms who sold their product to sugar mills.

Conduit (*canoa*)

In *ingenios*, a closed wooden channel closed off on each end and made from a single tree. It had various uses. Like the English "canoe," *canoa* also refers to a boat made by indigenous Americans from a large tree trunk.

Corral

Hog farm.

Corte

Clearing of trees and cutting of cane. *Corte de ingenio*, opening of the forest to set up a sugar farm. Corte del Rey (Royal Forest Reserve), logging for shipbuilding.

Corvette (*corbeta*)

Boat smaller than but otherwise similar to a frigate.

Cowherds (*boyeros*)

Workers charged with leading ox teams.

Crate (*caja*)

Container. Sugar crates usually had a capacity of 16 to 18 arrobas.

Dead time (*tiempo muerto*)

Time between harvests (*zafra* or *molienda*) during which much of the work of the sugar industry stops.

Dismantlement (*demolición*)

Subdivision of traditional livestock estates, *hatos* and *corrales*. To dismantle an *ingenio* was to demolish it and use its land for another purpose.

Distillery (*alambiques*)

Apparatus for the distillation of the final molasses, and the building in which it is housed.

Ecosystem (*ecosistema*)

Complex of relationships and interactions between the biotic and abiotic components of a given habitat.

Endemic (*endémico*)

Indigenous or native to a place.

Environment (*medioambiente*)

Physical surroundings and system that sustains life. In a broader sense, it includes socioeconomic factors.

Estate owner (*hacendado*)

Owner of a livestock farm (*hatos* and *corrales*). Also used for owners of *ingenios*, coffee plantations, and *potreros*.

Fat cows (*vacas gordas*)

Time of plenty for the economy in general and the sugar industry in particular.

Firewood (*leña*)

Pieces of tree trunks or branches used as fuel.

Frigate (*fragata*)

Three-masted cruising vessel, smaller than a ship. It had only one bridge or battery armed with cannons. It was used in the merchant marine and for military actions.

Furnace (*fornalla*)

Oven where the boiler *tren* was supplied with fuel.

Harvest

Has two equivalents in Cuban Spanish: *zafra* and *molienda*.

Hato

Cattle ranch.

Ingenio

The sugar plantation in its entirety. This term was also used to identify the mill itself, especially after the appearance of the *ingenio central*.

Lean cows (*vacas flacas*)

Time of crisis for the economy in general and the sugar industry in particular.

Length (*toza*)

Large piece of mahogany or cedar sometimes made from an entire tree.

Milling (*molienda*)

The grinding of sugarcane. The Spanish term also refers to the sugar harvest or refining period.

Molasses (*miel*)

By-product in the sugar-making process. The Spanish word also means "honey," produced by bees in hives located in trees or made by humans.

Monoculture (*monocultivo*)

Repeated cultivation of a single type of plant in terrain, area, or region.

Muscovado (*mascabado*)

Type of sugar with high molasses content that is packed without having gone through a purification process.

Potrero

Livestock farm. From the end of the eighteenth century and through much of the nineteenth, *portreros* specialized in the fattening (*engorde*) of animals.

Pounder (*maza*)

A cylinder in the *ingenio* that mills cane and extracts the syrup.

Pulp house (*casa de bagazo*)

Building where pulp is stored for use as fuel.

Purify (*purgar*)

Separate crystallized sugar from molasses, and operation performed in purification house (*casa de purga*).

Refine (*refinar*)

Whiten sugar. Reprocess unrefined sugar (muscovado) and broken sugar to make white sugar.

Sack (*saco*)

Made of twine during the eighteenth and nineteenth centuries, with a capacity of 5 arrobas (57.5 kg). Used to transport sugar from the *ingenio* to the city. In the nineteenth century sacks began to made of jute; later they were used directly for export.

Savanna (*sabana*)

Flat terrain with no trees or with a few isolated ones. These open landscapes include grasses, bushes, and palm or pine trees in some areas.

Schooner (*goleta*)

Vessel about 100 feet long, with two masts and fore and aft sails.

Ship (*navío*)

Large seagoing vessel with two, three, or four bridges or canon batteries on each side. *Ships of the line* were those considered suitable to participate in the formation of the battle line. They had more than sixty large-caliber cannons.

Syrup (*guarapo*)

Sugarcane juice.

Trapiche

Mill that extracts the syrup from the cane. Beginning in the late eighteenth century this term came to identify sugar farms with smaller production capacities.

Tren

Set of boilers used to extract the syrup. The term also was used for vacuum-evaporation technologies (e.g., the *tren Derosne*).

Woodland (*monte*)

Synonym for *forest* or *wooded area*. In Cuba, unlike in many other Spanish-speaking countries, *monte* is almost never used as a synonym for mountain.

Bibliographic Essay

In this essay I will evaluate the qualitative relevance of some of the sources I used for this book and their interest for the study of Cuban environmental history generally. To avoid unnecessarily lengthening the text, I have omitted some works cited in the notes and included others not mentioned that treat some of the themes discussed or the different stages and historical processes in such an extensive chronological period. Nevertheless, I hope that this historiographic commentary will be of use to readers.

David Watts's wide-ranging book on the Caribbean islands, *The West Indies: Patterns of Development, Culture and Environmental Change since 1492* (Cambridge, England, 1987), translated into Spanish as *Las Indias occidentales: Modalidades de desarrollo, cultura y cambio medio ambiental desde 1492* (Madrid, 1992), compares the environmental transformation caused by commercial agricultural plantations to great traumas of the region's common history, such as the complete disappearance of native populations and the forced transfer of African slaves as a labor force. Owing to the sugar industry's importance on the islands, the impact of cane cultivation on local ecosystems is a central topic of Watts's research. Other recent studies of Caribbean environmental history focus on different aspects of human interaction with the environment, as we see in Richard H. Grove, *Green Imperialism: Colonial Expansion, Tropical Island Edens and the Origins of Environmentalism, 1600–1860* (Cambridge, England, 1996); Stuart McCook, *States of Nature: Science, Agriculture, and Environment in the Spanish Caribbean, 1760–1940* (Austin, TX, 2002); and Bonham C. Richardson, *Igniting the Caribbean's Past: Fire in British West Indian History* (Chapel Hill, NC, 2004).

Its particular relevance to the subject of this book makes Richard P. Tucker's *Insatiable Appetite: The United States and the Ecological Degradation of the Tropical World* (Berkeley, CA, 2000) deserving of special mention. In one of his chapters Tucker discusses the environmental implications of the sugar industry in the Caribbean from the seventeenth to the early twentieth century. Here he also deals with the implantation in the provinces of Camagüey and Oriente of industrial agriculture on an unprecedented scale, as an early example of the flowering of U.S. ecological imperialism. Mark J. Smith's article "The Political Economy of Sugar Production and the Environment of Eastern Cuba, 1898–1923," *Environmental History Review* 19.4 (1995): 31–48, takes a similar approach, based on existing documentation about the Manatí *central*.

One finds fewer studies of the environmental history of the Caribbean's Spanish-speaking islands than of those colonized by the English or French (the latter to a lesser degree). Some of the works that mention Cuba conclude that there are few references to sugar's ecological impact and to the advance of the plantation economy generally. After claiming that the greatest environmental change in the nineteenth century occurred in Cuba, Watts observes that very little was known about the effects of deforestation on the environment, although it could be supposed that these were considerable. Tucker notes the difficulty of finding documentation about sugar's environmental cost in Cuba, since there is no detailed information about total forested area and about soil erosion, among other effects, although it is still possible to trace a general outline of the phenomenon.

This general lack of understanding in Cuba of sugar's environmental consequences may be considered relative when we take into account the different books and articles devoted to the history of what was for two centuries the island's principal economic activity, as well as the contributions of natural scientists and geographers. Nevertheless, it is true that few studies have explored the interactions between the island's economic development and the environment, or the evolution of environmentalist thought and government environmental policy. The case of the sugar industry can be considered, of course, in both senses: first, by examining the ecological limitations it entailed; second, by studying its impact on the forests, and the environmental consequences and socioeconomic implications of the process. With respect to topics such as labor, social conflicts, capital and business leaders, technology, and commerce, among others, sugar's interaction with the environment has received much less attention. We can see this reflected, for example, in the bibliographic study by José A. Piqueras, "El azúcar en Cuba y las fuentes para su estudio," *América Latina en la historia económica: Boletín de fuentes* (Mexico City), no. 11 (1999): 35–47.

The most detailed discussion of this topic among historians can be found in Manuel Moreno Fraginals, *El ingenio: Complejo económico social cubano del azúcar*, 3 vols. (Havana, 1964, 1978; New York, 1976), and Leví Marrero, *Cuba: Economía y sociedad*, 15 vols. (Madrid, 1971–86). Moreno Fraginals frequently refers to the sugar industry's relationship with Cuban forests between the late eighteenth century and 1860; he includes a paragraph titled "La muerte del bosque" (The Death of the Forest; in the chapter "La expansión y la transformación del medio [The Expansion and Transformation of the Environment], 1800–1860") that synthetically describes the accelerated deforestation of vast areas of the island as a result of the sugar fever. Marrero, for his part, does not limit his discussion to the impact of sugar; he broadens his spectrum to include forest history in general and a more encompassing period, from the beginning of colonization in the first half of the sixteenth century until 1868. His twin specialties of geography and history no doubt contributed to his greater interest in the exploitation of natural resources in general and their economic, social, and environmental implications, as well in the role different geographic limitations have played in Cuban history.

Most of the twentieth-century works that examine the interaction of Cuban society with the environment emerge out of this combining of history and geography. Rich examples of this fusion include Juan Pérez de La Riva's edition of and introductory articles to Antonio del Valle Hernández, *Sucinta noticia de la situación presente de esta colonia, 1800* (Havana, 1977); Antonio Núñez Jiménez, *La erosión desgasta a Cuba* (Havana, 1968); and Núñez Jiménez, *Hacia una cultura de la naturaleza* (Havana, 1998). Both authors deal amply with the transformation of Cuban space, the former with a greater emphasis on history and demography and the second concentrating more on geography. In these writers, as in Moreno Fraginals and Marrero, we can see the influence of the Annales school and of different aspects of human geography and historical geography, which were in vogue during these Cubans' most intellectually productive years.

The works most specifically about the history of Cuban forests and the relationship of the island's socioeconomic development with its natural environment are by less-known authors working in natural sciences or geography. Among these are two unpublished works that I consulted in the library of the Institute of Tropical Geography in Havana: Isabel Pruna, "Bosques y deforestación en Cuba a través de la historia" (Havana, 1956), and Eliseo Matos, "Breve historia de los montes en Cuba" (Havana, n.d. [early 1970s]). Matos's manuscript is made more valuable by its effort to quantify deforestation in different stages from the European conquest to the late 1960s. Other authors in the same fields examined the subject of the forests during the first half of the twentieth century. Juan A. Cosculluela included a brief historical review in his study *Cuatro años en la ciénaga de Zapata: Memorias de un ingeniero* (Havana, 1918). José Isaac del Corral Alemán, who for more than three decades was director of woodlands and mines in the Ministry of Agriculture, wrote prolifically about the forests, although he was most interested in solving practical problems; see, for instance, his *Derecho forestal cubano*, vol. 1, *Disposiciones fundamentales* (Havana, 1936). Also worth mentioning is the brochure by Juan Luis Martín, *Esquema elemental de temas sobre la caña de azúcar como factor topoclimático de la geografía social de Cuba* (Havana, 1944).

I cannot fail to mention here the debate over Cuba's original vegetation, which in the authoritative opinion of the Cuban geographer and botanist Onaney Muñiz (1937–2002) was perhaps the most important among flora specialists during the twentieth century. The first attempt to address this question specifically was by the German geographer Leo Waibel, in his article "Places Names as an Aid in the Reconstruction of the Original Vegetation of Cuba," *Geographical Review* 33 (1943): 376–96. In the early 1960s the School of Geography in the Faculty of Sciences at the University of Havana put out a modest edition that later was republished with Ricardo Herrera's "El origen de las sabanas cubanas" as the book *La toponimia en el paisaje cubano* (Havana, 1984). Both authors used historical data, as well as documentary and cartographic sources from the nineteenth century and early twentieth. Especially noteworthy is Waibel's use of toponyms and maps with remnants of wooded areas at the beginning of the twentieth century and Herrara's identification of possible savannas through maps of *hatos* and *corrales*.

Many of the writers who link the perspectives of history and geography, such as Marrero and Pérez de La Riva, begin with Waibel's estimates when attempting to determine the state of Cuba's vegetation on the arrival of the Spaniards. Another commonly used source is Earl Smith's estimate in *The Forests of Cuba* (Cambridge, MA, 1953), who to a certain degree follows that of Hugh H. Bennett and Robert V. Allison in *Los suelos de Cuba* (1928; Havana, 1962). Another example of the study of vegetation at the Europeans' arrival and the ensuing changes is the map estimating Cuba's sixteenth-century vegetation prepared by Enrique del Risco Rodríguez for the *Nuevo atlas nacional de Cuba* (Havana, 1989), by the Academia de Ciencias de Cuba, and for his book *Los bosques de Cuba: Su historia y características* (Havana, 1995). The debate over the island's original vegetation and the existence of forests in different historical periods is far from closed. An idea of the range of estimates of wooded area is offered in S. Díaz-Briquets and J. Pérez-López, *Conquering Nature: The Environmental Legacy of Socialism in Cuba* (Pittsburgh, 2000), 138–44.

Although most references to past Cuban forests mention the impact of sugar and other economic activities, they often cannot be categorized as rigorous scientific research. Professional geographers known for focusing on historical geography or environmental history have not had access to the ample information in archives and libraries, not yet consulted by "professional historians," that is usually their principal source. Among the farthest-reaching studies is the work of Enrique Fernández, *La historia como condicionante del territorio: El caso de Cuba* (Madrid, 1995), which stresses the importance of historical knowledge for understanding the settlement of the island, its demography, and the characteristics of Cuba's urbanization. More recently a collective of writers from the Institute of Tropical Geography in the Ministry of Science, Technology, and the Environment, headed by Carmen Mosquera, created a CD-ROM titled *Historia ambiental de Cuba* (Havana, 2004). It discusses the whole island generally, but with a focus on coastal areas (the Zapata Swamp and Southern Dike), basins (of the Itabo, Mayabeque, and Cauto rivers), and mountains (Guamuaya, Las Pizarras, Mayarí-Moa). Although its historical information is based on traditional sources, this remains an innovative attempt to study Cuba's history on the basis not of its administrative districts but of territories with common physico-geographic characteristics.

The literature on the history of Cuban forests has been enriched by various studies published in Spain, among them Vicente Casals Costa, "Las ideas sobre la protección del bosque en Cuba y Filipinas durante el siglo XIX," in *Estudios sobre la ciencia: Ciencia, vida y espacio en Ibero América*, ed. José Luis Pesset, vol. 3 (Madrid, 1989); Casals Costa, "Del cultivo de los árboles a las leyes de la espesura," in *El bosque ilustrado: Estudios sobre la política forestal española en América*, ed. Manuel Lucena (Madrid, 1991); Gaspar de Aranda y Antón, "Las maderas de Indias," *Asclepio*, no. 45 (1993): 217–48; and Aranda y Antón, *La administración forestal y los montes de Ultramar durante el siglo XIX* (Madrid, 1995). Both authors delve into the beginnings of forest administration during the second half of the nineteenth century and refer to sugar's impact on the forests, as well as to the importance of Cuban lumber for Spanish shipbuilding. Among the studies of scientific expeditions during the colonial period one can find examinations of Spain's interest in Cuban wood, such as Consuelo Naranjo, "Los reconocimientos madereros en Cuba (1780–1810)," in Lucena, *Bosque ilustrado*. Broader in scope is the article by Josef Opatrny, "Los cambios socio-económicos y el medio ambiente: Cuba, primera mitad del siglo XIX," *Revista de Indias* 56.207 (1996): 367–86, which pays detailed attention to the deforestation provoked by the advance of sugar and other crops.

Among the works devoted specifically to the history of the sugar industry in Cuba, the ones that give the most importance to sugar's impact on the environment, without this being their central topic (aside from the ones by Moreno Fraginals and Marrero that I have already mentioned), are Roland T. Ely, *Cuando reinaba Su Majestad el azúcar: Estudio histórico sociológico de una tragedia latinoamericana — El monocultivo en Cuba, Origen y evolución del proceso* (1963; Havana, 2001), and Laird W. Bergad, *Cuban Rural Society in the Nineteenth Century: The Social and Economic History of Monoculture in Matanzas* (Princeton, NJ, 1990). Ely devotes a paragraph to the specific problem of the exhaustion of soils, and Bergad frequently refers to the importance of forests in sugar's expansion in the Matanzas area and to the heavy impact of agroindustry on local ecosystems.

Authors more focused on the history of sugar in the eighteenth and early nineteenth centuries also mention the subject on occasion, although with less emphasis. See, for instance, Mercedes García Rodríguez, "Ingenios habaneros del siglo XVIII," *Arbor*, no. 547–48 (1991): 113–37; García, *Misticismo y capitales: La Compañía de Jesús en la economía habanera del siglo XVIII* (Havana, 2000); and Pablo Tornero, *Crecimiento económico y transformaciones sociales: Esclavos, hacendados y comerciantes en la Cuba colonial, 1760–1840* (Madrid, 1996). Inattentive to environmental transformation but useful for its discussion of the frontier of the slave sugar plantations in the mid-nineteenth century is Modesto González, *Ultimo escalón alcanzado por la plantación comercial azucarera esclavista (1827–1886)* (Havana, 2003). Dale Tomich, "Material Process and Industrial Architecture: Innovation on the Cuban Sugar Frontier, 1818–1857," *Nature, Raw Materials and Political Economy: Research in Rural Sociology and Development* 10 (2005): 289–309, offers suggestive reflections on the new phase of Cuban slavery after the changes in sugar production under the influence of the Industrial Revolution. Similarly, J. H. Galloway, *The Sugar Cane Industry: An Historical Geography from Its Origins to 1914* (Cambridge, England, 1989), provides a global view of the advance of sugar production in the different producing regions.

Other studies of Cuban sugar history devoted to the last third of the nineteenth and the early twentieth centuries place less emphasis on the direct importance of the forest as a supplier of lumber for mills and of fuel, owing to its relative loss of influence on the industry's fate. Nevertheless, aspects of interest to environmental history are always taken up, such as the changes in land ownership, technology, agricultural and industrial yield, and so on. Among the most influential of these works are Fe Iglesias García, *Del ingenio al central* (San Juan, Puerto Rico, 1998); Allan Dye, *Cuban Sugar in the Age of Mass Production: Technology and the Economics of the Cuban Sugar Central* (Stanford, CA, 1998); César J. Ayala, *American Sugar Kingdom: The Plantation Economy of the Spanish Caribbean, 1898–1934* (Chapel Hill, NC, 1999); and Antonio Santamaría, *Sin azúcar no hay país: La industria azucarera y la economía cubana (1919–1939)* (Seville, 2001).

In his *States of Nature*, mentioned above, McCook devotes a chapter to the role of agricultural science and its institutions in the introduction of new varieties of sugarcane in Cuba as a means to fight the diseases that affected the crop in the different producing areas and to increase yields. On the role of science in Cuban agriculture between the late nineteenth century and the early twentieth we also have studies such as Rolando Misas, "La ciencia agrícola en Cuba: Nacionalismo y modernidad (1898–1909)," in Mildred de la Torre et al., *La sociedad cubana en los albores de la República* (Havana, 2002), and Leida Fernández Prieto, *Cuba agrícola: Mito y tradición, 1878–1920* (Madrid, 2005).

A number of works on the island's socioeconomic evolution mention, in one way or another, the disappearance of the forests or the transformation of the island's landscapes generally. This is the case of railroad histories, prominent among them Oscar Zanetti and Alejandro García, *Caminos para el azúcar* (Havana, 1987), revised by the authors and translated by Franklin Knight and Mary Todd as *Sugar and Railroads: A Cuban History* (Chapel Hill, NC, 1998), and Eduardo L. Moyano, *La nueva frontera del azúcar: El ferrocarril y la economía cubana del siglo XIX* (Madrid, 1991).

This interaction also appears, explicitly or implicitly, in different publications dealing with the historical evolution of regions or localities on the island, such as in Ramiro Guerra y Sánchez, "Desarrollo de La Habana y su provincia: Un caso singular de determinismo geográfico," *Revista de la Sociedad Geográfica de Cuba*, January–June 1947, 5–17; Julio Le Riverend, *La Habana: Biografía de una provincia* (Havana, 1960); and Carlos Venegas, "La Habana y su región: Un proyecto de organización espacial de la plantación esclavista," *Revista de Indias* 56.207 (1996): 333–65. Other works are more focused on the sugar theme, such as Orlando García Martínez, "Estudio de la economía cienfueguera desde la fundación de la colonia Fernandina de Jagua hasta mediados del siglo XIX," *Islas*, no. 55–56 (1977): 117–69; Hernán Venegas, "Consideraciones en torno a la economía remediana colonial," *Islas*, no. 67 (1980): 11–79; Hernán Venegas, "Acerca del proceso de concentración y centralización de la industria azucarera en la región remediana a fines del siglo XIX," *Islas*, no. 73 (1982): 63–121; José M. Gómez, *Camajuaní: La plantación azucarera en el siglo XIX* (Santa Clara, 2001); and José Sánchez, *El azúcar en el valle de los ingenios guantanameros (1532–1899)* (Guantánamo, 2003).

For an overview of sugar's influence on different regions of the country, one can consult Eduardo Torres, "El azúcar y la formación de los complejos económico-sociales regionales," in *Le sucre dans l'espace Caraïbe hispanophone aux XIXe et XXe siècles: Stratégies et représentations* (Paris, 1998). María Aguiar Fons, "Un enfoque geográfico en la investigación cultural: Relación cultura-hombre-naturaleza y regionalización," in *Pensamiento y tradiciones populares: estudios de identidad cultural cubana y latinoamericana*, ed. Ana Vera Estrada (Havana, 2000): 291–327, offers an interesting study of the connections between Cuba's physico-natural and sociocultural regionalization.

One study that stands out among regional approaches for its incorporation of environmental conditions and the transformation of the territory is Hernán Venegas's essay about Trinidad, "Apuntes sobre la decadencia trinitaria en el siglo XIX," *Islas*, no. 46 (1973): 159–251, which notes the impact on the area of the soils' lost fertility and of the decline of sugar production. Among investigations of problematics such as the evolution of the system of appropriation and of land use, there are important references to the changes in Cuban space, particularly those entailed by deforestation: see Julio Le Riverend, *Problemas de la formación agraria de Cuba, siglos XVI–XVII* (Havana, 1992), and Francisco Pérez de La Riva, *Origen y régimen de la propiedad territorial en Cuba* (Havana, 1946). The issues of land ownership conflicts and rapid ecological transformation also appear in studies of the economic and social implications of sugar plantations in central eastern Cuba in the last third of the nineteenth century and the first two decades of the twentieth, as illustrated, for instance, by Louis Pérez Jr., *Lords of the Mountain: Social Banditry and Peasant Protest in Cuba, 1878–1918* (Pittsburgh, 1989).

In pursuing the goals of this book, it was essential to go deeper into the history of Havana shipbuilding and forest harvesting by the Spanish royal navy between the seventeenth century and the early nineteenth. Among the most notable studies in this regard are Ovidio Ortega Pereyra, *El Real Arsenal de La Habana: La construcción naval en La Habana bajo la dominación colonial española* (Havana, 1998); Douglas Inglis, "The Spanish Naval Shipyard at Havana in the Eighteenth Century," in *New Aspects of Naval History* (Baltimore, 1985); and Leví Marrero, *Cuba: Economía y sociedad*, vol. 8 (Madrid, 1980), 1–24, and vol. 12 (Madrid, 1985), 174–85. These three authors refer to the Cortes del Rey's exploitation of forests for the Havana shipyard and for shipments of lumber to Spain, but they pay less attention to this aspect than to construction at the shipyard, the vessels that left its harbor, the orders of navy officers charged with running it, and Spain's imperial politics to reinforce its sea power.

In the future it would be worthwhile to undertake a more thorough study of the systems used by the Spanish navy to satisfy its wood needs (the Protocolo de Marina documents at the Cuban National Archive could prove an excellent documentary source). In this way one could weigh the successes and failures of forest activity on the island related to shipbuilding. This would allow us to compare the Cuban experience with that of, say, Brazil, for which there are contrary interpretations of the effects of Europe's imperial policies of control and exploitation of its American colonies' forest resources, as we see in Warren Dean, *With Broadax and Firebrand: The Destruction of the Brazilian Atlantic Forest* (Berkeley, CA, 1995); and Shawn W. Miller, *Fruitless Trees: Portuguese Conservation and Brazil's Colonial Timber* (Berkeley, CA, 2000).

In summary, many works about Cuba allude to the history of the interaction between economic, social, and political processes with the forests (or nature in general), but they do so usually as isolated references largely unconnected to the main theme, whether this is the sugar industry, shipbuilding, or some other topic. In the few works on forest administration itself, in contrast, little connection is made with other areas of Cuba's economic, social, and political evolution.

Interest in the disappearance of the forests was greater in nineteenth-century works, which can be explained by the lost resources' relatively greater importance in Cuba's economy and living conditions at that time. Writers who lived through the periods of greatest deforestation resulting from sugar's advance warned of the dangers to which the island exposed itself in losing its forest cover. They thus devoted special attention to the subject, hoping to intervene before it was too late. Many of these writings have no more than testimonial value, but others are important forerunners of efforts to study the evolution of the relationship between nature and society in Cuban history.

Most prominent in this regard are the naturalists Ramón de La Sagra and Miguel Rodríguez Ferrer, who incorporated much historical material into their analyses, which became fundamental sources for all the studies that followed. La Sagra was prolific, but we need only mention his *Historia económica-política y estadística de la isla de Cuba, o sea de sus progresos en la población, la agricultura, el comercio y las rentas* (Havana, 1831) and *Cuba en 1860, o sea cuadro de sus adelantos en la población, la agricultura, el comercio y las rentas públicas* (Paris, 1862). Rodríguez Ferrer, in the first volume of his *Naturaleza y civilización de la grandiosa isla de Cuba* (Madrid, 1876), devoted two chapters to a historical perspective on the forest question and to the rapid deforestation that occurred during his years living on the island (especially in Puerto Príncipe), between 1840 and 1870. Both scientists grounded their analyses on firsthand experience of the colony and were up to date on the most advanced ideas of the period on the physico-economic importance of the forest and the rise of a modern forest administration in Spain.

Illustrative of nineteenth-century interest in the history of the island's forests was the reproduction by the *Anales de la Junta de Fomento* (the name at the time of the *Memorias de la Sociedad Económica de La Habana*) in 1850 and 1851 of documents in which the sugar planters and the royal navy engaged in a lengthy conflict over property rights and the exploitation of forests. A series of seven articles appeared under the heading "Cortes de maderas: Relación de las disposiciones gubernativas desde la prohibición de la tala de árboles hasta la completa libertad de abatir los bosques" (Logging: Account of Government Measures from the Ban on Felling Trees to the Complete Freedom to Clear Forests). The final essay was devoted to the rapid disappearance of Cuba's forests in the mid-nineteenth century. Several well-known writers, Cuban and foreign, alluded to the island's forests and their disappearance, among them Alexander von Humboldt, José Antonio Saco, the Count de Pozos Dulces, Jacobo de La Pezuela, Alvaro Reynoso, Francisco Javier de Balmaceda, and José María Fernández y Jiménez. But in none of these cases was the historical element given great attention.

The central topic of this book links it with numerous studies of the environmental implications of different Latin American and Caribbean plantation crops destined for export, such as coffee, bananas, cocoa, henequen, and of course sugar, essentially beginning in the nineteenth century. Among the specific works, these include the ones I have already mentioned by Watts, Tucker, McCook, and Dean, as well as José Augusto Pádua, *Um sopro de destruição: Pensamento político e crítica ambiental no Brasil escravista (1786–1888)* (Rio de Janeiro, 2002); Stefania Gallini, "A Maya Mam Agro-ecosystem in Guatemala's Coffee Revolution: Costa Cuca, 1830–1880s," in *Territories, Commodities and Knowledges: Latin American Environmental Histories in the Nineteenth and Twentieth Centuries*, ed. Christian Brannstrom (London, 2004); and John Soluri, *Banana Cultures: Agriculture, Consumption, and Environmental Change in Honduras and the United States* (Austin, TX, 2006). The list could be much longer and include pioneering works such as Gilberto Freyre, *Nordeste: Aspectos da influência da cana sobre a vida e a paisagem do Nordeste do Brasil* (1937; São Paulo, 2004).

For the subject of this book, however, the most important studies are those done from the specific perspective of environmental history. To get an idea of this movement in scientific research on Latin America and the Caribbean, one can consult the introduction by Brannstrom and Gallini in Brannstrom, *Territories, Commodities and Knowledges*. We owe some of the most precise references to environmental history "done" from the very region under study to Guillermo Castro Herrera — for example, in his *Para una historia ambiental latinoamericana* (Havana, 2004). The list of collective national or regional contributions continues to lengthen. See, for example, Germán Palacio, ed., *Naturaleza en disputa: Ensayos de historia ambiental de Colombia, 1850–1995* (Bogotá, 2001); Bernardo García Martínez and Alba González Jácome, comps., *Estudios sobre historia y ambiente en América*, vol. 1 (Mexico City, 1999 [the second volume, compiled by García Martínez and M. del Rosario Prieto, appeared in 2003]); and the special issues of *Varia história* (Belo Horizonte) organized by Regina Horta: "História e naturaleza" (no. 26 [2002]), and "História ambiental (feita) na América Latina" (no. 33 [2005]).

This book set out to expand the existing literature on Cuba. I took an initial step toward my treatment here of the interaction of sugar and the destruction of the island's forests in "Azúcar y deforestación: Una aproximación a la historia ambiental en Cuba," in *Naturaleza transformada: Estudios de historia ambiental en España* (Barcelona, 2001). The list of works specifically on Cuban environmental history is still quite short. In addition to some of the books and essays cited above that directly or indirectly take on the problematics of society's interaction with its surroundings from the perspective of historical geography, the history of science, the history of technology, or environmental history, a good example of the potential of this field is Louis A. Pérez Jr., *Winds of Change: Hurricanes and the Transformation of Nineteenth-Century Cuba* (Chapel Hill, NC, 2001).

The book you hold in your hands seeks to be one contribution to the immense task of discovering and analyzing the evolution of the interaction with the rest of nature of the human beings who have inhabited Cuba's territory (the island and its archipelago) since the Europeans' arrival. It will have achieved its goal if it eases the way for those who are interested in writing or understanding the environmental history of the Largest of the Antilles.

dismantlement, 91, 92, 112, 115–16; and Royal Forest Reserves, 92; and Arango y Parreño, 92, 116, 304 (n. 59); and Wood Committee, 105; on property rights, 106–7, 303 (n. 47); on supply of woodlands, 107–8, 302 (n. 26), 303 (n. 48); and Spanish royal navy's logging operations, 110; and suspension of permits, 118, 304 (n. 64)

Artemisa Plain, 42, 45, 63, 87–89, 188

Artificial forests, 214–15, 258–59

Atkins, Edwin, 193, 316 (n. 41)

Balmaceda, Francisco Javier de, 190, 214–15

Barbados, 3, 30

Bartlet, Jorge, 142

Bauduy, Pedro, 148

Bauer, Erich, 172, 290 (n. 50)

Bautista Jiménez, Juan, 190

Bayamo, 15, 25

Becerra Betancourt, Manuel, 33

Beehives: and wood use, 77, 79–80, 81, 95, 118

Beet sugar, 128, 180, 218

Bennett, Hugh H., 9, 10, 145, 204, 250, 259, 295 (n. 38), 325 (n. 74)

Berchon, Charles, 243–44

Betancourt, Pedro E., 252–53

Betancourt Cisneros, Gaspar, 242

Birds: of forests, 8, 19, 139; and deforestation, 152, 214, 259–60, 273–74; protection of, 325 (n. 83)

Biscay: Havana compared to, 21, 289 (n. 42); iron imported from, 52, 81, 301 (n. 19)

Boiler houses, 30, 49, 56–57, 130, 131

Bonet, Juan Bautista, 50, 62, 64, 65, 66, 67–69, 74, 298 (nn. 84, 92)

Borja, Francisco de, 51, 52, 75–78, 299 (n. 103)

Bosh y Juliá, Miguel, 207

Boussingault, Jean-Baptiste, 151–52

Bouyóon, Honorato, 105, 160, 303 (n. 43)

Brazil, 128, 148

Bucarely, Antonio María de, 297 (n. 79)

Cabañas Bay, 24

Cabello de Robles, Domingo, 81, 302 (n. 38)

Cagigal y de La Vega, Francisco, 23, 27, 28, 298 (n. 96)

Calvo, Nicolás, 88, 89, 301 (n. 18)

Camagüey Province: and U.S. capitalists, 2, 220–21, 228, 248; and harvesting of wood, 195; and impact of sugar expansion, 219, 221–22, 224, 227, 232, 238–51 passim, 271; colossal *ingenios* in, 220, 249; and deforestation, 229, 238, 239, 241–42, 249–50, 260, 262, 325 (n. 74); change in natural region, 230–40; and *centrales*, 237, 238, 244–45, 247, 248, 249, 251, 324–25 (n. 70); and lumber trade, 241–42, 243; and Ten Years' War, 242; woodland area of, 243–44, 250, 251, 324 (n. 59), 325 (n. 77); boundaries of, 323 (n. 52)

Cambre *ingenio*, 129

Canary Islands, 25, 186

Canel, Eva, 215

Canet, Gerardo, 275

Canga Argüelles, José, 121

Cantero, Justo Germán, 131

Cárdenas, 140, 157

Caribbean islands: and sugar industry, 2, 3, 26, 28, 29, 41, 291 (n. 73); and sugar cultivation, 30, 31, 264, 265; and plantation colonies, 128; deforestation of, 147–48; U.S. investment in, 219, 321 (n. 7); land area of, 286 (n. 2)

Carlist War of 1833–40, 172

Carlos III (king of Spain), 28, 40, 298 (n. 96)

Carlos IV (king of Spain), 41, 123

Carreño, Francisco, 21

Carrera, Manuel, 202

Casals Costa, Vicente, 172

Casaseca, José Luis, 130
Castelló, José, 121
Castro Palomino, Gabriel de, 190
Central Department, 131, 230
Centrales: emergence of, 179, 191, 201; raw materials supplied by *colonato*, 180; and mechanized *ingenios*, 181; productive capacity of, 182–83, 219, 232–33; size of, 183; and railroads, 183, 195, 235–36, 237, 265; location of, 185, 186; and virgin land, 186, 187, 237, 238; and sugar cultivation, 195; and World War I, 218; and land use, 219; and pastures, 219; and colossal *ingenios*, 219–21; and U.S. capitalists, 233; and Camagüey Province, 237, 238, 244–45, 247, 248, 249, 251, 324–25 (n. 70); and Verdeja Law, 258
Central Railroad, 197, 233–37, 238, 243–44, 245, 249, 317 (n. 51)
Centrifuges, 181, 182, 200
Chaunu, Pierre, 289 (n. 42)
Cienfuegos, 160–62, 165, 195, 196
Cienfuegos, José, 160
Civil Superior Government, 175
Clark, William J., 222, 322 (n. 20)
Clear-cutting: and sugar plantations, 1, 27; sugar industry's dependence on, 3; and indigenous Cubans, 8–9; license for, 23–24; and private landowners, 24, 70, 301 (nn. 23, 25); and soil fertility, 128, 154; and deforestation, 132–33, 159, 187, 227, 260, 272; and artificial clearing, 154–55; and expansion of sugar production, 224; impact on pastures, 241
Clouet, Louis de, 160–61
Coal, 138, 149, 151, 152, 191, 192, 194, 265
Coca, Josef de, 90–91
Coffee industry, 45, 54, 84, 85, 108, 296 (n. 50)
Colonato system, 180, 183, 185, 187, 189–90, 271
Colonias, 183, 184, 197, 204

Colón Plain region, 129, 130–31, 134, 135, 184, 188, 193, 230
Columbus, Christopher, 7, 8, 25
Communal property, 18, 32–33, 268, 269, 288 (n. 32)
Compañía de Caminos de Hierro de La Habana (Havana Railroads Company), 134, 137
Corn cultivation, 46, 295 (n. 33)
Corrales (hog farms): reconstructed maps of, 10; and land distribution, 17; size of, 17, 288 (n. 29); and forests, 18–19, 71; increase in, 20; and conflicts over forest use, 31; sale of, 34; coexistence of tobacco plantations with, 35; dismantlement of, 35, 73, 107, 219, 293 (n. 97), 302 (n. 35)
Corte of Alquízar, 62–63, 77
Corte of Casiguas, 63–64, 77, 90, 95
Cortes of Cádiz, 119–24, 128, 173, 305 (n. 78)
Cosculluela, Juan A., 5, 152, 188
Council of the Indies, 21, 27, 104, 107, 115, 116, 122–24, 126
Cowley, Rafael A., 85
Crawley, Josiah T., 224, 227, 239, 322 (n. 24)
Cremata, Marcelino, 260
Crop rotation, 149–50
Cuadrado, Gastón Alonso, 191, 194
Cuba: land area of, 3, 286 (n. 2), 287 (n. 13); role of forests in formation of Cuban nation, 5; forested area of, 8, 9, 125, 222, 228, 255, 256–57, 270, 322 (n. 17), 327 (n. 6); colonization of, 15, 17–25; choice between "big Cuba" and "little Cuba," 86; early use of railroads, 134, 307 (n. 20); and war for independence, 158, 217; U.S. investment in, 219; elevation of, 309 (n. 48)
Cuban Railroad Company, 235–37, 238
Curbelo, José, 186–87

160–71 passim, 175, 176, 195, 222, 224, 231–32, 242, 243, 322 (n. 22)

Faunal diversity, 273–74
Felipe Poey Cuban Society for Natural History, 261–62
Felipe II (king of Spain), 19, 25
Fernández y Jiménez, José María, 213, 260–61
Fernando VII (king of Spain), 122, 172
Ferrocarril Central, 197, 233–37, 238, 243–44, 245, 249, 317 (n. 51)
Ferrocarril de Cárdenas, 135–36, 138, 307 (n. 22)
Ferrocarril de Júcaro, 136, 138
Ferrocarril del Norte de Cuba, 248, 325 (n. 71)
Ferrocarril de Sagua la Grande, 136, 143
Ferrocarriles de Cárdenas y Júcaro, 136
Finlay, Carlos J., 218
Firewood: and forest exploitation, 1, 2, 4; and Havana's municipal woodland, 21; in sugar industry, 30, 31–32, 35, 191; quality of, 31; sugar plantations' consumption of, 55–59; Moreno Fraginals on, 57–58, 296 (nn. 62, 67); reserves of, 128; and semimechanized and mechanized *ingenios*, 131; and deforestation, 133, 148, 270, 271; and railroads, 137–38; eliminating dependence on, 147, 148, 150, 184, 189; and steam engines, 149, 152, 159, 164, 265; and lumber trade, 160; and forest administration, 212; and Camagüey Province, 244–45
Fiske, Samuel, 193, 317 (n. 42)
Floral diversity, 273, 274
Forest administration: establishment of, 5, 206, 210; in Spain, 173–74, 177, 208, 211, 269, 313 (n. 132); private landowners' opposition to, 206; and ordinances, 207, 208; and lumber trade, 207, 208, 210, 211, 212, 213, 251–52, 253, 257, 258, 262, 319

(n. 87); and organization of forest property, 208, 209, 210–11; and private woodlands, 208, 210, 211, 270; structure of, 209; and deforestation, 214, 252, 256; and artificial forests, 214–15, 258–59; and conservation, 252, 253–56, 261; and demarcation of public woodlands, 252, 269–70; and reforestation, 253, 254, 255–56, 258–59, 261; and decrees, 253–58, 270, 326 (n. 84); and rehabilitation of Cuba, 264
Forest exploitation: and soil fertility, 1, 2, 4, 227–28; and Royal Forest Reserves, 1, 62–66, 73, 74, 76, 90, 297 (n. 73); conflicts over, 1–2, 267; and shipbuilding industry, 2, 24–25, 49, 61–62, 79–80, 89, 127, 267; and sugar planters, 2, 90–99, 101–3, 160, 269; and European colonization, 17; and woodcutting licenses, 66–75, 97, 298 (n. 83); and individual rights, 119–26; and property rights, 128, 175, 268; and railroads, 137, 138–39; in Sagua la Grande, 144, 199; and advocates of state intervention, 147; and domestic market, 172; organization of, 172–78; and latifundios, 227–28, 233
Forests: and sugar industry, 1, 3, 4–5, 274–75; and Spanish royal navy's conservation regulations, 1, 23–24, 50, 51, 61–62, 117, 174, 175, 290 (n. 50), 298 (n. 96); private landowners' absolute right over, 1, 73–74, 93–94, 103, 119–26, 133–34, 157, 158–59, 166, 167, 173–74, 175, 240, 241, 268–69, 270, 275, 298 (n. 98), 305 (n. 78), 310 (n. 80); lack of replacement of resources of, 4; disappearance of, 5; role in formation of Cuban nation, 5; on arrival of Europeans, 7–11, 13, 15; area of, 8, 9, 125, 222, 228, 255, 256–57, 270, 322 (n. 17), 327 (n. 6); and colonization of Cuba, 15, 17–25; precious woods of,

19–20; virgin forests, 72, 222, 257, 322
(n. 20); responsibility for conservation
of, 92–93, 96, 156, 157–58, 165–67, 172,
173, 174, 177–78, 212, 213, 252, 253–56,
261–62; and royal edict of August 30,
1815, 146–47, 156–57; exhaustion of, 181;
and reconstruction after Ten Years'
War, 194; artificial forests, 214–15,
258–59; and forest reserves, 239–40,
254; as essential resource, 274–75

Forest science, 158, 172–73

Fors, Alberto, 240

Fossil fuels, 4, 131, 194, 265

Foutant, Santiago, 67

France, 2, 44–45, 84, 172

Frasquieri, Tranquilino, 227, 258–59

Free workers, 3, 86, 128, 153, 186, 198,
271

Frías y Jacott, José Jacinto de, 153, 181

Friedlaender, Heinrich, 306 (n. 2)

Gálvez, José de, 68, 74, 78, 298 (n. 93)

García Barreras, Miguel, 91

García Herreros, Manuel, 121

García Osés, Ramón, 262

García Rodríguez, Mercedes, 29

Gil, Manuel, 92, 93, 94

Godoy, Manuel, 115

Gómez Mendoza, Josefina, 173

Goróstegui, Joaquín María, 319 (n. 81)

Great Britain: control of Havana, 1–2,
28, 36, 39–40, 59; war with Spain,
40; blockade of, 85; and economic
liberalism, 101, 104; slave trade treaty
of 1817, 306 (n. 4)

Greater Antilles, 286 (n. 2)

Green-pulp burners, 181, 189, 191, 192–93,
316 (nn. 39, 40), 317 (nn. 42, 43)

Guanabacoa, 32, 33–34, 42, 44

Guanajay, 88, 301 (n. 15)

Guantánamo Plain, 196, 230

Guerra, Luis, 97

Guerra y Sánchez, Ramiro, 2, 3, 40, 218,
221, 321 (n. 2)

Güines, 42, 88, 129, 301 (n. 15)

Güines River, 47, 152

Gundlach, Johannes, 214

Haciendas, 17, 18, 24, 43, 50, 51, 71–75,
98–99

Haiti, 3, 4, 6, 39, 41, 83, 84, 89

Haitian immigrants, 47, 55, 58, 84, 118

Haitian Revolution, 39, 41, 85, 89, 127, 147,
267, 268

Hall, A. D., 227

Hatos (cattle ranches): reconstructed
maps of, 10; size of, 17, 287 (n. 15),
288 (n. 29); and forests, 18–19, 71;
increase in, 20; coexistence of tobacco
plantations with, 35; dismantlement
of, 107, 219

Havana: English control of, 1–2, 28, 36,
39–40, 59; as port of call for Spanish
royal navy, 6, 20; establishment of, 15;
shipbuilding industry of, 20, 21–23,
36–37, 289 (nn. 42, 44, 45); and Plains
of Ariguanabo–Almendares–San
Juan, 20–21; and conservationist
regulation, 21, 22–24, 289 (n. 45), 290
(n. 50); sugar industry in, 25–29, 230,
290–91 (n. 60), 291 (n. 65); Spain's
recovery of, 28; sugar mills of, 29–32;
and geographical distribution of sugar
plantations, 32–37; deforestation of,
118; woodland area of, 324 (n. 60)

Havana Academy of Sciences, 239, 259

Havana-Matanzas district, 15, 20, 135, 147,
198, 219, 230, 289 (n. 38)

Hawaii, 180

Heights of Bejucal-Madruga-Coliseo,
20, 48

Heights of the Northern Range, 129, 139,
196, 198

Heights of the North of Havana and
Matanzas, 48, 86

Heights of the Sierra de Cubitas, 241

Herrera, Ricardo, 9–10, 287 (n. 15)

Hill, Robert T., 222

Humboldt, Alexander von, 8, 44, 45–46, 58, 59, 86, 151, 264, 295 (n. 33)

Ibáñez, Francisco Feliciano, 186, 201
Iglesias García, Fe, 29, 181
Indigenous Cubans, 8, 17, 33, 34–35, 287 (n. 6)
Industrial era: and sugar industry, 3, 4, 6, 83, 128, 129–30, 266; and industrialized agriculture, 4, 224, 264, 270, 271; and semimechanized *ingenios*, 129, 130; and mechanized *ingenios*, 130, 131, 181; and railroads, 134; and colossal *ingenios*, 220
Ingenios: and small farms' sugar cultivation, 31; location of, 32–33; increase in number and size of, 39, 41–42, 48, 84–87; distribution of, 42–43, 48, 176; types of, 43–44; and soil types, 45; wood use in, 48–55, 76, 92, 160–61, 162, 164, 324 (n. 57); and regulations on use of woods, 52, 267; dismantlement of, 55, 183; and firewood consumption, 55–59; authorization for development of, 96; semimechanized and mechanized *ingenios*, 127–34, 139, 180, 265; animal-powered *ingenios*, 130, 265; in Sagua la Grande, 142, 143–44, 145, 146; and technical and scientific knowledge, 144, 179; and problem of fuel, 150, 151, 152; and deforestation, 159; and virgin terrain, 176, 180; and agricultural and refining sectors, 180–81; decrease in, 182–83; and war of 1895–98, 183, 315 (n. 8); abandonment of, 184, 315 (n. 13); and *centrales*, 185, 186, 191; colossal *ingenios*, 219–21, 249. *See also* Sugar mills
Ingenios centrales, 186, 194, 196–98, 204, 231, 239, 265, 271
Isaac del Corral Alemán, José, 228, 253, 254, 255, 256, 259–60

Jamaica, 44, 45, 104, 147, 148, 160, 161, 286 (n. 2), 309 (n. 48)
Jatibonico River, 139, 200
Jáuregui, Andrés de, 105, 106, 108–10, 112, 120, 121, 303 (n. 51)
Java, 180, 193
Jenks, Leland H., 218, 228, 229, 238, 248
Jibacoa, Count de, 67–68, 298 (n. 84)
Jorge, Leandro Luis, 33
Jústiz de Santa Ana, Marquis de, 67–68, 298 (n. 84)

Keuthe, Allan James, 28

Labat, Jean-Baptiste, 30
La Condamine, Marie de, 151
La Cruz Aguilar, Emilio de, 290 (n. 50), 305 (n. 67)
La Ensenada, Marquis de, 23, 290 (n. 50)
La Explotadora, S.A., 167–68
La nueva era, 185–86, 189, 191–93, 197, 198, 201, 214, 215
La Paz, Antonio de, 40–41
La Pezuela, Jacobo de, 133, 144, 307 (n. 15)
La Puente, Juan de, 65
La Puente, Miguel de, 65, 105, 106, 108–10, 112–14, 118, 303 (nn. 43, 51), 304 (nn. 53, 55, 56)
La Sagra, Ramón de, 8, 44, 132, 142, 156–57, 158, 181, 191, 213, 263, 264, 272
Las Casas, Bartolomé de, 7, 9, 10, 139
Las Casas, Luis de, 91, 92, 95, 103, 104, 301 (n. 18)
Las Delicias de Tempú, Marquis de, 206
Las Villas Province, 139–46, 198, 199–202, 204, 308 (n. 27)
Latifundios: and division of population, 2–3; and *centrales*, 220, 221; and forest exploitation, 227–28, 233; and absentee landlords, 228; and Camagüey Province, 248, 251; percentage of land occupied by, 266; and foreign investors, 275; protests against, 327 (n. 106)

La Torre, Marquis de, 55, 66, 67, 68–69, 88, 298 (n. 93), 323 (n. 53)
Le Reverend, Julio, 31, 35
Lesser Antilles, 286 (n. 2)
Lira, Araujo de, 164–65
Livestock farming: as principal economic activity, 17; impact on landscape, 18; and pastures, 19, 24, 92, 264, 267; and conflicts over forest use, 31, 36; and sugar production, 35, 267, 272; and *potreros*, 35–36, 54, 293 (n. 99); wood used in, 54, 57, 79, 108–9, 267, 296 (n. 50); and *potreros del Rey*, 62, 64; and dismantlement, 90, 98, 99, 100, 219; decline of, 95, 98, 99, 146; and ban on cutting cedar braces, 96; and Sagua la Grande River, 142; increase in, 183; and Las Villas, 199; and savannas, 241; and Camagüey Province, 245, 251
Los Arabos–Real Campiña Plain, 129
Louisiana, 55, 66–67, 168–69, 192–93
Luaces, Roberto, 261
Lumber trade: and forest exploitation, 3, 267; and municipal woodlands, 21; and imports, 55, 66–67, 110, 137, 138, 149, 160, 168–71, 172, 224, 261, 270, 312 (n. 114), 313 (n. 127); and exports, 133, 160–71 passim, 175, 176, 195, 222, 224, 231–32, 242, 243, 322 (n. 22); and private landowners, 160, 164–65, 187; and Nuevitas, 165, 242, 323 (n. 54); and war of 1868–78, 167; and *centrales*, 187; and Manzanilla, 197, 317 (n. 53); and Yaguajay, 202, 204; and forest administration, 207, 208, 210, 211, 212, 213, 251–52, 253, 257, 258, 262, 319 (n. 87); and U.S. capitalists, 222; and World War I, 222, 224, 270; and Camagüey Province, 241–42, 243

Machado, Gerardo, 229, 256, 261
Macuriges, Count de, 67, 72, 108
Maldonado, Juan, 290–91 (n. 60)
Managua, 33, 42

Manzaneda, Severino de, 26, 36
Manzanillo, 195, 197, 317 (n. 53)
Manzanillo Plain, 196, 197, 230
Marabú, 250–51, 274, 328 (n. 14)
Marrero, Leví, 21, 23, 30, 31, 293 (nn. 97, 99)
Martí, Carlos, 237–38
Martí, José, 276
Matos, Eliseo, 10, 133, 187, 222, 228, 287 (n. 17), 322 (n. 31)
Mayabeque River, 21, 47, 152
McKinley, William, 204
McKinley Tariff, 182
McNeill, John, 269
Melchor de Jovellanos, Gaspar, 119, 176, 268, 306 (n. 2)
Menéndez de Avilés, Pedro, 21
Menéndez Márquez, Pedro, 21
Merchant, Carolyn, 327 (n. 4)
Meyreles, Manuela, 100
Ministry of Agriculture, 258, 270, 326 (n. 91)
Ministry of Overseas Territories, 206, 209
Molinet, Eugenio, 261
Montalvo, Lorenzo, 22, 59
Montalvo y Castillo, José, 151, 309 (n. 59)
Monte Hermoso, Marquis de, 105
Montes vedados (private woodlands preserves), 31, 36
Mopox y de Jaruco, Count de, 149–50, 156, 310 (n. 74)
Morales, Francisco Javier de, 79
Morales, Sebastián Alfredo de, 212–13
Morejón y Gato, Antonio de, 45
Morelet, Arthur, 158
Morell de Santa Cruz, Pedro, 33, 34, 42
Moreno Fraginals, Manuel: on precious woods, 20; on Havana Company of Commerce, 28; on average land area for sugar mills, 29; on British colonial plantations, 39–40; on sugar production, 41, 294 (n. 23); on Otahití cane, 48; on firewood

consumption, 57–58, 296 (nn. 62, 67); on semimechanized *ingenio*, 129; on railroad, 134; on mechanized *ingenios*, 181; on slaveholding system, 306 (n. 1); on effect of steam power, 306 (n. 6); on lumber imports, 312 (n. 114)

Moya de Colón, Diego, 72–73, 74

Municipalities: concession of land by, 17, 18, 20, 72, 128, 268, 269; wood use of, 92, 118

Napoleonic wars, 85

Naumann, Friedrich, 165–66, 167

Navarro, Diego José, 69–70, 74

Neolithic communities, 8–9, 287 (n. 6)

New Guinea, 25

New Spain, 288 (n. 28)

Nipe, 195–96

Nipe Plain, 233, 238

North American colonies, 28, 40–41, 293 (n. 4). *See also* United States

Northern Cuba Railroad, 248, 249, 325 (n. 71)

Norton, Albert J., 222

Nuevitas, 129, 165, 197, 242, 244, 323 (n. 54), 324 (n. 55)

O'Donnell, Leopoldo, 175

O'Farrill, José Ricardo, 43–49, 56–57, 91–95, 148, 295 (n. 33)

O'Gavan, Juan Bernardo, 120, 121

Oliván, Alejandro, 148

Ordinances of Cáceres, 17, 292 (n. 89)

O'Reilly, Alejandro, 28, 40, 105

Oriente Province: and U.S. capitalists, 2, 220–21, 228; and concession of land, 17; sugar plantations in, 129; and harvesting of wood, 195; impact of sugar expansion in, 219, 221–22, 224, 227, 232, 233, 238, 239, 271; colossal *ingenios* in, 220; and deforestation, 229, 238, 239, 251, 260, 262; change in natural region, 230–40; and *centrales*, 237, 238, 245; Perpiña on,

242; and sugar production, 244; forest administration in, 253

Ortega Pereyra, Ovidio, 22

Otahití cane, 47–48, 295 (n. 36)

Overseas Committee for the Revising of Laws of the Indies, 174, 314 (n. 139)

Ozés y Alzúa, Joaquín de, 118

Palma–San Luis, 230

Patriotic Society of Havana, 43

Patriotic Society of Seville, 92, 302 (n. 27)

Peñalver, Francisco, 97, 105, 112

Peñalver, Ignacio, 27

Pera y Peralta, Rafael, 244

Pérez de La Riva, Juan, 87, 230–31

Pérez de Oporto, Juan, 22, 289 (n. 45)

Perpiña, Escolapio Antonio, 242, 324 (n. 57)

Petroleum, 194, 224

Physico-natural regions, 5, 13, 15, 286 (n. 8)

Pichardo Tapia, Esteban, 138–39, 273

Pimienta, E., 192

Piña, Tomás de, 95–97, 100

Pinar del Río district, 219, 288 (n. 24)

Pino Santos, Oscar, 219

Piqueras Arenas, José, 121

Pizarro y Gardín, José, 150

Plain of Corralillo-Yaguajay, 129, 136, 139, 196, 200

Plain of Júcaro-Morón, 240–41, 249

Plain of Manacas-Cienfuegos, 129, 136

Plain of North-Central Camagüey, 241

Plain of Northern Camagüey-Maniabón, 241, 249

Plain of Sagua de Tánamo, 238

Plain of Santa Clara–Sancti Spíritus, 129, 196

Plain of South-Central Camagüey, 241

Plain of Southern Camagüey, 241

Plains and Heights of Banes-Cacocum, 233

Plains and Heights of Cauto, 238

Rebello, Carlos, 129, 144, 199

Remedios, 15, 24, 64, 140, 141, 199, 200, 204, 317 (n. 60), 318 (n. 61)

Reverberatory furnaces, 55–57, 58, 296 (n. 59)

Revista de agricultura, 184, 189

Revista de agricultura, comercio y trabajo, 229, 240, 260

Reynell, Gómez, 25

Reynoso, Alvaro, 58, 59, 154–56, 181, 189, 192, 227, 261, 271, 273, 310 (n. 70)

Ribera, Nicolás Joseph de, 19, 27–28

Rice cultivation, 46, 295 (n. 33)

Ricla, Count de, 28, 40

Rionda, Manuel, 232

Roa, Francisco Manuel, 36

Rodríguez Ferrer, Miguel, 132–33, 156–58, 163–65, 177–78, 206, 207, 308 (n. 26), 314 (n. 150)

Rodríguez Ledesma, Francisco, 31–32

Roig, Juan Tomás, 239–40

Romay, Tomás, 142

Royal Consulate of Agriculture, Industry, and Commerce of Havana, 43, 47–48, 56, 84, 127–28, 148, 160, 168–69

Royal edict of August 30, 1815, 1, 124, 125, 127, 146–47, 156–57, 166, 174–75, 268, 275

Royal Forest Reserves (Cortes del Rey): as obstacle to sugar industry, 1, 43, 77–78, 112, 127; and forest exploitation, 1, 62–66, 73, 74, 76, 90, 297 (n. 73); and shipbuilding, 39, 62–63, 267; and dismantlement, 51, 63, 64, 88, 89, 102, 106; and exploration of woodlands, 64–65; and elimination of boundaries, 81; and Araoz, 92; Acevedo on, 94–95; and woodcutting licenses, 101; location of, 109, 110, 111, 115, 160, 305 (n. 73); infrastructure of, 134

Royal palms, 150, 254–55

Ruiz Melo, Ernesto, 209

Rural areas: wood use in, 108–9, 113, 118

Saccharum officinarum L., 25

Saco, José Antonio, 148–49

Sagua la Chica River, 64, 139, 140–41, 199

Sagua la Grande, 139, 140–46, 196, 198, 199, 200

Sagua la Grande River, 64, 139, 140–41, 142, 143, 146

Salas y Quiroga, Jacinto de, 152

Sancti Spíritus, 15, 24

Santa Cruz, 165, 195

Santa Cruz del Sur, 242, 244, 249, 323 (n. 54), 324 (n. 65), 325 (n. 73)

Santiago de Cuba, 15, 25, 117–18, 195, 222, 230, 231, 243, 324 (n. 60)

Savannas: and indigenous Cubans, 8, 287 (n. 5); studies of, 9–11; and lack of suitability for planting, 46; Borja on, 75; and *hatos*, 91; and ban on burning woodlands, 93, 118; and savannization, 131, 149, 266; and soil fertility, 233, 241

Secretariat of Agriculture, Commerce, and Industry, 252, 253, 254, 260

Sedano, Diego José, 85–86, 171

Semicaducifolious forests, 11, 13, 33, 139

Serrano, Francisco, 206

Shipbuilding industry: and forest exploitation, 2, 24–25, 49, 61–62, 79–80, 89, 127, 267; lumber for, 5, 33, 112, 114, 161; in Havana, 20, 21–23, 36–37, 289 (nn. 42, 44, 45); strategic importance of, 20, 36–37, 39; and conservationist regulation, 21; and Spanish royal navy, 22–23, 43, 60, 61–62; conflict with sugar industry, 36–37, 39, 41, 43, 49, 51–53, 59, 62, 66, 74, 82, 89; and Royal Forest Reserves, 39, 62–63, 267; and regeneration of woodlands, 59; growth of, 59–60; and Wood Committee, 102; effects of regulation on, 108; decline of, 125, 267

Showalter, William, 218, 227

Slaves and slavery: and sugar industry, 3, 4; private landowners' use of, 6; and conservationist regulation, 21;

in Indies, 25; and Havana's sugar industry, 26, 27, 28, 30, 34, 41; and area under sugar cultivation, 29–30; average number per estate, 42, 44, 294 (n. 23); working conditions of, 58; increase in importation of, 84, 86, 128, 301 (n. 19); and plantation economy, 128; effect of steam power on, 129; and semimechanized and mechanized *ingenios*, 131; free labor replaces, 153; abolition of, 179, 180, 186, 193, 271; role of, 275; effect on agricultural improvements, 306 (n. 1); and slave trade treaty of 1817, 306 (n. 4)

Small farms: licenses to establish, 17; and clear-cutting, 23; and sugar cultivation, 26, 31, 88, 128; wood used by, 32, 54, 57, 92, 108–9, 161, 296 (n. 50); and Guanabacoa, 33; diversification of, 86; and livestock farming, 98; and Sagua la Grande River, 142

Smith, Adam, 306 (n. 2)

Smith, Earl, 10

Smith, Mark J., 233

Soil fertility: and forest exploitation, 1, 2, 4, 227–28; and agricultural use of soils, 15; and Plains of Ariguanabo–Almendares–San Juan, 21; and Havana's sugar mills, 30; and soil types, 45, 48, 230, 239, 250, 295 (nn. 29, 38); and traditional system of cultivation, 46, 224; and clear-cutting, 128, 154; and Sagua la Grande River, 142, 145; prolonging of, 147; deterioration of, 149; and exhaustion of soil, 152–59, 264, 271, 272; and sugar cultivation, 191, 227, 239; and Ten Years' War, 197; of eastern soils, 238–39; and Camagüey Province, 241, 251; and deforestation, 259, 263, 264, 271; and low cane yields, 259, 272, 327 (n. 7)

Soil studies, 9–11

Someruelos, Marquis de, 105, 106, 114, 122, 303 (n. 46), 304 (n. 57)

Spain: free trade reforms of, 4, 29, 40, 293 (n. 3); and sugar industry, 25; peace treaty with Great Britain, 39; war with Great Britain, 40; war with France, 84; decline in forests of, 93; woodlands ordinances of, 123; forest science in, 158, 173; and transfer of Louisiana to France, 169, 312 (n. 119); forest administration in, 173–74, 177, 208, 211, 269, 313 (n. 132); slave trade treaty of 1817, 306 (n. 4); and effect of royal edict of August 30, 1815, 311 (n. 94)

Spanish metropole: and Cuban forests, 1, 20, 60, 65, 66, 267; and traditional agriculture, 4; Cuba as model for colonial relations, 28–29, 62; and role of Havana in naval power development, 62; and railroads, 134; and forest administration, 173–74, 269

Spanish royal navy: and conflicts with sugar planters, 1, 2, 52–53, 77–78, 89, 90–99, 101–3, 122, 123, 128, 159, 264, 268; and conservation regulations, 1, 23–24, 50, 51, 61–62, 117, 174, 175, 290 (n. 50), 298 (n. 96); Havana as port of call for, 6, 20; and Havana's shipbuilding industry, 22–23, 43, 60, 61–62; and restrictions on sugar planters, 49, 59, 69, 86; privileges of, 61–62, 72–74, 81–82, 90, 91, 99–100, 103, 114, 116, 119, 120, 121, 124, 267, 268, 304 (n. 55); dismantlement process controlled by, 75–82, 88, 91, 100, 103, 267; and intensive settlement, 88, 89; Prendis on, 98, 302 (n. 34); and cost of moving logging operations, 110, 304 (n. 53); jurisdiction north of Colón Plain, 134; on wood shortages, 146; and state intervention, 156; and control of forest exploitation, 158; and lumber trade, 160, 165, 166; and exclusive use of forests, 303 (n. 40); and maintaining watch over uncultivated areas, 314 (n. 148)

Special School of Woodlands Engineers, 173, 177, 206, 207

State intervention, 147, 156, 157–58, 173, 206–15

Steam engines: and sugar production, 3, 265; and *trapiches*, 129, 131, 306–7 (n. 10); and sugar mills, 129, 142; and use of firewood, 149, 152, 159, 164, 265; effect of, 306 (n. 6)

Subperennifolious forests, 11, 13, 139

Subsistence crops, 31, 35, 85–86, 188, 221, 264, 268, 275

Sugar cultivation: evolution of, 3; and small farms, 26, 31, 88, 128; and slavery, 29–30; and lack of regeneration of woodlands, 43; traditional system of, 45–48, 224, 227, 257, 265–66, 272; and use of woodlands, 46, 47, 48, 125; and virgin terrain, 128, 176, 180, 186, 187, 191, 202, 204, 227, 230, 237, 238, 250, 266, 320 (n. 102), 322 (n. 24); and land under cultivation, 129–30; and exhaustion of soil, 152–59; separation of cane refining from, 179, 180, 181, 183; improvement of, 186, 189, 227, 266, 271, 272; and soil fertility, 191, 227, 239

Sugar industry: and forest use, 1, 2, 4–5, 31–32, 36; and land-exploitation regime, 2–3; and industrial era, 3, 4, 6, 83, 128, 129–30, 266; in Havana, 25–29, 230, 290–91 (n. 60), 291 (n. 65); itinerant nature of, 30, 180, 184, 187, 189, 266, 271; and conflict with shipbuilding industry, 36–37, 39, 41, 43, 49, 51–53, 59, 62, 66, 74, 82, 89; British influence on, 39–40; and free trade reforms, 40, 293 (n. 3); growth of, 66, 83, 86, 90, 91, 117, 125, 127, 182, 229, 269, 276; privileges for, 84, 86; effect of railroads on, 134–39; centralization of, 179–80, 184–86, 187, 200, 219, 271; legacy of, 275–76; and *intensivismo*, 326 (n. 90)

Sugar Islands, 2, 3, 28, 29, 147, 264

Sugar kettle batteries, 58, 129, 130, 149, 151, 153

Sugar mills: construction of, 1, 2, 26, 27, 30–31, 48, 49–51, 53–55, 219; productive capacity of, 5; and haciendas, 17; and license for clear-cutting, 23–24; and debt-seizure regulations, 25; average land area of, 29; and correlation between open land and woodlands, 29–30; of Havana, 29–32; geographic distribution of, 33; and Cuban plantation economy, 41; distribution of, 42–43; and steam engines, 129, 142; environmental impact of, 153; technological advances of, 179. See also *Ingenios*

Sugar plantations: and clear-cutting, 1, 27; environmental impact of spread of, 3, 6, 129; geographical concentration of, 32–37; and deforestation, 33, 34, 35, 131, 133, 168, 171, 177–78; expansion of, 42, 85, 147, 185, 188, 219; and sugar production, 44; dismantlement of, 55, 127; firewood consumption of, 55–59; and Ten Years' War, 180, 199; and *centrales*, 184; and *ingenios centrales*, 194; decrease in, 199, 200; and forest reserves, 254

Sugar planters: and conflicts with Spanish royal navy, 1, 2, 52–53, 77–78, 89, 90–99, 101–3, 122, 123, 128, 159, 264, 268; and forest exploitation, 2, 90–99, 101–3, 160, 269; Spanish royal navy's restrictions on, 49, 59, 69, 86; wood used by, 54, 66; and importing cypress from Louisiana, 55, 66–67, 69; and woodcutting licenses, 66–70, 97; O'Farrill on tree-planting requirements for, 93; and Wood Committee, 104–5, 106, 112, 119, 125–26; as large-scale landowners, 127

Sugar production: and conflicts over forest use and exploitation, 1–2, 31–32, 36; increase in, 4, 41–42, 84, 85, 128,

Velázquez, Diego, 15
Venegas, Francisco de, 289 (n. 45)
Venegas, Hernán, 200, 202
Verdeja Law, 258
Viana Hinojosa, Antonio de, 36
Vianas, Alfonso de, 117
Vigurí, Luis de, 106, 303 (n. 45)
Villa, Alférez de Navío Nicolá de, 54
Villa Clara, 142, 143
Villanueva, Count de, 175–76, 314 (n. 144)
Villaurruitia, Wenceslao de, 130
Villavicencio, Juan María de, 119
Villena, José Manuel de, 79–82, 92, 102, 297 (n. 72), 299 (nn. 113, 114), 299–300 (n. 118), 303 (n. 42)
Vivanco, Idelfonso, 142

Waibel, Leo, 9–10, 231, 287 (n. 13)
War of 1895–98, 183, 204, 215, 218, 242, 315 (n. 8)
Watts, David, 9, 30, 276, 291 (n. 73)
Western Department, 129, 131, 242
Wood Committee: and tariffs on iron pounders, 52; on woodlands for public, 53, 70, 74, 77–78; and dismantlement, 70–71, 72, 75, 79, 80, 90–91, 92, 98, 99, 105–19, 122, 299 (n. 101); and woodcutting licenses, 91, 101; and rule of director, 100, 102, 112, 116, 302 (n. 37); composition of, 104–5, 112, 116, 124, 125; and Cortes of Cádiz,

120–21, 122; and Spaniards' taking of peninsula timber, 301 (n. 19); and Cabello, 302 (n. 38)
Woodlands Engineers Corps, 173, 178, 206, 211
Woodlands Inspection, 210, 212, 251
Woodlands Ordinance of 1748, 119
Woodlands Ordinances for Cuba and Puerto Rico, 177, 206, 208
Woodlands Ordinances of 1833, 172
Woodlands Ordinances of 1876, 252, 256, 269
Woodlands Protection Commission for the Island of Cuba, 175, 176–77
Woodlands Reconnaissance Commission, 206
World War I: and sugar production, 218–19, 227, 237–38, 245, 248, 266; and lumber trade, 222, 224, 270; and deforestation, 224, 252, 260, 270

Yaguajay, 200–202, 204, 318 (n. 75)

Zaldivar, Count de, 105, 125
Zanetti, Oscar, 183
Zanjón Accord, 242
Zapata Swamp, 188, 274
Zayas, Alfredo, 252–53
Zayas, Andrés de, 151
Zayas, Francisco, 227
Zayas y Jiménez, Francisco de, 190

Envisioning Cuba

Reinaldo Funes Monzote, *From Rainforest to Cane Field in Cuba: An Environmental History since 1492* (2008).

Matt D. Childs, *The 1812 Aponte Rebellion in Cuba and the Struggle against Atlantic Slavery* (2006).

Eduardo González, *Cuba and the Tempest: Literature and Cinema in the Time of Diaspora* (2006).

John Lawrence Tone, *War and Genocide in Cuba, 1895–1898* (2006).

Samuel Farber, *The Origins of the Cuban Revolution Reconsidered* (2006).

Lillian Guerra, *The Myth of José Martí: Conflicting Nationalisms in Early Twentieth-Century Cuba* (2005).

Rodrigo Lazo, *Writing to Cuba: Filibustering and Cuban Exiles in the United States* (2005).

Alejandra Bronfman, *Measures of Equality: Social Science, Citizenship, and Race in Cuba, 1902–1940* (2004).

Edna M. Rodríguez-Mangual, *Lydia Cabrera and the Construction of an Afro-Cuban Cultural Identity* (2004).

Gabino La Rosa Corzo, *Runaway Slave Settlements in Cuba: Resistance and Repression* (2003).

Piero Gleijeses, *Conflicting Missions: Havana, Washington, and Africa, 1959–1976* (2002).

Robert Whitney, *State and Revolution in Cuba: Mass Mobilization and Political Change, 1920–1940* (2001).

Alejandro de la Fuente, *A Nation for All: Race, Inequality, and Politics in Twentieth-Century Cuba* (2001).

CPSIA information can be obtained at www.ICGtesting.com
Printed in the USA
BVOW02s1445280116

434198BV00003B/37/P